THE DRIVE FOR KNOWLEDGE

Humans constantly search for and use information to solve a wide range of problems related to survival, social interactions, and learning. While it is clear that curiosity and the drive for knowledge occupies a central role in defining what being human means to ourselves, where does this desire to know the unknown come from? What is its purpose? And how does it operate? These are some of the core questions this book seeks to answer by showcasing new and exciting research on human information-seeking. The volume brings together perspectives from leading researchers at the cutting edge of the cognitive sciences, working on human brains and behavior within psychology, computer science, and neuroscience. These vital connections between disciplines will continue to lead to further breakthroughs in our understanding of human cognition.

IRENE COGLIATI DEZZA is a Research Fellow in the Department of Experimental Psychology & The Max Planck UCL Centre for Computational Psychiatry and Ageing Research, University College London; Department of Experimental Psychology, Ghent University.

ERIC SCHULZ is a Max Planck Research Group Leader at the Max Planck Institute for Biological Cybernetics.

CHARLEY M. WU is Research Group Leader in the Human and Machine Cognition Lab at the University of Tübingen.

T0371536

THE DRIVE FOR KNOWLEDGE

The Science of Human Information Seeking

EDITED BY

IRENE COGLIATI DEZZA

University College London

ERIC SCHULZ

Max Planck Institute for Biological Cybernetics, Tübingen

CHARLEY M. WU

University of Tübingen

CAMBRIDGE
UNIVERSITY PRESS

Shaftesbury Road, Cambridge CB2 8EA, United Kingdom

One Liberty Plaza, 20th Floor, New York, NY 10006, USA

477 Williamstown Road, Port Melbourne, VIC 3207, Australia

314–321, 3rd Floor, Plot 3, Splendor Forum, Jasola District Centre, New Delhi – 110025, India

103 Penang Road, #05–06/07, Visioncrest Commercial, Singapore 238467

Cambridge University Press is part of Cambridge University Press & Assessment, a department of the University of Cambridge.

We share the University's mission to contribute to society through the pursuit of education, learning and research at the highest international levels of excellence.

www.cambridge.org
Information on this title: www.cambridge.org/9781009013048

DOI: 10.1017/9781009026949

First published 2022
First paperback edition 2023

A catalogue record for this publication is available from the British Library

Library of Congress Cataloging-in-Publication data
Names: Dezza, Irene Cogliati, editor. | Schulz, Eric (Cognitive scientist), editor. | Wu, Charley M., editor.
Title: The drive for knowledge : the science of human information seeking / edited by Irene Cogliati Dezza, University College London, Eric Schulz, Max-Planck-Institut für biologische Kybernetick, Tübingen, Charley M. Wu, University of Tübingen.
Description: Cambridge, United Kingdom ; New York, NY : Cambridge University Press, 2022. | Includes bibliographical references and index.
Identifiers: LCCN 2021051465 (print) | LCCN 2021051466 (ebook) | ISBN 9781316515907 (hardback) | ISBN 9781009013048 (paperback) | ISBN 9781009026949 (ebook)
Subjects: LCSH: Cognition. | Belief and doubt. | Knowledge, Theory of – Psychological aspects. | Inquiry (Theory of knowledge) – Psychological aspects.
Classification: LCC BF311 .D74 2022 (print) | LCC BF311 (ebook) | DDC 153–dc23/eng/ 20211104
LC record available at https://lccn.loc.gov/2021051465
LC ebook record available at https://lccn.loc.gov/2021051466

ISBN   978-1-316-51590-7   Hardback
ISBN   978-1-009-01304-8   Paperback

Contents

Figures

Tables

Notes on Contributors

DANIELLE S. BASSETT

University of Pennsylvania

MARCEL BINZ

MPI Biological Cybernetics

FRANZISKA BRÄNDLE

MPI Biological Cybernetics

CAROLINE CHARPENTIER

Division of Humanities and Social Sciences, California Institute of Technology, Institute of Cognitive Neuroscience, University College London

NICK CHATER

University of Warwick

IRENE COGLIATI DEZZA

Department of Experimental Psychology & The Max Planck UCL Centre for Computational Psychiatry and Ageing Research, University College London; Department of Experimental Psychology, Ghent University

VINCENZO CRUPI

University of Turin, Italy

FIERY CUSHMAN

Department of Psychology, Harvard University

LANCELOT DA COSTA

Wellcome Centre for Human Neuroimaging, University College London, London, UK, Department of Mathematics, Imperial College London, London, UK

COSTANZA DE SIMONE

Max Planck Institute for Human Development, Germany

ED DONNELLAN

Department of Experimental Psychology, University College London, UK School of Psychology and Clinical Language Sciences, University of Reading, UK

KARL FRISTON

Wellcome Centre for Human Neuroimaging, University College London, London, UK

JACQUELINE GOTTLIEB

Department of Neuroscience, The Kavli Institute for Brain Science, The Mortimer B. Zuckerman Mind Brain Behavior Institute, Columbia University

THOMAS HILLS

University of Warwick

GEORGE LOEWENSTEIN

Carnegie Mellon University

NANCY B. LUNDIN

Indiana University

MAHI LUTHRA

Indiana University

DAVID M. LYDON-STALEY

University of Pennsylvania

BJÖRN MEDER

Health and Medical University Potsdam, Germany, Max Planck Institute for Human Development, Berlin, Germany

CLÉMENT MOULIN-FRIER

Inria / University of Bordeaux / Ensta ParisTech, France

KOU MURAYAMA

Hector Research Institute of Education Sciences and Psychology,
University of Tübingen, Germany School of Psychology and Clinical
Language Sciences, University of Reading, UK

JONATHAN D. NELSON

Max Planck Institute for Human Development, Berlin, Germany,
University of Surrey, Guildford, UK

PIERRE-YVES OUDEYER

Inria / University of Bordeaux / Ensta ParisTech, France

THOMAS PARR

Wellcome Centre for Human Neuroimaging, University College
London, London, UK

AZZURRA RUGGERI

Technical University Munich, Germany

NOOR SAJID

Wellcome Centre for Human Neuroimaging, University College
London, London, UK

MICHIKO SAKAKI

Hector Research Institute of Education Sciences and Psychology,
University of Tübingen, Germany School of Psychology and Clinical
Language Sciences, University of Reading, UK

ERIC SCHULZ

Computational Principles of Intelligence, Max Planck Institute for
Biological Cybernetics

ALEXANDER TEN

Inria / University of Bordeaux / Ensta ParisTech, France

PETER M. TODD

Indiana University

NATALIA VÉLEZ

Department of Psychology, Harvard University

ZACHARY WOJTOWICZ

Carnegie Mellon University

CHARLEY M. WU

Human and Machine Cognition Lab, University of Tübingen

DALE ZHOU

University of Pennsylvania

PERRY ZURN

American University

Preface

Irene Cogliati Dezza, Eric Schulz, and Charley M. Wu

What defines us as humans? Named *Homo Sapiens*, or "Wise Person" by Carl Linnaeus in the eighteenth century, what seems to distinguish us from our nearest primate relatives is our knowledge – or rather, our appetite for knowledge. Indeed, Aristotle begins his volume on Metaphysics with the simple statement "all people by nature desire to know."[1] This central role of human curiosity also permeates life and culture well beyond dusty academic tomes, abounding in the creation myths that define our cultural identities, from Adam and Eve seduced by the fruit of the tree of knowledge to Pandora tempted by the irresistible mysteries of a locked box.

While it is clear that curiosity and the drive for knowledge occupies a central role in defining what being human means to ourselves, an important concern is where this desire to know the unknown comes from. What is its purpose? And how does it operate? These are some of the core questions we seek to answer in this book. These are not new questions, of course, since they have occupied the minds of innumerable thinkers over countless generations. But today, we have new tools and methods for providing answers, from computational models of human information-seeking behavior to peering into the brain using an arsenal of neuro-imaging techniques. With these new tools has come the advent of new theories that unite previously disparate fields: connecting neuroscience with recent advances in artificial intelligence, bridging the psychology of childhood development with mathematical theories of learning, and countless other criss-crossing avenues of interdisciplinary research. Emerging from this hotbed of innovative and collaborative research is a new science of human information-seeking, which we proudly showcase between the covers of this book.

---

[1] Linnæus, C. 1758. Systema naturæ per regna tria naturæ, secundum classes, ordines, genera, species, cum characteribus, differentiis, synonymis, locis. Tomus I. Editio decima, reformata. 1–824. Holmiæ. (Salvius).

The drive to seek information can come from diverse motives, fulfilling different biological and neurological functions, and producing disparate outcomes when paired in opposition to other drives, such as toward reward or avoidance of pain. Acquiring new information serves the crucial functions of making sense of reality, improving our internal representations of the world, and driving the development of our skills and intellect. In general, acquiring more information empowers us to solve increasingly sophisticated problems, from the mundane "What should I eat for lunch?" to pivotal life-or-death survival scenarios such as "Should I fight or flee?" Yet we do not only desire useful or relevant knowledge; rather, new information and novel sensations seem to be enjoyed for their own sake. Information thus seems to have hedonic value and can induce sadness, joy, or fear. Our drive for knowledge is therefore tangled up in the regulation of emotions and affective states, perhaps providing a key piece of the puzzle for understanding clinical disorders, such as depression and anxiety. Moreover, humans not only engage in information-seeking when interacting with the external world, they also search for information internally, when dredging up an old memory, searching for a prelearned motor sequence (e.g., shooting a basketball after a long absence from the court), or selecting which sensory information to attend to (e.g., at a busy cocktail party). The search for information is thus a crucial process anytime we act, learn, and decide in the world.

Today, with modern advances in global communication through the Internet and social media, people have access to more information than ever before. The sum of scientific and medical knowledge is at our fingertips, and constant updates about world events and insight into the personal lives of friends and celebrities are available to continually ping us on our phones, tablets, and computers. With more information, however, comes more choice about what knowledge we wish to seek out. The current crisis of misinformation and belief polarization on social media may be partly explained by our cognitive mechanisms for information-seeking – tuned over long evolutionary timescales – doing its best to adapt to the new information landscape we now find ourselves in.

One consequence of the complexity and breadth of research on information-seeking behavior is that the research landscape spans a rich but scattered manifold, encompassing diverse disciplines including psychology, economics, neuroscience, and computer science. This means that the terminology can vary widely across and within disciplines. Terms such as "curiosity," "novelty," and "interest" are often used to ground the science of information-seeking in the intuitive concepts we all share through common experience. These terms are often related to more technical terms, such as "information gain," "entropy minimization," or "prediction error," which provide a mathematical and computational framework for quantifying and comparing the informational value of different behaviors.

To make sense of these different approaches, this book is organized according to three simple questions: **What** drives humans to seek information? **How** do humans search for information? **Which** machinery supports the drive for knowledge? Each question is targeted in three separate parts, but with plenty of spillover and connections across parts.

Part I aims to answer the question "What drives humans to seek information?" Humans are internally driven to make sense of the world in the same fashion as they are driven to seek primary rewards such as food, water, sex, etc. Wojtowicz et al. (Chapter 1) explore the motivational factors that drive humans to make sense of the world through acquiring novel information. Acquiring novel information is also achieved at different time scales. Donnellan et al. (Chapter 2) discuss a novel framework of knowledge acquisition which unifies one-time information-seeking (i.e., curiosity) and long-term development of information-seeking motivations (i.e., interest). Information-seeking is also key to autonomous learning in the real world. By facilitating faster, more efficient learning, intrinsically motivated curiosity prepares both artificial and biological agents to perform better in future problems. Ten et al. (Chapter 3) focus on the functions, mechanisms, and usage of intrinsic motivation as a mechanism to promote information-seeking and boost the rate of learning. Lastly, De Simone and Ruggeri (Chapter 4) provide an overview of how different forms of information-seeking behaviors develop over the lifespan. They plot a developmental trajectory of active learning, unified by the three core capacities of "sensitivity" to environmental inputs, "competence" in selecting and generating informative queries, and "adaptiveness" in tailoring learning strategies to the structure of the environment.

Part II attempts to answer "how" people search for information. In particular, different theoretical frameworks are presented to describe the computational principles underlying information-seeking. Meder et al. (Chapter 5) provide an overview of different formalizations for quantifying the value of information based on the principles of Bayesian experimental design. This provides an organizational layout for different probabilistic models and heuristics used to model human information acquisition, based on different approaches for characterizing uncertainty. Sajid et al. (Chapter 6) further bridge domains by exploring how active inference unifies Bayesian experimental design with Bayesian decision theory: when removing prior outcome preferences, active inference reduces to Bayesian experimental design, while in the absence of ambiguity and relative risk, active inference reduces to Bayesian decision theory. Brändle et al. (Chapter 7) discusses the limitations of traditional decision-making tasks (i.e., multiarmed bandits) used to study human information seeking, and proposes a shift toward more real-world problems, where empowerment-based exploration strategies can expand the study of human exploration to a richer repertoire of scenarios. Lastly, since most of what we learn is from other people, the study of information-seeking must also consider how information is exchanged both between and within minds in a social context. Wu et al. (Chapter 8) present a novel framework for studying human social learning, oriented around the representations involved (e.g., behavioral policies, values, and beliefs). This framework provides new insights into how people select from different social learning strategies and combine socially acquired information with their own mental representations.

Part III seeks to answer "Which machinery supports the drive for knowledge?" Since information is valuable, similar to primary or monetary rewards, the neural machinery used to process information may mimic that of reward processing. However, by exploring the neural mechanisms and motives underlying information-seeking behaviors, Charpentier and Cogliati Dezza (Chapter 9) review recent discoveries showing two different neural networks involved in information-seeking: one network sharing similar neural codes with reward processing and another independent of it. Furthermore, since the brain has resource-limited capacity, it has to select only information relevant for behavioral benefits. Gottlieb (Chapter 10) explores the neural mechanisms underlying the selection of relevant information, suggesting that these processes are modulated by learning, individual goals, biological constraints, and behavioral contexts. Another indication of neural machinery shared between different cognitive systems is when comparing commonalities of search behavior in internal and external spaces. Hills et al. (Chapter 11) argue that the strategies adapted for search in external spatial environments are similar to those used to seek information internally from memory, as demonstrated by the use of classic models of spatial foraging used to predict internal search in memory. This framework suggests that the representational structure of inner space may be shaped by the processes people apply to search within it. Lastly, information-seeking is not only a drive to acquire new knowledge, but also to connect ideas and relate knowledge about different things in the world. Zurn et al. (Chapter 12) discuss a novel framework that moves away from an acquisitional account of curiosity to a connectional one. In doing so, this chapter describes how humans build their own network of knowledge and how both personal traits and states influence this building process.

In the conclusion of the book, we discuss the open questions and future challenges the field may face in the coming years. For example, how is information-seeking related to reward-seeking? What are the principles that enable us to acquire useful information with computational efficiency, despite possessing limited cognitive capacities and knowledge? Which aspects of our neural machinery are unique to information-seeking, and what is shared across other cognitive systems? We conclude by discussing how the science of information-seeking informs important societal issues. Just as limitless as our appetite for knowledge, so too is the science of information-seeking bounded only by the limits of our curiosity.

PART I

What Drives Humans to Seek Information?

CHAPTER I

The Motivational Processes of Sense-Making

Zachary Wojtowicz, Nick Chater, and George Loewenstein

> Humboldt thought ... A hill whose height remained unknown was an insult to the intelligence and made him uneasy ... A riddle, no matter how small, could not be left by the side of the road.
>
> Kehlmann, *Measuring the World*

1.1 Introduction

Our innate drive to make sense of things is one of the most powerful forces shaping both individual human cognition and collective societal progress. Consider the huge impetus behind the accumulation and critique of knowledge, which touches on all subjects – whether they be scientific, historical, or cultural – and proceeds at a grand scale to fill every corner of life, from the lectures of academic halls to the chatter of coffee houses. Sometimes knowledge is sought with some immediate objective in mind, but this makes up, on the whole, a surprisingly small part of our intellectual life. The force driving us to identify the causes of the Bolshevik revolution, map the deep oceans or the surface of the moon, chart the history of jazz, and understand the origins of life is powerful enough to drive millions of hours of scholarly activity – often without obvious direct application and even without pay. Daily life, too, is filled with myriad activities that provoke our interest, from exploring new cities, music, or cuisine to tracing our family history, becoming intrigued by gossip at the next table, and following the news. Indeed, these pleasures are so great that vast sectors of human activity are devoted to creating objects whose primary purpose is to stimulate the delights of sense-making: novels, movies, works of art, puzzles, and many more.

Although we generally take our undirected urge to make sense of the world for granted, it may seem strange upon reflection, especially because it frequently does not confer obvious near-term benefits. One might expect that the brutal logic of natural selection would have favored creatures interested only in practical concerns that directly enhance survival and reproduction. One might imagine, too, that societies with a laser-like focus on knowledge with immediate utility, rather than those promoting apparently purposeless inquiry, would be the ones to get ahead. Yet the opposite seems to be true: just "figuring stuff out" often yields unpredictable, but enormous, practical benefits. Indeed, the aimlessness of human curiosity may, paradoxically, be the secret of our species' success (if it can be called that). This chapter focuses on the rationale for, and nature of, the motivational processes underlying the drive for sense-making: the intrinsic human desire to make sense of the world. We explore why the drive for sense-making is so valuable and, crucially, how particular features of its implementation can at times lead us astray into systematically incorrect beliefs.

In Section 1.2 ("The Drive for Sense-Making"), we start by discussing why sense-making generates a drive, similar to those associated with the primary reinforcers of food, water, sleep, sex, shelter, and air. The essence of our argument is that the drive for sense-making helps us balance the immediate benefits of satisfying tangible wants against the delayed benefits of investing in knowledge about ourselves and the world around us. The task of optimally making such trade-offs, which are incumbent upon all agents capable of self-directed learning, presents a formidable challenge because explicitly forecasting the beneficial consequences of each and every potential cognitive investment is often more trouble than it is worth. For many of the decisions we are faced with every day, such calculations would require a great deal of computational effort and yield inaccurate results, if they are even possible at all.

The drive for sense-making circumvents this problem by directly incentivizing our ability to make sense of the world in the here and now. It operates under the general assumption that "knowledge is power" – that is, that an enriched understanding of the world will benefit us in the future even if we cannot foresee exactly how. In the absence of a drive for sense-making, a limited ability to prospectively evaluate, and hence appreciate, the benefits of cognitively enriching activities would lead us to persistently underinvest in them. In this way, the drive for sense-making fills a critical gap that arises in purely goal-oriented cognition.

An economic framing of this argument reveals that the motivational incentive generated by the sense-making drive is analogous to the monetary incentive generated by a subsidy on knowledge-producing activities. We glean insights from this analogy by discussing why societies do in fact subsidize what is called basic research: "systematic study directed toward greater knowledge or understanding of the fundamental aspects of phenomena and of observable facts without specific applications."[1] Analogous to our argument that the drive for sense-making exists to enhance future pay-offs, the quoted definition continues by noting that basic research is "farsighted high payoff research that provides the basis for technological progress."

While Section 1.2 examines reasons why humans have a drive for sense-making, Section 1.3 ("The Objectives Governing Sense-Making") examines three different factors that guide the particular form sense-making takes: (1) the practical utility of accurate beliefs for attaining concrete goals, (2) the desire to make sense of the world in a way that feels good, and (3) the impact of computational limitations on the sense-making process, including our limited ability to explicitly predict what information will turn out to be useful.

Of note, only the first of these categories is accounted for by standard rational theories of human behavior. Standard economics treats cognition as strictly a means to material ends. Accordingly, it holds that both cognitive states (e.g., knowledge, understanding, beliefs) and functions (e.g., information acquisition and processing) are only valuable to the degree that they are "instrumental" in helping us achieve concrete goals, such as increasing consumption or reducing labor. According to this view, because a rational agent is better prepared to maximize utility when they have an accurate understanding of their environment (Blackwell, 1953), the goal of information acquisition and processing should be to arrive at beliefs that are as accurate (and hence useful) as possible.

Some cognitive scientists, for their part, have recently proposed that correctly predicting the environment is all that matters to agents – essentially inverting the classical economist's long-standing position by entirely subordinating material objectives to cognitive ones (Friston, 2010). Such "predictive processing" accounts take a different conceptual and mathematical form than rational economic models, but they share the fundamental conclusion that our cognition is exclusively aimed at generating accurate predictions about the future.

These perspectives yield important insights, but they also leave out critical aspects of sense-making. First, theories that exclusively focus on instrumental value (e.g., standard economics) fail to explain why we so fervently pursue activities, such as solving puzzles or reading mystery

---

[1] www.law.cornell.edu/cfr/text/32/272.3

novels, that seem to yield little instrumental value relative to other readily available uses of our time.[2] On the other hand, theories that exclusively focus on inferential value (e.g., predictive processing models) do not readily explain the purposeful, goal-oriented nature of much of our cognition: the obvious fact that we do care about eating, sleeping, attracting the attention of potential mates, and achieving innumerable other material objectives. Predictive processing theories also seem to make the implausible prediction that agents should seek a maximally predictable environment and stay there forever (known as the "dark room problem"; see Friston, Thornton, & Clark, 2012; Sun & Firestone, 2020).

Both the standard instrumental and the predictive processing theories of sense-making also leave out the fact that motivation and beliefs frequently interact with one another. In recent years, however, economists have begun to recognize that certain cognitive states and processes seem to be valued in themselves and confer strong motivational significance for agents. Work on "belief-based utility" (Loewenstein & Molnar, 2018) has shown that the desire to make sense that feels good plays a significant role in determining how we seek, interpret, and act upon information. In a similar vein, psychologists outside of the predictive processing tradition have long recognized the importance of motivated reasoning in shaping our beliefs (Kunda, 1990).

Motivational factors are also crucial for ensuring we make the best use of our limited cognitive resources when gathering and processing information. For example, the motivational signals of flow and curiosity direct us toward the most valuable new information we might gather through reading, observing, discussing, or experimenting (Wojtowicz, Chater, & Loewenstein, 2020; Wojtowicz & Loewenstein, 2020), and the sense of "cognitive dissonance" (Festinger, 1957) alerts us to inconsistencies in our beliefs that require further analysis and scrutiny. As a result, understanding what interpretation an individual will arrive at requires, at least in part, accounting for the motivational factors that guide our uptake and processing of information.

The standard instrumental and predictive accounts also generally overlook the impact of computational constraints on the sense we can and do make of the world. In particular, these accounts leave out the fact that considering each of the myriad possible interpretations of a given body of information as prescribed by Bayes' rule is often intractable (Jeffrey, 2004),

---

[2] Notably, most people spend a shockingly small fraction of their free time purposefully investing in economically valuable forms of human capital.

even for relatively simple problems (Kwisthout, 2011; Van Rooij, 2008). Evidence suggests that our cognitive system instead approximates this normative standard by sampling interpretations one at a time (e.g., we see the duck-rabbit as either a duck, or a rabbit, but not both at once; see Figure 1.1). As we will argue, this has huge ramifications for how sense-making operates (Chater, 2019; Pashler, 1999).

Perhaps the most important practical limitation of both the standard instrumental and predictive processing accounts of sense-making, however, is that they fail to explain the troubling predominance of nonnormative belief patterns in society or to provide adequate guidance as to how they might be addressed. Recent developments – such as the precipitous growth of online radicalization, conspiracy theory communities, religious extremism, political polarization, anti-science rhetoric, climate change skepticism, antivaccination sentiment, COVID-19 denial, and hate groups – have heightened concerns about the descriptive adequacy of rational frameworks. Such phenomena are especially puzzling for rational theories given that their growth has coincided with (and, arguably, been fueled by) the rise of the Internet, which enables free and instantaneous access to much of human knowledge. According to a purely rational conception of belief-formation, such a dramatic increase in access to high-quality information should have resulted in a commensurate increase in the accuracy of popular beliefs, contrary to recent events. Finally, Section 1.4 ("Implications") shows how the alternative perspective we lay out in the preceding sections can be used to better understand these phenomena.

The core argument of this chapter is that analyzing the multiplicity of objectives governing sense-making can help to explain the scientific and practical puzzles that vex current theories. According to our account, instrumental, inferential, and computational factors work together to guide our decisions. The drive for sense-making is primarily directed at maximizing predictive accuracy, but the other above-noted factors – belief-based utility and cognitive efficiency – also shape the sense we make. The interaction of these (sometimes competing) factors gives rise to characteristic patterns of irrationality, which leave us vulnerable to seductive mistruths that are increasingly amplified, both passively (by technologies that spread misinformation with unprecedented speed) and actively (by social movements dedicated to propagating abnormal patterns of beliefs). A comprehensive picture of how sense-making fits into the broader psychology of motivation explains characteristic distortions in our relationship with truth and, in turn, sheds new light on these concerning trends.

1.2   The Drive for Sense-Making

In this section, we develop a functional account of the drive for sense-making that explains its characteristic features by analyzing the cognitive problem it solves. Our account starts with the general observation that many – if not all – motivational states exist to address the boundedness of our rationality (Hanoch, 2002; MacLeod, 1996; Muramatsu & Hanoch, 2005; Samuelson & Swinkels, 2006; Sorg, Singh, & Lewis, 2010). Immediate drives, feelings, and urges help us make decisions quickly and cheaply by circumventing the need to prospectively calculate the costs and benefits of each potential option explicitly. More specifically, these visceral states circumvent the (often intractable) task of forecasting the consequences of our actions arbitrarily far into an uncertain future (Bechara & Damasio, 2005; Damasio, 2006) by encoding the expected survival value associated with evolutionarily significant behaviors, such as consuming key nutrients, copulating, nurturing offspring, and avoiding bodily harm (Cabanac, 1971; Cosmides & Tooby, 2000).

A subset of these states specifically function to shape our information seeking and processing behavior: boredom, flow (Wojtowicz et al., 2020), curiosity (Wojtowicz & Loewenstein, 2020), mental effort (Kurzban et al., 2013; Shenhav et al., 2017), and, as we will argue, the drive for sense-making. Although these states are psychologically distinct, they share many theoretical connections and overlap operationally due to the interrelated nature of their underlying functions. Indeed, we have argued elsewhere that curiosity may in fact be a special case of the drive for sense-making (Chater & Loewenstein, 2016; Wojtowicz & Loewenstein, 2020), and that flow and boredom partly reflect deviations from the amount of cognitive enrichment one has come to expect from similar environments (Wojtowicz et al., 2020).

As we have suggested, explicitly appraising the value of an increase in information, knowledge, or understanding is computationally intractable and would exhaust our finite cognitive resources in most situations. In most cases, our models of the external world are so underspecified that they do not provide meaningful answers to the question of how useful a particular piece of information is likely to be. But even if such models were available and could in principle yield well-defined answers, the computational costs of generating accurate predictions would still be prohibitive in most circumstances. This is because explicitly assessing the value of a piece of information or knowledge requires that we consider the many instances where a piece of information or knowledge would be applied. In general, the number of potential futures grows exponentially with the time horizon one considers; because cognitive resources can be applied arbitrarily far in the future, this explosion can be difficult to contend with (Bellman, 1957; Savage, 1972; Sutton & Barto, 2018). Planning the optimal sequence of information-acquisition behaviors also requires that one anticipate how information gained at each stage will impact the interpretation and usefulness of information gained at all later stages (Meder et al., 2019).

Our hypothesis is that the brain circumvents these computational challenges by directly incentivizing actions that result in increased understanding using a motivational state that we experience as the drive for sense-making (Chater & Loewenstein, 2016). This approach avoids the need to prospectively calculate the potential usefulness of knowledge explicitly because "sense" is quantified using a contemporaneous measure of our ability to explain empirical regularities in the world. This is principally a backward-looking appraisal that operates on fixed data and, critically, does not require us to simulate the exponential number of diverging possible futures where that sense might be applied.

The exact nature of how the brain quantifies sense is still an area of active research, but one hypothesis is that sense measures our ability to *compress* the information we encounter into explanations. Data can be compressed to the extent that patterns can be found in that data, so the degree of compression achieved provides a natural measure of how well patterns in that data have been uncovered, irrespective of whether those patterns will turn out to help achieve any practical goal. Viewed in this way, the amount of *sense* we make out of a particular piece of information corresponds to the reduction in representational code length that we can achieve when we discover successively better (i.e., compressive) explanations for it. *Sense-making* occurs when we strike upon insights or critical pieces of new information that help us to resolve ambiguities or recognize regularities in an existing set of facts, thereby enabling us to compress them further.

As an example, consider the text "GNIKAMESNES." While this might at first appear to be meaningless, it acquires more sense – especially in the context of this chapter – once we recognize it as "SENSEMAKING" spelled backwards. Under the compression hypothesis, this insight *makes sense* of the original text precisely because it reduces an unfamiliar and unwieldy jumble of letters to two simple cognitive operations: recalling a familiar word ("sense-making") plus applying a familiar transformation (left–right transposition), enabling us to cognitively represent, manipulate, encode, and recall the string more efficiently. If, for illustration, we imagine all "units" are equal (whether letters, words, or transpositions), then we can see that spotting this new representation of "GNIKAMESNES" counts as definite progress. For a hypothetical cognitive system that encoded text using such a system – that is, either by storing it letter by letter or by applying a transformation to previously stored text – detecting this pattern would reduce the representational length of "GNIKAMESNES" from eleven to just two units, thus yielding nine "units of sense."

While more research is needed to determine what form the representations underlying a fully domain-general measure of sense-making might take, a variety of candidates have been proposed that range from the most comprehensive model of computation – programs compiled by a Turing complete language (Chater, 1996; Chater & Loewenstein, 2016; Chater & Vitányi, 2003) – to less powerful automata capable of expressing more restricted grammars (i.e., ones at a lower level of the Chomsky hierarchy; see Griffiths & Tenenbaum, 2003; Simon, 1972). For now, the question of how these mathematically abstracted computational-level measures might be implemented in the brain is a largely unexplored – but exciting – topic for future research.

According to this perspective, the *drive for sense-making* is an innate source of motivation that rewards us for each marginal increase (and, perhaps, punishes us for each marginal decrease) in our ability to compress information into efficient representations (Chater & Loewenstein, 2016). While the goal of compressing the information we encounter is certainly valuable for its own sake (e.g., because it enables us to store information more efficiently in the brain), its primary benefit is that it directs our cognitive machinery to actively search for regularities in the phenomena we observe, thus enabling us to better describe, predict, and control the world.[3]

Given that sense-making and the classical drives serve similar psychological functions, they also share many basic characteristics. For example, classical drives consist of both a "carrot" and a "stick": pleasure when we fulfill the drive's target behavior and pain when we abstain from it. For example, eating when hungry feels good, but failing to do so for long

---

[3] This hypothesized correspondence between sense-making and compression may also help explain why memorization is such a critical component of pedagogy. In many educational contexts, no one truly expects that students will retain most of the information they learn after the course is finished. Nevertheless, the challenge of memorizing a large domain of related facts efficiently enough to reproduce them on a test forces students to search for the underlying connections, structures, and regularities that are the true marrow of knowledge. Even if the particulars are themselves forgotten, the concepts which bind them together are generally retained, and these are often the most useful.

periods of time becomes highly aversive, especially while in the presence of food. Paralleling these mechanisms, a few studies have shown that curiosity activates the same areas of the brain that process extrinsic rewards (Jepma et al., 2012; Kang et al., 2009), suggesting that sense-making considerations may enter into standard reward calculation as an intrinsic reward (or punishment) signal (Gottlieb et al., 2013; Kidd & Hayden, 2015).

In the case of sense-making, the carrot corresponds to the pleasure we experience when we succeed at uncovering regularities that generate new sense. In moments of profound insight, the sudden rush of sense-making pleasure can be quite intense (Gopnik, 1998), as exemplified by Archimedes' famous exclamation of "Eureka!" upon discovering the principle of buoyancy. Less acute instances of sense-making pleasure also permeate many aspects of our daily life and range from the delight of discovering the answer to a riddle to the satisfaction of arriving at a mystery novel's grand reveal. The stick, on the other hand, consists of the unpleasant sense of deprivation we feel when we are faced with a salient lack of understanding, as exemplified by the torment of leaving a riddle unanswered or a mystery novel unfinished. This deprivation is stronger the more apparent the gap in our understanding becomes, and the less easily it can be closed (Golman & Loewenstein, 2018; Loewenstein, 1994).

The drive for sense-making is related to, and may even entirely subsume, other motivational states that guide how we gather and process information. The most obvious example is curiosity, which shares the same drive-like features (Loewenstein, 1994), solves the same cognitive problem (Wojtowicz & Loewenstein, 2020), and has overlapping behavioral implications (Chater & Loewenstein, 2016) as sense-making. Other examples include boredom, which redirects our attention away from understimulating activities when more promising opportunities seem to exist in our environment, and flow, which keeps our attention focused on the task at hand when other, better opportunities seem unlikely to exist. Both of these states emerge from a counterfactual comparison between the current and anticipated value of engagement, which is largely determined by the degree of sense-making achieved (Chater & Loewenstein, 2016; Wojtowicz et al., 2020). Sense-making is also closely related to our preferences for creating and resolving uncertainty (Ruan, Hsee, & Lu, 2018) and may underpin the states of suspense and surprise (Ely, Frankel, & Kamenica, 2015). Finally, the explanatory values we use to evaluate everything from scientific hypotheses to quick excuses – such as how simple, descriptive, or unifying an account is – are key implements of sense-making and arguably exist to further the same overall inferential objective (Wojtowicz & DeDeo, 2020).

According to our account, the drive for sense-making makes up for our limited ability to appreciate the true long-term value of investing in knowledge. This parallels the way in which governments use subsidies to overcome the inherent tendency of private enterprise to underinvest in knowledge-generating activities. In a social setting, it is virtually free to include, and very difficult to exclude, others from using knowledge once it has been created. Knowledge is therefore an example of what economists refer to as "public goods," which are chronically undersupplied relative to the socially efficient optimum because potential producers cannot capture the full value they create by investing in them.

Modern societies address this problem through government funding of public universities, scientific institutions, and basic research. Just as the drive for sense-making is necessary to motivate undirected inquiry, this funding is necessary to sustain learning for its own sake, without any immediate expectation of profit. As it turns out, however, such research often lays the groundwork for a variety of unforeseen applications that more than pay for the initial outlay through increased long-term economic growth. Also like sense-making, our inability to predict which types of knowledge will eventually be useful for particular problems means that continued broad investment in basic research often turns out to be the best way of ensuring we eventually solve them. Moreover, heavy-handed attempts to override research curiosity and narrowly optimize the direction of their work often end up backfiring because the process of justifying the value of scientific projects (including, sometimes, their practical value) through grant writing and related activities takes up time that could be used for actual research. In much the same way, forecasting the future value of sense-making uses up the very mental resources one needs to make sense of the world.

The function of the drive for sense-making is also illustrated by an analogy to education. Students perpetually complain that what they learn has no obvious value or relevance to their daily lives or future careers. While out-of-date education is certainly a problem, these critiques are often overstated, especially in young children who have no conception of what adult life is like and consequently cannot accurately gauge the importance of the knowledge and skills they are learning. Indeed, the distinction between *education* and *training* nicely captures the difference between the provision of knowledge which has no immediate application and that which is focused on learning an applicable skill. While *training* is, of course, extremely important, a school and university system focused purely on immediately applicable skills would fail to cultivate the growth of general knowledge that is crucial to long-term development. The main goal of *education*, therefore, is to provide a broad base of fundamental knowledge that helps students get a sense of the overall "geography" of knowledge in its broadest outlines. As students get older and their particular interests, proclivities, and goals become more clear, a greater degree of specialization is gradually introduced, but education is not, and cannot be, perfectly tailored.

If, as this analysis suggests, the purpose of formal education is to ensure that students acquire skills that are *unexpectedly* useful (and therefore would not seek out themselves), initiatives to shift the curriculum toward more apparently useful material may miss the point entirely. In much the same way, sense-making drives us to enrich our cognitive capacities in numerous directions, only some of which will turn out to be useful. Like a good teacher, the sense-making drive encourages us to engage in enriching activities, even in the absence of foreseeable benefits. Given that sense-making functions as "nature's endogenous teacher," it is not surprising that its derivative states, most notably curiosity, play a critical role in supporting learning, both in and out of the classroom (Deci & Ryan, 1981; Litman, 2005; Markey & Loewenstein, 2014; Pluck & Johnson, 2011; Wade & Kidd, 2019).

These points are corroborated by research in machine learning, which has shown that intrinsically generated sense-making rewards help to foster robust learning by encouraging structured exploration. Schmidhuber (1991, p. 222) points out that these incentives not only instill a desire for an artificial system to improve its understanding of the world, but also "to model its own ignorance, thus showing a rudimentary form of self-introspective behavior." Lopes, Lang, Toussaint, and Oudeyer (2012) further show that such rewards can be generated using heuristic online estimates of learning progress, closely matching our conception of the drive for sense-making as rewarding gains in our ability to compress existing information. In a similar vein, Pathak, Agrawal, Efros, and Darrell (2017) demonstrated the benefits of combining standard reinforcement learning with an "intrinsic curiosity module" that learns to predict which actions might expose the shortcomings in an agent's model of the environment. They show that adding these predictions to the stream of extrinsic reward feedback an agent receives from the environment speeds up learning; in fact, their agents learn to successfully navigate video games when motivated by intrinsic curiosity alone (see also Burda et al., 2018).

1.3 The Objectives Governing Sense-Making

In this section, we describe three objectives that shape sense-making, either directly, through motivational signals that orient sense-making, or indirectly, through constraints on the cognitive processes that underlie it.

1.3.1   Instrumental Objectives

The most obvious goal of sense-making is to help people make decisions that reliably lead to desired outcomes. From the perspective of decision theory, a rational agent acting in isolation is better equipped to pursue concrete ends when armed with more accurate beliefs (Blackwell, 1953), so the instrumental objective of sense-making often boils down to developing beliefs that are as accurate as possible. Indeed, in extreme cases, holding beliefs that are too divorced from reality (e.g., believing that one knows how to swim when one does not) can be fatal. Consequently, there seem to be strong constraints on the sense-making process: we cannot simply believe whatever we wish, and we labor to justify even our most fanciful beliefs to ourselves and others.

However, the fact that humans are both boundedly rational and highly social adds several important caveats to the truth-orienting function of sense-making, such that inaccurate beliefs may sometimes be advantageous when other psychological factors are taken into account. For example, the autonomic effects of nervousness evolved because they are usually adaptive, but they have the unintended consequence of degrading performance in some circumstances, such as test taking (Zeidner, 2010), public speaking (Beatty 1988), high-stakes games (Ariely, Gneezy, Loewenstein, & Mazar, 2009), athletic performance (Kleine, 1990), and sexual function (McCabe, 2005). Conditional on being subject to these autonomic forces, overconfidence in our objective abilities might benefit us in situations in which performance anxiety would otherwise hold us back. Systematic cognitive errors can also be beneficial if and when they compensate for other types of errors. As one example, Kahneman and Lovallo (1993) argue that overconfidence can be beneficial to the degree that it compensates for the conservatism and extreme avoidance of risk that would, in its absence, arise from loss aversion.

The beliefs we hold also change the way others regard us. For example, people are more likely to trust the leadership and advice of those who are self-confident. Anderson, Brion, Moore, and Kennedy (2012) present a series of studies showing that overconfidence leads other people to view an individual as more competent, and generally enhances their social status. Some strategic interactions, such as the game of chicken, also favor those who can convince others of their irrational commitment to undertake risky actions (Colman, 2003; Rapoport & Chammah, 1966; Schelling, 1980). While it is always possible, in principle, for a well-calibrated individual to fake confidence, such an act can, in practice, be difficult to sustain. In some domains, the most effective way to convince others of one's exceptional abilities may be to first convince oneself.

Mercier and Sperber (2011) go even further, advancing the provocative hypothesis that the principle function of reasoning is to develop arguments that will be convincing to others. Needless to say, it is not always in one's personal best interest to reason in good faith when the objective is to sway someone else. According to this account, many apparently irrational aspects of cognition are actually driven by the benefits associated with successfully influencing others.

1.3.2   Hedonic Objectives

Although beliefs primarily function to help us achieve desired outcomes, people also care about what happens purely in their own minds. In other words, beliefs are not merely a means to an end, but can also become an end in themselves. While this general phenomenon – known in economics as belief-based utility – is at odds with basic tenets of rational thought (and, as we will describe, can undercut the instrumental function of beliefs outlined in the preceding section), it nevertheless performs an indispensable cognitive function by motivating us to pursue complex goals that would be hard to define without the aid of sense-making.

Evolution has, as we have noted, endowed us with a variety of motivational mechanisms that encode the value of various goals and push us to pursue beneficial actions, most notably the visceral feeling states and hedonic signals associated with classic drives that incentivize us to maintain homeostasis and satisfy various biological imperatives. While the satisfaction of many basic physiological goals can be determined automatically and without conscious awareness (e.g., monitoring the blood for a satisfactory glucose level), measuring progress on other goals, especially social goals, depends on nuanced inferences that must be assessed using higher-level cognitive processing. For instance, we care about considerations such as our standing in the world – whether we are liked and respected by others – and, with especially obvious evolutionary significance, whether we are found attractive by potential mates. Our motivational system induces us to pursue these goals by making certain belief states directly valuable. The pleasure associated with, for example, believing that others view us favorably provides an incentive for us to behave in a fashion that makes it true. This may, in turn, lead to substantial long-term benefits, such as the cooperative support of others, although the specific nature of these benefits will, of course, be difficult to foresee precisely.

Belief-based utility exists to motivate behaviors that bring about desirable situations, but it is an imperfect mechanism for achieving this goal from a purely hedonic point of view. After all, simply believing what makes us feel good, irrespective of reality, would be a more direct route to unlocking the pleasures of the mind. Fortunately for the survival of our species, there seem to be significant limitations on our ability to believe whatever makes us feel good (Loewenstein & Molnar, 2018). So, for example, we cannot, by sheer force of will, perceive low teaching feedback scores as high praise – though we may be able to avoid looking at our teaching ratings entirely. However, despite such constraints on our ability to see what we want to see, the motives induced by belief-based utility can, in some instances, distort our relationship with truth and undermine our ability to achieve material goals. For example, an overestimate of our ability might feel good, but it can also lead us to expend time, energy, and money on endeavors where we are overwhelmingly likely to fail.

Exactly how motivational forces influence the direction that sense-making takes is an interesting and underexplored question. The influence of motivational processes on sense-making is undoubtedly aided by the fact that sense-making is, like most cognitive processes, sequential. That means that motivations can influence the *direction* that information processing takes. As Epley and Gilovich (2016, p. 133) note, "People don't simply believe what they want to believe ... People generally reason their way to conclusions they favor, with their preferences influencing the way evidence is gathered, arguments are processed, and memories of past experience are recalled. Each of these processes can be affected in subtle ways by people's motivations." "For propositions we want to believe," Gilovich (2008, pp. 83–84) writes in his classic *How We Know What Isn't So*, "we ask only that the evidence not force us to believe otherwise. . . For propositions we want to resist, however, we ask whether the evidence compels such a distasteful conclusion. . . For desired conclusions, in other words, it is as if we ask ourselves, 'Can I believe this?', but for unpalatable conclusions we ask 'Must I believe this?'." Or, as Kunda (1990, pp. 482–483) expressed it, people "draw the desired conclusion only if they can muster up the evidence necessary to support it."

As the above-quoted passages hint, the processes that people use to achieve sense-making that feels good bear a striking resemblance to the biased processes that scientists use to collect and analyze data in a fashion that supports the conclusions they want to arrive at (c.f. John,

Loewenstein, & Prelec, 2012; Simmons, Nelson, & Simonsohn, 2011) –
a set of practices that have come to be known, collectively, as "p-hacking."
Much as scientists may collect just enough information to support their
favored hypothesis and no more, people who want to behave selfishly
without perceiving themselves as such will avoid collecting new information about the consequences of their actions when their current data
supports the conclusion that their actions will not hurt others (Chen,
et al., 2020).

One potential consequence of motivated processing is a phenomenon
known as belief polarization, which occurs when exposure to the same new
piece of evidence causes individuals who hold different beliefs to diverge
even further (Batson, 1975; Liberman & Chaiken, 1992; Lord, Ross, &
Lepper, 1979). Some have rightly pointed out that this pattern of updating
is not necessarily irrational given that it can result from Bayes' rule in
certain circumstances (Cook & Lewandowsky, 2016; Jern, Chang, &
Kemp, 2014). However, by the same token, consistency with Bayes' rule
does not, on its own, necessarily preclude the influence of motivational
factors. Indeed, the many degrees of freedom available to a mischievous
Bayesian – what evidence to consider and how, exactly, to interpret that
evidence – provide a variety of opportunities for motivation to influence an
otherwise mechanical application of Bayes' rule (c.f., Rabin & Schrag,
1999).

In Cook and Lewandowsky (2016), for example, Bayes' theorem is
made to accommodate belief polarization through the addition of variables
such as "a pro-market worldview" and "trust in scientists" that influence an
agent's priors and interpretation of evidence about global warming. This,
however, only pushes the question of motivational influence up a level:
while it may indeed be Bayesian for someone to reject the academic
consensus on global warming conditional on the belief that climate science
is a communist conspiracy to undermine the free market, this hypercritical
approach to evidence may itself not be warranted, especially if it were only
adopted to protect a cherished belief.

The question of what normative constraints, if any, can be said to limit
how a rational agent constructs their likelihood function and prior is
a fascinating, complex, and as-yet unresolved problem; our goal here is
simply to point out that the apparent use of Bayesian inference at one level
does not necessarily preclude the influence of motivational factors at
another. At the same time, it is important to note that post-hoc rationalization and other forms of motivated reasoning are not necessarily
irrational once the many practical considerations that constrain cognition

have been taken into account. Cushman (2020), for instance, argues that adjusting beliefs to rationalize our actions is a functional mechanism that transfers knowledge from the decision processes that underlie instinct, intuition, and habit to our rational mind. We turn to the influence of cognitive constraints next.

1.3.3   Cognitive Efficiency

Sense-making, like all cognitive processes, is subject to computational constraints. This has the implication that we generally cannot consider every potential interpretation of information in strict accordance with Bayes' rule (Aragones, Gilboa, Postlewaite, & Schmeidler, 2005; Kwisthout, 2011; Van Rooij, 2008). Recent work suggests that our brain instead approximates Bayesian inference using a step-by-step process of sampling – that is, we adopt a single working hypothesis and update it over time as we think of alternative hypotheses and gather new data (Bramley, Dayan, Griffiths, & Lagnado, 2017; Dasgupta, Schulz, & Gershman, 2017; Dayan, 1998; Gershman, Vul, & Tenenbaum, 2009; Griffiths, Vul, & Sanborn, 2012; Levy, Reali, & Griffiths, 2009; Sanborn & Chater, 2016; Vul, Goodman, Griffiths, & Tenenbaum, 2014; Vul & Pashler, 2008). Randomly selecting potential hypotheses for consideration is inefficient because most of them would turn out to be nonsensical, so the alternatives we consider are usually local, piecewise modifications of the working hypothesis we already have and are heavily informed by prior beliefs (Bramley et al., 2017; Tenenbaum, Griffiths, & Niyogi, 2007). This strategy brings otherwise intractable problems within reach, but it also leads to a number of biases (Chater et al., 2020; Sanborn & Chater, 2016).

The ambiguous visual patterns of Figure 1.1 demonstrate the constraint that we only perceive one interpretation at a time. Each image appears to flip back and forth between two distinct percepts, exhibiting "multistability." Both interpretations are equally correct, but we experience one – and only one – as the concrete, definitive, and exclusive truth at each point in time. Thus, rather than being able to average over possible perceptual interpretations, we seem limited to sampling interpretations one at a time (Moreno-Bote, Knill, & Pouget, 2011). In the examples of Figure 1.1, these shifts happen quickly enough that the subjectivity of our perception is made apparent and can be tempered by rational self-reflection, but this is likely the exception, not the rule. When extrapolated to higher-order epistemic (rather than perceptual) beliefs, it is easy to imagine how such

(a) Necker Cube   (b) Duck-Rabbit   (c) Rubin Face-Vase

Figure 1.1 Three examples of perceptual multistability. Each image can be interpreted in two ways, but we only perceive one interpretation at a time. Evidence
suggests that this phenomenon extends to higher cognitive processes such as
explanatory inference. See text for details.

illusions of objectivity might exacerbate interpersonal conflict between
people who arrive at different conclusions from common information.

Another implication of this cognitive strategy is that sense-making
proceeds much like evolution, which "tinkers" by creatively repurposing
existing biological machinery to address new environmental challenges
rather than redesigning each species, cell-type, organ, physiological process, or behavior from scratch. Jacob (1977) illustrates this with the
examples of the woodpecker and the aye-aye (a type of lemur), both of
which exploit the same ecological niche of extracting insects from small
crevices in dead wood. Each has adapted to accomplish this task using
features already possessed by their evolutionary forebears: the woodpecker,
whose ancestors possessed beaks but lacked hands, developed an elongated
beak; the aye-aye, whose ancestors lacked beaks but had hands, developed
unusually long and thin fingers. While there may, in principle, be an
optimal solution to this ecological problem involving neither beak nor
hand, evolution cannot discover it except by way of intermediate forms.
Each evolutionary lineage is, in the near term, fated to build on what it has
already developed.

In much the same way, reconsidering our entire worldview in light of
every new piece of information would be computationally prohibitive: we
do not update globally. Instead, we take the bulk of our beliefs as given and
re-examine only those that bear most directly on new evidence we encounter. In Otto Neurath's famous metaphor, knowledge is like a boat that is
always on the high seas, never able to rebuild from scratch but always
forced to repair using whatever existing materials are to hand (Bramley
et al., 2017; Cat, 2021). In cases when our deeply held beliefs and evidence

come into conflict, the latter is usually made to yield. Only rarely do we reflect upon and take stock of "core" beliefs, foundational assumptions, and axiomatic commitments; crises of faith are the exception, not the rule. Such phenomena are, to a degree, already a feature of hierarchical Bayesian models, where priors descending from higher levels can override the bottom-up flow of information (Friston & Kiebel, 2009; Tenenbaum et al., 2007; Yuille & Kersten, 2006). Note, however, that these dynamics are greatly exacerbated by the process of local updating that makes a sampling approximation to Bayesian inference computationally efficient.

The ambiguous patterns in Figure 1.1 demonstrate that we do not control certain aspects of how our brain performs inference; no matter how hard we try, it is simply impossible to see both interpretations of a multistable image simultaneously. There are, however, other aspects of sense-making that we are able to influence through deliberative choice. To the degree that these choices bear upon our use of scarce cognitive resources, we might expect them to be mediated by motivational signals. In the same way that physical exhaustion exists to force us to reckon with the physiological consequences of continued exertion, some mental states may exist to "price in" the cognitive costs of sense-making operations.

This observation suggests a possible functional reinterpretation of dogmatic thinking, which Christensen (1994, p. 69) paraphrases as the epistemological attitude that "I happen to believe it – and that's all the justification I need for continuing to believe it." The process of updating beliefs imposes costs that range from the physical (e.g., rewiring neurons) to the practical (e.g., sapping cognitive resources from other important uses). Moreover, if belief updating is a serial, step-by-step process, it will inevitably be both limited and slow (although changing one belief may then, of course, have a cascade of implications for others). This means that the tendency to maintain one's beliefs in the absence of any reason to do otherwise may be unavoidable – and possibly also normatively justified (a philosophical position that Gilbert Harman calls "general foundationalism"; Harman, 2003). In the presence of such considerations, a motivational force that pushes back against the free revision of belief might be beneficial, even if it led to epistemic distortions. Such an account might also help to explain why we are more dogmatic about certain types of beliefs than others; for example, a higher real cost of uprooting more fundamental beliefs would explain our greater resistance to questioning them.

1.4 Implications

The fact that sense-making is a drive helps to explain why humans are so enthusiastic about many activities that make no obvious contribution to survival or reproduction – for example, reading fiction, watching films, and solving puzzles that we ourselves create. Sense-making, like other drives, originally emerged to promote biological fitness, but operates even when this function is obviously nonoperative, similarly to when we have sex using birth control or consume "empty calories." Indeed, forms of entertainment that provide the least amount of informational enrichment (and are therefore arguably the most heavily driven by sense-making, e.g., mystery novels) are often precisely structured to build and release suspense artificially. This characteristic strategy of drive buildup and consummation is seen across the many other drives we cultivate for pleasure. Take, for instance, hunger, which we actively protect by avoiding snacks that will "ruin our appetite," then tease over many courses before finally indulging. Viewed from this perspective, much of what we call culture appears, indeed, to be a grand collection of machines that produce the pleasure of sense-making through the origination, elaboration, and resolution of fascinating complexities.

All drives are, of course, imperfect regulators. A starving person exposed to unlimited amounts of food will overconsume to the point of sickness or even death; extreme levels of pain and fear can, in some cases, become counterproductive. Sense-making, likewise, is not always perfectly calibrated to the provision of long-term benefits in every situation. The mass appeal of conspiracy theories and pseudoscientific frameworks, as exemplified by the widespread rejection of life-saving vaccines against COVID-19, illustrate sense-making taken beyond the point of functionality. The potential for sense-making to reach dysfunctional levels is also vividly illustrated by delusional schizophrenia, which is marked by a tendency to attribute "too much" coherence to meaningless or inconclusive information while dismissing contrary evidence (DSM-5, 2013; McLean, Mattiske, & Balzan, 2017). Of note, individual differences in conspiracy-mindedness and schizotypal personality disorder are interrelated (Bruder, Haffke, Neave, Nouripanah, & Imhoff, 2013; Darwin, Neave, & Holmes, 2011), raising the intriguing possibility that shared cognitive foundations may help explain these excesses of sense-making.

The rapid proliferation of new digital information technologies poses both great promise and great peril for sense-making. On one hand, the "information explosion" occasioned by the rise of the Internet has drastic-ally expanded access to nourishment for sense-making, ranging from the most extensive encyclopedia in history (Voß, 2005) to tens of thousands of digitized books (Coyle, 2006) and millions of user-generated videos (Cheng, Dale, & Liu, 2008). At the same time, social media has also greatly increased our exposure to the sense-making produced by others, leading to a dense cross-fertilization of ideas and the almost instantaneous transmission of new insights between people, leading to a kind of global-ization of knowledge.

On the other hand, changes to the topological structure of communica-tion have profoundly disrupted how sense-making flows through society, often in troubling ways. Homophily (the preferential tendency for similar individuals to form network connections; McPherson, Smith-Lovin, and Cook (2001)) combined with the sense-making distortions introduced by belief-based utility (as discussed in Section 1.2) has led to concern about the emergence of online "echo chambers": massive networks of individuals who see and propagate information or explanations that corroborate their existing worldview with little critical feedback (Bakshy, Messing, & Adamic, 2015; Colleoni, Rozza, & Arvidsson, 2014; Sunstein, 2002; but see also the moderating evidence of Dubois & Blank, 2018; Flaxman, Goel, & Rao, 2016). These effects are, no doubt, exacerbated by the failure of individuals to take account of just how biased their media diet is (Enke & Zimmermann, 2019; Eyster & Rabin, 2014; Pronin, Lin, & Ross, 2002; Vallone, Ross, & Lepper, 1985), worsening the recalcitrance and illusions of objectivity already inherent to our inferential cognition.

Even outside echo chambers, certain of these belief dynamics threaten to reduce diversity in how we interpret the world. Rather than, quite literally, thinking for ourselves, the proliferation of public commentary has made it all too easy to simply adopt the explanations of the people and media we surround ourselves with. This is appealing to each individual in the short run, as doing so yields an immediate sense-making boost with little cogni-tive investment, but it is potentially disastrous to the health of social discourse as a whole, which depends on the diversity of public opinion.

For all its many benefits, the rapid democratization of information and mass communication has also had the side-effect of destabilizing mechanisms that societies have historically relied upon to filter informa-tion and vet explanations. Those who in ages past claimed privileged sense-making authority – most notably academic scholars, religious leaders, journalists, and political officials – are now frequently reduced to shouting their opinions over the din of popular commentary.

Increasingly, the most valuable commodity in the marketplace of ideas is not a reputation for careful consideration, but rather the sheer ability to garner attention (Heath & Heath, 2007). Newly ascendant counter-normative belief communities fueled by these dynamics – antivaxxers, climate deniers, flat earthers, conspiracy theorists, and religious extremists – have begun to undermine the ability of social institutions to function properly by out-competing their traditional counterparts when it comes to harnessing public attention, and, with it, opinion.

As the sense-making landscape has been upended, those who seek to influence society's understanding have adapted their strategies to take advantage of the new opportunities it provides. Technology has created an increasingly sophisticated set of tools that grant the ability to precisely target and massively amplify both the dissemination (Goldfarb, 2014; Kramer, Guillory, & Hancock, 2014) and the suppression (Bamman, O'Connor, & Smith, 2012) of information. These efforts are becoming increasingly sophisticated now that insights from behavioral and data science are being applied to predict what will engage and persuade us (Matz, Kosinski, Nave, & Stillwell, 2017; Zarouali, Dobber, De Pauw, & de Vreese, 2020).

These intra- and interindividual-level processes that determine the direction of sense-making can have profound consequences for society. As highlighted in George Marshall's (2015) insightful treatise *Don't Even Think About It: Why Our Brains Are Wired to Ignore Climate Change*, our collective ability to grapple with existential problems facing humanity depends on how we collect and make sense of information. Different nations' success in combating the coronavirus pandemic has likewise been affected by the sense that citizens have made of the virus and of interventions intended to stem its spread, often in ways that link to wider political attitudes and group affiliations.

The analysis of sense-making's cognitive foundations that we have pursued in this chapter is only the start of a much broader intellectual project, one which will involve an analysis of how the quirks of our fixed sense-making capacity can be deceived by shifting environmental forces, especially those created by technological advances. As has been illustrated by some of the recent trends that have emerged from this dynamic, the psychological foundations of sense-making have far-reaching consequences for society that we are only just beginning to understand.

References

Anderson, C., Brion, S., Moore, D. A., & Kennedy, J. A. (2012). A status enhancement account of overconfidence. *Journal of Personality and Social Psychology*, 103(4), 718.

Aragones, E., Gilboa, I., Postlewaite, A., & Schmeidler, D. (2005). Fact-free learning. *American Economic Review*, 95(5), 1355–1368.

Ariely, D., Gneezy, U., Loewenstein, G., & Mazar, N. (2009). Large stakes and big mistakes. *The Review of Economic Studies*, 76(2), 451–469.

Bakshy, E., Messing, S., & Adamic, L. A. (2015). Exposure to ideologically diverse news and opinion on Facebook. *Science*, 348(6239), 1130–1132.

Bamman, D., O'Connor, B., & Smith, N. (2012). Censorship and deletion practices in Chinese social media. *First Monday*, 17(3). https://doi.org/10.5210/fm.v17i3.3943.

Batson, C. D. (1975). Rational processing or rationalization? The effect of disconfirming information on a stated religious belief. *Journal of Personality and Social Psychology*, 32(1), 176.

Beatty, M. J. (1988). Situational and predispositional correlates of public speaking anxiety. *Communication Education*, 37(1), 28–39.

Bechara, A., & Damasio, A. R. (2005). The somatic marker hypothesis: A neural theory of economic decision. *Games and Economic Behavior*, 52(2), 336–372.

Bellman, R. E. (1957). *Dynamic programming*. Princeton University Press.

Blackwell, D. (1953). Equivalent comparisons of experiments. *The annals of mathematical statistics*, 24(2), 265–272. www.jstor.org/stable/2236332.

Bramley, N. R., Dayan, P., Griffiths, T. L., & Lagnado, D. A. (2017). Formalizing Neurath's ship: Approximate algorithms for online causal learning. *Psychological Review*, 124(3), 301.

Bruder, M., Haffke, P., Neave, N., Nouripanah, N., & Imhoff, R. (2013). Measuring individual differences in generic beliefs in conspiracy theories across cultures: Conspiracy mentality questionnaire. *Frontiers in Psychology*, 4, 225.

Burda, Y., Edwards, H., Pathak, D., Storkey, A., Darrell, T., & Efros, A. A. (2018). Large-scale study of curiosity-driven learning. *arXiv preprint arXiv:1808.04355*.

Cabanac, M. (1971). Physiological role of pleasure. *Science*, 173(4002), 1103–1107.

Cat, J. (2021). Otto Neurath. In Zalta, E. N. (Ed.), *The Stanford encyclopedia of philosophy* (Spring 2021 ed.). Metaphysics Research Lab, Stanford University. https://plato.stanford.edu/archives/spr2021/entries/neurath/.

Chater, N. (1996). Reconciling simplicity and likelihood principles in perceptual organization. *Psychological Review*, 103(3), 566.

Chater, N. (2019). *The mind is flat*. Yale University Press.

Chater, N., & Loewenstein, G. (2016). The under-appreciated drive for sensemaking. *Journal of Economic Behavior & Organization*, 126, 137–154.

Chater, N., & Vitányi, P. (2003). Simplicity: A unifying principle in cognitive science? *Trends in Cognitive Sciences*, 7(1), 19–22.

Chater, N., Zhu, J., Spicer, J., Sundh, J., León-Villagrá, P., & Sanborn, A. (2020). Probabilistic biases meet the Bayesian brain. *Current Directions in Psychological Science*, 29(5), 506–512.

Chen, S., & Heese, C. (2021). "Fishing for Good News: Motivated Information Acquisition." CRC TR 224 Discussion Paper Series crctr224_2021_223v3, University of Bonn and University of Mannheim, Germany.

Cheng, X., Dale, C., & Liu, J. (2008). Statistics and social network of YouTube videos. In *2008 16th International Workshop on Quality of Service* (pp. 229–238). IEEE. https://ieeexplore.ieee.org/document/4539688.

Christensen, D. (1994). Conservatism in epistemology. *Noûs*, 28(1), 69–89.

Colleoni, E., Rozza, A., & Arvidsson, A. (2014). Echo chamber or public sphere? Predicting political orientation and measuring political homophily in Twitter using big data. *Journal of Communication*, 64(2), 317–332.

Colman, A. M. (2003). Cooperation, psychological game theory, and limitations of rationality in social interaction. *Behavioral and Brain Sciences*, 26(2), 139–153.

Cook, J., & Lewandowsky, S. (2016). Rational irrationality: Modeling climate change belief polarization using Bayesian networks. *Topics in Cognitive Science*, 8(1), 160–179.

Cosmides, L., & Tooby, J. (2000). Evolutionary psychology and the emotions. In Lewis, M. & Haviland-Jones, J. M. (eds.), *Handbook of Emotions* (pp. 91–115). Guilford.

Coyle, K. (2006). Mass digitization of books. *The Journal of Academic Librarianship*, 32(6), 641–645.

Cushman, F. (2020). Rationalization is rational. *Behavioral and Brain Sciences*, 43, E28.

Damasio, A. R. (2006). *Descartes' error*. Random House.

Darwin, H., Neave, N., & Holmes, J. (2011). Belief in conspiracy theories. The role of paranormal belief, paranoid ideation and schizotypy. *Personality and Individual Differences*, 50(8), 1289–1293.

Dasgupta, I., Schulz, E., & Gershman, S. J. (2017). Where do hypotheses come from? *Cognitive Psychology*, 96, 1–25.

Dayan, P. (1998). A hierarchical model of binocular rivalry. *Neural Computation*, 10(5), 1119–1135.

Deci, E. L., & Ryan, R. M. (1981). Curiosity and self-directed learning: The role of motivation in education. In Katz, L. (Ed.), *Current topics in early childhood education* (Vol. 4). Ablex Publishing Co.

DSM-5. (2013). *Diagnostic and statistical manual of mental disorders*. American Psychiatric Association.

Dubois, E., & Blank, G. (2018). The echo chamber is overstated: The moderating effect of political interest and diverse media. *Information, Communication & Society*, 21(5), 729–745.

Ely, J., Frankel, A., & Kamenica, E. (2015). Suspense and surprise. *Journal of Political Economy*, 123(1), 215–260.

Enke, B., & Zimmermann, F. (2019). Correlation neglect in belief formation. *The Review of Economic Studies*, 86(1), 313–332.

Epley, N., & Gilovich, T. (2016). The mechanics of motivated reasoning. *Journal of Economic perspectives*, 30(3), 133–140.

Eyster, E., & Rabin, M. (2014). Extensive imitation is irrational and harmful. *The Quarterly Journal of Economics*, 129(4), 1861–1898.

Festinger, L. (1957). *A theory of cognitive dissonance* (Vol. 2). Stanford University Press.

Flaxman, S., Goel, S., & Rao, J. M. (2016). Filter bubbles, echo chambers, and online news consumption. *Public Opinion Quarterly*, 80(S1), 298–320.

Friston, K. (2010). The free-energy principle: A unified brain theory? *Nature Reviews Neuroscience*, 11(2), 127–138.

Friston, K., & Kiebel, S. (2009). Predictive coding under the free-energy principle. *Philosophical Transactions of the Royal Society B: Biological Sciences*, 364(1521), 1211–1221.

Friston, K., Thornton, C., & Clark, A. (2012). Free-energy minimization and the dark-room problem. *Frontiers in Psychology*, 3, 130.

Gershman, S., Vul, E., & Tenenbaum, J. B. (2009). Perceptual multistability as Markov chain Monte Carlo inference. In *Advances in neural information processing systems 22* (pp. 611–619). https://proceedings.neurips.cc/paper/2009/hash/692f93be8c7a41525c0baf2076aecfb4-Abstract.html.

Gilovich, T. (2008). *How we know what isn't so*. Simon and Schuster.

Goldfarb, A. (2014). What is different about online advertising? *Review of Industrial Organization*, 44(2), 115–129.

Golman, R., & Loewenstein, G. (2018). Information gaps: A theory of preferences regarding the presence and absence of information. *Decision*, 5(3), 143.

Gopnik, A. (1998). Explanation as orgasm. *Minds and Machines*, 8(1), 101–118.

Gottlieb, J., Oudeyer, P.-Y., Lopes, M., & Baranes, A. (2013). Information seeking, curiosity, and attention: Computational and neural mechanisms. *Trends in Cognitive Sciences*, 17(11), 585–593.

Griffiths, T. L., & Tenenbaum, J. B. (2003). Probability, algorithmic complexity, and subjective randomness. In *Proceedings of the annual meeting of the cognitive science society* (Vol. 25). https://escholarship.org/uc/item/6ts3j7bw.

Griffiths, T. L., Vul, E., & Sanborn, A. N. (2012). Bridging levels of analysis for probabilistic models of cognition. *Current Directions in Psychological Science*, 21(4), 263–268.

Hanoch, Y. (2002). "Neither an angel nor an ant": Emotion as an aid to bounded rationality. *Journal of Economic Psychology*, 23(1), 1–25.

Harman, G. (2003). Skepticism and foundations. In Luper, S. (ed.), *The skeptics: Contemporary essays* (pp. 1–11). Routledge.

Heath, C., & Heath, D. (2007). *Made to stick: Why some ideas survive and others die*. Random House.

Jacob, F. (1977). Evolution and tinkering. *Science*, 196(4295), 1161–1166.

Jeffrey, R. C. (2004). *Subjective probability: The real thing*. Cambridge University Press.

Jepma, M., Verdonschot, R. G., Van Steenbergen, H., Rombouts, S. A., & Nieuwenhuis, S. (2012). Neural mechanisms underlying the induction and relief of perceptual curiosity. *Frontiers in Behavioral Neuroscience*, 6, 5. www.frontiersin.org/article/10.3389/fnbeh.2012.00005.

Jern, A., Chang, K.-M. K., & Kemp, C. (2014). Belief polarization is not always irrational. *Psychological Review*, 121(2), 206.

John, L. K., Loewenstein, G., & Prelec, D. (2012). Measuring the prevalence of questionable research practices with incentives for truth telling. *Psychological Science*, 23(5), 524–532.

Kahneman, D., & Lovallo, D. (1993). Timid choices and bold forecasts: A cognitive perspective on risk taking. *Management Science*, 39(1), 17–31.

Kang, M. J., Hsu, M., Krajbich, I. M., Loewenstein, G., McClure, S. M., Wang, J. T.-y., & Camerer, C. F. (2009). The wick in the candle of learning: Epistemic curiosity activates reward circuitry and enhances memory. *Psychological Science*, 20(8), 963–973.

Kehlmann, D. (2009). *Measuring the world: A novel*. Vintage.

Kidd, C., & Hayden, B. Y. (2015). The psychology and neuroscience of curiosity. *Neuron*, 88(3), 449–460.

Kleine, D. (1990). Anxiety and sport performance: A meta-analysis. *Anxiety Research*, 2(2), 113–131.

Kramer, A. D., Guillory, J. E., & Hancock, J. T. (2014). Experimental evidence of massive-scale emotional contagion through social networks. *Proceedings of the National Academy of Sciences*, 111(24), 8788–8790.

Kunda, Z. (1990). The case for motivated reasoning. *Psychological Bulletin*, 108 (3), 480.

Kurzban, R., Duckworth, A., Kable, J. W., & Myers, J. (2013). An opportunity cost model of subjective effort and task performance. *Behavioral and Brain Sciences*, 36(6), 661–679.

Kwisthout, J. (2011). Most probable explanations in Bayesian networks: Complexity and tractability. *International Journal of Approximate Reasoning*, 52(9), 1452–1469.

Levy, R. P., Reali, F., & Griffiths, T. L. (2009). Modeling the effects of memory on human online sentence processing with particle filters. In *Advances in neural information processing systems* (pp. 937–944). https://cocosci.princeton.edu/tom/papers/sentencepf1.pdf.

Liberman, A., & Chaiken, S. (1992). Defensive processing of personally relevant health messages. *Personality and Social Psychology Bulletin*, 18(6), 669–679.

Litman, J. (2005). Curiosity and the pleasures of learning: Wanting and liking new information. *Cognition & Emotion*, 19(6), 793–814.

Loewenstein, G. (1994). The psychology of curiosity: A review and reinterpretation. *Psychological Bulletin*, 116(1), 75.

Loewenstein, G., & Molnar, A. (2018). The renaissance of belief-based utility in economics. *Nature Human Behaviour*, 2(3), 166–167.

Lopes, M., Lang, T., Toussaint, M., & Oudeyer, P.-Y. (2012). Exploration in model-based reinforcement learning by empirically estimating learning progress. In Pereira, F., Burges, C. J. C., Bottou, L. & Weinberger, K. Q. (eds.),

Advances in neural information processing systems (pp. 206–214). Curran Associates, Inc.

Lord, C. G., Ross, L., & Lepper, M. R. (1979). Biased assimilation and attitude polarization: The effects of prior theories on subsequently considered evidence. *Journal of Personality and Social Psychology*, 37(11), 2098.

MacLeod, W. B. (1996). Decision, contract, and emotion: Some economics for a complex and confusing world. *Canadian Journal of Economics*, 29(4), 788–810.

Markey, A., & Loewenstein, G. (2014). Curiosity. In Linnenbrink-Garcia, L. (ed.) *International handbook of emotions in education* (pp. 228–245). Routledge.

Marshall, G. (2015). *Don't even think about it: Why our brains are wired to ignore climate change*. Bloomsbury Publishing USA.

Matz, S. C., Kosinski, M., Nave, G., & Stillwell, D. J. (2017). Psychological targeting as an effective approach to digital mass persuasion. *Proceedings of the National Academy of Sciences*, 114(48), 12714–12719.

McCabe, M. P. (2005). The role of performance anxiety in the development and maintenance of sexual dysfunction in men and women. *International Journal of Stress Management*, 12(4), 379.

McLean, B. F., Mattiske, J. K., & Balzan, R. P. (2017). Association of the jumping to conclusions and evidence integration biases with delusions in psychosis: A detailed meta-analysis. *Schizophrenia Bulletin*, 43(2), 344–354.

McPherson, M., Smith-Lovin, L., & Cook, J. M. (2001). Birds of a feather: Homophily in social networks. *Annual Review of Sociology*, 27(1), 415–444.

Meder, B., Nelson, J. D., Jones, M., & Ruggeri, A. (2019). Stepwise versus globally optimal search in children and adults. *Cognition*, 191, 103965.

Mercier, H., & Sperber, D. (2011). Why do humans reason? Arguments for an argumentative theory. *Behavioral and Brain Sciences*, 34(2), 57–74.

Moreno-Bote, R., Knill, D. C., & Pouget, A. (2011). Bayesian sampling in visual perception. *Proceedings of the National Academy of Sciences*, 108(30), 12491–12496.

Muramatsu, R., & Hanoch, Y. (2005). Emotions as a mechanism for boundedly rational agents: The fast and frugal way. *Journal of Economic Psychology*, 26(2), 201–221.

Pashler, H. (1999). *The psychology of attention*. MIT Press.

Pathak, D., Agrawal, P., Efros, A. A., & Darrell, T. (2017). Curiosity-driven exploration by self-supervised prediction. In *Proceedings of the IEEE Conference on Computer Vision and Pattern Recognition Workshops* (pp. 16– 17). http://proceedings.mlr.press/v70/pathak17a/pathak17a.pdf.

Pluck, G., & Johnson, H. (2011). Stimulating curiosity to enhance learning. *GESJ: Education Sciences and Psychology*, 2(19). ISSN 1512-1801.

Pronin, E., Lin, D. Y., & Ross, L. (2002). The bias blind spot: Perceptions of bias in self versus others. *Personality and Social Psychology Bulletin*, 28(3), 369–381.

Rabin, M., & Schrag, J. L. (1999). First impressions matter: A model of confirmatory bias. *The Quarterly Journal of Economics*, 114(1), 37–82.

Rapoport, A., & Chammah, A. M. (1966). The game of chicken. *American Behavioral Scientist*, 10(3), 10–28.

Ruan, B., Hsee, C. K., & Lu, Z. Y. (2018). The teasing effect: An underappreciated benefit of creating and resolving an uncertainty. *Journal of Marketing Research*, 55(4), 556–570.

Samuelson, L., & Swinkels, J. M. (2006). Information, evolution and utility. *Theoretical Economics*, 1(1), 119–142.

Sanborn, A. N., & Chater, N. (2016). Bayesian brains without probabilities. *Trends in Cognitive Sciences*, 20(12), 883–893.

Savage, L. J. (1972). *The foundations of statistics*. Courier Corporation.

Schelling, T. C. (1980). *The strategy of conflict: With a new preface by the author*. Harvard University Press.

Schmidhuber, J. (1991). A possibility for implementing curiosity and boredom in model-building neural controllers. In Meyer, J. A. and Wilson, S. W. (eds.), *Proc. of the international conference on simulation of adaptive behavior: From animals to animats* (pp. 222–227). MIT Press/Bradford Books.

Shenhav, A., Musslick, S., Lieder, F., Kool, W., Griffiths, T. L., Cohen, J. D., & Botvinick, M. M. (2017). Toward a rational and mechanistic account of mental effort. *Annual Review of Neuroscience*, 40, 99–124.

Simmons, J. P., Nelson, L. D., & Simonsohn, U. (2011). False-positive psychology: Undisclosed flexibility in data collection and analysis allows presenting anything as significant. *Psychological Science*, 22(11), 1359–1366.

Simon, H. A. (1972). Complexity and the representation of patterned sequences of symbols. *Psychological Review*, 79(5), 369.

Sorg, J., Singh, S. P., & Lewis, R. L. (2010). Internal rewards mitigate agent boundedness. In *Proceedings of the 27th International Conference on Machine Learning (ICML-10)* (pp. 1007–1014). https://icml.cc/Conferences/2010/papers/442.pdf.

Sun, Z., & Firestone, C. (2020). The dark room problem. *Trends in Cognitive Sciences*, 24. https://doi.org/10.1016/j.tics.2020.02.006.

Sunstein, C. R. (2002). The law of group polarization. *The Journal of Political Philosophy*, 10(2), 175–195.

Sutton, R. S., & Barto, A. G. (2018). *Reinforcement learning: An introduction*. MIT press.

Tenenbaum, J. B., Griffiths, T. L., & Niyogi, S. (2007). Intuitive theories as grammars for causal inference. In *Causal learning: Psychology, philosophy, and computation*, 301–322. https://oxford.universitypressscholarship.com/view/10.1093/acprof:oso/9780195176803.001.0001/acprof-9780195176803-chapter-20.

Vallone, R. P., Ross, L., & Lepper, M. R. (1985). The hostile media phenomenon: Biased perception and perceptions of media bias in coverage of the Beirut massacre. *Journal of Personality and Social Psychology*, 49(3), 577–585.

Van Rooij, I. (2008). The tractable cognition thesis. *Cognitive Science*, 32(6), 939–984.

Voß, J. (2005). Measuring Wikipedia. In *International Conference of the International Society for Scientometrics and Informetrics: 10th, Stockholm (Sweden), 24–28 July 2005* (pp. 221–231). http://eprints.rclis.org/6207/.

Vul, E., Goodman, N., Griffiths, T. L., & Tenenbaum, J. B. (2014). One and done? Optimal decisions from very few samples. *Cognitive Science, 38*(4), 599–637.

Vul, E., & Pashler, H. (2008). Measuring the crowd within: Probabilistic representations within individuals. *Psychological Science, 19*(7), 645–647.

Wade, S., & Kidd, C. (2019). The role of prior knowledge and curiosity in learning. *Psychonomic Bulletin & Review, 26*(4), 1377–1387.

Wojtowicz, Z., Chater, N., & Loewenstein, G. (2020). Boredom and flow: An opportunity cost theory of attention-directing motivational states. *Available at SSRN 3339123*. https://papers.ssrn.com/sol3/papers.cfm?abstract_id=3339123.

Wojtowicz, Z., & DeDeo, S. (2020). From probability to consilience: How explanatory values implement Bayesian reasoning. *Trends in Cognitive Sciences, 24*(12), 981–993.

Wojtowicz, Z., & Loewenstein, G. (2020). Curiosity and the economics of attention. *Current Opinion in Behavioral Sciences, 35*, 135–140.

Yuille, A., & Kersten, D. (2006). Vision as Bayesian inference: Analysis by synthesis? *Trends in Cognitive Sciences, 10*(7), 301–308.

Zarouali, B., Dobber, T., De Pauw, G., & de Vreese, C. (2020). Using a personality-profiling algorithm to investigate political microtargeting: Assessing the persuasion effects of personality-tailored ads on social media. *Communication Research*, 0093650220961965.

Zeidner, M. (2010). Test anxiety. In Weiner, I. B., & Craighead, W. E. (eds.), *The Corsini encyclopedia of psychology*, pp. 1–3. John Wiley.

CHAPTER 2

From Curiosity to Interest
Accumulated Knowledge Supports Long-Term Persistence of Information-Seeking Behavior

Ed Donnellan, Michiko Sakaki, and Kou Murayama

2.1 Introduction

Accounts of information-seeking attempt to explain how a person is motivated to seek information when there is no apparent tangible or instrumental reward for finding it. Intriguingly, research on information-seeking emerges from two separate traditions that rely on independent theory and investigative methods: one focusing on information-seeking motivated by "curiosity," the other on information-seeking motivated by "interest" (Murayama, 2022; Peterson & Hidi, 2019). This dichotomy between curiosity and interest as seemingly distinct motivational forces persists despite both traditions claiming lineage from early psychological research that used the terms synonymously (Berlyne, 1949, 1950; Day, 1982). Beyond terminology, however, the different traditions provide unique insights into the motivations underlying information-seeking behavior. Researchers studying curiosity typically provide detailed quantitative investigations into one-time information-seeking behavior, using cognitive, neuroscientific and computational methods (e.g., Gottlieb et al., 2013; Lau et al., 2020). For example, Lau et al., (2020) investigated how peoples' risky decision making (i.e., that potentially involved electric shocks) was influenced by their motivation to satisfy their curiosity about how a magic trick was done. In contrast, interest researchers provide strong qualitative theoretical accounts of the long-term development of information-seeking behavior on a particular topic, which is functionally important in applied psychological disciplines, such as education (e.g., Hidi & Renninger, 2006; Sansone & Thoman, 2005; Schiefele, 2009). For example, Hidi & Renninger (2006) provide a theoretical account of how students' interest in a subject develops from initial engagements (e.g., intrigued by some historical facts) to an established predisposition toward re-engagement (e.g., in-depth, voluntarily study of an historical period over a prolonged period).

As a consequence of these siloed research traditions, on the one hand we have extensive quantitative empirical investigations of one-time information-seeking behavior, and, on the other hand, we have detailed theoretical models of long-term task engagement. Yet these aspects remain unintegrated – that is, we lack a coherent and empirically supported account of how people's motivation to seek information in specific domains develops over time. In this chapter we provide a brief overview of these separate research traditions, and aim to connect their relative strengths using the recently proposed reward-learning framework of knowledge acquisition (Murayama, 2022; Murayama et al., 2019). This conceptual framework explains long-term development of information-seeking behavior (focused on by interest research) by extending existing reward-learning models that mainly account for one-time information-seeking behavior (focused on by curiosity research). By linking these two research traditions, we aim to highlight and facilitate much-needed empirical investigations into long-term development of information-seeking that research on curiosity has hitherto somewhat overlooked.

2.2   Interest Research: Long-Term Development of Information-Seeking

Researchers studying interest from an educational perspective focus on theoretical models accounting for the long-term development of information-seeking. In other words, the big question they seek to answer is: "How do learners sustain engagement in information-seeking behavior on a particular topic over a long period of time?" In doing so, they seek plausible (nonquantitative) models of development to account for and foster the process by which students might become interested in a topic and become self-motivated learners (selective persistence; Prenzel, 1992), generating questions and independently seeking out information on that topic. To this end, they offer two key insights on information-seeking. First, individuals' information-seeking in particular domains develops, progressing from momentary information-seeking on a topic to repeated, self-sustained engagement in information-seeking on that topic (Section 2.2.1). Second, this development toward self-sustained engagement is driven by accumulated knowledge (Section 2.2.2).

2.2.1 Development of Information-Seeking

A common distinction made in interest research is between momentary experiences of focused attention on a subject caused by environmental factors (termed situational interest) and a predisposition to re-engage with a particular subject (termed individual interest; Hidi & Renninger, 2006; Krapp, 2000). The four-phase model of interest development attempts to model the development of students' interest in a topic, from initial momentary experiences to sustained self-motivated re-engagement (Hidi & Renninger, 2006; Renninger & Hidi, 2016). Under this model, in the "triggered situational interest" phase, an individual focuses their attention on a subject when they notice incongruous information or recognize personal relevance in it (e.g., reading an article about the French revolutionary Maximilien Robespierre). Following this, in the "maintained situational interest" phase, individuals continue to focus attention on the subject over an extended period (or perhaps re-engage after the initial instance of triggered interest subsides – e.g., returning to the original article on Robespierre). The model proposes that it is possible to develop individual interest following these phases of situational interest. The "emerging individual interest" phase (phase three) relates to a developing predisposition to re-engage with a subject (e.g., seeking out more articles about notable French revolutionaries), which becomes "well-developed individual interest" (phase four) when this predisposition is established (e.g., regularly engaging with historical sources about the French Revolution). Though the phases chart a potential developmental trajectory, Hidi & Renninger (2006) note that not all instances of triggered situational interest necessarily develop into an individual interest (and not all emerging interests become well-developed) – that is, a person with an individual interest can still experience situational interest in that subject. Therefore, the phases of the model are not exactly akin to unidirectional developmental stages. Nevertheless, the model provides a theoretical framework for how one-time information-seeking triggered by environmental stimuli can develop into an established disposition for a person to engage in self-motivated information-seeking (not requiring environmental triggering).

2.2.2 Knowledge Accumulation

The second particularly insightful observation made by interest researchers concerns the role of knowledge in driving the development of long-term information-seeking. In the four-phase model, students' individual inter-ests are characterized in part by stored knowledge on a topic. In turn, this stored knowledge allows students to self-sustain their engagement by posing questions based on the knowledge that they do have, resulting in more engagement ("curiosity questions"; see Hidi & Renninger, 2006). This hypothesis has some empirical support. Alexander et al. (1994) demonstrated that students' interest in a specific topic was predicted by their prior knowledge of the topic. For example, students' scores on a test of key concepts and principles in physics, as well as their specific knowledge about black holes, predicted their interest in reading a passage of text about the work of physicist Stephen Hawking. More recently, Fastrich & Murayama (2020) showed that people's interest in a topic grew as they were presented with more information about it. In this study, participants repeatedly rated their interest in a lesser-known country (e.g., Bahrain, Lesotho) as they were given step-by-step information about that country (e.g., relating to geography or politics). This allowed the researchers to plot a trajectory for participants' interest as they acquired knowledge, and they demonstrated that participants' ratings of their interest in lesser-known countries increased as they received more information. Finally, Witherby & Carpenter (2021) found that people's ability to learn new information about a subject (e.g., American football or cooking) was better, and ratings of curiosity were higher, for subjects where they had more prior knowledge compared to those where they had less prior knowledge.

2.3   Curiosity Research: Momentary Information-Seeking Behavior Driven by the Reward Value of Information

Curiosity research typically relies on experiments investigating one-time information-seeking evoked by state curiosity (see Section 2.6.1). State curiosity is typically conceived of as the experience of an uncomfortable gap in a person's knowledge that needs satiation with specific and in-principle obtainable information, dissipating when this information is acquired (Grossnickle, 2016; Gruber et al., 2016; Kobayashi et al., 2019; Loewenstein, 1994; Peterson & Cohen, 2019). To this end, this research offers two key contributions to the study of information-seeking. First, it provides empirically supported reward-learning models for why humans seek information even when the information is noninstrumental in obtain-ing an extrinsic reward (e.g., money/food). Second, it provides a detailed investigation into what knowledge states are a prerequisite to motivate a person to seek information in a situation.

2.3.1   Information as a Reward

Recent curiosity research has mainly posited that information is rewarding in and of itself (i.e., it is intrinsically valuable), and therefore reward-learning processes can explain people's information-seeking behavior (Gruber & Ranganath, 2019; Kidd & Hayden, 2015). Research has demonstrated that people seek information even when it is not instrumentally valuable and may be costly or pointless to obtain (i.e., not directly leading to tangible reward; Charpentier et al., 2018; Kobayashi et al., 2019; Lanzetta & Driscoll, 1966; Rodriguez Cabrero et al., 2019; Van Lieshout et al., 2018). Furthermore, recent work indicates that people seek information even when it knowingly brings overtly negative consequences such as receiving electric shocks or experiencing feelings of regret (FitzGibbon et al., 2021; Hsee & Ruan, 2016; Oosterwijk, 2017). Since Berlyne (1960) argued that the resolution of states of novelty, uncertainty, conflict, or complexity is rewarding in and of itself, researchers have proposed various reward-learning models (or reinforcement-learning models) to explain such curiosity-driven information-seeking behavior. Historically, reward-learning models have attempted to explain why humans repeat actions that are instrumental in obtaining extrinsic rewards (e.g., food or money; see Berridge, 2000 for a review). Simply put, traditional reward-learning models posit that if an action leads to some reward in some situation, the value of the action increases and so is more likely to be performed when encountering the same situation again, and can be generalized to different contexts on repeated success.

In information-seeking research, reward-learning models treat information itself as a reward (not some directly resulting extrinsic reward from the action, e.g., food/money). Information-seeking behavior can therefore be reinforced simply by obtaining information, increasing the value of information-seeking behavior (making this behavior more likely in the future). This explains why people seek information even when it might result in negative consequences (e.g., electric shocks) – namely, because information-seeking behavior has an expected reward value that is strong enough to override the expectation of negative consequences. The hypothesis that information has inherent value (like extrinsic rewards do) has been supported by evidence that the neural reward networks associated with extrinsic rewards (Iigaya et al., 2020; see also O'Doherty, 2004; Rushworth et al., 2009 for reviews) are activated when someone wants to know answers to trivia questions (Gruber et al., 2014; Kang et al., 2009) and when uncertainty over ambiguous pictures is resolved (Jepma et al., 2012). Furthermore, the same brain areas activate both when we are curious and when we are hungry, and this activation predicts information-seeking and food-seeking behavior respectively (Lau et al., 2020; see also Kobayashi & Hsu, 2019). Based on these findings, there has been an explosion of computational models aiming to provide quantitative accounts for how and what type of new information is valued (see Oudeyer & Kaplan, 2009 for a review).

2.3.2   Information Gaps

Curiosity research focuses on the role of knowledge for motivating one-time information-seeking. One good example is the information-gap theory of curiosity (Loewenstein, 1994), which articulates the mechanisms by which people initiate information-seeking behavior in the first place. Information-gap theories of curiosity require two interacting components regarding an individual's knowledge about a situation. First, an individual needs to have some level of retrievable knowledge that they can apply when encountering the situation. Second, based on that knowledge retrieval, the individual needs to have a metacognitive representation of how much they do not know about the situation – that is, whether there is an information gap in their knowledge. It should be noted that whether this representation accurately represents a person's "true" knowledge level is irrelevant – for example, if someone "knows" some information (i.e., has it stored in their memory) but fails to retrieve it, this representation is technically inaccurate (yet this is unproblematic for the account). The theory suggests that curiosity is triggered when someone encounters a situation where they metacognitively believe that they have an information gap (Loewenstein, 1994; Metcalfe et al., 2020). As such, information-seeking behavior is most highly motivated in a metacognitive sweet-spot where an individual retrieves enough knowledge about a situation to believe that they lack knowledge. This view suggests that you need some knowledge base about a topic to estimate the plausible extent or bounds of potential information about the topic and therefore build a representation of how complete your knowledge is. Accordingly, curiosity is unlikely to be triggered when someone retrieves very little or no knowledge pertaining to a situation, because they cannot estimate how much of a knowledge gap they have without a certain amount of knowledge. It is also worth noting that, according to this perspective, knowledge level and curiosity (motivation for information-seeking) have an inverted-U shape function; whereas a certain amount of knowledge is a prerequisite for triggering curiosity, curiosity is unlikely when someone retrieves a lot of knowledge about the situation, because they are unlikely to believe that they lack some knowledge. In fact, experimental work suggests that individuals reporting that the answer to a trivia question is on the tip of their tongue report being more curious about the answer compared to when they report not knowing or knowing the answer (Dubey et al., 2021; Kang et al., 2009; Litman, Hutchins, et al., 2005).

2.4 Interim Summary: Commonalities and Differences of the Two Research Traditions

Clearly, there are important commonalities across curiosity and interest research. Both traditions aim to explain information-seeking behavior with a focus on people's motivation to acquire information which is not contingent on immediate extrinsic incentives. Both underscore the intricate relationship between a person's pre-existing knowledge and their information-seeking behavior; one's learning history has a considerable impact on whether information-seeking is initiated and sustained.

On the other hand, the research traditions show marked differences in their focus. In contrast to interest research, curiosity research does not typically consider how curiosity might drive repeated engagement with a subject over time. While there is a growing body of empirical studies on curiosity, these more exclusively focus on one-time or momentary experiences of information-seeking behavior. In fact, these studies mainly use short (i.e., less than one hour), arbitrary experimental tasks or quiz-style self-contained stimuli where uncertainty can be resolved and information learned in a moment – for example, the answer to a trivia question (Kang et al., 2009) or the identity of an unknown card (Rodriguez Cabrero et al., 2019). This focus may result from the roots of modern theories of curiosity in theories that treated curiosity as an appetitive drive, analogous to other drives such as hunger (Berlyne, 1960; see also Grossnickle, 2016). Under these accounts, information sates curiosity, as food sates hunger, so it is perhaps unsurprising that contemporary accounts do not consider how continued information-seeking may occur and develop after curiosity has been sated or subsided. However, by focusing on momentary information-seeking, this provides no insight into the important dimension central to accounts of interest, namely how individuals develop and sustain information-seeking in a particular domain over time (selective persistence). In contrast, interest researchers focus on stimuli that might promote re-engagement. Therefore, the information stimuli that participants engage with are large bodies of information to be worked through – for example, an entire introductory university psychology course (Harackiewicz et al., 2008), and information-seeking behavior is examined across relatively long periods, such as weeks or even years (Frenzel et al., 2012; Rotgans & Schmidt, 2017).

Consequently, work investigating knowledge (or representation of knowledge) prerequisites for triggering curiosity may not generalize outside of one-time information-seeking to more sustained information-seeking. For example, theoretical accounts of interest suggest that knowledge is accumulated over time when we repeatedly seek information in the same domain, which helps us generate new questions concerning that domain, leading to more information-seeking behavior (Alexander et al., 1994, 1995). This idea seemingly contradicts the view in curiosity research that knowledge and information-seeking behavior have an inverted-U shape relationship. From the standpoint of interest research, this curve could simply result from the type of stimuli used in curiosity research, because knowledge concerning these stimuli can be bounded: for instance, it is possible to be certain (or almost certain) that you know the answer to a trivia question, and so you may not need to seek information any further. In contrast, models of long-term engagement focus on knowledge of subject areas that are unlikely to be saturated: for instance, it is highly unlikely that you are certain that you know everything about the modern study of psychology.

2.5   An Integrative Approach: The Reward-Learning Framework of Knowledge Acquisition

We propose that unique contributions of the research traditions discussed earlier can be integrated into a coherent account of long-term information-seeking by conceptually extending existing reward-learning models of information-seeking, explicitly consolidating the role of existing knowledge in the reward-learning process. The proposed "reward-learning framework of knowledge acquisition" (Murayama, 2022; Murayama et al., 2019) is not a formal quantitative model unlike other models of curiosity, but rather aims to serve as a guiding framework for further development of quantitative models of people's real-life knowledge acquisition behavior (see Figure 2.1). The framework uses the term "knowledge acquisition" rather than "information-seeking" to stress the critical importance of individuals' knowledge base (built through experience of information-seeking).

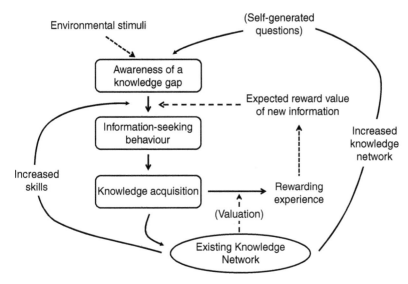

Figure 2.1 The reward-learning framework for knowledge acquisition.
Note. For a more detailed figure, see Murayama (2022).

Like previous reward-learning models typically used in curiosity research, the framework holds that information itself is valuable, and so information-seeking is motivated by the expected reward value of information-seeking behavior. However, the framework holds that information gained about a topic can lead to further information-seeking, because the information itself has unique *self-boosting* properties that other rewards lack (i.e., food/money), which result from knowledge accumulation (see Murayama, 2022). This framework therefore applies a critical aspect of theories of interest to modify current theories of curiosity to account for long-term information-seeking, attempting to provide a more comprehensive account for people's information-seeking. In the following sections we explain three ways in which knowledge accumulation fosters the prolonged and increased engagement of people's information-seeking behavior.

2.5.1   Knowledge Accumulation Influences Awareness of Knowledge Gaps

The core component of the framework is that knowledge accumulation can lead to self-boosting of information-seeking behavior – that is, long-term engagement with information-seeking resulting from a feedback loop when someone successfully seeks information (see "Increased knowledge network" in Figure 2.1). When information is found, as well as reinforcing information-seeking behavior because the information is rewarding, it also means that the information is consolidated into a person's knowledge base. When a knowledge base increases, this can result in the potential for more unknown information to become apparent than before – that is, when a person increases their knowledge base on a topic, this increases the amount of potential information gaps in their knowledge that they could become aware of. This seems slightly counterintuitive, but see Figure 2.2

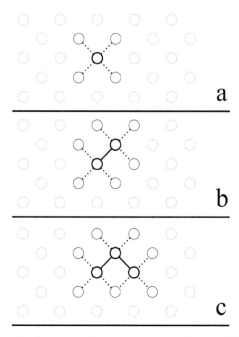

Figure 2.2 Expanding knowledge base results in increased potential for awareness of information gaps

Note. Nodes represent pieces of information; bold outlines represent known information (i.e., knowledge), light outlines represent unknown information that is related to known information, and lighter dotted outlines represent information more distantly related to known information. Edges between nodes denote the relationship between information; dashed edges represent information gaps (i.e., between known and unknown information), and solid lines show that there is no information gap (i.e., the information is connected). As more information is acquired (i.e., connections are made between known and unknown information), the number of potential knowledge gaps increases (e.g., from 4 potential gaps in figure 2a, to 6 in figure 2b, and 8 in figure 2c).

for a demonstration using a simple network (note that the basic idea holds for more complicated real-world networks; see Murayama, 2022). To give a real-world example, consider a person watching a nature documentary featuring a great ape, the species of which they do not recognize (maybe they think it is a gorilla, but they are not confident). They seek the information and find out it is a "western lowland gorilla." This information gain (i.e., an added node in their knowledge network) would result in a larger number of possible links to new information, not yet in their knowledge base, compared to if they had not made the information gain (compare number of dashed edges in Figure 2a and 2b from addition of one node). This increases the chance for them to become aware that they have more gaps in their knowledge (e.g., gaps about the multiple species/ subspecies of gorilla). The way in which a person actually becomes aware of gaps resulting from an expanded knowledge base, and boosts their information-seeking in a specific domain, can occur through both bottom-up and top-down processes.

Regarding the bottom-up process, because of an expanding knowledge base in a specific domain, a person may be more likely to engage in information-seeking in that domain when encountering further environmental stimuli that could trigger it (see "Environmental stimuli" in Figure 2.1). This is boosting domain-specific information-seeking through bottom-up processes, and it relies on environmental stimuli that can cause individuals to become aware of a knowledge gap to trigger it. Returning to the gorilla example: initial information gain about the "western lowland gorilla" (itself a bottom-up, stimuli-driven information search) expanded the individual's knowledge base to make it more likely that they will become aware of the possibility that there are multiple unknown subspecies of gorilla. When that person by chance encounters a picture of a different looking gorilla (environmental stimuli), they may become aware of this information gap (they may not know what type of gorilla this is), and be motivated to seek out information about it. This sustains their engagement with the topic; initial information-seeking makes the probability of further stimuli-driven (e.g., bottom-up) information-seeking more likely (i.e., increases their likelihood of information-seeking being triggered by environmental stimuli). In contrast, another individual who did not make initial information gain about gorillas (therefore not expanding their knowledge base) lacks the same increased potential to become aware of the same gap when having the chance encounter with the picture and so would not seek more information (see Murayama, 2022 for a discussion of the Matthew effect).

Regarding the top-down process, a person may self-generate their own questions about a subject as a result of newly gained information (and an expanded knowledge base), leading them to engage in independent research (as proposed by interest researchers: e.g., Renninger & Hidi, 2016; see "Self-generated questions" in Figure 2.1). This is top-down boosting of domain-specific information-seeking; it is self-generated, not relying on environmental stimuli to trigger it. In terms of the reward-learning model, increased knowledge allows people to interrogate their expanded knowledge base to become aware of gaps and motivate themselves to actively seek information. Returning to the example, the initial and spontaneous information-seeking may motivate a person to actively seek more information about gorillas (e.g., reading books or journal articles, watching nature documentaries), sustaining their engagement with the topic. In contrast, a person who did not initially seek the information about the specific type of gorilla lacks the expanded knowledge base that could facilitate the generation of these questions, and would therefore be less likely to engage in further information-seeking.

2.5.2   Knowledge Accumulation Increases Skills or Perceived Competence

The process of information-seeking can also facilitate long-term engagement in information-seeking in a particular domain because of skills acquired through repeated information-seeking. The importance of perceived skills or competence to acquire and comprehend information has been relatively underexamined in the curiosity literature (for notable exceptions, see Mirolli & Baldassarre, 2013), but plays a critical role in explaining our information-seeking behavior in daily life. Importantly, in accumulating knowledge, people's ability to comprehend new information (incorporating it into their knowledge base) improves simply because people with more knowledge have more internal resources to resolve knowledge gaps. As a result, the increased confidence in their perceived skills for information-seeking promotes further information-seeking (see "Increased skills" in Figure 2.1). This would support long-term engagement in a specific domain for an individual, because of domain-specific and domain-general boosting effects. Regarding the former, information-seeking in a certain domain may require more specialization than others, which would increase as a person engages in more information-seeking in that domain, honing their skills in seeking specific types of information (e.g., finding that a particular journal is the best place to find information about gorillas). This would increase the likelihood of people engaging in information-seeking in that domain when presented with new opportunities (i.e., environmental situations that make an information gap pertinent) or when they self-generate questions. Regarding the latter, one's information-seeking in a particular domain can be self-sustained or boosted by domain-general skills for information-seeking resulting from knowledge accumulation in other domains (e.g., their skill in interpreting journal articles relating to their undergraduate psychology course may generalize to interpreting articles about gorilla ecology, and vice versa).

2.5.3 *Knowledge Accumulation Increases Expected Reward Value of New Information*

Not all information is valued equally. Topic-specific knowledge accumulation means it is likely that a person will assign greater value to information about that topic, providing a feedback loop that facilitates domain-specific long-term information-seeking (see "Valuation" in Figure 2.1). For example, people tend to value knowledge that is associated with their own goals and identities, which together form the core value of the self (Sedikides & Strube, 1997). This "self-scheme" reflects one's learning history: people's goals and identities are strongly influenced by what they have experienced and learned in their daily life (Conway & Pleydell-Pearce, 2000). Therefore, every piece of new information one acquires becomes part of the existing self-scheme, in turn providing a basis for the valuation of upcoming information. In other words, domain-specific knowledge acquisition may enhance the value of the new information in that domain, selectively facilitating information-seeking behavior (e.g., if someone views themselves as an expert in gorillas, they will value information about gorillas over information about cooking, preferentially seeking information about gorillas).

In sum, we have shown that knowledge accumulation can influence three critical components of the reward-learning process of information-seeking. Knowledge acquisition increases (1) awareness of knowledge gaps, (2) skill and perceived competence in comprehending new information, and (3) the reward value of new information. The reward-learning framework of knowledge acquisition extends previous reward-learning models by incorporating the role of knowledge accumulation. Importantly, these processes work in a way that facilitates further information-seeking behavior, making the knowledge acquisition process increasingly self-reinforcing and sustainable. Thus, the framework not only explains one-time information-seeking behavior (already captured by existing reward-learning models), but also how this one-time information-seeking behavior can be sustainable over a long time period. We should emphasize that the proposed framework aims to present a way in which to link curiosity and interest research with reward-learning models. It does not aim to provide a full computational account of long-term engagement in knowledge acquisition. Recently, there have been various computational accounts for many important aspects of information-seeking behavior: for example, how knowledge gaps are quantified and transform depending on the value of information (Oudeyer & Kaplan, 2009), how hedonic value of information is integrated in the information-seeking process (Kobayashi et al., 2019; Sharot & Sunstein, 2020; see also Murayama, 2022), and how predicted value for certain information generalizes to related but novel information (Schulz, Bhui, et al., 2019; Wu et al., 2018). The proposed framework leaves detailed computational accounts to ongoing work, while providing a bigger picture view on how these studies should be expanded in the future. For example, the proposed framework underscores the importance of understanding how knowledge is structured in our mental representations, suggesting the potential benefit to be gained from memory research in examining long-term information-seeking behavior.

2.6   Going Further: Information-Seeking over Situations and the Life Course

To conclude the chapter, we consider two important related areas based on the reward-learning framework of knowledge acquisition: how the development of a tendency to seek information in a particular domain sometimes extends to formation of a more general attitude for information-seeking, and how long-term engagement takes place over the life course.

2.6.1   Development of Attitudes Toward Information-Seeking: Trait Curiosity

Trait curiosity represents another strand of research not yet discussed in this chapter. This refers to people's general tendency to experience (state) curiosity in situations where they have opportunity to be curious, namely their domain-general inquisitiveness (Kashdan et al., 2004; Litman & Spielberger, 2003). Importantly, this is not analogous to individual interest as trait curiosity is seen as a stable and domain-general trait, and so unlike models considering individual interest it does not provide a clear way of investigating how an individual's information-seeking in a *specific* domain *develops* over time. However, we believe that trait curiosity can be considered as an extended and generalized outcome of long-term information-seeking in multiple specific domains.

First, the fact that some people tend to be generally more or less inquisitive, or open to new experiences (explicitly linked to curiosity: see John & Srivastava, 1999; McCrae & Costa, 1987), clearly impacts on long-term engagement, interacting with the factors discussed earlier. If a person is more inquisitive or open to novelty (i.e., novelty-seeking), then we expect them to seek information more across all domains. This plausibly leads to an increase in domain-general skills for information-seeking, which in turn supports long-term engagement in specific domains (as discussed earlier). Inquisitive people (i.e., high in traits associated with curiosity) are also more likely to interrogate their own knowledge to find information gaps, or to seek information when gaps are presented (Harrison et al., 2011; Litman, Collins, et al., 2005), thus increasing the boosting effects of knowledge accumulation.

Second, trait curiosity levels may be increased by a person's domain-specific information-seeking. Under reward-learning (and reinforcement-learning) models, once a specific action-reward contingency is learned and reinforced, people may generalize, expecting that similar actions will be similarly rewarding. By engaging in repeated information-seeking behavior in one domain, people learn to expect a high reward value for information in that domain (reinforcement). Therefore, they may generalize the expectation, expecting similar reward value for information gained by information-seeking behavior in other domains, thus increasing domain-general inquisitiveness (generalization). Such cross-domain generalization mechanisms may be realized in computational terms under a hierarchical process (e.g., hierarchical Bayesian generalization; see Gershman & Niv, 2015). In other words, the expected reward value of information in a specific domain (reinforced by repeated information-seeking) may be generalized to information across domains, although this generalization may be countered by various factors in the new domain (e.g., prior knowledge about the new domain).

2.6.2 Life-Long Development of Information-Seeking

It is typically believed that children are more curious than adults, and adults become increasingly less curious as they age. But by considering information-seeking as the function of knowledge structure, we can delineate a more nuanced view on how motivation for information-seeking develops over the lifespan. For example, while it may be true that children are more curious in that they actively seek information, their information-seeking behavior may be unsustainable and less sophisticated due to the lack of an established knowledge base. In fact, Schulz, Wu, et al. (2019) found that children showed more directed exploration (i.e. purposefully exploring uncertain options) than adults, but failed to generalize their knowledge to efficiently explore the environment (see also Somerville et al., 2017).

What about older adults? Curiosity research has mainly focused on children and young adults, with less examination of information-seeking in middle or old age. Limited research suggests that older adults typically show reduced levels of trait curiosity and reduced exploration behavior compared to younger adults (Chu et al., 2020; Mata et al., 2013; Robinson et al., 2017). Thus, previous research suggests that there are age-related declines in information-seeking behavior, which is consistent with stereotypic portrayal of older adults. However, by incorporating the idea that knowledge is the basis for long-term engagement, we can provide more fine-grained explanations about developmental changes in information-seeking behavior in older adults. As described earlier, information-seeking behavior is supported by reward value of new knowledge as well as individuals' existing knowledge (Hidi & Renninger, 2006). Neuroimaging research suggests that the reward value of new knowledge may decline with age due to detrimental effects of age on the brain (see Sakaki et al., 2018 for a review). However, this reduced sensitivity to new information may be compensated for by the fact that individuals' knowledge develops with age; older adults tend to have richer and more extensive knowledge about the world (Dodson et al., 2007; Kavé & Halamish, 2015). Such age-related increases in knowledge may help preserve or even boost older adults' information-seeking behavior. In addition, the increased knowledge base that comes with age may result in qualitative changes in information-seeking behavior; as individuals age, their existing knowledge may play a bigger role in motivating their information-seeking behavior, and thus they may seek information relevant to their existing knowledge more than novelty (cf. Frenzel et al., 2012).

2.7 Concluding Remarks

The terms "curiosity" and "interest" are clearly related, but there are no agreed-upon scientific definitions. Both terms are used in common parlance, and so people have conceptualizations of their meaning which are perhaps naïve to, and pre-date, their scientific study. Therefore, there is no guarantee that they are underlined by distinct psychological processes (Murayama et al., 2019). However, this is not to say that this terminology should be entirely ignored; the terms may highlight important distinctions in people's intuitive understanding about information-seeking processes (Donnellan et al., 2021). This chapter illustrates how the two growing research fields identifying with their respective terminologies can be unified to provide a comprehensive understanding of information-seeking behavior. We hope that the integrated framework explored here serves as a call to action for the future investigation of "selective persistence" in information-seeking that has been examined in interest research – that is, people's extended engagement of information-seeking behavior in specific domains over time.

References

Alexander, P. A., Jetton, T. L., & Kulikowich, J. M. (1995). Interrelationship of knowledge, interest, and recall: Assessing a model of domain learning. *Journal of Educational Psychology*, 87(4), 559–575. https://doi.org/10.1037/0022-0663 .87.4.559.

Alexander, P. A., Kulikowich, J. M., & Schulze, S. K. (1994). How subject-matter knowledge affects recall and interest. *American Educational Research Journal*, 31(2), 313–337.

Berlyne, D. E. (1949). "Interest" as a psychological concept. *British Journal of Psychology: General Section*, 39(4), 184–195. https://doi.org/10.1111/j.2044-8 295.1949.tb00219.x.

Berlyne, D. E. (1950). Novelty and curiosity as determinants of exploratory behaviour. *British Journal of Psychology*, 41(1), 68–80.

Berlyne, D. E. (1960). *Conflict, Arousal, and Curiosity*. McGraw-Hill Book Company. https://doi.org/10.1037/11164-000.

Berridge, K. C. (2000). Reward learning: Reinforcement, incentives, and expectations. *Psychology of Learning and Motivation – Advances in Research and Theory*, 40, 223–278. https://doi.org/10.1016/s0079-7421(00)80022-5.

Charpentier, C. J., Bromberg-Martin, E. S., & Sharot, T. (2018). Valuation of knowledge and ignorance in mesolimbic reward circuitry. *Proceedings of the National Academy of Sciences of the United States of America*, 115(31), E7255–E7264. https://doi.org/10.1073/pnas.1800547115.

Chu, L., Tsai, J. L., & Fung, H. H. (2020). Association between age and intellectual curiosity: The mediating roles of future time perspective and importance of curiosity. *European Journal of Ageing*. https://doi.org/10.1007/s 10433-020-00567-6.

Conway, M. A., & Pleydell-Pearce, C. W. (2000). The construction of autobiographical memories in the self-memory system. *Psychological Review*, 107(2), 261–288. https://doi.org/10.1037/0033-295X.107.2.261.

Day, H. I. (1982). Curiosity and the interested explorer. *Performance & Instruction*, 21(4), 19–22. https://doi.org/10.1002/pfi.4170210410.

Dodson, C. S., Bawa, S., & Krueger, L. E. (2007). Aging, metamemory, and high-confidence errors: A misrecollection account. *Psychology and Aging*, 22(1), 122–133. https://doi.org/10.1037/0882-7974.22.1.122.

Donnellan, E., Aslan, S., Fastrich, G. M., & Murayama, K., (2021). How are curiosity and interest different? Naïve Bayes classification of people's beliefs. *Educational Psychology Review*. https://doi.org/10.1007/s10648-021-09622-9.

Dubey, R., Mehta, H., & Lombrozo, T. (2021). Curiosity is contagious: A social influence intervention to induce curiosity. *Cognitive Science*, 45(2). https://doi.org/10.1111/cogs.12937.

Fastrich, G. M., & Murayama, K. (2020). Development of interest and role of choice during sequential knowledge acquisition. *AERA Open*, 6(2), 233285842092998. https://doi.org/10.1177/2332858420929981.

FitzGibbon, L., Komiya, A., & Murayama, K. (2021). The lure of counterfactual curiosity: People incur a cost to experience regret. *Psychological Science*, 32(2), 241–255. https://doi.org/10.1177/0956797620963615.

Frenzel, A. C., Pekrun, R., Dicke, A. L., & Goetz, T. (2012). Beyond quantitative decline: Conceptual shifts in adolescents' development of interest in mathematics. *Developmental Psychology*, 48(4), 1069–1082. https://doi.org/10.1037/a0026895.

Gershman, S. J., & Niv, Y. (2015). Novelty and inductive generalization in human reinforcement learning. *Topics in Cognitive Science*, 7(3), 391–415. https://doi.org/10.1111/tops.12138.

Gottlieb, J., Oudeyer, P.-Y., Lopes, M., & Baranes, A. (2013). Information-seeking, curiosity, and attention: computational and neural mechanisms. *Trends in Cognitive Sciences*, 17(11), 585–593. https://doi.org/10.1016/j.tics.2013.09.001.

Grossnickle, E. M. (2016). Disentangling curiosity: Dimensionality, definitions, and distinctions from interest in educational contexts. *Educational Psychology Review*, 28(1), 23–60. https://doi.org/10.1007/s10648-014-9294-y.

Gruber, M. J., Gelman, B. D., & Ranganath, C. (2014). States of curiosity modulate hippocampus-dependent learning via the dopaminergic circuit. *Neuron*, 84(2), 486–496. https://doi.org/10.1016/j.neuron.2014.08.060.

Gruber, M. J., & Ranganath, C. (2019). How curiosity enhances hippocampus-dependent memory: The prediction, appraisal, curiosity, and exploration (PACE) framework. *Trends in Cognitive Sciences*, 23(12), 1014–1025. https://doi.org/10.1016/j.tics.2019.10.003.

Gruber, M. J., Ritchey, M., Wang, S. F., Doss, M. K., & Ranganath, C. (2016). Post-learning hippocampal dynamics promote preferential retention of rewarding events. *Neuron*, 89(5), 1110–1120. https://doi.org/10.1016/j.neuron.2016.01.017.

Harackiewicz, J. M., Durik, A. M., Barron, K. E., Linnenbrink-Garcia, L., & Tauer, J. M. (2008). The role of achievement goals in the development of interest: Reciprocal relations between achievement goals, interest, and performance. *Journal of Educational Psychology*, 100(1), 105–122. https://doi .org/10.1037/0022-0663.100.1.105.

Harrison, S. H., Sluss, D. M., & Ashforth, B. E. (2011). Curiosity adapted the cat: The role of trait curiosity in newcomer adaptation. *Journal of Applied Psychology*, 96(1), 211–220. https://doi.org/10.1037/a0021647.

Hidi, S. E., & Renninger, K. A. (2006). The four-phase model of interest development. *Educational Psychologist*, 41(2), 111–127. https://doi.org/10 .1207/s15326985ep4102_4.

Hsee, C. K., & Ruan, B. (2016). The Pandora Effect: The power and peril of curiosity. *Psychological Science*, 27(5), 659–666. https://doi.org/10.1177 /0956797616631733.

Iigaya, K., Hauser, T. U., Kurth-Nelson, Z., O'Doherty, J. P., Dayan, P., & Dolan, R. J. (2020). The value of what's to come: Neural mechanisms coupling prediction error and the utility of anticipation. *Science Advances*, 6(25), eaba3828. https://doi.org/10.1126/sciadv.aba3828.

Jepma, M., Verdonschot, R. G., van Steenbergen, H., Rombouts, S. A. R. B., & Nieuwenhuis, S. (2012). Neural mechanisms underlying the induction and relief of perceptual curiosity. *Frontiers in Behavioral Neuroscience*, 6, 1–9. https://doi.org/10.3389/fnbeh.2012.00005.

John, O. P., & Srivastava, S. (1999). The Big Five Trait taxonomy: History, measurement, and theoretical perspectives. In L. A. Pervin & O. P. John (Eds.), *Handbook of personality: Theory and research (2nd edition)* (pp. 102–138). Guildford.

Kang, M. J., Hsu, M., Krajbich, I. M., Loewenstein, G., McClure, S. M., Wang, J. T., & Camerer, C. F. (2009). The wick in the candle of learning. *Psychological Science*, 20(8), 963–973. https://doi.org/10.1111/j.1467-9280 .2009.02402.x.

Kashdan, T. B., Rose, P., & Fincham, F. D. (2004). Curiosity and exploration: Facilitating positive subjective experiences and personal growth opportunities. *Journal of Personality Assessment*, 82(3), 291–305. https://doi.org/10.1207 /s15327752jpa8203_05.

Kavé, G., & Halamish, V. (2015). Doubly blessed: Older adults know more vocabulary and know better what they know. *Psychology and Aging*, 30(1), 68–73. https://doi.org/10.1037/a0038669.

Kidd, C., & Hayden, B. Y. (2015). The psychology and neuroscience of curiosity. *Neuron*, 88(3), 449–460. https://doi.org/10.1016/j.neuron.2015.09.010.

Kobayashi, K., & Hsu, M. (2019). Common neural code for reward and infor- mation value. *Proceedings of the National Academy of Sciences of the United States of America*, 116(26), 13061–13066. https://doi.org/10.1073/pnas .1820145116.

Kobayashi, K., Ravaioli, S., Baranès, A., Woodford, M., & Gottlieb, J. (2019). Diverse motives for human curiosity. *Nature Human Behaviour*, 3(6), 587–595. https://doi.org/10.1038/s41562-019-0589-3.

Krapp, A. (2000). Interest and human development during adolescence: An educational-psychological approach. In J. Heckhausen (Ed.), *Motivational psychology of human development: Developing motivation and motivating development* (pp. 109–128). Elsevier Science. https://doi.org/10.1016/S0166-4115 (00)80008-4.

Lanzetta, J. T., & Driscoll, J. M. (1966). Preference for information about an uncertain but unavoidable outcome. *Journal of Personality and Social Psychology.* https://doi.org/10.1037/h0022674.

Lau, J. K. L., Ozono, H., Kuratomi, K., Komiya, A., & Murayama, K. (2020). Shared striatal activity in decisions to satisfy curiosity and hunger at the risk of electric shocks. *Nature Human Behaviour.* https://doi.org/10.1038/s41562-020-0848-3.

Litman, J. A., Collins, R. P., & Spielberger, C. D. (2005). The nature and measurement of sensory curiosity. *Personality and Individual Differences,* 39(6), 1123–1133. https://doi.org/10.1016/j.paid.2005.05.001.

Litman, J. A., Hutchins, T., & Russon, R. (2005). Epistemic curiosity, feeling-of-knowing, and exploratory behaviour. *Cognition & Emotion,* 19(4), 559–582. https://doi.org/10.1080/02699930441000427.

Litman, J. A., & Spielberger, C. D. (2003). Measuring epistemic curiosity and its diversive and specific components. *Journal of Personality Assessment,* 80(1), 75–86. http://dx.doi.org/10.1207/S15327752JPA8001_16.

Loewenstein, G. (1994). The psychology of curiosity: A review and reinterpretation. *Psychological Bulletin,* 116(1), 75–98. https://doi.org/10 .1037/0033-2909.116.1.75.

Mata, R., Wilke, A., & Czienskowski, U. (2013). Foraging across the life span: is there a reduction in exploration with aging? *Frontiers in Neuroscience,* 7, 1–7. https://doi.org/10.3389/fnins.2013.00053.

McCrae, R. R., & Costa, P. T. (1987). Validation of the five-factor model of personality across instruments and observers. *Journal of Personality and Social Psychology,* 52(1), 81–90. https://doi.org/10.1037/0022-3514.52.1.81.

Metcalfe, J., Schwartz, B. L., & Eich, T. S. (2020). Epistemic curiosity and the region of proximal learning. *Current Opinion in Behavioral Sciences,* 35, 40–47. https://doi.org/10.1016/j.cobeha.2020.06.007.

Mirolli, M., & Baldassarre, G. (2013). Functions and mechanisms of intrinsic motivations. In G. Baldassarre & M. Mirolli (Eds.), *Intrinsically motivating learning in natural and artificial systems* (pp. 49–72). Springer.

Murayama, K. (2022). A reward-learning framework of knowledge acquisition: An integrated account of curiosity, interest, and intrinsic-extrinsic rewards. *Psychological Review,* https://doi.org/10.1037/rev0000349.

Murayama, K., FitzGibbon, L., & Sakaki, M. (2019). Process account of curiosity and interest: A reward-learning perspective. *Educational Psychology Review,* 31(4), 875–895. https://doi.org/10.1007/s10648-019-09499-9.

O'Doherty, J. P. (2004). Reward representations and reward-related learning in the human brain: Insights from neuroimaging. *Current Opinion in Neurobiology,* 14(6), 769–776. https://doi.org/10.1016/j.conb.2004.10.016.

Oosterwijk, S. (2017). Choosing the negative: A behavioral demonstration of morbid curiosity. *PloS One,* 12(7), 1–20. https://doi.org/10.1371/journal .pone.0178399.

Oudeyer, P.-Y., & Kaplan, F. (2009). What is intrinsic motivation? A typology of computational approaches. *Frontiers in Neurorobotics*, 1, 1–14. https://doi.org /10.3389/neuro.12.006.2007.

Peterson, E. G., & Cohen, J. (2019). A case for domain-specific curiosity in mathematics. *Educational Psychology Review*, 31(4), 807–832. https://doi.org/ 10.1007/s10648-019-09501-4.

Peterson, E. G., & Hidi, S. E. (2019). Curiosity and interest: Current perspectives. *Educational Psychology Review*, 31(4), 781–788. https://doi.org/10 .1007/s10648-019-09513-0.

Prenzel, M. (1992). Selective persistence of interest. In K. A. Renninger, S. E. Hidi, & A. Krapp (Eds.), *The role of interest in learning and development* (pp. 71–98). Erlbaum.

Renninger, K. A., & Hidi, S. E. (2016). *The power of interest for motivation and engagement*. Routledge. www.taylorfrancis.com/books/9781317674214.

Robinson, O. C., Demetre, J. D., & Litman, J. A. (2017). Adult life stage and crisis as predictors of curiosity and authenticity. *International Journal of Behavioral Development*, 41(3), 426–431. https://doi.org/10.1177/0165025416645201.

Rodriguez Cabrero, J. A. M., Zhu, J.-Q., & Ludvig, E. A. (2019). Costly curiosity: People pay a price to resolve an uncertain gamble early. *Behavioural Processes*, 160, 20–25. https://doi.org/10.1016/j.beproc.2018.12.015.

Rotgans, J. I., & Schmidt, H. G. (2017). Interest development: Arousing situational interest affects the growth trajectory of individual interest. *Contemporary Educational Psychology*, 49, 175–184. https://doi.org/10.1016/j.cedpsych .2017.02.003.

Rushworth, M. F. S., Mars, R. B., & Summerfield, C. (2009). General mechanisms for making decisions? *Current Opinion in Neurobiology*, 19(1), 75–83. https://doi.org/10.1016/j.conb.2009.02.005.

Sakaki, M., Yagi, A., & Murayama, K. (2018). Curiosity in old age: A possible key to achieving adaptive aging. *Neuroscience and Biobehavioral Reviews*, 88, 106–116. https://doi.org/10.1016/j.neubiorev.2018.03.007.

Sansone, C., & Thoman, D. B. (2005). Interest as the missing motivator in self-regulation. *European Psychologist*, 10(3), 175–186. https://doi.org/10 .1027/1016-9040.10.3.175.

Schiefele, U. (2009). Situational and individual interest. In K. R. Wenzel & A. Wigfield (Eds.), *Educational psychology handbook series: Handbook of motivation at school* (pp. 197–222). Routledge/Taylor & Francis Group.

Schulz, E., Bhui, R., Love, B. C., Brier, B., Todd, M. T., & Gershman, S. J. (2019). Structured, uncertainty-driven exploration in real-world consumer choice. *Proceedings of the National Academy of Sciences*, 116(28), 13903–13908. https:// doi.org/10.1073/pnas.1821028116.

Schulz, E., Wu, C. M., Ruggeri, A., & Meder, B. (2019). Searching for rewards like a child means less generalization and more directed exploration. *Psychological Science*, 30(11), 1561–1572. https://doi.org/10.1177/0956797619863663.

Sedikides, C., & Strube, M. J. (1997). Self-evaluation: To thine own self be good, to thine own self be sure, to thine own self be true, and to thine own self be better. *Advances in Experimental Social Psychology*, 29, 209–269. https://doi.org /10.1016/S0065-2601(08)60018-0.

Sharot, T., & Sunstein, C. R. (2020). How people decide what they want to know. *Nature Human Behaviour*, 4(1), 14–19. https://doi.org/10.1038/s41562-019-0793-1.

Somerville, L. H., Sasse, S. F., Garrad, M. C., Drysdale, A. T., Abi Akar, N., Insel, C., & Wilson, R. C. (2017). Charting the expansion of strategic exploratory behavior during adolescence. *Journal of Experimental Psychology: General*, 146(2), 155–164. https://doi.org/10.1037/xge0000250.

Van Lieshout, L. L. F., Vandenbroucke, A. R. E., Müller, N. C. J., Cools, R., & de Lange, F. P. (2018). Induction and relief of curiosity elicit parietal and frontal activity. *Journal of Neuroscience*, 38(10), 2579–2588. https://doi.org/10.1523 /JNEUROSCI.2816-17.2018.

Witherby, A. E., & Carpenter, S. K. (2021). The rich-get-richer effect: Prior knowledge predicts new learning of domain-relevant information. *Journal of Experimental Psychology: Learning, Memory, and Cognition*. https://doi.org/10 .1037/xlm0000996.

Wu, C. M., Schulz, E., Speekenbrink, M., Nelson, J. D., & Meder, B. (2018). Generalization guides human exploration in vast decision spaces. *Nature Human Behaviour*, 2(12), 915–924. https://doi.org/10.1038/s41562-018-0467-4.

CHAPTER 3

Curiosity-Driven Exploration
Diversity of Mechanisms and Functions

Alexandr Ten, Pierre-Yves Oudeyer, and Clément Moulin-Frier

3.1 Introduction

If you are reading this chapter, chances are you are seeking information; you might even be curious about what you are about to read. Whatever the case, you are certainly familiar – as much as the next person – with what being curious feels like. It is this paradoxically palpable gap you perceive in your knowledge that makes you long for information.

Contemporary cognitive psychological theory maintains that curiosity is a crucial developmental element that allows humans to acquire useful knowledge (Oudeyer & Smith, 2016; Gopnik, 2020). Curiosity lets us seek out certain experiences for the inherent value of learning from them, not because they are rewarding in a more tangible way. The feeling of curiosity itself is borne out by a cognitive mechanism that prioritizes potential learning experiences in order to prepare the learner for future challenges that are as yet unknown (Oudeyer, 2018; Gopnik, 2020).

Precisely how the curiosity-inducing mechanism operates in biological organisms is poorly understood (Gottlieb & Oudeyer, 2018), but the undeniable significance of curiosity for the eventual acquisition of useful knowledge continues to spur researchers in artificial intelligence (AI) to develop curious learning algorithms. These efforts have generated a great diversity of mechanisms enabling curiosity-driven learning in artificial agents. This chapter identifies common structural dimensions of these mechanisms and relates variation along these dimensions to possible evolutionary functions. To be able to discuss these ideas, we need to recount how machines learn.

Although defining learning can be controversial (Barron et al., 2015), we will adopt a straightforward formulation from machine learning (ML; Jordan & Mitchell, 2015), where learning is defined as improvement on a task (or a set of tasks) with experience. An artificial agent is said to have improved on a task if – according to some well-defined criterion – it is able to perform the task better than it did prior to receiving learning experience. Thus, what drives improvement is a combination of the experience that comes in the form of data that the agent can represent and the learning algorithm (also called learning, or update rule) that specifies how the agent's innards change by processing the incoming data.

For a long time, major ML paradigms have been elaborating increasingly efficient and powerful learning algorithms that optimize prespecified task criteria. For example, all traditional supervised and unsupervised learning (respectively, SL and UL) algorithms depend on a formally defined objective function which evaluates the agent's responses to stimuli and thus drives structural changes that result in better responses in the future. While these algorithms can learn many different tasks (e.g., image classification, natural language processing, visual scene parsing, etc.), they are typically trained on datasets and objective functions assigned by the engineer. On the other hand, active learning agents (Thrun, 1995; Cohn, Ghahramani & Jordan, 1996) feature algorithms that autonomously sample the data they learn from. This is particularly the case in reinforcement learning (RL; Sutton & Barto, 2018), where agents have control over the sampled data by virtue of causal interactions with their environments. Here, learning is driven by an evaluative objective criterion which comes in the form of a reward function. Like in SL and UL, what the agent ends up learning is determined by a predefined criterion, but additional complications arise because of the need to sample experiences that help the agent improve. In realistic settings, only a tiny fraction of all possible experiences are relevant, which can be further complicated by the sparsity or deceptiveness of rewards. Sampling relevant experiences while avoiding noise is an important problem which will receive much attention in this chapter.

In contrast to ML agents that learn externally assigned tasks, biological agents, particularly humans, often have autonomy not only in how they choose experiences to learn tasks, but also in choosing what tasks to learn. We seek information when we become curious without being told what to be curious about. Seeking information out of curiosity, rather than to achieve a separable outcome such as food or money, is characterized in psychology as intrinsically motivated (Harlow, Harlow, & Meyer, 1950; Ryan & Deci, 2000). In addition to information-seeking phenomena like curiosity (Bazhydai, Twomey, & Westermann, 2021) and interest (Hidi & Renninger, 2006), intrinsic motivation (IM) is also linked to other hallmarks of human behavior, such as creativity (Gross, Zedelius, & Schooler, 2020) and play (Chu & Schulz, 2020).

Similarly to humans, but unlike the traditional ML systems mentioned above, intrinsically motivated artificial agents control what they learn through autonomous and task-independent sampling of learning experiences. In order to collect learning experiences, agents explore learning situations. To better appreciate what we mean by learning situations and how they relate to various mechanisms and functions of intrinsic motivation, consider the following scenarios:

1. A virtual robot trying random actions in its environment.
2. A toddler trying to build the tallest possible tower with toy blocks.
3. A curious student raising his hand to ask a question.
4. A human infant looking at where her mother is pointing.
5. A rat exploring a maze to get familiar with its environment.
6. A scientist designing the next experiment.

All of these scenarios describe an agent interacting with its environment and thereby engaging in a learning situation.[1] Importantly, these situations are not merely different due to the different kinds of agents involved, but because they involve different mechanisms that have distinct functions. Mechanisms of curiosity-driven exploration are composed of (a) the interface through which agents sample learning situations (i.e. the space in which they can make choices); and (b) the principle by which agents rank learning situations within this space. We describe these dimensions more thoroughly in Section 3.2 (Mechanisms), but the examples above already illustrate that agents can sample learning situations by choosing what actions to take (1), what goals to pursue (2), or whom to ask (3). Moreover, the decisions between the alternatives may be based on prior knowledge (3), driven by competence (2), or influenced socially (4). Note that the different mechanisms illustrated by the examples imply distinct consequences, suggesting that they may serve distinct functions. In Section 3.2 (Functions), we locate these functions on the axis of causal proximity to evolutionary fitness: from the rat exploring a maze (5) to the scientist exploring an obscure domain (6). Finally, in Section 3.4 (Usages) we discuss the relationships between AI and psychology and briefly survey some of the use cases for various intrinsically motivated algorithms outside the realm of AI research.

---

[1] Of course, the agent may not learn from every single interaction with the environment, but any interaction creates a situation where learning could happen.

3.2   Mechanisms

As mentioned in the introduction, researchers in AI have proposed a wealth of algorithms for curiosity-driven exploration. These algorithms differ by how they address two related subproblems:

1. How to parameterize learning situations?
2. How to choose learning situations?

The first subproblem is addressed by defining the choice space to drive exploration (Moulin-Frier & Oudeyer, 2013). Intuitively, a choice space serves as a basis for assessing different learning situations. Actualizing choices in a choice space results in agent–environment interactions from which the agent can learn. This chapter reviews three kinds of choice spaces that consist of either actions, goal states, or social partners. These choice spaces correspond to different ways in which learning situations can be parameterized. Parameterizing learning situations on the basis of actions lets the agent consider what can be learned by performing these actions; parameterizing learning situations on the basis of goals lets the agent consider what can be learned by pursuing goals; parameterizing learning situations on the basis of social partners lets the agent consider what can be learned by interacting with others. We discuss the main ways in which choice spaces are specified and how they differ in Section 3.2.1 (Exploration Bases).

Given a fully specified choice space, the agent can make decisions within that space. Specifying this decision-making process addresses the second subproblem. Agents choose what to learn by following a certain strategy by which they assign "interestingness" to the available choices, thereby determining which learning situations are more likely to be approached. For example, choices can be driven by features of learning situations, such as the amount of knowledge a situation might bring or how novel it is; they can also be made completely at random (e.g., Colas, Sigaud, & Oudeyer, 2018; Colas, Karch, Lair, et al., 2020). We provide a brief survey of these methods in Section 3.2.2 (Exploration strategies).

3.2.1   Exploration Bases

As stated, a learning situation arises whenever an agent interacts with its environment. Active interactions entail that the agent has to decide how to act in a given context, and upon deciding and acting, gets to observe the effects of its actions. How the agent explores, therefore, depends primarily on how the agent contextualizes its interactions. Specifically, the agent can explore by considering what actions to take, what goals to pursue, or what social partners to engage. Sets of actions, goals, or social partners provide a basis for comparing potential interactions. The rest of this section reviews different ways in which such bases are defined, used, and represented.

3.2.1.1 *Exploring by Choosing Actions*

One family of approaches considers agents which observe the current state of the environment as a context, choose actions to execute, and observe the resulting following state. Here, the objective of exploration is to select the actions which generate informative data for learning an internal model of causal dynamics through SL, UL, or RL. For example, several SL-based robotic agents (Oudeyer, Kaplan, & Hafner, 2007; Caligiore et al., 2008; Baranes & Oudeyer, 2009; Saegusa et al., 2009; Lefort & Gepperth, 2015) maintain world models representing their knowledge about either forward dynamics (inferring future states from specific actions), or inverse dynamics (inferring the right actions to bring about specific states), or both. These systems learn from observations borne out of the actions they choose. Therefore, exploration of learning situations in these approaches corresponds to making choices in the action space. Examples of action-space exploration can also be found in RL settings (Singh et al., 2010; Bellemare et al., 2016; Jaderberg et al., 2016; Pathak et al., 2017; Tang et al., 2017; Burda et al., 2018; Haber et al., 2018; Bougie & Ichise, 2021). In intrinsically motivated RL, agents learn behavioral policies by maximizing intrinsic rewards (e.g., rewards based on state novelty, as in Tang et al., 2017; on model prediction error, as in Pathak et al., 2017; or on surprise, as in Berseth et al., 2021). In these systems, actions that bring about rewarding states get reinforced. Thus, the agent collects learning data (state transitions) by ranking actions according to their capacity to yield intrinsic rewards.

3.2.1.2 *Exploring by Choosing Goals*

Another family of approaches considers agents making choices in a goal space instead of an action space. In the general case, such agents learn to represent and sample their own goals: that is, they are autotelic (Colas, Karch, Sigaud, et al., 2021). This family of approaches is referred to as Intrinsically Motivated Goal-Exploration Processes (or IMGEP for short; Forestier et al., 2017; Colas, Karch, Sigaud, et al. 2021). Here, the notion of a goal is generalized: it refers to any set of constraints on any set of future sensorimotor representations (Colas, Karch, Sigaud, et al., 2021).

This abstract conceptualization enables researchers to express all kinds of goals, ranging from particular world states (e.g., coordinates of the agent's hand must be equal to a specific x, y, and z), to constraints on entire behavioral trajectories and their linguistic descriptions (e.g., "water the plant and then feed the dog"; Colas, Karch, Lair, et al., 2020). In all cases, goals are specified by two essential components: (1) goal representation that specifies the criteria, and (2) goal-achievement function that signals whether the criteria are met. Goals are usually represented as numerical vectors (sometimes called goal embeddings) that comprise abstract goal spaces from which specific goals can be sampled, while goal achievement is evaluated using logical operations.

Examples of IMGEPs can be found in SL and UL contexts (Jordan & Rumelhart, 1992; Rolf, Steil, & Gienger, 2010; Baranes & Oudeyer, 2013; Moulin-Frier & Oudeyer, 2013; Forestier et al., 2017; Takahashi et al., 2017; Reinke, Etcheverry, & Oudeyer, 2020; Laversanne-Finot, Péré, & Oudeyer, 2018). In these frameworks, agents autonomously engage in learning situations by attempting to reach self-selected goals. Note that this process is markedly different from the one described above, where the agent accesses learning situations by choosing among the available actions. In IMGEPs, the agent can consider any goal it may imagine, not just the states that its actions may bring about.

The domain of goal-conditioned RL works with agents that learn action-policies conditioned on goals. These agents base their actions not only on the current state (as in traditional RL) but also the goal encoding, which means they can act differently in the same situation depending on what they are after (Schaul et al., 2016). Intrinsically motivated goal-conditioned RL builds upon that framework and allows agents to generate their own goals (see Colas, Karch, Sigaud, et al., 2021, for a recent review). Some notable examples include Colas, Sigaud, & Oudeyer, 2018; Nair et al., 2018; Colas, Fournier, et al., 2019; Pong et al., 2020; Colas, Karch, Lair, et al., 2020. While there is a great deal of variability among strategies for sampling interesting goals (see Section 3.2.2: Exploration Strategies), all of these goal-oriented agents make decisions in a goal space rather than in an action space. Goal-oriented intrinsically motivated learning has a number of advantages compared to action-oriented intrinsically motivated learning: it improves the performance and convergence time when learning inverse models in high-dimensional spaces with highly nonlinear mappings (Baranes & Oudeyer, 2013); it automatically generates learning curricula from easy to more complex skills (Moulin-Frier, Nguyen, & Oudeyer, 2014); and, finally, it enables hindsight learning (Forestier et al., 2017; Andrychowicz et al., 2018; Colas, Fournier, et al., 2019). We discuss these positive practical implications in more detail in Section 3.3 (Functions).

3.2.1.3 *Exploring by Choosing Social Partners*

A few contributions have explored how IM can be coupled with social interaction. The SGIM-ACTS architecture (Nguyen & Oudeyer, 2012) considers an IM agent that is able to choose whether and when to learn from a social peer or by autonomous goal generation, from which social peer to learn, and what to ask the chosen social peer. Interacting with the social peer becomes part of the choice space and the agent makes hierarchical decisions: it first decides to interact or to self-explore its own goals, then which social peer or self-generated goal to focus on. The SGIM-ACTS framework was also applied to agents equipped with a realistic computer model of the human vocal tract and was able to reproduce the main developmental stages of infant vocal development (Moulin-Frier, Nguyen, & Oudeyer, 2014). More recent contributions consider social influence as intrinsic motivation for achieving coordination and communication in multiagent RL (Jaques et al., 2019). Other works in multiagent RL have theorized and demonstrated how competition and cooperation display intrinsic dynamics resulting in a naturally emergent curriculum (Leibo et al., 2019; Baker et al., 2020).

3.2.1.4 *Representing Choice Spaces*

Precisely what do choices in choice spaces represent? In the case of action-space exploration, actions can represent micro-actions responsible for transitions between temporally adjacent momentary states, like pixel images (e.g., Bellemare et al., 2016; Pathak et al., 2017). In this case, the agent can only learn from short-term transitions, which limits their ability to efficiently learn regularities spanning larger time scales.[2] However, the agent can sample learning situations by making decisions in the space of macro-actions (e.g., action-policies), rather than micro-actions, which enables exploration of more temporally extended effects of its actions (see Baranes & Oudeyer, 2013).

---

[2] Model-free RL agents (e.g., Bellemare et al., 2016; Pathak et al., 2017) do not learn from the transitions per se – they learn from rewards. Specifically, the agent usually learns a value function V, mapping states to their expected cumulative reward. Even if the transitions are momentary, the agent can still maximize their long-term cumulative reward using techniques such as bootstrapping (Sutton & Barto, 2018). Another exception is when the world model is represented by a recurrent neural network (RNN; Takahashi et al., 2017) as RNNs can encode time series.

In the case of goal sampling, the choice space can correspond entirely to the state space, so that a given goal represents a particular state. This can be problematic for very high-dimensional spaces – for example, if the state space is a space of pixel images, because sampling directly from this space yields white noise most of the time, just like blindly picking alphabet letters would produce mostly gibberish (Nair et al., 2018). One solution to this problem is to define the goal space as some high-level feature space (also called latent or embedding space) of the raw-image space (e.g., Laversanne-Finot, Péré, & Oudeyer, 2021). Following the letter-picking analogy, this would correspond to composing and sampling from a higher-level space of syllables or words, which is more likely to produce meaningful strings. A related issue in cases when the goal space is defined over some abstraction over the raw sensory experience (e.g., 2D positions of objects vs. raw pixel images), is whether to assume that this abstract space is given to the agent (like in Forestier et al. 2017) or whether the agent needs to learn a latent goal space from scratch (e.g., Nair et al., 2018; Laversanne-Finot, Péré, & Oudeyer, 2021).

3.2.2   *Exploration Strategies*

Given a well-defined choice space for exploration, what strategies can an artificial agent follow to decide which learning situations are more or less interesting? Comprehensive reviews of different approaches can be found elsewhere (Oudeyer & Kaplan, 2009; Mirolli & Baldassarre, 2013; Aubret, Matignon, & Hassas, 2019; Linke et al., 2020), so we provide only a short survey of different approaches, with a focus on their diversity rather than precise implementations.

We group existing approaches into three main categories: undirected, knowledge-based, and competence-based exploration. While all learning situations are equally interesting in undirected exploration, directed exploration strategies scale interestingness with the agent's abilities. Directed exploration can be divided into two broad classes: knowledge-based and competence-based strategies (Oudeyer & Kaplan, 2009). Sometimes the distinction between the two can be subtle because knowledgeable systems can also be competent and competent systems can be knowledgeable (Mirolli & Baldassarre, 2013). The point of divergence for these families of mechanisms is that to a knowledge-based system, the interestingness of a learning situation is determined by its relation to the system's knowledge. On the other hand, to a competence-based system, a given learning situation may be more or less interesting because it relates to the system's ability to reach a specific self-generated goal.

3.2.2.1   Undirected Exploration

Undirected exploration (sometimes random or uniform exploration) refers to a strategy that assigns interest uniformly across the choice space (making all learning situations equally interesting). The effectiveness of this simple strategy is inconsistent across different settings. When applied to action-space exploration, for example, undirected exploration is only effective for simplistic problems (Baranes & Oudeyer, 2013; Benureau & Oudeyer, 2016), such as when the environment provides dense rewards or when actions have simple and consistent effects. In more challenging settings, where the mapping between actions and their effects exhibits a combination of nonlinearity, stochasticity, and redundancy, motor exploration is not sufficient for effective learning, but goal exploration could be (Moulin-Frier & Oudeyer, 2013). This is largely because learning how to reach goals contributes to the agent's competence and thus its ability to control the environment, while learning about various outcomes of all of one's actions in all possible contexts may be worthless in practice (Mirolli & Baldassarre, 2013). Besides, trying out random actions from a particular state may be futile for reaching certain hard-to-reach regions of the state space. Think of how hard it would be to learn how to drive from home to work by performing random actions (you would end up crashing your car most of the time). If instead you were to learn how to drive to various places from home (your driveway, a cornershop, a nearby gas station) your chances of finding your way to your office eventually would be much higher.

Despite its simplicity, random goal exploration has proven to be surprisingly efficient, leading to some forms of novelty search as an emergent feature and surpassing directed approaches operating in the action space in the learning of redundant inverse mappings (Benureau & Oudeyer, 2016; Colas, Sigaud, & Oudeyer, 2018). Because it is simple and computationally cheap, random goal exploration is often combined with other strategies, either to jumpstart the primary mode of directed exploration by collecting initial data, or sometimes as a complementary strategy at a certain level of hierarchical sampling decisions in modular spaces (e.g., Forestier et al. 2017), and sometimes as an epsilon-greedy strategy (see Sutton & Barto, 2018) to balance between random and directed exploration (e.g., Colas, Fournier, et al., 2019). Still, in many situations, undirected exploration may not be as efficient or effective as more sophisticated guided exploration approaches. For example, random (goal) exploration performs poorly when the space of effects has a hierarchical structure, so that certain states are only accessible through reaching some prerequisite states (e.g., Forestier et al., 2017). An agent exploring goals randomly is unlikely to ever get to practice these "out-of-reach" goals, unless there is a mechanism for imagining them that leverages structured representations of goals, such as natural language encodings (e.g., Colas, Karch, Lair et al., 2020).

3.2.2.2 Knowledge-Based Exploration

Knowledge-based exploration is perhaps the most diverse family of intrinsically motivated strategies. Not only are there many ways in which one can characterize a relation between learning situations and the agent's knowledge, there are many kinds of knowledge that agents represent. For example, an agent can maintain a predictive causal model of the effects of its actions and have a metacognitive monitoring system track errors that this predictive model commits. Equipped with such a system, the agent can measure interestingness of actions based on, for example, outcome prediction error of the forward model (e.g., Saegusa et al., 2009). Specifically, the agent can be more (or less) interested in taking actions for which the forward model does accurately predict the consequences (known as prediction-error strategy). Alternatively, the agent can track changes in prediction accuracy (a strategy known as learning progress; e.g., Schmidhuber, 1991b; Oudeyer, Kaplan, & Hafner, 2007; Kim et al., 2020). Here the agent would be more (or less) interested in actions, predictions for which get more accurate with time. While the measure of interestingness in these approaches is based on the predictions from a forward model, exploring agents can also monitor the behavior of an inverse dynamics model (Pathak et al., 2017; Haber et al., 2018).

A distinct subclass of knowledge-based strategies relies on knowledge about frequencies of observed states. In so-called count-based approaches (Bellemare et al., 2016; Tang et al., 2017), this knowledge is represented explicitly, allowing the agent to selectively explore over- or under-visited states. Other systems in this subclass of approaches incorporate different variants of autoencoder networks to learn latent spaces (Twomey & Westermann, 2018; Bougie & Ichise, 2021) or generative models (Nair et al., 2018; Pong et al., 2020) of states observed by the agent. Specifically, Twomey and Westerman defined several interestingness measures based on backpropagation computation of their category-learning neural network, including measures of weight update, prediction error, and activation-function derivative (which model, respectively, the system's curiosity, novelty, and plasticity; Twomey & Westermann, 2018). Bougie & Ichise introduced auxiliary tasks of image reconstruction with context-based autoencoders and defined an intrinsic reward measure derived from reconstruction errors from these tasks (Bougie & Ichise, 2021). Others (Nair et al., 2018; Pong et al., 2020) employed variational autoencoders to estimate valid state distributions in order to guide exploration. Although these models do not explicitly encode state visitation counts, the interestingness measures defined on their basis are related to frequencies of the observed states. Autoencoder prediction error, for instance, should decrease with repeated exposure to a given state. Variational autoencoders additionally represent the statistics of the latent space – a feature that can be used to estimate the likelihood of any state (including completely novel states) given what has been observed in the past.

3.2.2.3 *Competence-Based Exploration*

Another family of strategies assigns interestingness based on competence. These approaches do not need to assume any explicit world-dynamics knowledge model (although they can), so they can be readily incorporated in model-free learning systems without the need to introduce any auxiliary tasks. Competence-based exploration strategies are especially well suited for intrinsically motivated agents that explore self-imposed goals, since the notion of competence corresponds naturally to goal achievement. A simple competence-based heuristic in a goal-oriented context is to sample goals according to the agent's ability to achieve them. For example, Bougie and Ichise reward the agent in a given state based on how incompetent the agent perceives itself to be in that state (Bougie & Ichise, 2020). Here the agent generates its data set by taking interest in actions that lead it to states at which it deems itself incompetent, namely by choosing actions that maximize incompetence. In a different approach, Florensa and colleagues leveraged the generative power of adversarial networks for generating goals, which the agent evaluates based on the probability of reaching them (Florensa et al., 2018). Thanks to this evaluation, their agent can prioritize goals of intermediate difficulty, thereby avoiding goals that it already knows how to achieve and goals that it knows it cannot achieve. Santucci et al. compared the efficacy of several interestingness measures for autonomous mastering of a set of tasks that included unreachable distractor tasks. The best-performing measure that allowed their agent to learn all learnable tasks in the least amount of time was based on competence prediction-error (Santucci, Baldassarre, & Mirolli, 2013). Several other teams have explored modular goal spaces using measures of competence progress

(Stout & Barto, 2010; Forestier et al., 2017; Colas, Fournier, et al., 2019). Agents in these studies were incentivized to sample goals from the predefined regions (modules) of the goal space where competence was either improving or deteriorating. Oudeyer and colleagues used a similar competence progress-based strategy but in settings where the singular goal-space was progressively modularized (Baranes & Oudeyer, 2013; Moulin-Frier, Nguyen, & Oudeyer, 2014).

3.3 Functions

The previous section reviewed the diversity of approaches to specifying intrinsically motivated mechanisms in AI. We mentioned in the introduction that these mechanisms are useful for autonomous learning in the absence of externally assigned objectives, but what specific functional consequences do different intrinsic motivation mechanisms bear? This section focuses on the functional aspects of intrinsically motivated systems, addressing the question of how different intrinsic-motivational systems are useful for both artificial and biological agents.

Singh et al., (2010) provide a useful connection between the concepts of extrinsic and intrinsic motivation and the concepts of primary and secondary rewards. While the reception of primary rewards (e.g., related to nutrients, sex, or pain) contributes to an agent's survival and, thus, its reproductive success, secondary reinforcers signal anticipation of primary rewards, but are neutral a priori and have to be learned. In RL, outputs of the reward function can be analogous to primary reward signals, because the reward function is given to the agent. However, value functions evaluate states based on their learned expected cumulative reward, and therefore outputs of the value function are analogous to secondary reinforcers. In this formulation, intrinsic motivators (e.g., novelty, uncertainty, learning progress, etc.) are primary reinforcers because their rewardingness is a given. On the other hand, predictors of intrinsic primary reinforcers can acquire rewarding qualities through the learning of secondary reinforcers, in the same way as nonrewarding states gain value due to extrinsic reinforcers. Therefore, intrinsic primary rewards differ from extrinsic primary rewards, mostly due to their causal proximity to evolutionary success. As it is often the case in biology (Dobzhansky, 1973), it is sensible to analyze the functional aspect of artificial intrinsic-motivational mechanisms in light of evolution – an exercise that allows us to consider the possible bio-ecological roles of engineered curiosity-driven systems.

In what follows, we build upon Singh et al.'s framework as well as the taxonomy of mechanisms we proposed in the previous section in order to extract key functional aspects of intrinsic motivation in both biological and artificial agents. We start from the more evolutionarily proximal functions (direct procurement of primary rewards) and gradually consider increasingly distal ones (learning of internal models, goal discovery, and cultural innovation).

3.3.1 Procurement of Extrinsic Primary Rewards

In relatively dense primary-reward environments, unstructured random exploration in the action space is sufficient to efficiently elicit extrinsic primary rewards (as is the case in some standard AI benchmarks based on video games: e.g., Mnih et al., 2015). This points to the most proximal function of intrinsic motivation: the generation of diverse sensorimotor experiences. The direct benefit of generating diverse experiences is to increase the probability of eliciting primary extrinsic rewards. However, the diversity generated by random exploration is usually not sufficient in sparser reward environments (e.g., Pathak et al., 2017). Knowledge-based exploration can increase the diversity of learning experiences by guiding exploration based on different measures of interestingness (see Section 3.2.2). Discovering extrinsic primary rewards such as food, water, or shelter through exploration is clearly linked to the agent's well-being.

3.3.2 Learning Internal Models

A more distal function of intrinsic motivation is the learning of internal models of the agent–environment interaction (e.g., forward or inverse models) that can enhance the agent's decision-making abilities. Learning such a model can be formalized as an UL or an SL problem and strongly relies on the information contained in the training dataset. Autonomous agents generate this dataset by interacting with the environment, and the key role of intrinsic motivation is to generate informative training data. Research in intrinsically motivated SL extensively studied two main cases. On the one hand, knowledge-based approaches have proven to be efficient in generating informative data for learning forward models (Oudeyer, Kaplan, & Hafner, 2007). On the other hand, competence-based approaches have proven to be more efficient than knowledge-based approaches for learning inverse models (Baranes & Oudeyer, 2013). RL agents can also benefit from internal models, be they in the form of a value function and an action policy in model-free RL (Pathak et al., 2017), or in the form of a world-dynamics model (forward or inverse) in model-based RL (Haber et al., 2018). Understanding how the world works per se does not put proverbial food in the agent's mouth, but it allows the agent to act more intelligently in novel situations and plan ahead in order to obtain what it needs more reliably.

3.3.3   Goal Discovery

The third level of functions we propose is related to the discovery and learning of novel goals and the associated skills to achieve them. This is the main function of competence-based approaches, where exploration is guided by the pursuit of self-imposed goals. These approaches can automatically organize exploration from simple to more complex skills (Forestier et al., 2017; Pong et al., 2020), as well as discover the full range of the achievable behavioral repertoire, possibly in an open-ended manner (Colas, Fournier, et al., 2019). There are multiple functional advantages to discovering and mastering novel goals that are not extrinsically rewarding. First, in environments where eliciting extrinsic primary rewards requires the acquisition of complex skills (e.g., hunting), it is crucial to structure learning in a curriculum from simple (e.g., locomotion) to more complex skills. Complex skill sets often display a hierarchical structure, where mastering easier skills is a prerequisite for acquiring more complex ones. Second, the ability to autonomously explore and discover new goals and skills provides a crucial advantage in changing environments. For example, paleoclimatological data provides evidence for strongly varying climate conditions in the Rift Valley in East Africa approximately 7 million years ago, and it is hypothesized that the ability to rapidly and flexibly reorganize a diverse behavioral repertoire was a key requirement to adapt to such unprecedented conditions (Potts, 2013). Thus, the ability to autonomously generate and master novel goals and thereby acquire a diverse repertoire of complex skills provides a crucial advantage for a species' success in such settings of strong environmental variability (see Nisioty, Jodogne-del Litto, & Moulin-Frier, 2021, for a recent proposition to apply this principle in AI).

3.3.4   Cultural Innovation

Finally, the fourth and most distal level of functions we propose concerns cultural innovation. Several theoretical contributions proposed a potential role of curiosity-driven exploration in both language acquisition (Oller, 2000) and evolution (Oudeyer & Smith, 2016). From a sensorimotor perspective, active exploration can spontaneously generate diverse behaviors from modality-independent and task-independent internal drives. Such spontaneous behavior can result in vocal activity that may have bootstrapped the emergence of communication. This hypothesis is supported by computational simulations showing a role of curiosity-driven exploration in vocal development (Moulin-Frier, Nguyen, & Oudeyer, 2014), social affordance discovery (Oudeyer & Kaplan, 2006), and active control of the emerging conventions in social lexicon (Schueller, Loreto, & Oudeyer, 2018). From a cognitive perspective, compositional language itself is a powerful cognitive tool to imagine novel out-of-distribution goals in competence-based intrinsic motivation (Colas, Karch, Lair, et al., 2020). Moreover, recent contributions in multiagent RL have shown how an autocurriculum of increasingly complex behaviors displaying features of open-ended innovation can emerge from agents' coadaptation in mixed cooperative-competitive environments (Baker et al., 2020). Such mechanisms are potential precursors of cultural evolution in the human species. Cultural evolution has triggered increasingly complex technological innovation across generations (Fogarty & Creanza, 2017). A prime example of this is the industrial revolution, which has resulted in a rapid acceleration of global population growth in the nineteenth century (Lucas, 2004).

3.4 Usages

Other than helping artificial agents explore learning situations in abstract task-independent contexts, how can intrinsically motivated learning algorithms be used? We identify two main directions in which such algorithms can have high impact. On the one hand, they can be a great tool for advancing research in cognitive psychology and neuroscience. Outside cognitive research, these algorithms can be applied directly to problems that require intelligent automated exploration. We review both of these domains of application in the rest of this section.

3.4.1 Cognitive Modeling

The notion of intrinsically motivated exploration in psychology has been developing – for the most part – independently of AI (Kaplan & Oudeyer, 2007). Psychological investigations can be traced back to psychophysiological perspectives on exploration in the early 1940s (Hull 1943). Since then, psychological views on curiosity and information-seeking have undergone multiple changes (Loewenstein, 1994; Bazhydai, Twomey, & Westermann, 2021) and are now becoming more integrated with the computational perspective (Kaplan & Oudeyer, 2007; Gottlieb, Oudeyer, et al., 2013). On the other hand, early formulations of intrinsic motivation in AI were either "discovered by accident" (Andreae & Andreae, 1978, p. 5) or influenced by relatively distant research areas, such as biological autopoiesis (Maturana & Varela, 1980) and aesthetic information theory (Nake, 1976, as cited in Schmidhuber 1991a), yet not the aforementioned psychological literature (see Kaplan & Oudeyer, 2007, for a historical overview). Over the course of history, psychology and AI have actually been converging on similar ideas for why certain behaviors could be intrinsically rewarding: due to some kind of mismatch between bottom-up observations and top-down predictions (Kaplan & Oudeyer, 2007).

Evolutionary implications of artificial intrinsic-motivational systems discussed earlier (see Section 3.3: Functions) reinforce the need to seriously consider them as good candidate models for human curiosity-driven learning. A major advantage that comes naturally with these systems is their precise formulation. Such a formal description unambiguously discloses crucial structural and functional properties of the system in question and thus enables to advance the related theory more efficiently (McClelland 2009).

Cognitive models based on artificial exploring agents are becoming increasingly common. For instance, Moulin-Frier et al. explained the progression of human vocal behavior through distinct developmental stages as an intrinsically motivated, competence-progress-based goal-exploration process with an emergent curriculum (Moulin-Frier, Nguyen, & Oudeyer, 2014). (Such computational accounts of curiosity-driven learning have led to novel hypotheses on the role of curiosity in the evolution of language; see Oudeyer & Smith, 2016). More recently, Twomey and Westermann used an actively exploring autoencoder network to hypothesize an algorithmic-level description of visual exploration in infants (Twomey & Westermann, 2018); Poli et al. compared several knowledge-based sampling strategies to predict visual-attention control in infants (Poli et al., 2020). Moreover, computational models of intrinsic motivation are invoked to explain self-determined instrumental (Gershman, 2019) and noninstrumental (Ten et al., 2021) choices in human adults.

Relating specific mechanistic implementations of curiosity to a common underlying structure can be beneficial for revealing potential theoretical and empirical gaps in the scientific understanding of human information-seeking. For instance, while the information-seeking literature is brimming with work investigating episodic curiosity-driven sampling over short time scales (see Bazhydai, Twomey, & Westermann, 2021, for a recent review), only a handful of studies have looked at active time-extended curiosity-driven exploration (e.g., Holm, Wadenholt, & Schrater, 2019; Ten et al., 2021). Similarly, while most behavioral paradigms study mechanisms with action-based choice spaces (e.g., Twomey & Westermann, 2018), hardly any studies investigate intrinsically motivated exploration of goals in humans, specifically of how humans generate and choose new goals in unfamiliar sensorimotor environments.

Of course, successful curiosity-driven systems developed in AI should not be simply adopted as cognitive models of human exploration. Data from carefully designed behavioral studies should place more weight on the truthfulness of propositions about the mechanisms implemented in biological organisms than the success of these mechanisms in virtual settings. Behavioral studies employing model comparison techniques (e.g., Poli et al., 2020; Ten et al., 2021) can evaluate different AI-inspired proposals by their ability to explain human or animal data. Such studies could also fuel novel ideas to improve existing AI systems, as was done in instrumental problem settings (Lin et al., 2020). These are exciting areas of future research that can promote synergy between the two fields, allowing us to home in on a more comprehensive mechanistic understanding of intrinsically motivated information-seeking in biological organisms.

3.4.2 Practical Applications

The functional diversity of intrinsic-motivational mechanisms makes them useful for practical applications, such as automated knowledge discovery and education. Mechanisms of intrinsic motivation help autonomous agents learn in settings with complex sensorimotor spaces and sparse or nonexistent rewards. They are crucial for building autonomous control systems that can learn efficiently in open-ended environments. The practical effectiveness of these mechanisms has been recently demonstrated in studies of automated discovery in complex systems, where curious agents learn to control diverse effects in complex nonlinear settings, such as smartphone applications (Pan et al., 2020), continuous cellular automata (Etcheverry, Moulin-Frier, & Oudeyer, 2021), and real-world chemical systems (Grizou et al., 2020). Automated discovery can have a high societal impact by assisting both scientific research and artistic creation. Moreover, since one of the functions of curiosity-driven systems is knowledge acquisition, directed exploration strategies of such systems can be used to assist learners when they behave suboptimally. Importantly, such intelligent tutoring systems can be tailored to the current levels of knowledge or competence of individual learners (Clement, Oudeyer, & Lopes, 2016) and have shown promising results in pedagogical settings (Clement, Roy, et al., 2015; Delmas et al., 2018), where they assist learners in selecting topics and exercises that maximize their individual learning progress.

3.4   Conclusion

The goal of this chapter was to familiarize the reader with the diversity of computational mechanisms and possible evolutionary functions of curiosity-driven exploration. We identified an important problem facing autonomous agents that have control over their learning experiences. Specifically, such agents must decide how to sample learning data in the absence of externally imposed tasks. We briefly reviewed several ways in which artificial agents choose actions, goals, or social peers in order to engage in learning situations. We presented distinct families of exploration strategies, including undirected, knowledge-based, competence-based, and socially influenced approaches. We then discussed how these mechanisms can contribute to evolutionary success at different levels: by helping agents to approach primary rewards, acquire world models, discover goals, and bootstrap a cultural repertoire. Finally, we provided some contemporary examples of how IM algorithms are used in practical applications as well as in cognitive research. We hope that this concise bird's-eye perspective – organized along the proposed mechanistic, functional, and pragmatic dimensions of curiosity-driven exploration – can serve as a stepping stone toward a unified taxonomy of this fascinating and important field.

References

Andreae, P. M., & Andreae, J. H. (1978). A teachable machine in the real world. *International Journal of Man-Machine Studies*, 10(3), 301–312.

Andrychowicz, M., Wolski, F., Ray, A., Schneider, J., Fong, R., Welinder, P., … & Zaremba, W. (2018). Hindsight experience replay. *arXiv preprint arXiv:1707.01495*.

Aubret, A., Matignon, L., & Hassas, S. (2019). A survey on intrinsic motivation in reinforcement learning. *arXiv preprint arXiv:1908.06976*.

Baker, B., Kanitscheider, I., Markov, T., Wu, Y., Powell, G., McGrew, B., & Mordatch, I. (2020). Emergent tool use from multi-agent autocurricula. *arXiv preprint arXiv:1909.07528*.

Baranes, A., & Oudeyer, P. Y. (2009). R-iac: Robust intrinsically motivated exploration and active learning. *IEEE Transactions on Autonomous Mental Development*, 1(3), 155–169.

Baranes, A., & Oudeyer, P. Y. (2013). Active learning of inverse models with intrinsically motivated goal exploration in robots. *Robotics and Autonomous Systems*, 61(1), 49–73.

Barron, A. B., Hebets, E. A., Cleland, T. A., Fitzpatrick, C. L., Hauber, M. E., & Stevens, J. R. (2015). Embracing multiple definitions of learning. *Trends in Neurosciences*, 38(7), 405–407.

Bazhydai, M., Twomey, K., & Westermann, G. (2021). Curiosity and Exploration. In J. B. Benson (Ed.), *Encyclopedia of Infant and Early Childhood Development* (2nd ed.). Elsevier, pp. 370–378.

Bellemare, M., Srinivasan, S., Ostrovski, G., Schaul, T., Saxton, D., & Munos, R. (2016). Unifying count-based exploration and intrinsic motivation. *Advances in Neural Information Processing Systems*, 29, 1471–1479.

Benureau, F. C., & Oudeyer, P. Y. (2016). Behavioral diversity generation in autonomous exploration through reuse of past experience. *Frontiers in Robotics and AI*, 3, 8.

Berseth, G., Geng, D., Devin, C., Rhinehart, N., Finn, C., Jayaraman, D., & Levine, S. (2021). SMiRL: Surprise Minimizing Reinforcement Learning in Unstable Environments. *arXiv preprint arXiv:1912.05510*.

Bougie, N., & Ichise, R. (2020). Skill-based curiosity for intrinsically motivated reinforcement learning. *Machine Learning*, 109(3), 493–512.

Bougie, N., & Ichise, R. (2021). Fast and slow curiosity for high-level exploration in reinforcement learning. *Applied Intelligence*, 51(2), 1086–1107.

Burda, Y., Edwards, H., Pathak, D., Storkey, A., Darrell, T., & Efros, A. A. (2018). Large-scale study of curiosity-driven learning. *arXiv preprint arXiv:1808.04355*.

Caligiore, D., Ferrauto, T., Parisi, D., Accornero, N., Capozza, M., & Baldassarre, G. (2008). Using motor babbling and hebb rules for modeling the development of reaching with obstacles and grasping. In *International Conference on Cognitive Systems* (Vol. 13, pp. 22–23). www.researchgate.net/publication/2 27945187_Using_Motor_Babbling_and_Hebb_Rules_for_Modeling_the_Dev elopment_of_Reaching_with_Obstacles_and_Grasping.

Chu, J., & Schulz, L. E. (2020). Play, curiosity, and cognition. *Annual Review of Developmental Psychology*, 2, 317–343.

Clement, B., Oudeyer, P. Y., & Lopes, M. (2016). A Comparison of Automatic Teaching Strategies for Heterogeneous Student Populations. *Proceedings of the 9th International Conference on Educational Data Mining*, Raleigh, USA.

Clement, B., Roy, D., Oudeyer, P. Y., & Lopes, M. (2015). Multi-armed bandits for intelligent tutoring systems. *arXiv preprint arXiv:1310.3174*.

Cohn, D. A., Ghahramani, Z., & Jordan, M. I. (1996). Active learning with statistical models. *Journal of Artificial Intelligence Research*, 4, 129–145.

Colas, C., Fournier, P., Chetouani, M., Sigaud, O., & Oudeyer, P. Y. (2019, May). CURIOUS: intrinsically motivated modular multi-goal reinforcement learning. In *International conference on machine learning* (pp. 1331–1340). PMLR. http://proceedings.mlr.press/v97/colas19a.html.

Colas, C., Karch, T., Lair, N., Dussoux, J. M., Moulin-Frier, C., Dominey, P. F., & Oudeyer, P. Y. (2020). Language as a cognitive tool to imagine goals in curiosity-driven exploration. *arXiv preprint arXiv:2002.09253*.

Colas, C., Karch, T., Sigaud, O., & Oudeyer, P. Y. (2021). Intrinsically motivated goal-conditioned reinforcement learning: a short survey. *arXiv preprint arXiv:2012.09830*.

Colas, C., Sigaud, O., & Oudeyer, P. Y. (2018). Gep-pg: Decoupling exploration and exploitation in deep reinforcement learning algorithms. In *International conference on machine learning* (pp. 1039–1048). PMLR. http://proceedings .mlr.press/v80/colas18a.html.

Delmas, A., Clement, B., Oudeyer, P. Y., & Sauzéon, H. (2018). Fostering health education with a serious game in children with asthma: pilot studies for assessing learning efficacy and automatized learning personalization. In *Frontiers in Education* (Vol. 3, p. 99). Frontiers. https://doi.org/10.3389/feduc.2018.00099.

Dobzhansky, T. (1973). Nothing in biology makes sense except in the light of evolution. *The American Biology Teacher*, 75(2), 87–91.

Etcheverry, M., Moulin-Frier, C., & Oudeyer, P. Y. (2021). Hierarchically organized latent modules for exploratory search in morphogenetic systems. *arXiv preprint arXiv:2007.01195*.

Florensa, C., Held, D., Geng, X., & Abbeel, P. (2018, July). Automatic goal generation for reinforcement learning agents. In *International conference on machine learning* (pp. 1515–1528). PMLR. http://proceedings.mlr.press/v80/ florensa18a.html.

Fogarty, L., & Creanza, N. (2017). The niche construction of cultural complexity: interactions between innovations, population size and the environment. *Philosophical Transactions of the Royal Society B: Biological Sciences*, 372(1735), 20160428.

Forestier, S., Portelas, R., Mollard, Y., & Oudeyer, P. Y. (2017). Intrinsically motivated goal exploration processes with automatic curriculum learning. *arXiv preprint arXiv:1708.02190*.

Gershman, S. J. (2019). Uncertainty and exploration. *Decision*, 6(3), 277.

Gopnik, A. (2020). Childhood as a solution to explore–exploit tensions. *Philosophical Transactions of the Royal Society B*, 375(1803), 20190502.

Gottlieb, J., & Oudeyer, P. Y. (2018). Towards a neuroscience of active sampling and curiosity. *Nature Reviews Neuroscience*, 19(12), 758–770.

Gottlieb, J., Oudeyer, P. Y., Lopes, M., & Baranes, A. (2013). Information-seeking, curiosity, and attention: computational and neural mechanisms. *Trends in Cognitive Sciences*, 17(11), 585–593.

Grizou, J., Points, L. J., Sharma, A., & Cronin, L. (2020). A curious formulation robot enables the discovery of a novel protocell behavior. *Science Advances*, 6(5), eaay4237.

Gross, M. E., Zedelius, C. M., & Schooler, J. W. (2020). Cultivating an understanding of curiosity as a seed for creativity. *Current Opinion in Behavioral Sciences*, 35, 77–82.

Haber, N., Mrowca, D., Fei-Fei, L., & Yamins, D. L. (2018). Learning to play with intrinsically-motivated self-aware agents. *arXiv preprint arXiv:1802.07442*.

Harlow, H. F., Harlow, M. K., & Meyer, D. R. (1950). Learning motivated by a manipulation drive. *Journal of Experimental Psychology*, 40(2), 228.

Hidi, S., & Renninger, K. A. (2006). The four-phase model of interest development. *Educational Psychologist*, 41(2), 111–127.

Holm, L., Wadenholt, G., & Schrater, P. (2019). Episodic curiosity for avoiding asteroids: Per-trial information gain for choice outcomes drive information seeking. *Scientific Reports*, 9(1), 1–16.

Hull, C. L. (1943). *Principles of behavior: An introduction to behavior theory*. Appleton-Century.

Jaderberg, M., Mnih, V., Czarnecki, W. M., Schaul, T., Leibo, J. Z., Silver, D., & Kavukcuoglu, K. (2016). Reinforcement learning with unsupervised auxiliary tasks. *arXiv preprint arXiv:1611.05397*.

Jaques, N., Lazaridou, A., Hughes, E., Gulcehre, C., Ortega, P., Strouse, D. J., . . . & De Freitas, N. (2019, May). Social influence as intrinsic motivation for multi-agent deep reinforcement learning. In *International Conference on Machine Learning* (pp. 3040–3049). PMLR. http://proceedings.mlr.press/v97/jaques19a .html.

Jordan, M. I., & Mitchell, T. M. (2015). Machine learning: Trends, perspectives, and prospects. *Science*, 349(6245), 255–260.

Jordan, M. I., & Rumelhart, D. E. (1992). Forward models: Supervised learning with a distal teacher. *Cognitive Science*, 16(3), 307–354.

Kaplan, F., & Oudeyer, P. Y. (2007). In search of the neural circuits of intrinsic motivation. *Frontiers in Neuroscience*, 1, 17.

Kim, K., Sano, M., De Freitas, J., Haber, N., & Yamins, D. (2020). Active world model learning with progress curiosity. In *International conference on machine learning* (pp. 5306–5315). PMLR. https://proceedings.mlr.press/v119/kim20e .html.

Laversanne-Finot, A., Péré, A., & Oudeyer, P. Y. (2018). Curiosity driven exploration of learned disentangled goal spaces. In *Conference on Robot Learning* (pp. 487–504). PMLR. https://proceedings.mlr.press/v87/laver sanne-finot18a.html.

Laversanne-Finot, A., Péré, A., & Oudeyer, P. Y. (2021). Intrinsically motivated exploration of learned goal spaces. *Frontiers in Neurorobotics*, 14, 109.

Lefort, M., & Gepperth, A. (2015). Active learning of local predictable representations with artificial curiosity. In *2015 Joint IEEE International Conference on Development and Learning and Epigenetic Robotics (ICDL-EpiRob)* (pp. 228–233). IEEE. https://ieeexplore.ieee.org/abstract/document/7346145.

Leibo, J. Z., Hughes, E., Lanctot, M., & Graepel, T. (2019). Autocurricula and the emergence of innovation from social interaction: A manifesto for multi-agent intelligence research. *arXiv preprint arXiv:1903.00742*.

Lin, B., Cecchi, G., Bouneffouf, D., Reinen, J., & Rish, I. (2019). A story of two streams: Reinforcement learning models from human behavior and neuro-psychiatry. *arXiv preprint arXiv:1906.11286*.

Linke, C., Ady, N. M., White, M., Degris, T., & White, A. (2020). Adapting behavior via intrinsic reward: A survey and empirical study. *Journal of Artificial Intelligence Research*, 69, 1287–1332.

Loewenstein, G. (1994). The psychology of curiosity: A review and reinterpretation. Psychological Bulletin, 116(1), 75.

Lucas, R. E. (2004). The industrial revolution: Past and future. *Economic Education Bulletin*, 44(8), 1–8. www.aier.org/wp-content/uploads/2013/11/EEB-8.04-IndustRev.pdf.

Maturana, H. R., & Varela, F. J. (1980). *Autopoiesis and cognition: The realization of the living* (Vol. 42). Springer Science & Business Media.

McClelland, J. L. (2009). The place of modeling in cognitive science. *Topics in Cognitive Science*, 1(1), 11–38.

Mirolli, M., & Baldassarre, G. (2013). Functions and mechanisms of intrinsic motivations. In G. Baldassarre & M. Mirolli (Eds.), *Intrinsically Motivated Learning in Natural and Artificial Systems* (pp. 49–72). Springer.

Mnih, V., Kavukcuoglu, K., Silver, D., Rusu, A. A., Veness, J., Bellemare, M. G., ... & Hassabis, D. (2015). Human-level control through deep reinforcement learning. *Nature*, 518(7540), 529–533.

Moulin-Frier, C., Nguyen, S. M., & Oudeyer, P. Y. (2014). Self-organization of early vocal development in infants and machines: the role of intrinsic motivation. *Frontiers in Psychology*, 4, 1006.

Moulin-Frier, C., & Oudeyer, P. Y. (2013, August). Exploration strategies in developmental robotics: A unified probabilistic framework. In *2013 IEEE Third Joint International Conference on Development and Learning and Epigenetic Robotics (ICDL)* (pp. 1–6). IEEE. https://doi.org/10.1109/DevLrn.2013.6652535.

Nair, A., Pong, V., Dalal, M., Bahl, S., Lin, S., & Levine, S. (2018). Visual reinforcement learning with imagined goals. *arXiv preprint arXiv:1807.04742*.

Nake, F. (1976). Ästhetik als Informationsverarbeitung: Grundlagen und Anwendungen der Informatik im Bereich ästhetischer Produktion und Kritik. *Journal of Aesthetics and Art Criticism*, 34(3).

Nguyen, S. M., & Oudeyer, P. Y. (2012). Active choice of teachers, learning strategies and goals for a socially guided intrinsic motivation learner. *Paladyn*, 3(3), 136–146.

Eleni Nisioti, Katia Jodogne-del Litto, Clément Moulin-Frier. Grounding an Ecological Theory of Artificial Intelligence in Human Evolution. NeurIPS 2021 - Conference on Neural Information Processing Systems / Workshop: Ecological Theory of Reinforcement Learning, Dec 2021, virtual event, France. (hal-03446961v2)

Oller, D. K. (2000). *The emergence of the speech capacity.* Psychology Press.

Oudeyer, P. Y. (2018). Computational theories of curiosity-driven learning. *arXiv preprint arXiv:1802.10546.*

Oudeyer, P. Y., & Kaplan, F. (2006). Discovering communication. *Connection Science,* 18(2), 189–206.

Oudeyer, P. Y., & Kaplan, F. (2009). What is intrinsic motivation? A typology of computational approaches. *Frontiers in Neurorobotics,* 1, 6.

Oudeyer, P. Y., Kaplan, F., & Hafner, V. V. (2007). Intrinsic motivation systems for autonomous mental development. *IEEE Transactions on Evolutionary Computation,* 11(2), 265–286.

Oudeyer, P. Y., & Smith, L. B. (2016). How evolution may work through curiosity-driven developmental process. *Topics in Cognitive Science,* 8(2), 492–502.

Pan, M., Huang, A., Wang, G., Zhang, T., & Li, X. (2020). Reinforcement learning based curiosity-driven testing of android applications. In *Proceedings of the 29th ACM SIGSOFT International Symposium on Software Testing and Analysis* (pp. 153–164). https://doi.org/10.1145/3395363.3397354.

Pathak, D., Agrawal, P., Efros, A. A., & Darrell, T. (2017). Curiosity-driven exploration by self-supervised prediction. In *International conference on machine learning* (pp. 2778–2787). PMLR. http://proceedings.mlr.press/v70/pathak17a.html.

Poli, F., Serino, G., Mars, R. B., & Hunnius, S. (2020). Infants tailor their attention to maximize learning. *Science Advances,* 6(39), eabb5053.

Pong, V. H., Dalal, M., Lin, S., Nair, A., Bahl, S., & Levine, S. (2020). Skew-fit: State-covering self-supervised reinforcement learning. *arXiv preprint arXiv:1903.03698.*

Potts, R. (2013). Hominin evolution in settings of strong environmental variability. *Quaternary Science Reviews,* 73, 1–13.

Reinke, C., Etcheverry, M., & Oudeyer, P. Y. (2020). Intrinsically motivated discovery of diverse patterns in self-organizing systems. *arXiv preprint arXiv:1908.06663.*

Rolf, M., Steil, J. J., & Gienger, M. (2010). Goal babbling permits direct learning of inverse kinematics. *IEEE Transactions on Autonomous Mental Development,* 2(3), 216–229.

Ryan, R. M., & Deci, E. L. (2000). Self-determination theory and the facilitation of intrinsic motivation, social development, and well-being. *American Psychologist,* 55(1), 68.

Saegusa, R., Metta, G., Sandini, G., & Sakka, S. (2009). Active motor babbling for sensorimotor learning. In *2008 IEEE International Conference on Robotics and Biomimetics* (pp. 794–799). IEEE. https://doi.org/10.1109/ROBIO.2009.4913101.

Santucci, V. G., Baldassarre, G., & Mirolli, M. (2013). Which is the best intrinsic motivation signal for learning multiple skills? *Frontiers in Neurorobotics,* 7, 22.

Schaul, T., Quan, J., Antonoglou, I., & Silver, D. (2016). Prioritized experience replay. *arXiv preprint arXiv:1511.05952.*

Schmidhuber, J. (1991a). A possibility for implementing curiosity and boredom in model-building neural controllers. In *Proc. of the International Conference on Simulation of Adaptive Behavior: From Animals to Animats* (pp. 222–227). https://doi.org/10.7551/mitpress/3115.003.0030.

Schmidhuber, J. (1991b). Curious model-building control systems. In *Proc. International Joint Conference on Neural Networks*, Singapore City, November 18–21, 1991, (pp. 1458–1463). www.scirp.org/(S(lz5mqp453ed%20 snp55rrgjct55))/reference/referencespapers.aspx?referenceid=1385254.

Schueller, W., Loreto, V., & Oudeyer, P. Y. (2018). Complexity reduction in the negotiation of new lexical conventions. *arXiv preprint arXiv:1805.05631*.

Singh, S., Lewis, R. L., Barto, A. G., & Sorg, J. (2010). Intrinsically motivated reinforcement learning: An evolutionary perspective. *IEEE Transactions on Autonomous Mental Development*, 2(2), 70–82.

Stout, A., & Barto, A. G. (2010, August). Competence progress intrinsic motivation. In *2010 IEEE 9th International Conference on Development and Learning* (pp. 257–262). IEEE. http://citeseerx.ist.psu.edu/viewdoc/summary;jsessioni d=837FA22F4803E257348D38A7397B2774?doi=10.1.1.224.71.

Sutton, R. S., & Barto, A. G. (2018). *Reinforcement learning: An introduction*. MIT press.

Takahashi, K., Ogata, T., Nakanishi, J., Cheng, G., & Sugano, S. (2017). Dynamic motion learning for multi-DOF flexible-joint robots using active–passive motor babbling through deep learning. *Advanced Robotics*, 31(18), 1002–1015.

Tang, H., Houthooft, R., Foote, D., Stooke, A., Chen, X., Duan, Y., ... & Abbeel, P. (2017). #Exploration: A study of count-based exploration for deep reinforcement learning. *Advances in Neural Information Processing Systems*. Presented at the 31st Conference on Neural Information Processing Systems (NIPS), 2017. In *31st Conference on Neural Information Processing Systems (NIPS)* (Vol. 30, pp. 1–18).

Ten, A., Kaushik, P., Oudeyer, P. Y., & Gottlieb, J. (2021). Humans monitor learning progress in curiosity-driven exploration. *Nature Communications*, 12(1), 1–10.

Thrun, S. (1995). A lifelong learning perspective for mobile robot control. In *Intelligent robots and systems* (pp. 201–214). *Elsevier Science BV*.

Twomey, K. E., & Westermann, G. (2018). Curiosity-based learning in infants: a neurocomputational approach. *Developmental Science*, 21(4), e12629.

CHAPTER 4

Searching for Information, from Infancy to Adolescence

Costanza De Simone and Azzurra Ruggeri

4.1 Introduction

As adults, we spend a lot of our time seeking and consuming information, reading newspapers and magazines, watching the daily news on TV, browsing the web, scrolling the latest posts on Twitter, and more or less obsessively checking the status updates of our contacts on Facebook or Instagram. Admittedly, this massive, almost compulsive consumption of information is a byproduct of our digital era, characterized by unlimited, overflowing, and often overwhelming availability of ever-accessible, easy-to -ingest information. Yet it is also a reflection – or some might argue, a degeneration – of the intrinsic curiosity and thirst for knowledge that we start displaying in our first months of life, which motivates and drives our learning throughout childhood and beyond. This is evident in the way infants attentively observe and listen to what happens around them, and later in their desire to actively engage with their physical and social environment, tinkering with toys and tools, curiously exploring the space around them, or asking questions. Children's active involvement with the world around them has been considered a crucial component of learning by early developmental psychologists (e.g., Dewey, 1986; Piaget, 1952; Vygotsky, 1987). In particular, Piaget theorized that children's exploration may be triggered and driven by the "discomfort of uncertainty" or by what he refers to as "cognitive disequilibrium" – that is, a mismatch between what is expected and what is observed, which does not fit their existing conceptual structures. This cognitive disequilibrium motivates children to adapt or develop new conceptual structures that better accommodate the new information. Piaget (1952) was probably the first to propose the idea of children as active learners, describing the behavior of his own children as resembling hypothesis testing with self-generated data. Although Piaget and other early constructivists never proposed a full-fledged developmental theory of active learning, as described throughout this chapter, more recent

77

research has not only supported the idea that children are indeed active learners, but has grounded robust evidence that children are efficient and effective information gatherers from a very early age in behavioral, cognitive, and computational work.

In this chapter we review previous developmental literature on active learning, examining the various forms active learning can take across the life span, as well as the novel paradigms and analytical approaches developed to investigate it. In Section 4.2, we review the most recent evidence documenting infants' and toddlers' sensitivity to environmental ambiguity and unexpectedness, triggering increasingly sophisticated forms of information solicitation from others. In Sections 4.3 and 4.4 we draw a developmental trajectory of the effectiveness of children's exploratory and sampling strategies, and of their question asking.

Across sections, we will touch upon three main themes: first, children's *sensitivity* to environmental inputs – that is, their ability to recognize whether a piece of information or observation is novel, and meaningful, and their intrinsic desire to explore it further to make sense of it; second, children's developing *competence* to identify, select, and generate effective active learning strategies from scratch, both on their own and in social contexts; third, children's *adaptiveness* – that is, their ability to tailor their active learning strategies to the specific characteristics of the environment they are presented with. We conclude the chapter by discussing some of the most pressing open questions and promising avenues for future developmental research on active learning and information search.

4.2 Information Search in Infants and Toddlers

Before children develop locomotor and verbal abilities, thereby becoming able to indulge their curiosity through firsthand exploration and question asking, information seeking relies on observations and some rudimentary forms of solicitation of information from their caregivers. Infants' information-seeking strategies are usually investigated by measuring their visual exploration patterns and selective attention, for example, by implementing looking-time paradigms (for critical reviews, see Oakes, 2010, 2017) that observe the direction and duration of participants' eye gaze to infer their degree of interest in stimuli, scenes, or people. A growing body of work has demonstrated that infants tend to look longer at stimuli that are more perceptually salient (e.g., they are more sensitive and pay more attention to changes in color than in speed; Kaldy & Blasser, 2013). In particular, recent work has shown that by 11 months, infants selectively attend to events that violate their expectations and naïve theories across different domains (e.g., emotional, Wu & Gweon, 2019; numerical, McCrinck & Wynn, 2004; social, Henderson & Woodward, 2011; perceptual, Walden et al., 2007). Kidd and colleagues (2012, 2014) demonstrated that this attentional capture can be characterized in terms of information gain, with infants focusing their attention on situations of intermediate visual complexity, thus optimizing their learning by avoiding wasting cognitive resources trying to process overly simple or overly complex events. Along these lines, previous work suggested that at 5 months, infants are already sensitive to the likelihood of a social partner being informative – that is, they look longer at partners who express willingness to convey information, for instance, by making eye contact, calling their name, and using infant-directed speech (e.g., Cooper & Aslin, 1990; Csibra & Gergely, 2009; Kampe et al., 2003; Senju & Csibra, 2008). However, recent evidence suggests that, beyond being selective in deciding what information and information source to attend to (i.e., those most likely to be informative), infants may look at other people to *actively solicit* information, indicating that pretty much the same events and stimuli that trigger infants' perceptual interest may also result in increased references to their social informants (see Dunn & Bremner, 2017). For instance, infants are more likely to direct their gaze to social partners when they encounter novel versus familiar objects (Kutsuki et al., 2007), witness events violating their expectations (e.g., puppets appearing or disappearing from a stage; Dunn & Bremner, 2017; Walden et al., 2007), or are presented with confounded evidence (e.g., they are provided with one label that could refer to any of two novel objects; Hembacher et al., 2017; Vaish et al., 2011). This work offers a brand new perspective on infants' social referencing, which was originally proposed as merely a means for infants to modulate their emotional response to unknown events by seeking reassurance in their caregivers' proximity and reactions to the same event (e.g., Ainsworth, 1992; Dickstein et al., 1984).

Such perspective is further supported by evidence that infants' references to others are *selective*, and emerge only under certain circumstances, such as when they are presented with potentially unknown plants, but not with novel artifacts (Elsner & Wertz, 2019). Infants' selectivity is also evident when they are choosing whom to look at for information. For instance, when confronted with an ambiguous toy, infants prefer to look at unfamiliar individuals who in that specific context are more likely to be knowledgeable (e.g., experimenters in the lab) over caregivers (e.g., Stenberg, 2009). Similarly, when asked to locate which of two novel objects a "pseudoword" refers to, 12-month-olds prefer to look at a knowledgeable informant (one they had previously seen accurately labeling familiar objects) over an ignorant one (Bazhydai et al., 2020).

Around 12 months of age, infants selectively signal their epistemic uncertainty and explicitly solicit information from others through the use of gestures and sounds (i.e., pointing and babbling; see Begus & Southgate, 2018). For instance, 16-month-olds were found to increase their pointing rate in the presence of adults who demonstrated knowledge-ability (Begus & Southgate, 2012). Similarly, 24-month-olds showed increased pointing rates when presented with more cognitively demanding tasks (e.g., when asked to remember which of three identical boxes arranged on a rotating table contained a target object; Delgado et al., 2011), and 20-month-olds were found to use pointing strategically to improve their performance by asking adults for help with the location of a hidden toy (Goupil et al., 2016).

Infants' expectation to receive information from others has also been recently associated with neural correlates of information encoding and reward processing (see Begus & Bonawitz, 2020). By complementing the behavioral evidence mentioned above, these findings suggest that the intrinsic drive to seek information is perceived as a rewarding experience, and as such may lead to superior learning outcomes early on. For example, 30-month-old children showed more robust learning of novel word–object associations in categories they were more interested in, as assessed through their pupillary change (Ackermann et al., 2020). More generally, infants' information-seeking behavior has been found to be predictive of superior learning of objects' labels and functions (pointing; Lucca & Wilbourn, 2019), expressive language development (e.g., babbling; Donnellan et al., 2020) and general vocabulary size (pointing; Goldin-Meadow, 2007).

Overall, the evidence reviewed in this section demonstrates that infants' engagement with their physical and social environment is not merely motivated by a general desire for attention, affiliation, or comfort, but is driven by an urge to resolve the discrepancy between what they know and what they encounter (e.g., Loewenstein, 1994). As a result of this drive, systematic patterns of efficient information seeking start emerging during the first months of life and become increasingly explicit and selective between the first and second year of life, when infants can promptly and effectively signal their uncertainty and elicit information from the most informative sources available.

4.3 Developmental Changes in Exploration and Sampling

Recent research on early exploration provides evidence that children are sensitive, competent, and adaptive explorers from a very young age, and that their explorative actions are meaningfully aimed at testing their naïve theories about the environment. Indeed, even 6-month-olds prefer to explore objects that violate their expectations (Stahl & Feigenson, 2015; for a review, see Stahl & Feigenson, 2019), and their willingness to explore decreases when they are provided with explanations for the surprising events they have witnessed (Perez & Feigenson, 2020).

With increasingly fine-grained motor skills and greater familiarity with the environment around them, preschoolers spontaneously engage in systematic hypothesis-testing behavior, looking for the causes underlying observed violations of their expectations (e.g., pushing a button to see if it is connected to a light that was turning on randomly; Muentener & Schulz, 2014) and exploring confounded or ambiguous evidence (i.e., 4- to 9-year-olds exploring why two identical objects had shadows of different sizes; van Schijndel et al., 2015; see also Cook et al., 2011, L. E. Schulz & Bonawitz, 2007). For example, Bonawitz and colleagues found that 4- to 6-year-olds are more likely to explore an asymmetrically weighted block when the asymmetry violated their prior beliefs, compared to when it was consistent with their beliefs. That is, children who believed that objects balance at their geometrical center (i.e., *center theorists)* explored more when the block was balanced on the object's mass, whereas *mass theorists*, who believed that objects balance at their mass center, explored more when the block was balanced on its geometrical center. Moreover, recent work shows that preschoolers tailor their exploring effort (e.g., time) to the complexity, or "degree of discriminability" between two variables, with 4- and 5-year-olds shaking a box for a longer time when tasked to guess whether it contained 8 or 9 marbles, compared to conditions in which the discrimination was easier (e.g., 2 vs. 9; Siegel et al., 2021).

This meaningful exploratory behavior, clearly guided by hypothesis testing, has often been associated with learning, and thus with a general drive to reduce current uncertainty while increasing accuracy to predict future events (for reviews, see Gottlieb et al., 2013; Kidd & Hayden, 2015). Indeed, studies using the "blicket detector" paradigm (Gopnik & Sobel, 2000) – a machine that lights up and plays music when only some objects (blickets) are placed on it – have shown that an increase in preschoolers' successful active exploration supports causal learning (e.g., McCormack et al., 2015), counterfactual reasoning (Nyhout & Ganea,

2019), better, evidence-based verbal arguments to disconfirm false claims (Köksal-Tuncer & Sodian, 2018), and higher-order generalizations of the causal rules learned (Sim & Xu, 2017).

Recent work also showed that preschoolers adapt their exploratory strategies to the characteristics of the task presented to them, demonstrating the *ecological learning* competence previously attributed only to older children and adults. For example, Ruggeri and colleagues (2019) asked 3- to 5-year-olds to choose which of two exploratory actions (open vs. shake) to perform to find an egg shaker hidden in one of four small boxes, contained in two larger boxes. Prior to this game, children learned that the egg was either equally likely to be found in any of the four small boxes (uniform condition) or most likely to be found in one particular small box (skewed condition). The authors found that children successfully tailored their exploratory actions to the different likelihood distributions: They were more likely to shake first in the uniform compared to the skewed condition. These results are in line with those from Domberg et al. (2020) showing that children as young as 4 years can already successfully adapt their predecisional information search to given goals, for instance, deciding to observe the arms of a monster to predict its throwing ability, but to observe their legs when they have to predict the monster's jumping success.

As shown in these studies above, from a developmental perspective, early childhood has been traditionally described as a spike for exploration's breadth and frequency. For instance, a key finding in the psychological literature is that before focusing on smaller subsets of possibilities, children tend to try out far more options than adults, and this has been interpreted as evidence for higher levels of random exploration. This high *temperature* parameter supposedly "cools off" with age, leading to lower levels of random exploration in late childhood and adulthood. However, more contemporary accounts suggest that exploration rather changes in qualitative, complex ways, which could be understood in terms of the resolution of the explore–exploit dilemmas (Gopnik, Frankenhuis and Tomasello, 2020). In particular, changes in exploration may also be associated to *uncertainty-driven sampling* and/or with a more fine-grained ability to *generalize* what is learned beyond observed outcomes. E. Schulz, Wu, and colleagues (2019) demonstrated the individual contribution of these three nonmutually exclusive mechanisms through a spatial search task, wherein 7- to 11-year-olds and adult participants were given a limited number of clicks to explore a grid and acquire as many points as possible. Rewards were spatially correlated across the grid, such that nearby tiles had similar reward values, providing traction for generalization, which could be used to guide search. To maximize rewards, participants had to decide whether to explore (i.e., clicking a new tile) or exploit (i.e., reclick an open tile) a limited number of tiles on a grid. Using a computational model with parameters directly corresponding to the three hypothesized mechanisms of developmental change, the authors found that, compared to adults, children generalized less from observed to unobserved tiles, rarely exploiting and more often showing uncertainty-directed exploration. They did not, however, find differences in random sampling. Using the same paradigm, they also found that although younger children tended to be more random in their search compared to older children and adults, even 4-year-olds showed uncertainty-directed exploratory patterns (Meder et al., 2021). Adding to these findings, Pelz and Kidd (2020) suggest that developmental changes in exploratory behavior may also be explained in terms of response inhibition. In particular, by analyzing 2- to 12-year-old children's free play during an interactive touch-screen game, they found that their exploratory patterns became increasingly efficient and sophisticated with age, as repetitive sampling decreased.

Competence in exploration strategies is reached much later in development if we consider more real-word-like complex scenarios, wherein to make a decision we often have to explore many options, and evaluate multiple, complex causal relations. For example, studies implementing information board paradigms, where participants have to look up information about different available cues for a set of options (e.g., for a set of bikes: the price, number of gears, and color) to make a decision (e.g., which bike to buy), show consistent developmental improvements in search efficiency. On the one hand, younger children tend to search more exhaustively and in a less systematic manner than older children (Betsch et al., 2014, 2016; Gregan-Paxton & John, 1995; Howse et al., 2003). On the other hand, when compared to adults, adolescents' sampling has been found to be characterized by shorter and more superficial predecisional search (see van den Bos & Hertwig, 2017). Similar patterns also emerge from work focusing on teenagers' *information literacy* – that is, their ability to search, navigate, discriminate, and acquire information on the web. Generally, this work converges to suggest that adolescents often do not implement optimal search strategies when navigating the web to make decisions, and this ineffectiveness may be linked to inaccurate judgments (e.g., about health-related risks; see Freeman et al., 2018, for a comprehensive review). For instance, they struggle to formulate efficient and correct queries, (e.g., Gossen et al., 2011), and have trouble filtering the search engines' results page – being, for instance, more likely than adults to click on higher-ranked results, and spend less time on each web address (i.e., URL; Duarte & Weber, 2011). Moreover, they often fail to evaluate the reliability of the sources they are presented with, as well as the accuracy of their content (e.g., Macedo-Rouet and colleagues, 2019), obtaining quite poor learning outcomes (see De Simone et al., 2021).

4.4   Children's Developing Ability to Ask Informative Questions

As soon as they start talking, children ask an impressive number of questions when engaged in conversations with adults – about eighty per hour, according to the verbal transcripts analyzed by Chouinard and colleagues (2007). Asking questions is one of the most powerful learning tools children possess, as it allows young learners to be more precise about the information they want from social partners, select which informants to query, inquire about absent objects or events, address abstract concepts or emotions, target specific attributes of the same object, and, importantly, make queries at different levels of abstraction (e.g., "Do you like apples?" vs. "Do you like fruit?").

Research with 2- to 5-year-olds indicates that children's question asking becomes increasingly more sophisticated throughout the childhood years (see Jones, Swaboda, & Ruggeri, 2020; Ronfard et al., 2018, for reviews). Around age 2, children begin inquiring about causal explanations, besides being just interested in asking about facts or labels, as they do during the first year of life (Callanan & Oakes, 1992; Chouinard et al., 2007; Hickling & Wellman, 2001). By age 3, children have reasonable expectations about what responses count as satisfying answers to their questions: They tend to agree and ask follow-up questions when adults provide explanatory answers, but re-ask their original question or provide their own explanations otherwise (Frazier et al., 2009; Kurkul & Corriveau, 2018).

Preschool-aged children ask domain-appropriate questions; for example, they are more likely to ask about the functions of artifacts but about category membership, food choices, and typical locations of animals (Greif et al., 2006). Previous work has also demonstrated that preschoolers as young as 4 years are competent at generating questions that are mostly informative, as opposed to redundant, uninformative, or irrelevant, and that by age 5 they reliably use the information they receive to solve problems (see Legare et al., 2013).

However, preschoolers still struggle to formulate *the most informative* questions. Analyses of naturalistic and semistructured adult–child conversations have shown that children's questions are usually constrained by their knowledge domains and intuitions (e.g., social and biological phenomena vs. artifacts; Kelemen et al., 2005) and are often unclear with respect to the specific information they would like to acquire. For instance, when presented with novel artifacts, 3- to 5-year-olds often ask ambiguous questions (e.g., "what is it?"), rather than expressing their specific interest in the object's function (and not in the object's name; Kemler Nelson, Egan & Holt, 2004). Yet, preschoolers' difficulty has been also documented in experimental settings, mostly using variations of the twenty-questions game, in which participants have to identify a target object within a given set by asking as few yes–no questions as possible. This work has found that children do not start to implement effective question-asking strategies consistently until age 10 years (Herwig, 1982; Mosher et al., 1966; Ruggeri & Feufel, 2015; Ruggeri & Lombrozo, 2015; Ruggeri et al., 2016).

In particular, this work shows that younger children predominantly, if not exclusively, ask "hypothesis-scanning" questions, which offer tentative solutions by targeting individual hypotheses or objects (e.g., "Is it the dog?"; see Figure 4.1) and typically support a less efficient path to the correct solution. For example, in a traditional version of the game, Herwig (1982) found that about 95 percent of the questions asked by preschoolers, 90 percent of those asked by first graders, and 83 percent of those asked by second graders were hypothesis scanning (see also Ruggeri et al., 2021). In contrast, older children and adults more readily ask "constraint-seeking" questions (see Figure 4.1), which can more efficiently partition the hypothesis space by targeting superordinate categories or features that are shared by multiple hypotheses (e.g., "Is it an animal?" or "Does it have a tail?"; see Herwig, 1982; Mosher et al., 1966; Ruggeri et al., 2016). Moreover, previous research has shown that although even 4- and 5-year-olds are able to spontaneously generate constraint-seeking questions to some extent, these questions are often not the most efficient available (see Legare et al., 2013; Ruggeri et al., 2021).

Why is this the case? To ask constraint-seeking questions from scratch, one needs to identify features that can be used to group hypotheses into different categories, categorize objects correctly according to those features, label those categories, and, finally, formulate the question. That is, generating constraint-seeking questions taps into children's developing vocabulary, categorization skills, and previous experience. Indeed, the developmental change and individual variability in the effectiveness of children's questions has often been explained by an increasing ability to generate object-general features that can be used to cluster similar objects

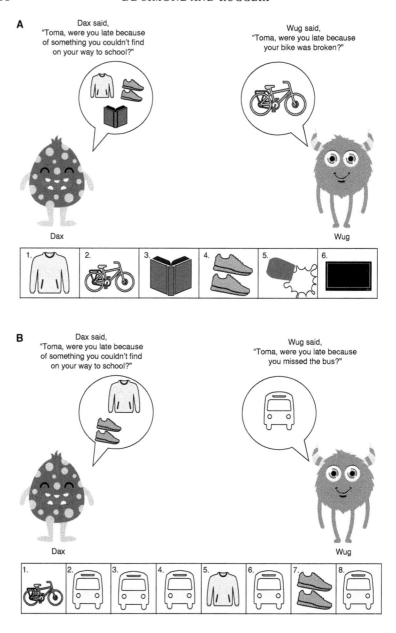

Figure 4.1 Adaptation of the scenarios presented in Ruggeri et al. (2016). Children were asked to select which monster would find out first why *Toma* was late for school. *Dax* asked a *constraint-seeking* question targeting multiple hypothesis, whereas *Wug* asked a *hypothesis-scanning* question targeting a single hypothesis. The icons at the bottom of the page illustrated the reasons why Toma had been late over the previous days (i.e., the hypotheses space). Crucially, in the *Uniform* condition, when the reasons were all equally likely (A), the constraint-seeking question was the most informative. However, in the *Skewed* condition, when one reason was more likely than the others (B), the hypothesis-scanning question was more informative.

into categories (e.g., quadrupeds vs. nonquadrupeds; see Ruggeri & Feufel, 2015), and to identify and flexibly categorize objects on the basis of alternative features (e.g., color and pattern; Legare et al., 2013). Similarly, recent work has found that supporting children's categorization performance, for example, by providing the object-related features needed to ask constraint-seeking questions, helped 4- to 6-year-olds ask more effective questions, target higher category levels, and reach the solution with fewer questions (Ruggeri et al., 2021). Moreover, Swaboda and colleagues (2020) found that 4- to 6-year-olds made more informative queries in a spatial search task, in which they had to find a target monster by tracing a path through a maze, compared to a computationally and structurally analogous twenty-questions game, where they had to identify the monster from a set of eight by asking yes–no questions.

Supporting this further, Ruggeri and colleagues found that even 3-year-olds, when they were not required to verbally *generate* questions from scratch, could reliably identify the most informative between two given questions (Ruggeri et al., 2017), adapting their reliance on the likelihood distribution of the presented hypotheses (see Figure 4.1), showing a capacity for *ecological learning*. Only later, by age 7, were children increasingly able to *generate* different types of queries depending on the likelihood distribution of the hypotheses under consideration, in order to maximize the questions' informativeness (Ruggeri & Lombrozo, 2015). Children's ability to tailor their search to the characteristics of the environment they are presented with is further illustrated by the work of Nelson et al., (2014), showing that, in a variant of the twenty-questions game, children selected more informative queries when the task environment was *representative* of the real-world likelihood distribution (i.e., when gender was uniformly distributed), compared to when the likelihood distribution of the presented features was artificial.

While it is important to know *what* to ask and *how*, and what to expect as an answer, it is also crucial, especially from a developmental perspective, to be able to determine *whom* to ask. A significant body of literature has examined preschoolers' selective trust when discriminating between different sources of information (see Harris et al., 2018; Mills, 2013, for reviews). Results from these studies suggest that children's ability to distinguish reliable from unreliable sources improves over the preschool years for two main reasons. First, there is increasing sophistication in how children interpret the necessary characteristics of a reliable informant. As an example, children younger than 4 years discount claims made by informants who lack relevant episodic knowledge (e.g., Palmquist & Jaswal, 2015), express absolute uncertainty (e.g., Sabbagh & Baldwin, 2001), or show a stable history of inaccuracy (Koenig & Harris, 2005). Yet, only at around age 6 do they take into account the *degree* of inaccuracy, the number of past errors, or even the deceptive intentions that an informant might demonstrate (e.g., Einav & Robinson, 2010). Second, there are developmental improvements in preschoolers' understanding that different individuals may possess different kinds of knowledge. For instance, 3- to 5-year-olds ask their peers when they want to know how to play with a novel toy but refer to adults for information about the nutritional value of foods (VanderBorght & Jaswal, 2009). Three- to 5-year-olds think that doctors know more than car mechanics about how to fix a broken arm, whereas mechanics know more than doctors about how to fix a flat tire. Yet in the same study, 3-year-olds did not make the same judgment about topics that would lie within broader areas of expertise (e.g., who would know more about why plants need sunlight to grow or how to build a treehouse), and without familiar experts as a base for attribution, 4- and 5-year-olds also failed to do so (Lutz & Keil, 2002). Crucially, although by age 5 children focus on the relevant clues when deciding whom to trust, at age 6 they still struggle to use this information to direct their questions or ask the proper experts for help (e.g., De Simone & Ruggeri, 2021; Fitneva et al., 2013).

4.5   Concluding Remarks, Open Questions, and Promising Avenues for Future Research

In this chapter we have reviewed the most recent work to shed light on the developmental trajectory of active learning from infancy to adolescence. In contrast to what Piaget assumed, we now know that infants do not act exclusively on reflexes. Not at all! They intentionally indulge their curiosity about novel and surprising events by actively soliciting information from others through looks, sounds, and gestures. Early information seeking is often driven by perceptually ambiguous or surprising cues and – as a consequence – the ensuing exploratory actions often serve to test and find out about the causes underlying this evidence. Preschoolers can already ask questions and demand explanations in an effective, adaptive fashion, although this ability continues to improve across childhood and until adulthood, in tandem with their increasingly sophisticated verbal and cognitive skills.

Despite its deep roots tracing back to the pioneering work of Piaget and Vygotsky, this field is still fairly young and uncharted, and therefore fertile and wide open to new perspectives and methods. We conclude this chapter by briefly discussing what we deem the most pressing questions and promising directions for future developmental research on active learning.

First, to develop a more fine-grained developmental trajectory of active learning and information search strategies over the life span, it is important to include those age groups that have been generally underrepresented in research on active learning (e.g., adolescent and elderly populations). This broader developmental focus could contribute to the development of more precise computational models and theories, which would shed further light on the *mechanisms* underlying the observed developmental changes at a deeper, process level.

Second, and connected to the previous point, the existing research on active learning reviewed above has mostly focused on identifying key developmental differences in the efficiency and adaptiveness of children's search. However, we do not yet understand why these changes occur or what factors underlie the observed developmental trajectories. More specifically, we do not know what task-related, cultural, environmental, or individual factors (e.g., differences in cognitive abilities, vocabulary, motivation, personality, education, parenting style) drive developmental changes in active learning, how they interact with each other, or how their relative importance changes with age. As a first step in this direction, we developed an exploratory analysis aiming to identify the factors contributing to active learning performance, beyond the broad developmental differences captured in previous research. On the one hand, the project aims to measure different aspects of active learning (e.g., effectiveness, adaptiveness, speed, accuracy) on a wide range of tasks (e.g., question asking, question evaluation, spatial search) to comprehensively assess 6- to 11-year-old children's active learning performance. On the other hand, we will systematically examine the cognitive, social, motivational, cultural, and socioeconomic factors impacting and contributing to active learning performance, to identify the sources of the developmental differences and interpret the individual differences observed.

Third, it is crucial to trace the relative importance of these contributing factors *longitudinally*, in addition to cross-sectionally. This perspective is even more important when considering that it is still unclear, on the one hand, if active learning efficiency or propensity has an impact on later outcomes, such as school achievement, and, on the other, if factors such as parenting and schooling styles impact children's active learning ability or propensity.

Finally, even if the work reviewed in this chapter makes it crystal clear that young children are indeed curious and that this contributes to their impressive learning abilities (see Alvarez & Booth, 2014), it is still unclear what exactly motivates children to explore and learn, and how this can be mathematically modeled. In a recent paper, E. Schulz, Pelz, Gopnik & Ruggeri (2019) showed that the mere opportunity to gain information can serve as an intrinsic reward and suffices to motivate 2- to 4-year-olds to persist in their exploration. This work further highlights the importance of understanding why children explore and what drives their curiosity in the absence of external rewards – a question we believe will keep psychologists, educators, computer scientists, and roboticists busy for a while longer.

References

Ackermann, L., Hepach, R., & Mani, N. (2020). Children learn words easier when they are interested in the category to which the word belongs. *Developmental Science*, 23(3), Article e12915. https://doi.org/10.1111/desc.12915.

Ainsworth, M. D. S. (1992). A consideration of social referencing in the context of attachment theory and research. In S. Feinman (Ed.), *Social referencing and the social construction of reality in infancy* (pp. 349–367). Plenum.

Alvarez, A. L., & Booth, A. E. (2014). Motivated by meaning: Testing the effect of knowledge-infused rewards on preschoolers' persistence. *Child Development*, 85, 783–791. https://doi.org/10.1111/cdev.12151.

Bazhydai, M., Westermann, G., & Parise, E. (2020). "I don't know but I know who to ask": 12-month-olds actively seek information from knowledgeable adults. *Developmental Science*, 23(5), Article e12938. https://doi.org/10.1111/desc.12938.

Begus, K., & Bonawitz, E. (2020). The rhythm of learning: Theta oscillations as an index of active learning in infancy. *Developmental Cognitive Neuroscience*, 45, Article 100810. https://doi.org/10.1016/j.dcn.2020.100810.

Begus, K., & Southgate, V. (2012). Infant pointing serves an interrogative function. *Developmental Science*, 15, 611–617. https://doi.org/10.1111/j.1467-7687.2012.01160.x.

Begus, K., & Southgate, V. (2018). Curious learners: How infants' motivation to learn shapes and is shaped by infants' interactions with the social world. In M. Saylor & P. Ganea (Eds.), *Active learning from infancy to childhood* (pp. 13–37). Springer. https://doi.org/10.1007/978-3-319-77182-3_2.

Betsch, T., Lang, A., Lehmann, A., & Axmann, J. M. (2014). Utilizing probabilities as decision weights in closed and open information boards: A comparison of children and adults. *Acta Psychologica*, 153, 74–86. https://doi.org/10.1016/j.actpsy.2014.09.008.

Betsch, T., Lehmann, A., Lindow, S., Lang, A., & Schoemann, M. (2016). Lost in search: (Mal-)adaptation to probabilistic decision environments in children and adults. *Developmental Psychology*, 52(2), 311–325. https://doi.org/10.1037/dev0000077.

Callanan, M. A., & Oakes, L. M. (1992). Preschoolers' questions and parents' explanations: Causal thinking in everyday activity. *Cognitive Development*, 7(2), 213–233. https://doi.org/10.1016/0885-2014(92)90012-G.

Chouinard, M. M., Harris, P. L., & Maratsos, M. P. (2007). Children's questions: A mechanism for cognitive development. *Monographs of the Society for Research in Child Development*, 72(1), i–179. https://doi.org/10.1111/j.1540-5834 .2007.00412.x.

Cook, C., Goodman, N. D., & Schulz, L. E. (2011). Where science starts: Spontaneous experiments in preschoolers' exploratory play. *Cognition*, 120(3), 341–349. https://doi.org/10.1016/j.cognition.2011.03.003.

Cooper, R. P., & Aslin, R. N. (1990). Preferences for infant-directed speech in the first month after birth. *Child Development*, 61(5), 1584–1595. https://doi.org /10.2307/1130766.

Csibra, G., & Gergely, G. (2009). Natural pedagogy. *Trends in Cognitive Sciences*, 13(4), 148–153. https://doi.org/10.1016/j.tics.2009.01.005.

Delgado, B., Gómez, J. C., & Sarriá, E. (2011). Pointing gestures as a cognitive tool in young children: Experimental evidence. *Journal of Experimental Child Psychology*, 110(3), 299–312. https://doi.org/10.1016/j.jecp.2011.04.010.

De Simone, C., Battisti, A., & Ruggeri, A. (2021). Differential impact of web habits and active navigation on adolescents' online learning. *PsyArXiv*. https:// doi.org/10.31234/osf.io/hsvc4.

De Simone, C., & Ruggeri, A. (2021). What is a good question asker better at? From unsystematic generalization to adult-like selectivity across childhood. *Cognitive Development*, 59, 101082. https://doi.org/10.1016/j.cogdev.2021.101082.

Dewey, J. (1986). Experience and education. *The Educational Forum*, 50(3), 241–252. https://doi.org/10.1080/00131728609335764.

Dickstein, S., Thompson, R. A., Estes, D., Malkin, C., & Lamb, M. E. (1984). Social referencing and the security of attachment. *Infant Behavior and Development*, 7(4), 507–516. https://doi.org/10.1016/S0163-6383(84) 80009-0.

Domberg, A., Koskuba, K., Rothe, A., & Ruggeri, A. (2020). Goal-adaptiveness in children's cue-based information search. In S. Denison., M. Mack, Y. Xu, & B.C. Armstrong (Eds.), *Proceedings of the 42nd Annual Conference of the Cognitive Science Society* (pp. 1437–1443). Cognitive Science Society. https:// cogsci.mindmodeling.org/2020/papers/0298/0298.pdf.

Donnellan, E., Bannard, C., McGillion, M. L., Slocombe, K. E., & Matthews, D. (2020). Infants' intentionally communicative vocalizations elicit responses from caregivers and are the best predictors of the transition to language: A longitudinal investigation of infants' vocalizations, gestures and word produc-tion. *Developmental Science*, 23, Article e12843. https://doi.org/10.1111/desc .12843.

Duarte Torres, S., & Weber, I. (2011). What and how children search on the web. In *Proceedings of the 20th ACM International Conference on Information and Knowledge Management* (pp. 393–402). Association for Computing Machinery. https://doi.org/10.1145/2063576.2063638.

Dunn, K., & Bremner, J. G. (2017). Investigating looking and social looking measures as an index of infant violation of expectation. *Developmental Science*, 20, Article e12452. https://doi.org/10.1111/desc.12452.

Einav, S., & Robinson, E. J. (2010). Children's sensitivity to error magnitude when evaluating informants. *Cognitive Development*, 25(3), 218–232. https://doi.org/10.1016/j.cogdev.2010.04.002.

Elsner, C., & Wertz, A. E. (2019). The seeds of social learning: Infants exhibit more social looking for plants than other object types. *Cognition*, 183, 244–255. https://doi.org/10.1016/j.cognition.2018.09.016.

Fitneva, S. A., Lam, N. H. L., & Dunfield, K. A. (2013). The development of children's information gathering: To look or to ask? *Developmental Psychology*, 49(3), 533–542. https://doi.org/10.1037/a0031326.

Frazier, B. N., Gelman, S. A., & Wellman, H. M. (2009). Preschoolers' search for explanatory information within adult–child conversation. *Child Development*, 80(6), 1592–1611. https://doi.org/10.1111/j.1467-8624.2009.01356.x.

Freeman, J. L., Caldwell, P. H., Bennett, P. A., & Scott, K. M. (2018). How adolescents search for and appraise online health information: A systematic review. *The Journal of Pediatrics*, 195, 244–255. https://doi.org/10.1016/j.jpeds.2017.11.031.

Goldin-Meadow, S. (2007). Pointing sets the stage for learning language – and creating language. *Child Development*, 78, 741–745. https://doi.org/10.1111/j.1467-8624.2007.01029.x.

Gopnik, A., & Sobel, D. M. (2000). Detecting blickets: How young children use information about novel causal powers in categorization and induction. *Child Development*, 71(5), 1205–1222. https://doi.org/10.1111/1467-8624.00224.

Gopnik, A., Frankenhuis, W. E., & Tomasello, M. (2020). Introduction to special issue: "Life history and learning: how childhood, caregiving and old age shape cognition and culture in humans and other animals." *Philosophical Transactions of the Royal Society B*. https://doi.org/10.1098/rstb.2019.0489.

Gossen, T., Low, T., & Nürnberger, A. (2011). What are the real differences of children's and adults' web search. In *Proceedings of the 34th International ACM SIGIR Conference on Research and Development in Information Retrieval* (pp. 1115–1116). Association for Computing Machinery. https://doi.org/10.1145/2009916.2010076.

Gottlieb, J., Oudeyer, P.-Y., Lopes, M., & Baranes, A. (2013). Information-seeking, curiosity, and attention: Computational and neural mechanisms. *Trends in Cognitive Sciences*, 17(11), 585–593. https://doi.org/10.1016/j.tics.2013.09.001.

Goupil, L., Romand-Monnier, M., & Kouider, S. (2016). Infants ask for help when they know they don't know. *Proceedings of the National Academy of Sciences of the United States of America*, 113(13), 3492–3496. https://doi.org/10.1073/pnas.1515129113.

Gregan-Paxton, J., & John, D. R. (1995). Are young children adaptive decision makers? A study of age differences in information search behavior. *Journal of Consumer Research*, 21(4), 567–580. https://doi.org/10.1086/209419.

Greif, M. L., Kemler Nelson, D. G., Keil, F. C., & Gutierrez, F. (2006). What do children want to know about animals and artifacts? Domain-specific requests for information. *Psychological Science*, 17(6), 455–459. https://doi.org/10.1111/j .1467-9280.2006.01727.x.

Harris, P. L., Koenig, M. A., Corriveau, K. H., & Jaswal, V. K. (2018). Cognitive foundations of learning from testimony. *Annual Review of Psychology*, 69, 251–273. https://doi.org/10.1146/annurev-psych-122216-011710.

Hembacher, E., deMayo, B. & Frank, M. C. (2017). Children's social referencing reflects sensitivity to graded uncertainty. In G. Gunzelmann, A. Howes, T. Tenbrink, & E. Davelaar (Eds.), *CogSci 2017: Proceedings of the 39th Annual Meeting of the Cognitive Science Society* (pp. 496–500). Cognitive Science Society. https://cogsci.mindmodeling.org/2017/papers/0101/paper0101 .pdf.

Henderson, A. M., & Woodward, A. L. (2011). "Let's work together": What do infants understand about collaborative goals? *Cognition*, 121(1), 12–21. https:// doi.org/10.1016/j.cognition.2011.05.008.

Herwig, J. E. (1982). Effects of age, stimuli, and category recognition factors in children's inquiry behavior. *Journal of Experimental Child Psychology*, 33(2), 196–206. https://doi.org/10.1016/0022-0965(82)90015-7.

Hickling, A. K., & Wellman, H. M. (2001). The emergence of children's causal explanations and theories: Evidence from everyday conversation. *Developmental Psychology*, 37(5), 668–683. https://doi.org/10.1037/0012-1649.37.5.668.

Howse, R. B., Best, D. L., & Stone, E. R. (2003). Children's decision making: The effects of training, reinforcement, and memory aids. *Cognitive Development*, 18(2), 247–268. https://doi.org/10.1016/S0885-2014(03)00023-6.

Jones, A., Swaboda, N., & Ruggeri, A. (2020). Developmental changes in ques- tion-asking. In L. Butler, S. Ronfard, & K. Corriveau (Eds.), *The questioning child: Insights from psychology and education* (pp. 118–143). Cambridge University Press. https://doi.org/10.1017/9781108553803.007.

Kaldy, Z., & Blaser, E. (2013). Red to green or fast to slow? Infants' visual working memory for "just salient differences." *Child Development*, 84, 1855–1862. https://doi.org/10.1111/cdev.12086.

Kampe, K. K., Frith, C. D., & Frith, U. (2003). "Hey John": Signals conveying communicative intention toward the self activate brain regions associated with "mentalizing," regardless of modality. *Journal of Neuroscience*, 23(12), 5258–5263. https://doi.org/10.1523/JNEUROSCI.23-12-05258.2003.

Kelemen, D., Callanan, M. A., Casler, K., & Pérez-Granados, D. R. (2005). Why things happen: Teleological explanation in parent-child conversations. *Developmental Psychology*, 41(1), 251–264. https://doi.org/10.1037/0012-1649 .41.1.251.

Kemler Nelson, D. G., Egan, L. C., & Holt, M. B. (2004). When children ask, "What is it?" what do they want to know about artifacts? *Psychological Science*, 15(6), 384–389. https://doi.org/10.1111/j.0956-7976.2004.00689.x.

Kidd, C., & Hayden, B. Y. (2015). The psychology and neuroscience of curiosity. *Neuron*, 88(3), 449–460. https://doi.org/10.1016/j.neuron.2015.09.010.

Kidd, C., Piantadosi, S. T., & Aslin, R. N. (2012) The Goldilocks effect: Human infants allocate attention to visual sequences that are neither too simple nor too complex. *PLoS One*, 7(5), Article e36399. https://doi.org/10.1371/journal.pone.0036399.

Kidd, C., Piantadosi, S. T., & Aslin, R. N. (2014). The Goldilocks effect in infant auditory attention. *Child Development*, 85, 1795–1804. https://doi.org/10.1111/cdev.12263.

Koenig, M. A., & Harris, P. L. (2005). Preschoolers mistrust ignorant and inaccurate speakers. *Child Development*, 76(6), 1261–1277. https://doi.org/10.1111/j.1467-8624.2005.00849.x.

Köksal-Tuncer, Ö., & Sodian, B. (2018). The development of scientific reasoning: Hypothesis testing and argumentation from evidence in young children. *Cognitive Development*, 48, 135–145. https://doi.org/10.1016/j.cogdev.2018.06.011.

Kurkul, K. E., & Corriveau, K. H. (2018). Question, explanation, follow-up: A mechanism for learning from others? *Child Development*, 89(1), 280–294. https://doi.org/10.1111/cdev.12726.

Kutsuki, A., Egami, S., Ogura, T., Nakagawa, K., Kuroki, M., & Itakura, S. (2007). Developmental changes of referential looks in 7- and 9-month-olds: A transition from dyadic to proto-referential looks. *Psychologia*, 50(4), 319–329. https://doi.org/10.2117/psysoc.2007.319.

Legare, C. H., Mills, C. M., Souza, A. L., Plummer, L. E., & Yasskin, R. (2013). The use of questions as problem-solving strategies during early childhood. *Journal of Experimental Child Psychology*, 114(1), 63–76. https://doi.org/10.1016/j.jecp.2012.07.002.

Loewenstein, G. (1994). The psychology of curiosity: A review and reinterpretation. *Psychological Bulletin*, 116(1), 75–98. https://doi.org/10.1037/0033-2909.116.1.75.

Lucca, K., & Wilbourn, M. P. (2019). The what and the how: Information-seeking pointing gestures facilitate learning labels and functions. *Journal of Experimental Child Psychology*, 178, 417–436. https://doi.org/10.1016/j.jecp.2018.08.003.

Lutz, D. J., & Keil, F. C. (2002). Early understanding of the division of cognitive labor. *Child Development*, 73(4), 1073–1084. https://doi.org/10.1111/1467-8624.00458.

Macedo-Rouet, M., Potocki, A., Scharrer, L., Ros, C., Stadtler, M., Salmerón, L., & Rouet, J.-F. (2019). How good is this page? Benefits and limits of prompting on adolescents' evaluation of web information quality. *Reading Research Quarterly*, 54(3), 299–321. https://doi.org/10.1002/rrq.241.

McCormack, T., Frosch, C., Patrick, F., & Lagnado, D. (2015). Temporal and statistical information in causal structure learning. *Journal of Experimental Psychology: Learning, Memory, and Cognition*, 41(2), 395–416. https://doi.org/10.1037/a0038385.

Meder, B., Wu, C. M., Schulz, E., & Ruggeri, A. (2021). Development of directed and random exploration in children. *Developmental Science*. Advance online publication. https://doi.org/10.1111/desc.13095.

Mills, C. M. (2013). Knowing when to doubt: Developing a critical stance when learning from others. *Developmental Psychology*, 49(3), 404–418. https://doi .org/10.1037/a0029500.

Mosher, F. A., Hornsby, J. R., Bruner, J., & Oliver, R. (1966). On asking questions. In J. Bruner (Ed.), *Studies in cognitive growth* (pp. 86–102). Wiley.

Muentener, P., & Schulz, L. (2014). Toddlers infer unobserved causes for spontaneous events. *Frontiers in Psychology*, 5, Article 1496. https://doi.org/10.3389 /fpsyg.2014.01496.

Nelson, J. D., Divjak, B., Gudmundsdottir, G., Martignon, L. F., & Meder, B. (2014). Children's sequential information search is sensitive to environmental probabilities. *Cognition*, 130(1), 74–80. https://doi.org/10.1016/j.cognition.2013.09.007.

Nyhout, A., & Ganea, P. A. (2019). Mature counterfactual reasoning in 4- and 5-year-olds. *Cognition*, 183, 57–66. https://doi.org/10.1016/j.cognition.2018 .10.027.

Oakes, L. M. (2010). Using habituation of looking time to assess mental processes in infancy. *Journal of Cognition and Development*, 11(3), 255–268. https://doi .org/10.1080/15248371003699977.

Oakes, L. M. (2017). Sample size, statistical power, and false conclusions in infant looking-time research. *Infancy*, 22, 436–469. https://doi.org/10.1111/infa .12186.

Palmquist, C. M., & Jaswal, V. K. (2015). Preschoolers' inferences about pointers and labelers: The modality matters. *Cognitive Development*, 35, 178–185. https://doi.org/10.1016/j.cogdev.2015.06.003.

Pelz, M., & Kidd, C. (2020). The elaboration of exploratory play. *Philosophical Transactions of the Royal Society B*, 375(1803), 20190503. https://doi.org/10 .1098/rstb.2019.0503.

Perez, J., & Feigenson, L. (2020). Violations of expectation trigger infants to search for explanations. *PsyArXiv*. https://doi.org/10.31234/osf.io/eahjd.

Piaget, J. (1952). *The origins of intelligence in children*. International University Press.

Ronfard, S., Zambrana, I. M., Hermansen, T. K., & Kelemen, D. (2018). Question-asking in childhood: A review of the literature and a framework for understanding its development. *Developmental Review*, 49, 101–120. https:// doi.org/10.1016/j.dr.2018.05.002.

Ruggeri, A., & Feufel, M. (2015). How basic-level objects facilitate question-asking in a categorization task. *Frontiers in Psychology*, 6, Article 918. https://doi.org/10.3389/fpsyg.2015.00918.

Ruggeri, A., & Lombrozo, T. (2015). Children adapt their questions to achieve efficient search. *Cognition*, 143, 203–216. https://doi.org/10.1016/j .cognition.2015.07.004.

Ruggeri, A., Lombrozo, T., Griffiths, T. L., & Xu, F. (2016). Sources of developmental change in the efficiency of information search. *Developmental Psychology*, 52(12), 2159–2173. https://doi.org/10.1037/dev0000240.

Ruggeri, A., Sim, Z. L., & Xu, F. (2017). "Why is Toma late to school again?" Preschoolers identify the most informative questions. *Developmental Psychology*, 53(9), 1620–1632. https://doi.org/10.1037/dev0000340.

Ruggeri, A., Swaboda, N., Sim, Z. L., & Gopnik, A. (2019). Shake it baby, but only when needed: Preschoolers adapt their exploratory strategies to the information structure of the task. *Cognition*, 193, Article 104013. https://doi.org/10.1016/j.cognition.2019.104013.

Ruggeri, A., Walker, C. M., Lombrozo, T., & Gopnik, A. (2021). How to help young children ask better questions? *Frontiers in Psychology*, 11, Article 2908. https://doi.org/10.3389/fpsyg.2020.586819.

Sabbagh, M. A., & Baldwin, D. A. (2001). Learning words from knowledgeable versus ignorant speakers: Links between preschoolers' theory of mind and semantic development. *Child Development*, 72(4), 1054–1070. https://doi.org/10.1111/1467-8624.00334.

Schulz, E., Pelz, M., Gopnik, A., & Ruggeri, A. (2019). Preschoolers search longer when there is more information to be gained. *PsyArXiv*. https://doi.org/10.31234/osf.io/5wegk.

Schulz, E., Wu, C. M., Ruggeri, A., & Meder, B. (2019). Searching for rewards like a child means less generalization and more directed exploration. *Psychological Science*, 30(11), 1561–1572. https://doi.org/10.1177/0956797619863663.

Schulz, L. E., & Bonawitz, E. B. (2007). Serious fun: Preschoolers engage in more exploratory play when evidence is confounded. *Developmental Psychology*, 43(4), 1045–1050. https://doi.org/10.1037/0012-1649.43.4.1045.

Senju, A., & Csibra, G. (2008). Gaze following in human infants depends on communicative signals. *Current Biology*, 18(9), 668–671. https://doi.org/10.1016/j.cub.2008.03.059.

Siegel, M., Pelz, M., Magid, M., Tenenbaum, J. B., & Schulz, L. E. (2021). Children's exploratory play tracks the discriminability of hypotheses. *Nature Communications*, 12(3598). https://doi.org/10.1038/s41467-021-23431-2.

Sim, Z. L., & Xu, F. (2017). Learning higher-order generalizations through free play: Evidence from 2- and 3-year-old children. *Developmental Psychology*, 53(4), 642–651. http://dx.doi.org/10.1037/dev0000278.

Stahl, A. E., & Feigenson, L. (2015). Observing the unexpected enhances infants' learning and exploration. *Science*, 348(6230), 91–94. https://doi.org/10.1126/science.aaa3799.

Stahl, A. E., & Feigenson, L. (2019). Violations of core knowledge shape early learning. *Topics in Cognitive Science*, 11, 136–153. https://doi.org/10.1111/tops.12389.

Stenberg, G. (2009). Selectivity in infant social referencing. *Infancy*, 14(4), 457–473. https://doi.org/10.1080/15250000902994115.

Swaboda, N., Meder, B., & Ruggeri, A. (2020). Finding the (most efficient) way out of a maze is easier than asking (good) questions. *PsyArXiv*. https://doi.org/10.31234/osf.io/tdaqg.

Vaish, A., Demir, Ö. E., & Baldwin, D. (2011). Thirteen- and 18-month-old infants recognize when they need referential information. *Social Development*, 20, 431–449. https://doi.org/10.1111/j.1467-9507.2010.00601.x.

van den Bos, W., & Hertwig, R. (2017). Adolescents display distinctive tolerance to ambiguity and to uncertainty during risky decision making. *Scientific Reports*, 7, Article 40962. https://doi.org/10.1038/srep40962.

VanderBorght, M., & Jaswal, V. K. (2009). Who knows best? Preschoolers sometimes prefer child informants over adult informants. *Infant and Child Development*, 18, 61–71. https://doi.org/10.1002/icd.591.

van Schijndel, T. J., Visser, I., van Bers, B. M., & Raijmakers, M. E. (2015). Preschoolers perform more informative experiments after observing theory-violating evidence. *Journal of Experimental Child Psychology*, 131, 104–119. http://doi.org/10.1016/j.jecp.2014.11.008.

Vygotsky, L. S. (1987). *Problems of general psychology*. In R. Rieber & A. Carton (Eds.), *The collected works of L. S. Vygotsky*. Plenum Press. https://doi.org/10.1007/978-1-4613-1655-8.

Walden, T., Kim, G., McCoy, C., & Karrass, J. (2007). Do you believe in magic? Infants' social looking during violations of expectations. *Developmental Science*, 10, 654–663. https://doi.org/10.1111/j.1467-7687.2007.00607.x.

Wu, Y., & Gweon, H. (2019). Preschool-aged children jointly consider others' emotional expressions and prior knowledge to decide when to explore. *PsyArXiv*. https://doi.org/10.1111/cdev.13585.

PART II

How Do Humans Search for Information?

CHAPTER 5

What Makes a Good Query?
Prospects for a Comprehensive Theory of Human Information Acquisition

Björn Meder, Vincenzo Crupi, and Jonathan D. Nelson

5.1 The Psychology of Human Information Acquisition

Searching for relevant information to support learning and reasoning is central to intelligent and goal-directed behavior. Cognitive development is guided by children's ability to actively acquire information about their physical and social environment. Doctors routinely perform tests to diagnose their patients. And, of course, scientists conduct experiments to test their theories and hypotheses.

Psychological research on how humans acquire information in a self-directed manner began in the wake of the cognitive revolution (Bruner et al., 1956; Mosher & Hornsby, 1966; Wason, 1960). Many of these earlier studies were inspired by Popper's (1959) philosophy of science and his method of falsification: that from a logical point of view scientific theories cannot be proven to be true, but they can be shown to be wrong if their predictions are inconsistent with the outcome of an experiment. Accordingly, queries (e.g., questions, tests, experiments) are only useful if they can yield data that could potentially falsify a hypothesis.

Adopting a logical framework and falsificationism as the normatively correct approach to information acquisition, psychologists devised empirical studies to find out whether people would intuitively seek out potentially disconfirming evidence. A prominent example is the *selection task*, in which participants can acquire information to test whether a conditional rule holds (Wason, 1968). Presented with four cards and a rule such as "If there is a vowel on one side of any card, then there is an even number on its other side," searchers could turn over one or multiple cards to attempt to falsify the rule. Contrary to the prescriptions of a logico-deductive method, and paralleling findings from related tasks (Wason, 1960), few participants selected queries in accordance with a falsificationist strategy. In line with the emerging heuristics-and-biases program (Kahneman & Tversky, 1974), Wason and others suggested that people's hypothesis-testing strategies are prone to a "confirmation bias" and other suboptimalities (Klayman & Ha, 1987; Nelson & McKenzie, 2009; Nickerson, 1996).

Around the 1980s, psychologists started using a different theoretical framework for conceptualizing and evaluating human search, inspired by approaches developed in information theory (Shannon, 1948), philosophy of science (Good, 1950), statistics (Lindley, 1956), and decision theory (Savage, 1954). A key idea in this framework, foreshadowed by Chamberlin's (1890) method of multiple working hypotheses, is that the goal of scientific information acquisition is to discriminate among multiple possible hypotheses, rather than to falsify a single hypothesis. Commonly referred to as the *Optimal Experimental Design* (OED) framework, query selection is conceptualized as probabilistic inductive inference, where the outcome of a query is used to revise beliefs about the considered hypotheses. Updating beliefs in light of new data provides a certain amount of information, with different ways of measuring this quantity in relation to a searcher's beliefs and goals. These models have informed theory and empirical research on central issues in perception, developmental and cognitive psychology, and neuroscience.

Here, we discuss four key questions. First, how can we formalize the value of information and how do different models differ conceptually and mathematically? Second, how can these models support the theoretical and empirical analysis of human information acquisition? Third, what normative and computational principles govern sequential search, and how can the tension between short- and long-run optimality inform research on people's ability to conduct an efficient series of queries? Fourth, what are the relations between probabilistic (Bayesian) models of the value of information and heuristic approaches to information acquisition, and what insights can be gained from bridging different levels of analysis? We conclude by discussing current challenges and prospects for a comprehensive theory of human information search.

5.2   What Makes a Good Query?

How can we quantify the informational value of a query – a verbal question, a medical test, an eye movement, or an experiment? Several models to address this issue have been proposed in different fields, including information theory, philosophy of science, statistics, and psychology. Placed within the broad OED framework, these models evaluate queries according to different conceptual ideas and corresponding measures, such as the expected reduction in uncertainty (Lindley, 1956) or the expected improvement in classification accuracy (Baron, 1985). The quantities underpinning OED models (e.g., entropy measures) are widely used, including applications in ecology (Crupi, 2019; Simpson, 1949), economics (Gini, 1921), machine learning (Settles, 2010), and physics (Beck, 2009). They also provide the foundation of active learning strategies used to adaptively sample high-dimensional search spaces, for instance in material sciences (Lookman et al., 2019), drug discovery (Murphy, 2011), or learning of protein interactions (Mohamed et al., 2010). How humans search large decision spaces has also been addressed in recent psychological research (Meder et al., 2021; Schulz et al., 2019; Wu et al., 2018).

In cognitive science, OED models serve as descriptive or normative models for assessing human information acquisition in different domains (for reviews, see Coenen et al., 2019; Crupi et al., 2018; Nelson, 2005; Gureckis & Markant, 2012). Key applications include perceptual tasks (Najemnik & Geisler, 2005; Nelson & Cottrell, 2007), categorization (Markant & Gureckis, 2014; Nelson et al., 2010), associative learning (Kruschke, 2008), causal induction (Bramley et al., 2015; Steyvers et al., 2003), and hypothesis testing (Austerweil & Griffiths, 2011; Crupi et al., 2009; Oaksford & Chater, 1994, 1996; Skov & Sherman, 1986). OED principles are also frequently used in developmental research (Kachergis et al., 2016; Nelson et al., 2014; Ruggeri & Lombrozo, 2015; Ruggeri et al., 2015) and neuroscience (Filimon et al., 2020; Nakamura, 2006). Applied issues include eye witness identification (Wells & Lindsay, 1980), medical diagnosis (Benish, 1999), reading (Legge et al., 1997), and the design of psychological experiments (Myung & Pitt, 2009).

5.3 Optimal Experimental Design (OED): Probabilistic Models of the Value of Information

OED models provide a formal account of the epistemic value of information and the usefulness of possible queries. Typically, OED models are defined solely in terms of the relevant probability model, and are therefore most adequate for situations where the goal of the searcher is purely epistemic. Accordingly, OED models provide *informational* (or *epistemic*) *utility functions*.

The general method for evaluating a query *Q* based on OED principles requires specifying the prior probabilities of the hypotheses, the likelihood of each query outcome given the hypotheses, and a measure of the epistemic utility of each outcome. For instance, the information value of a medical test (Benish, 1999) that can come out positive or negative is fully specified by the prior probabilities of the condition (e.g., prior probability of the disease, for instance derived from epidemiological data), and the likelihoods of a positive test given that the medical condition is present or absent, respectively. Other examples are classification tasks, where different features can be queried before making a prediction (Nelson et al., 2010), or visual search tasks, where eye movements must be directed toward informative parts of a scene to find a target item (Najemnik & Geisler, 2005).

Based on the probability model, a *preposterior analysis* (Raiffa & Schlaifer, 1961) can be conducted, where the amount of obtained information is quantified by comparing the prior probability distribution over the hypotheses *before* asking query Q with the posterior distribution *after* asking Q and obtaining outcome q_j. (Capital letters refer to random variables, such as a query Q, whose answer is not yet known. Lowercase variables refer to known values: for instance, q_j is a specific obtained answer.) If a query Q has m possible answers, then its expected informational utility, $eu(Q)$, is the weighted average usefulness of its possible answers:

$$eu(Q) = \sum_{j=1}^{m} P(q_j)u(q_j) \tag{1}$$

where $P(q_j)$ denotes the probability of observing outcome q_j and $u(q_j)$ denotes its information value.

Figure 5.1 illustrates the basic rationale of determining queries' information value using a search-and-classification task with a binary hypothesis space (species A vs. species B) and two binary features, the specimen's "eye" and "claw" (Nelson et al., 2010). The probabilistic structure of the environment is shown in Figure 5.1a – that is, the hypotheses' prior probabilities, $P(h_i)$, and the individual feature likelihoods $P(q_j \mid h_i)$ (numbers from Wu et al., 2017, experiment 1). The goal is to classify the specimen as species A or B, after querying one of the two features (Figure 5.1b). Each query could yield two outcomes (feature values) with varying implications for the hypotheses' posterior probabilities – that is, for each $P(h_i \mid q_j)$. But how exactly can we use these quantities to determine the information value of the two queries?

Many different value-of-information models within the broad OED framework have been proposed for quantifying the value of queries. These

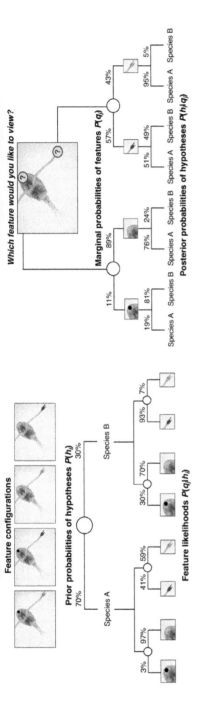
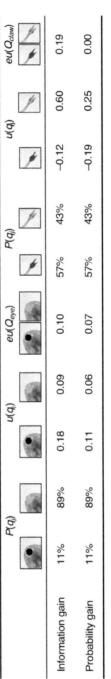

Figure 5.1 A search-and-classification task with a binary hypothesis (species A vs. B) and two binary features (the specimens' "eye" and "claw" feature, Nelson et al., 2010). **a)** Task structure, i.e., the hypotheses' prior probabilities $P(h_i)$, and the feature likelihoods, $P(q_{ij} \mid h_i)$. **b)** Information search task, where one of the two features can be queried before making a classification decision. The tree shows the marginal probabilities of the feature values, $P(q_{ij})$, and the posterior probabilities of the hypotheses given each feature value, $P(h_i \mid q_{ij})$. **c)** Informational utilities of outcomes, $u(q_{ij})$, and queries, $eu(Q)$, according to information gain and probability gain. Information gain considers querying the claw feature more useful than querying the eye feature, $eu(Q_{eye}) < eu(Q_{claw})$, whereas probability gain considers the eye feature more informative, $eu(Q_{eye}) > eu(Q_{claw})$.

models can make strongly diverging claims about the informational utility of a query (Nelson, 2005). Here, we briefly introduce some prominent entropy-based models of the value of information, which constitute the most widely used class of measures across different disciplines. Importantly, there are deep mathematical relationships among seemingly different models that allow them to be treated in a unified mathematical framework (Crupi et al., 2018; Sharma & Mittal, 1975).

5.4   Information Gain: Reducing Uncertainty

Information gain (IG; Lindley, 1956) values queries in accordance with the expected reduction in uncertainty, where uncertainty is measured via Shannon (1948) entropy. The model contrasts the entropy in the hypothesis space before conducting a query with the expected entropy after the query, with the information value of a query being the expected amount of entropy reduction.

The Shannon entropy of a random variable H, $ent(H)$, corresponding to the true hypothesis (e.g., the species in Figure 5.1), is defined as

$$ent_{Shannon}(H) = \sum_{i=1}^{n} P(h_i)\log_2 \frac{1}{P(h_i)} \tag{2}$$

where there are n possible hypotheses $h_1, h_2, \ldots h_n$. (The choice of base of logarithm is arbitrary; we use $\log_2$ such that IG is measured in bits; Figure 5.2a.) The corresponding informational utility of query outcome q_j is

$$u_{IG}(q_j) = \sum_{i=1}^{n} P(h_i)\log_2 \frac{1}{P(h_i)} - \sum_{i=1}^{n} P(h_i|q_j)\log_2 \frac{1}{P(h_i|q_j)} \tag{3}$$

where the first term corresponds to the prior entropy, $ent(H)$, and the second term denotes the expected posterior entropy of H, given answer q_j.

Figure 5.1c shows the IG of the individual query outcomes, $u(q_j)$, and the expected informational utility of the two queries, $eu(Q_{eye})$ and $eu(Q_{claw})$, given by the weighted average utility of the outcomes (Equation 1). According to IG, querying the claw feature is more useful than querying the eye feature, $eu(Q_{eye})$=0.1 bits vs. $eu(Q_{claw})$=0.19 bits.

IG is probably the most widely used measure for quantifying uncertainty reduction in information acquisition. Applications in psychology range from hypothesis testing (Austerweil & Griffiths, 2011; Nelson et al., 2001; Oaksford & Chater, 1994, 1996) and causal induction (Bramley et al.,

2015; Steyvers et al., 2003) to the analysis of eye movements (Legge et al., 1997; Najemnik & Geisler, 2005; Nelson & Cottrell, 2007) and cognitive development (Nelson et al., 2014; Ruggeri et al., 2015).

5.5 Probability Gain: Reducing Prediction Error

Probability gain (PG; Baron, 1985) measures improvement in classification accuracy. It can alternately be viewed as measuring a kind of information gain (see Crupi et al., 2018) in which error entropy (classification error), rather than Shannon entropy, is used to measure uncertainty. PG values answers in accordance with how much they improve the probability of making a correct prediction, assuming that if a searcher has to guess which hypothesis is correct (e.g., which disease is present or the species of a biological specimen) they will select the most likely hypothesis given all information obtained so far. The prediction error, $1 - \max P(h_i)$, provides the entropy function (Figure 5.2a):

$$ent_{Error}(H) = 1 - \max_{1 \leq i \leq n} P(h_i), \tag{4}$$

with the corresponding epistemic utility of a query outcome defined as

$$u_{Error}(q_j) = \max_{1 \leq i \leq n} P(h_i|q_j) - \max_{1 \leq i \leq n} P(h_i)$$

$$= \left(1 - \max_{1 \leq i \leq n} P(h_i)\right) - \left(1 - \max_{1 \leq i \leq n} P(h_i|q_j)\right). \tag{5}$$

In Figure 5.1, the probability of making a correct prediction before obtaining additional information is 70%, assuming one picks the most likely hypothesis (species A). According to PG, querying the eye feature is more useful than querying the claw feature, as the eye feature leads to 77% classification accuracy, $eu(Q_{eye})=0.07$ (Figure 5.1c). In contrast, the claw feature does not improve on the initial 70% accuracy based on the prior probabilities alone, $eu(Q_{eye})=0$. Thus, a reduction in uncertainty measured via Shannon entropy does not necessarily reduce prediction error.

PG has been widely used in psychology, including probabilistic multiple-cue categorization tasks (Nelson et al., 2010; Meder & Nelson, 2012; Wu et al., 2017), medical diagnostic test selection (Baron et al., 1988), and reasoning in the pseudodiagnosticity paradigm (Crupi et al., 2009). This research has also revealed important constraints on the ability of OED models to predict human behavior, namely the ways in which probability information is conveyed. In experience-based category learning with hundreds of learning trials, PG provides a robust predictive model of human query selection, compared to several other models (Nelson et al., 2010). With other presentation formats, for instance when probabilities are communicated with words-and-numbers or using visualizations of frequency information, the proportion of people searching in accordance with probability gain varies strongly, being as low as about 20% and as high as about 90% (Wu et al., 2017; where chance would be 50%). Thus, the predictive power of OED models to account for behavior cannot be judged in isolation, but requires a precise characterization of the task circumstances, especially in relation to how environmental probabilities are conveyed.

5.6   A Unifying Framework for Entropy and the Value of Information

5.6.1   The Sharma-Mittal-Space of Entropy Measures

Information gain and probability gain are two prominent measures of the epistemic utility of queries, with different entropies underpinning them. However, a variety of further entropy measures exist and are being used in different fields, including the measurement of species diversity in ecology (Keylock, 2005), genetic variability in evolutionary biology (Lewontin, 1972), and applications in physics (Beck, 2009). Different entropies offer alternative ways to formalize the notion of uncertainty contained in a probability distribution, with distinct mathematical properties of interest for theory and application (Crupi & Tentori, 2014; Nelson 2005). Analogously to Shannon and error entropy, these measures give rise to different informational utility functions, with the value of queries valued in terms of their ability to reduce alternative forms of entropy (Crupi et al., 2018).

One prominent model is Hartley (1928) entropy, which was an important precursor in the development of Shannon's seminal work:

$$ent_{Hartley}(H) = \log \sum_{i=1}^{n} P(h_i)^0. \qquad (6)$$

Hartley entropy computes the logarithm of the number of non-zero-probability hypotheses (assuming that $0^0 = 0$ and $P(h_i)^0 = 1$ for all

$P(h_i)>0$; Figure 5.2a). A value-of-information model based on Hartley entropy resembles Popper's (1959) method of falsification, as queries are valued by their ability to potentially rule out (falsify) at least one of the hypotheses considered. (Note though that ruling out any hypothesis – and not only the target hypothesis – would be equally valued in this information gain model.) If no outcome can potentially rule out a hypothesis, the query has no epistemic utility. This would be the case for the scenario in Figure 5.1, where no outcome yields certainty about the hypotheses.

Another important measure is *quadratic entropy* (Vajda & Zvárová, 2007; also known as *Gini-* or *Simpson-Gini index*), formally defined as

$$ent_{quadratic}(H) = 1 - \sum_{i=1}^{n} P(h_i)^2. \tag{7}$$

Quadratic entropy (Figure 5.2a) has been widely applied in many fields, including in economics to quantify income inequality (Gini, 1921) and in biology to measure species diversity (Patil & Taillie, 1982; Simpson, 1949). It is also frequently used in machine learning (Settles, 2010).

Different entropy measures are based on diverse conceptual and mathematical ideas about uncertainty and information. Notwithstanding these differences, several entropy measures arise as special cases in a unifying mathematical framework: the *Sharma–Mittal space of entropies* (SM; Sharma & Mittal, 1975; Crupi et al., 2018). The generalized SM-entropy measure has two parameters, the order parameter r and the degree parameter t:

$$ent_{SM}(H) = \frac{1}{t-1} \left[1 - \left(\sum_{i=1}^{n} P(h_i)^r \right)^{\frac{t-1}{r-1}} \right]. \tag{8}$$

The family of Sharma–Mittal entropies contains several other entropy measures as special cases (many of which exist only for well-defined limits): Shannon entropy is recovered for $r = t = 1$, Hartley entropy for $r = 0$ and $t = 1$, Quadratic entropy for $r = t = 1$, and Error entropy for $t = 2$ and $r \rightarrow \infty$ (Figure 5.2b). The family of Rényi (1961) entropies is recovered for $t = 1$, and the family of Tsallis (1988) entropies for $r = t$. Each of these entropy measures can be used to implement a corresponding model of the value of information that values query in accordance with the expected reduction of the chosen entropy.

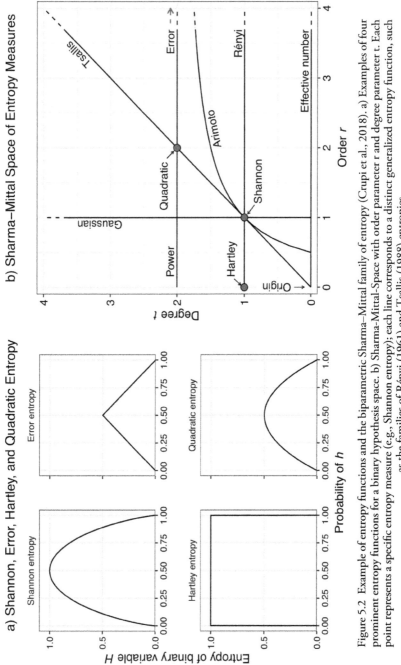

Figure 5.2 Example of entropy functions and the biparametric Sharma–Mittal family of entropy (Crupi et al., 2018). a) Examples of four prominent entropy functions for a binary hypothesis space. b) Sharma–Mittal-Space with order parameter r and degree parameter t. Each point represents a specific entropy measure (e.g., Shannon entropy); each line corresponds to a distinct generalized entropy function, such as the families of Rényi (1961) and Tsallis (1988) entropies.

In addition to providing a unified framework for quantifying entropy and uncertainty, the Sharma–Mittal framework offers prospects for cognitive modeling and empirical research. For instance, the logico-deductive interpretation of what constitutes rational information acquisition in Wason's (1968) selection task can be recovered in the Sharma–Mittal framework by using the reduction of Hartley entropy as a measure of epistemic utility (Crupi et al., 2018). Such analyses help to bridge seemingly incommensurate perspectives and models in a unifying mathematical framework, thereby fostering theory integration and providing guidance for empirical studies.

5.7 Short- vs. Long-Run Optimality of OED Models

OED models assess the epistemic utility of queries by considering each question's potential outcomes and their immediate implications for the hypotheses. These models were originally envisaged for situations in which only a single query can be conducted and thus they are *stepwise-optimal* in the sense that they optimize a particular informational utility function in the next time step. Since they disregard any future queries that could be conducted, such methods are also known as *myopic* or *greedy* models.

However, in many situations multiple queries can be conducted, for instance in medical diagnosis. In such cases, it is critical to search *efficiently* for information – to obtain as much information as possible with as few queries as possible (e.g., because medical tests can have intrinsic harms and are costly). Are stepwise OED models optimal in the long run when multiple queries can be conducted? The answer to this question is in the negative: Stepwise-optimal methods can provide a reasonable and tractable account for specific scenarios (Meder et al., 2019; Nelson et al., 2018), but they do not generally identify the most efficient sequence of queries – which in fact is a computationally intractable problem (Hyafil & Rivest, 1976).

The fact that what is in some sense optimal for a one-shot search decision can be distinctly suboptimal when multiple queries can be conducted has important implications for the theoretical and empirical analysis of human sequential search. For instance, stepwise models correspond to a valuation of individual queries, whereas planning a sequence of queries requires evaluating alternative search trees comprising multiple queries. However, in stark contrast to other domains such as reward-based learning (Bellman, 1957; Sutton & Barto, 1998), there is little research on the conflict between short- and long-term optimality and people's ability to search efficiently in situations where stepwise methods are distinctly suboptimal.

An exception is Meier and Blair (2013), who used a probabilistic classification task with four hypotheses and three (binary) queries, where the most informative first query according to several stepwise methods was not the most efficient first query in the long run (Figure 5.3a). Searchers were able to identify the most efficient query, but often required dozens or hundreds of learning trials to consistently select the most efficient feature first. These results show that people can learn from experience to search efficiently and overcome the limitations of stepwise approaches. However, further research is needed to achieve a better understanding of the interplay between learning processes, normative constraints imposed by sequential search scenarios, and the cognitive processes underlying query selection when stepwise methods are suboptimal.

The limitations of stepwise methods also apply in simpler situations with uniform priors over the hypotheses and deterministic likelihoods. Figure 5.3b shows a sequential search scenario based on the twenty-questions game (Meder et al., 2019), an experimental paradigm widely used in developmental and cognitive psychology to investigate sequential search in children and adults. The goal is to identify a randomly chosen hypothesis (here: monster) by asking as few yes–no questions about its features as possible (e.g., "Is the monster blue?"). Through a series of questions searchers move from a state of maximal uncertainty with equiprobable hypotheses to knowing the true hypothesis with certainty.

A common benchmark on this task is stepwise information gain (Kachergis et al., 2017; Nelson et al., 2014; Ruggeri et al., 2016, 2017). However, selecting questions according to their maximal stepwise information gain does not necessarily entail conducting as few queries as possible. For instance, in the task environment shown in Figure 5.3b, the color and shape feature tie for the maximum information gain query, but starting with the color feature is more efficient in the long run, because it allows for more informative queries on subsequent steps (Meder et al., 2019). Thus, similar to Meier and Blair (2013), selecting queries in accordance with the highest stepwise expected reduction of Shannon entropy (as well as various other entropy models) fails to identify the most efficient first query. Interestingly, in this task both children and adults show very limited sensitivity to long-run considerations, with behavior better accounted for by stepwise models (Meder et al., 2019). One explanation is that learning from experience is required to search efficiently across multiple queries.

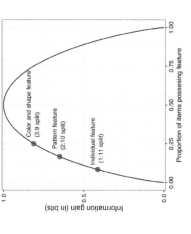

a) Suboptimality of Stepwise Methods in Probabilistic Classification

b) Suboptimality of Stepwise Methods in the 20-Questions-Game

c) Split-Half-Heuristic: Information Gain and Split

Figure 5.3 Suboptimality of stepwise methods and relationships between information gain and the split-half heuristic. a) Search trees in the classification task of Meier and Blair (2013). Q_1 to Q_3 denote possible queries (binary physical features of stimuli), the h_i denote four possible hypotheses (categories); + and – indicate the observed feature values. According to stepwise information gain (IG) and probability gain (PG), Q_2 is the most informative first query. In contrast, the globally optimal (=most efficient) search tree starts with Q_1. b) Stimuli from a twenty-questions game where stepwise-optimal methods fail to identify the most efficient first query (Meder et al., 2019). c) Relation between the split induced by a query and its stepwise information gain.

Another possibility is the use of heuristic methods that may somehow correspond to stepwise OED models.

The fact that selecting queries in accordance with stepwise methods does not ensure long-run efficiency is a critical issue for both the theoretical and the empirical analysis of human information acquisition, because it entails that stepwise OED models do not generally provide adequate benchmarks for evaluating people's search efficiency. While globally optimal solutions are generally unattainable due to the quickly increasing computational complexity, for smaller numbers of hypotheses and queries the most efficient search tree(s) can be determined through dynamic programming, such that empirical paradigms can be constructed that dissociate between short- and long-run efficiency (Meder et al., 2019; Nelson et al., 2018). Such paradigms also enable contrasting stepwise and multistep models of information acquisition, which can be more efficient because they plan multiple queries ahead (Nelson et al., 2018). To what extent multistep approaches can predict human sequential search is an important open question for developing a comprehensive theory of human sequential search.

5.8   From Heuristics to OED Models and Back

In cognitive science, OED models often serve as normative benchmarks that specify the problem faced by the searcher and the quantities required to solve the task from a computational point of view. Descriptively, OED models are able to predict human behavior well on a wide range of tasks, raising questions about the nature of the cognitive processes underlying query selection. It could be that the brain indeed carries out the relevant computations without searchers being consciously aware of these processes (e.g., in visual search tasks that recruit a dedicated neural machinery), but typically OED methods are considered computational-level models of behavior which provide a "rational description" rather than a "rational calculation" (Chater et al., 2003).

One promising approach to bridge different levels of analysis is to consider heuristic strategies that choose queries without resorting to the explicit calculation of the quantities underpinning OED models. In psychology, the use of heuristics is often assumed to lead to systematic errors in thinking and reasoning (Tversky & Kahneman, 1974). In a similar vein, it has frequently been argued that human search behavior does not conform to (supposedly) normative principles and suffers from a "confirmation bias" or other peculiarities. However, research has also revealed that the performance of heuristics can be on par with more computationally heavy models and sometimes even outperform them (Gigerenzer & Gaissmaier, 2011). A similar picture has emerged in the psychology of human inquiry, where intriguing connections between OED models and simple heuristics for query selection have been identified.

Consider the *split-half heuristic* (Navarro & Perfors, 2011; Nelson et al., 2014), which is applicable in the twenty-questions game (Figure 3b). This strategy does not rely on explicitly computing entropy, but rather evaluates queries in accordance with how they split the current set of hypotheses (items). According to the split-half heuristic, the closer a query comes to inducing a 50:50 split, the more informative it is. In Figure 3b, color and shape would be considered the most informative queries, as they induce a more even split (3:9) than the pattern feature (2:10) or querying individual monsters (1:11). Several papers have reported that human searchers frequently rely on this strategy, with the propensity to select features in accordance with the evenness of the induced split increasing with age (e.g., Denney & Denney, 1973; Mosher & Hornsby, 1966; Siegler, 1977).

How does the split-half heuristic relate to OED theories? It turns out that in the twenty-questions game the stepwise information gain of a query is a direct function of the induced split: The closer the split comes to 50:50, the higher the information gain of the query (Figure 5.3c). Thus, a searcher using the split-half heuristic will invariably select questions in accordance with their information gain. The analytic relation between the informativeness of a query and induced split also holds for several other entropy measures (Crupi et al., 2018) and particular nonentropic OED models (Nelson et al., 2018).

Another heuristic is the *likelihood difference heuristic* (Nelson, 2005; Nelson et al., 2020), which is sometimes used in binary classification tasks when probability information is conveyed through words and numbers (Slowiaczek et al., 1992). The heuristic is applicable in probabilistic search tasks with binary hypotheses and features, and values queries in accordance with the absolute difference in outcome likelihoods. Ranking queries in accordance with their likelihood difference corresponds to ranking queries in accordance with the OED model impact (Wells & Lindsay, 1980), which for the special case of equal priors also corresponds to ranking queries according to probability gain (Nelson, 2005). In particular circumstances the likelihood difference heuristic is provably optimal for selecting queries, whereas several OED models are not (Nelson et al., 2020).

5.9   Concluding Remarks: Open Questions and Challenges

Recent years have seen strong progress in building a comprehensive computational account of human inquiry based on applying OED principles to the theoretical and empirical analysis of cognition and behavior. What challenges need to be met to further advance theory, and what are important venues for empirical research?

One important issue concerns the relation between informational utilities and other kinds of reward structures. For instance, in medical diagnosis the information provided by a test is of course essential, but further costs and rewards are also highly relevant (Baron & Hershey, 1988; Nelson et al., 2020). This is because tests themselves can be intrinsically harmful (e.g., radiation) or because their outcomes have strong implications for subsequent actions (e.g., erroneously failing to quarantine an infectious person due to a false test result). While OED models evaluate queries in terms of their epistemic value, the general approach can be extended to incorporate situation-specific utilities (e.g., rewards and costs associated with decisions based upon obtained information). In this case, queries can be valued in accordance with their expected *utility gain*, rather than pure information value (Markant & Gureckis, 2012; Meder & Nelson, 2012). Incorporating other rewards and costs in the analysis of query selection might require invoking additional methods and considerations (Sharot & Sunstein, 2020). For instance, a doctor may need to choose between a highly informative test whose results may take several days to obtain, and a less informative test whose results are immediately available. Investigating how searchers balance information value and time (i.e., temporal discounting) and how they integrate other factors (e.g., hedonic value of query outcomes and other emotions related to the anticipation of information; Li et al., 2020) are important challenges for a broader characterization of information acquisition when searchers' goals are not purely epistemic.

A promising venue for applying the Sharma–Mittal framework to such questions is *deliberate ignorance* – the observation that people sometimes prefer to remain in a state of uncertainty rather than seeking out information that would resolve it (Hertwig & Engel, 2016). People may not want to know the sex of their child before birth or prefer to not know whether they have a genetic predisposition for a disease. Such behaviors raise interesting questions for theories of human inquiry, because OED models based on entropy reduction are usually strictly nonnegative, meaning that in the expectation a query can never have negative epistemic utility. The Sharma–Mittal framework, however, has the expressive power to devise models where queries can have negative information value, depending on which entropy measure is chosen to represent uncertainty and information (Crupi et al., 2018). Thus, the framework provides novel pathways to model situations where searchers consider information as contrary to their goals even in strictly informational terms and without introducing situation-specific costs.

Another key issue is the interplay between reinforcement learning and human inquiry. This is of particular importance in light of empirical findings showing that searchers can harness their learning experiences to overcome the limitations of stepwise methods (Meier & Blair, 2013), whereas absent such experiences behavior is better accounted for by stepwise models (Meder et al., 2019). Similarly, OED models provide a much better account of human behavior when learning environmental probabilities through experience, compared to other means of conveying probability information (Meder & Nelson, 2012; Nelson et al., 2010, Wu et al., 2017). Within the reinforcement learning framework (Sutton & Barto, 1998), inquiry could be modeled by using informational utilities as reward functions, extending the approach from reward-based to information-based reinforcement learning (Li et al., 2019). Importantly, the reinforcement learning framework offers different proposals to address the tension between short- and long-run optimality by assuming that future outcomes are temporally discounted. Stepwise OED methods could be implemented by setting the temporal discounting parameter to zero, such that only the immediate implications of query outcomes are considered. Multistep models with a longer planning horizon could be implemented by increasing the temporal discounting factor, in which case later inquiry steps are also considered (Butko & Movellan, 2010). Integrating ideas and models from the OED and reinforcement learning literature would offer new perspectives on the learning processes and how they are constrained by OED principles.

Besides these pathways for future research, several open questions about the psychology of human inquiry and OED models exist (Coenen et al., 2019). For instance, whereas OED models require a well-defined hypothesis space and probability model, many forms of human inquiry are more open ended in that the goal is not to discriminate between existing hypotheses, but to *generate* hypotheses in the first place, often in the absence of explicit learning goals or situation-specific incentives (e.g., self-guided inquiry in childhood or science). While the broad goal in such cases may also be epistemic in the sense of reducing uncertainty about the world more generally, fully accounting for such forms of open-ended inquiry might require integrating OED methods with other frameworks, such as theories of curiosity (Dubey & Griffiths, 2020). Conversely, applying

OED methods can be challenging in practice – for instance, in scientific experimentation, when the goal is to discriminate among complex models with free parameters and the data-generating distribution is unknown (Kleinegesse & Gutmann, 2020).

In sum, OED theories provide a computational framework for evaluating the informational value of different kinds of queries, including verbal questions, eye movements, medical tests, and experiments. Recent decades have yielded substantial progress in the understanding of the computational and behavioral principles underlying human information acquisition in different domains, from neuroscience to developmental and cognitive psychology. Notwithstanding these advances and breadth of applicability, many open questions remain, and addressing these challenges will be key to making further progress toward a comprehensive theory of human information acquisition.

References

Austerweil, J. L., & Griffiths, T. L. (2011). Seeking confirmation is rational for deterministic hypotheses. *Cognitive Science*, 35(3), 499–526. https://doi.org/10.1111/j.1551-6709.2010.01161.x.

Baron, J. (1985). *Rationality and intelligence*. Cambridge University Press.

Baron, J., & Hershey, J. C. (1988). Heuristics and biases in diagnostic reasoning: I. Priors, error costs, and test accuracy. *Organizational Behavior and Human Decision Processes*, 41(2), 259–279. https://doi.org/10.1016/0749-5978(88)90030-1.

Beck, C. (2009). Generalised information and entropy measures in physics. *Contemporary Physics*, 50(4), 495–510. https://doi.org/10.1080/00107510902823517.

Bellman, R. (1957). *Dynamic programming*. Princeton University Press.

Benish, W. A. (1999). Relative entropy as a measure of diagnostic information. *Medical Decision Making*, 19(2), 202–206. https://doi.org/10.1177/0272989X9901900211.

Bramley, N. R., Lagnado, D. A., & Speekenbrink, M. (2015). Conservative forgetful scholars: How people learn causal structure through sequences of interventions. *Journal of Experimental Psychology. Learning, Memory, and Cognition*, 41(3), 708–731. https://doi.org/10.1037/xlm0000061.

Bruner, J. S., Goodnow, J. J., & Austin, G. A. (1956). *A study of thinking*. John Wiley and Sons.

Butko, N. J., & Movellan, J. R. (2010). Infomax control of eye movements. *IEEE Transactions on Autonomous Mental Development*, 2(2), 91–107. https://doi.org/10.1109/TAMD.2010.2051029.

Chamberlin, T. C. (1890). The method of multiple working hypotheses. *Science*, 15, 92–96. https://doi.org/10.1126/science.148.3671.754

Chater, N., Oaksford, M., Nakisa, R., & Redington, M. (2003). Fast, frugal, and rational: How rational norms explain behavior. *Organizational Behavior and*

Human Decision Processes, 90(1), 63–86. https://doi.org/10.1016/S0749-597 8(02)00508-3.

Coenen, A., Nelson, J. D. & Gureckis, T. M. (2019). Asking the right questions about the psychology of human inquiry: Nine open challenges. *Psychonomic Bulletin & Review*, 26, 1548–1587. https://doi.org/10.3758/s13423-018-1470-5.

Crupi V. (2019). Measures of biological diversity: Overview and unified framework. In E. Casetta, J. Marques da Silva, and D. Vecchi (Eds.), *From assessing to conserving biodiversity* (pp. 123–136). Springer.

Crupi, V., Nelson, J. D., Meder, B., Cevolani, G., & Tentori, K. (2018). Generalized information theory meets human cognition: Introducing a unified framework to model uncertainty and information search. *Cognitive Science*, 42 (5), 1410–1456. https://doi.org/10.1111/cogs.12613.

Crupi, V., & Tentori, K. (2014). State of the field: Measuring information and confirmation. *Studies in History and Philosophy of Science Part A*, 47, 81–90. https://doi.org/10.1016/j.shpsa.2014.05.002.

Crupi, V., Tentori, K., & Lombardi, L. (2009). Pseudodiagnosticity revisited. *Psychological Review*, 116(4), 971–985. https://doi.org/10.1037/a0017050.

Denney, D. R., & Denney, N. W. (1973). The use of classification for problem solving: A comparison of middle and old age. *Developmental Psychology*, 9(2), 275–278. https://doi.org/10.1037/h0035092.

Dubey, R., & Griffiths, T. L. (2020). Reconciling novelty and complexity through a rational analysis of curiosity. *Psychological Review*, 127(3), 455–476. https://doi.org/10.1037/rev0000175.

Filimon, F., Nelson, J. D., Sejnowski, T. J., Sereno, M. I., & Cottrell, G. W. (2020). The ventral striatum dissociates information expectation, reward anticipation, and reward receipt. *Proceedings of the National Academy of Sciences*, 117 (26), 15200-15208. https://doi.org/10.1073/pnas.1911778117.

Gigerenzer, G., & Gaissmaier, W. (2011). Heuristic decision making. *Annual Review of Psychology*, 62, 451–482. https://doi.org/10.1146/annurev-psych-120709-145346.

Gini, C. (1921). Measurement of inequality of incomes. *The Economic Journal*, 31 (121), 124–126. https://doi.org/10.2307/2223319.

Good, I. J. (1950). *Probability and the weight of evidence.* Charles Griffin & Co.

Gureckis, T. M., & Markant, D. B. (2012). Self-directed learning: A cognitive and computational perspective. *Perspectives on Psychological Science*, 7(5), 464–481. https://doi.org/10.1177/1745691612454304.

Hartley, R. V. (1928). Transmission of information. *Bell System Technical Journal*, 7(3), 535–563.

Hertwig, R., & Engel, C. (2016). Homo Ignorans: Deliberately choosing not to know. *Perspectives on Psychological Science*, 11(3), 359–372. https://doi.org/10.1177/1745691616635594.

Hyafil, L., & Rivest, R. L. (1976). Constructing optimal binary decision trees is NP-complete. *Information Processing Letters*, 5(1), 15–17. https://doi.org/10.1016/0020-0190(76)90095-8.

Kachergis, G., Berends, F., Kleijn, R. D., & Hommel, B. (2016). Human reinforcement learning of sequential action. In A. Papafragou, D. Grodner, & D. Mirman (Eds.), *Proceedings of the 38th Annual Meeting of the Cognitive Science Society (CogSci 2016)*, pp. 193–198.

Kachergis, G., Rhodes, M., & Gureckis, T. (2017). Desirable difficulties during the development of active inquiry skills. *Cognition*, 166, 407–417. https://doi .org/10.1016/j.cognition.2017.05.021.

Keylock, C. J. (2005). Simpson diversity and the Shannon–Wiener index as special cases of a generalized entropy. *Oikos*, 109(1), 203–207. https://doi.org /10.1111/j.0030-1299.2005.13735.x.

Klayman, J., & Ha, Y.-W. (1987). Confirmation, disconfirmation, and information in hypothesis testing. *Psychological Review*, 94(2), 211–228. https://doi.org /10.1037/0033-295X.94.2.211.

Kleinegesse, S. & Gutmann, M. U. (2020). Bayesian experimental design for implicit models by mutual information neural estimation. *Proceedings of Machine Learning Research*, 119, 5316–5326.

Kruschke, J.K. (2008). Bayesian approaches to associative learning: From passive to active learning. *Learning & Behavior*, 36, 210–226. https://doi.org/10.3758 /LB.36.3.210.

Legge, G. E., Klitz, T. S., & Tjan, B. S. (1997). Mr. Chips: An ideal-observer model of reading. *Psychological Review*, 104(3), 524–553. https://doi.org/10 .1037/0033-295X.104.3.524.

Lewontin R.C. (1972) The apportionment of human diversity. In T. Dobzhansky, M. K. Hecht, and W. C. Steere (Eds.), *Evolutionary biology* (pp. 381–398). New York, NY: Springer. https://doi.org/10.1007/978-1-46 84-9063-3_14.

Li, S., Sun, Y., Liu, S., Sun, Y., Gureckis, T. M., & Bramley, N. R. (2019). Active physical inference via reinforcement learning. *Proceedings of the Cognitive Science Society* (pp. 2126–2132). Austin, TX: Cognitive Science Society.

Li, Z., Bramley, N. R., & Gureckis, T. M. (2020). Expectations about future learning influence moment-to-moment feelings of suspense. https://doi.org/10 .31234/osf.io/532tw.

Lindley, D. V. (1956). On a measure of the information provided by an experiment. *The Annals of Mathematical Statistics*, 27(4), 986–1005.

Lookman, T., Balachandran, P. V., Xue, D., & Yuan, R. (2019). Active learning in materials science with emphasis on adaptive sampling using uncertainties for targeted design. *NPJ Computational Materials*, 5(1), 1–17. https://doi.org/10 .1038/s41524-019-0153-8.

Markant, D., & Gureckis, T. M. (2012). Does the utility of information influence sampling behavior? *Proceedings of the 34th Annual Conference of the Cognitive Science Society* (pp. 719–724). Austin, TX: Cognitive Science Society.

Markant, D. B., & Gureckis, T. M. (2014). Is it better to select or to receive? Learning via active and passive hypothesis testing. *Journal of Experimental Psychology: General*, 143(1), 94–122. https://doi.org/10.1037/a0032108.

Meder, B., & Nelson, J. D. (2012). Information search with situation-specific reward functions. *Judgment and Decision Making*, 7(2), 119–148.

Meder, B., Nelson, J. D., Jones, M., & Ruggeri, A. (2019). Stepwise versus globally optimal search in children and adults. *Cognition*, 191, Article 103965. https://doi.org/10.1016/j.cognition.2019.05.002.

Meder, B., Wu, C. M., Schulz, E., & Ruggeri, A. (2021). Development of directed and random exploration in children. *Developmental Science*. e13095. https://doi.org/10.1111/desc.13095.

Meier, K. M., & Blair, M. R. (2013). Waiting and weighting: Information sampling is a balance between efficiency and error-reduction. *Cognition*, 126 (2), 319–325. https://doi.org/10.1016/j.cognition.2012.09.014.

Mohamed, T. P., Carbonell, J. G., & Ganapathiraju, M. K. (2010). Active learning for human protein-protein interaction prediction. *BMC Bioinformatics*, 11, S57. https://doi.org/10.1186/1471-2105-11-S1-S57.

Mosher, F. A., & Hornsby, J. R. (1966). On asking questions. In J. S. Bruner, R. R. Oliver, & P. M. Greenfield, et al. (Eds.), *Studies in cognitive growth* (pp. 86–102). Wiley.

Murphy, R. F. (2011). An active role for machine learning in drug development. *Nature Chemical Biology*, 7(6), 327–330. https://doi.org/10.1038/nchembio.576.

Myung, J. I., & Pitt, M. A. (2009). Optimal experimental design for model discrimination. *Psychological Review*, 116(3), 499–518. https://doi.org/10.1037/a0016104.

Najemnik, J., & Geisler, W. (2005). Optimal eye movement strategies in visual search. *Nature*, 434, 387–391. https://doi.org/10.1038/nature03390.

Nakamura, K. (2006). Neural representation of information measure in the primate premotor cortex. *Journal of Neurophysiology*, 96(1), 478–485. https://doi.org/10.1152/jn.01326.2005.

Navarro, D. J., & Perfors, A. F. (2011). Hypothesis generation, sparse categories, and the positive test strategy. *Psychological Review*, 118(1), 120–134. https://doi.org/10.1037/a0021110.

Nelson, J. D. (2005). Finding useful questions: On Bayesian diagnosticity, probability, impact, and information gain. *Psychological Review*, 112(4), 979–999. https://doi.org/10.1037/0033-295X.112.4.979.

Nelson, J. D., & Cottrell, G. W. (2007). A probabilistic model of eye movements in concept formation. *Neurocomputing*, 70, 2256–2272. https://doi.org/10.1016/j.neucom.2006.02.026.

Nelson, J. D., Divjak, B., Gudmundsdottir, G., Martignon, L. F., & Meder, B. (2014). Children's sequential information search is sensitive to environmental probabilities. *Cognition*, 130(1), 74–80.

Nelson, J. D., & McKenzie, C. R. M. (2009). Confirmation bias. In M. Kattan (Ed.), *The Encyclopedia of Medical Decision Making* (pp. 167–171). Sage.

Nelson, J. D., McKenzie, C. R. M., Cottrell, G. W., & Sejnowski, T. J. (2010). Experience matters: Information acquisition optimizes probability gain. *Psychological Science*, 21(7), 960–969. https://doi.org/10.1177/0956797610372637.

Nelson, J. D., Meder, B., & Jones, M. (2018). Towards a theory of heuristic and optimal planning for sequential information search. *PsyArXiv*.

Nelson, J. D., Rosenauer, C., Crupi, V., Tentori, K., & Meder, B. (2020). *On the likelihood difference heuristic and the objective utility of possible medical tests*. Manuscript submitted for publication.

Nelson, J. D., Tenenbaum, J. B., & Movellan, J. R. (2001). Active inference in concept learning. In J. D. Moore & K. Stenning (Eds.), *Proceedings of the 23rd Conference of the Cognitive Science Society*, 692–697.

Nickerson, R. S. (1996). Hempel's paradox and Wason's selection task: Logical and psychological puzzles of confirmation. *Thinking & Reasoning*, 2, 1–31. https://doi.org/10.1080/135467896394546.

Oaksford, M., & Chater, N. (1994). A rational analysis of the selection task as optimal data selection. *Psychological Review*, 101(4), 608–631. https://doi.org.10.1037/0033-295X.101.4.608.

Oaksford, M., & Chater, N. (1996). Rational explanation of the selection task. *Psychological Review*, 103(2), 381–391. https://doi.org/10.1037/0033-295X.103.2.381.

Patil, G. P., & Taillie, C. (1982) Diversity as a concept and its measurement. *Journal of the American Statistical Association*, 77(379), 548–561. https://doi.org/10.1080/01621459.1982.10477845.

Popper, K. R. (1959). *The logic of scientific discovery*. Hutchinson.

Raiffa, H., & Schlaifer, R. O. (1961). *Applied statistical decision theory*. Cambridge, MA: Division of Research, Graduate School of Business Administration, Harvard University.

Rényi, A. (1961). On measures of entropy and information. In J. Neyman (Ed.), *Proceedings of the Fourth Berkeley Symposium on Mathematical Statistics and Probability I* (pp. 547–556). University of California Press.

Ruggeri, A., & Lombrozo, T. (2015). Children adapt their questions to achieve efficient search. *Cognition*, 143, 203–216. https://doi.org/10.1016/j.cognition.2015.07.004.

Ruggeri, A., Lombrozo, T., Griffiths, T. L., & Xu, F. (2016). Sources of developmental change in the efficiency of information search. *Developmental Psychology*, 52(12), 2159–2173. https://doi.org/10.1037/dev0000240.

Ruggeri, A., Sim, Z. L., & Xu, F. (2017). "Why is Toma late to school again?" Preschoolers identify the most informative questions. *Developmental Psychology*, 53(9), 1620.

Savage, L. J. (1954). *The foundations of statistics*. Wiley.

Schulz, E., Wu, C. M., Ruggeri, A., & Meder, B. (2019). Searching for rewards like a child means less generalization and more directed exploration. *Psychological Science*, 30(11), 1561–1572. https://doi.org/10.1177/0956797619863663.

Settles, B. (2010). *Active learning literature survey*. Technical Report, University of Wisconsin-Madison.

Shannon, C. E. (1948). A mathematical theory of communication. *The Bell System Technical Journal*, 27, 379–423. https://doi.org/10.1002/j.1538-7305.1948.tb01338.x.

Sharma, B., & Mittal, D. (1975). New non–additive measures of entropy for discrete probability distributions. *Journal of Mathematical Sciences*, 10, 28–40.

Sharot, T., & Sunstein, C. R. (2020). How people decide what they want to know. *Nature Human Behaviour*, 4, 14–19. https://doi.org/10.1038/s41562-019-0793-1.

Siegler, R. S. (1977). The twenty questions game as a form of problem solving. *Child Development*, 395–403.

Simpson E. H. (1949). Measurement of diversity. *Nature*, 163, 688. https://doi.org/10.1038/163688a0

Skov, R. B., & Sherman, S. J. (1986). Information-gathering processes: Diagnosticity, hypothesis-confirmatory strategies, and perceived hypothesis confirmation. *Journal of Experimental Social Psychology*, 103, 278–282. https://doi.org/10.1016/j.beproc.2014.01.014.

Slowiaczek, L. M., Klayman, J., Sherman, S. J., & Skov, R. B. (1992). Information selection and use in hypothesis testing: What is a good question, and what is a good answer? *Memory & Cognition*, 20(4), 392–405. https://doi.org/10.3758/BF03210923.

Steyvers, M., Tenenbaum, J. B., Wagenmakers, E. J., & Blum, B. (2003). Inferring causal networks from observations and interventions. *Cognitive Science*, 27, 453–489. https://doi.org/10.1016/S0364-0213(03)00010-7.

Sutton, R. S., & Barto, A. G. (1998). *Reinforcement learning: An introduction.* Cambridge, MA: MIT Press.

Tsallis, C. (1988). Possible generalization of Boltzmann-Gibbs statistics. *Journal of Statistical Physics*, 52(1–2), 479–487. https://doi.org/10.1007/BF01016429.

Tversky, A., & Kahneman, D. (1974). Judgment under uncertainty: Heuristics and biases. *Science*, 185(4157), 1124–1131. https://doi.org/10.1126/science.185.4157.1124.

Vajda I. & Zvárová J. (2007). On generalized entropies, Bayesian decisions, and statistical diversity. *Kybernetika*, 43(5), 675–696.

Wason, P. C. (1960). On the failure to eliminate hypotheses in a conceptual task. *Quarterly Journal of Experimental Psychology*, 12, 129–140. https://doi.org/10.1080/17470216008416717.

Wason, P. C. (1968). Reasoning about a rule. *Quarterly Journal of Experimental Psychology*, 20, 273–281. https://doi.org/10.1080/14640746808400161.

Wells, G. L., & Lindsay, R. C. (1980). On estimating the diagnosticity of eyewitness nonidentifications. *Psychological Bulletin*, 88(3), 776–784. https://doi.org/10.1037/0033-2909.88.3.776.

Wu, C. M., Meder, B., Filimon, F., & Nelson, J. D. (2017). Asking better questions: How presentation formats influence information search. *Journal of Experimental Psychology: Learning, Memory, and Cognition*, 43(8), 1274–1297. https://doi.org/10.1037/xlm0000374.

Wu, C., Schulz, E., Speekenbrink, M., Nelson, J. D., & Meder, B. (2018). Generalization guides human exploration in vast decision spaces. *Nature Human Behavior*, 2, 915–924. https://doi.org/10.1038/s41562-018-0467-4.

CHAPTER 6

Active Inference, Bayesian Optimal Design, and Expected Utility

Noor Sajid, Lancelot Da Costa, Thomas Parr, and Karl Friston

6.1 Introduction

Humans contend with conflicting objectives when operating in capricious, nonstationary environments, including maximizing epistemic value or minimizing expected cost (Laureiro-Martínez, Brusoni, & Zollo, 2010; Schulz & Gershman, 2019; Schwartenbeck et al., 2019). A widely studied proposition for understanding how the balance between these distinct imperatives is maintained is active inference (Friston, FitzGerald, Rigoli, Schwartenbeck, & Pezzulo, 2017; Friston, Lin, et al., 2017), which brings together perception and action under a single objective of minimizing free energy across time (Da Costa, Parr, et al., 2020; Kaplan & Friston, 2018). Briefly, active inference is a formal way of describing the behavior of self-organizing (random dynamical) systems that interface with the external world, such as humans in their environment, with latent representations that maintain a consistent form (i.e., a particular steady-state) over time.

Active inference stipulates that by minimizing free energy (i.e., evidence upper bound) across time, agents will maintain sensed outcomes within a certain hospitable range (Friston, 2019; Friston et al., 2014). For this, agents optimize two complementary free energy functionals across time: variational and expected free energy.[1] Variational free energy measures the fit between an internal generative model and observed outcomes, while expected free energy scores each possible action trajectory in terms of its ability to reach a range of preferred latent states. Expected free energy equips the agent with a formal way to assess different hypothesis about the types of behavior that can be pursued, which guarantees realization of the agents' preferences over states and model parameters; c.f., planning as inference (Attias, 2003; Botvinick &

---

[1] Both free energies are closely related: systems at steady-state that minimize variational free energy also minimize expected free energy (Parr, Da Costa, & Friston, 2020)

Toussaint, 2012; Kaplan & Friston, 2018). The imperative to minimize expected free energy (or maximize expected model evidence) subsumes several important objectives that are prevalent in the psychological, economics, and engineering literatures: for example, Kullback–Leibler control (Todorov, 2008; van den Broek, Wiegerinck, & Kappen, 2010) and expected utility theory (Fleming & Sheu, 2002; Kahneman & Tversky, 1979). These special cases are revealed by removing particular sources of uncertainty from the problem setting.

In this chapter, we show how the expected free energy combines both Bayesian decision theory and optimal Bayesian design (Da Costa, Parr, et al., 2020; Friston, Da Costa, Hafner, Hesp, & Parr, 2020). Specifically, by removing prior preferences about outcomes from the expected free energy, active inference reduces to optimal Bayesian design (Chaloner & Verdinelli, 1995; Lindley, 1956; Pukelsheim, 2006; Stone, 1959). That is, it is only concerned with resolving uncertainty about the causes that generated particular outcomes. In contrast, by removing ambiguity and (posterior) predictive entropy from the expected free energy objective, active inference reduces to Bayesian decision theory (Harsanyi, 1978; Savage, 1972) – namely, the maximization of some utility function, expected under predictive posterior beliefs about the consequences of an action. Hence, Bayesian decision theory and optimal Bayesian design can be combined to equip agents with a rich trade-off between information-seeking and goal-directed behaviors.

Effectively, expected free energy minimization introduces a Bayes-optimal arbitration between intrinsic, information-seeking, and extrinsic goal-seeking behavior (Friston et al., 2015; Sajid, Ball, Parr, & Friston, 2021; Schwartenbeck et al., 2019). Here, information-seeking or uncertainty-resolving behavior come in two flavors. The first is uncertainty about beliefs about the state of the world and how they unfold (Parr & Friston, 2019a): agents will actively sample outcomes that have an unambiguous (i.e., low conditional entropy) relationship to latent states. Second, this kind of behavior resolves uncertainties about beliefs over particular model parameters (Schwartenbeck et al., 2019). Therefore, agents will expose themselves to observations that enable learning of the probabilistic structure of unknown – and unexplored – contingencies (Friston, Lin, et al., 2017; Schmidhuber, 2006). Consequently, expected free energy minimization entails information-seeking behavior that equips active inference agents with a deterministic way to explore unknown states – responding optimally to epistemic affordances.

We review these aspects of active inference and show that the minimization of expected free energy subsumes Bayesian decision theory and optimal Bayesian design principles as special cases. First, we briefly introduce active inference. This sets the scene to derive optimal Bayesian design principles and Bayesian decision theory as limiting cases of active inference. We then evaluate differences in behavior simulated under active inference – namely, optimal Bayesian design (i.e., by removing prior preferences about outcomes) and Bayesian decision theory (i.e., by removing ambiguity and relative risk) – in a T-maze setting. For simplicity, we focus on uncertainty about states of the world, noting that the same principles apply to lawful contingencies, parameterized by a generative model. The ensuing simulations show that goal-directed, information-seeking behavior is a direct consequence of minimizing expected free energy under active inference (Millidge, Tschantz, & Buckley, 2020; Parr & Friston, 2019b). That is, agents selectively sample options that are associated with the highest information gain (i.e., the most informative) when engaging with their environment. Conversely, expected utility maximizing agents exhibit suboptimal behavior by failing to sample – and exploit – epistemic or informative cues (Tschantz, Seth, & Buckley, 2020). We conclude with a brief discussion about the relevance of active inference as a way to characterize and quantify information-seeking behavior in relation to goal-seeking.

6.2 Active Inference

Active inference describes how goal-directed, information-seeking agents navigate their environments (Da Costa, Parr, et al., 2020; Friston et al., 2017). For this, it stipulates three essential components: 1) a generative model of the agent's environment (eq. 1), 2) fitting the model to (sampled) observations to reduce surprise (i.e., variational free energy: eq. 2), and 3) selecting actions that minimize uncertainty (i.e., expected free energy: eq. 3).

This is formalized as a partially observable Markov decision process (POMDP), with the following random variables:

- $s \in S$; where s is a particular latent state and S a finite set of all possible latent states,
- $o \in O$; where o is a particular observation and O a finite set of all possible observations,
- $\pi \in \Pi$; where $\pi = \{a_1, a_2, ..., a_t\}$ is a policy (i.e., action trajectory) and Π a finite set of all possible policies up to a given time horizon $T \in N^+$, and

- $T = \{1, ..t, ..\tau, T\}$; a finite set which stands for discrete time: t and τ are some current and future time, respectively.

From this, we define the agent's generative model as the following probability distribution, omitting model parameters for simplicity:

$$P(o_{1:T}, s_{1:T}, \pi) = \underbrace{P(s_1)P(\pi)}_{Priors} \left(\prod_{t=1}^{T} \underbrace{P(o_t|s_t)}_{Likelihood} \right) \left(\prod_{t=2}^{T} \underbrace{P(s_t|s_{t-1}, \pi)}_{Transition} \right) \quad (1)$$

Accordingly, the agent minimizes surprise about observations (i.e., fits a model to observations), that is, $-\log P(o_{1:t})$, through optimization of the following objective:

$$-\log P(o_{1:t}) \leq E_{Q(s_{1:T}, \pi)}[\log Q(s_{1:T}, \pi) - \log P(o_{1:t}, s_{1:T}, \pi)] \quad (2)$$

where $Q(s_{1:T}, \pi)$ is the variational distribution over s and π. Eq.2 undergirds the imperative to update beliefs about latent states to align them with observed outcomes. The inequality is derived using Jensen's inequality. The right-hand side is commonly referred to as variational free energy (F) (Friston, 2010; Friston, Daunizeau, Kilner, & Kiebel, 2010) or the evidence lower bound in the variational inference literature (Beal, 2003; Blei, Kucukelbir, & McAuliffe, 2017). Furthermore, uncertainty about anticipated observations is reduced by selecting policies that a priori minimize expected free energy (G); $\log P(o_\tau)$ where $\tau \geq t$(Parr & Friston, 2019b):

$$G(\pi, \tau) = E_{P(o_\tau|s_\tau)Q(s_\tau|\pi)}[\log Q(s_\tau|\pi) - \log P(o_\tau, s_\tau)] \quad (3)$$

Note the resemblance to the terms in eq. 2, which can be transformed into eq. 3 by supplementing the expectation under the approximate posterior with the likelihood, resulting in the following predictive distribution: $\tilde{Q} = P(o_\tau|s_\tau)Q(s_\tau|\pi)$. This treats planning as inference (Attias, 2003; Botvinick & Toussaint, 2012), where we can evaluate plausible policies before outcomes have been observed. Additionally, we condition upon the policy in the approximate posterior and omit the policy from the generative model. Consequently, expected free energy is the main construct of interest because it determines the behavior of an agent when planning or selecting its course of action. We reserve description of its main features and relationship to other Bayesian objectives for the next section.

In active inference, decision-making entails the selection of the most likely action from the following distribution:

$$P(\pi) = \sigma\left(-G(\pi)\right) = \sigma\left(-\sum_{\tau > t} G(\pi, \tau)\right) \qquad (4)$$

where $\sigma(.)$ is the softmax function and $G(\pi)$ is the expected free energy of a policy. The action associated with the sampled policy at the next timestep is then selected.

Using these components, expectations about latent states and policies can be optimized through inference and model parameters optimized through learning. This involves converging on the solution using gradient descent on free energy, F, which offers a biophysically plausible account of inference and learning (Da Costa, Parr, et al., 2020; Friston et al., 2017; Parr, Markovic, Kiebel, & Friston, 2019), and furnishing the expected free energy of various actions (Çatal, Wauthier, Verbelen, De Boom, & Dhoedt, 2020; Fountas, Sajid, Mediano, & Friston, 2020; van der Himst & Lanillos, 2020).

6.3   Expected Free Energy Decomposed

Expected free energy, a central quantity within active inference, is (loosely speaking) the free energy functional of future trajectories. It evaluates the goodness of plausible policies determined by outcomes that have yet to be observed – that is, anticipated future outcomes (Parr & Friston, 2019b). Accordingly, its minimization allows the agent to influence the future by taking actions in the present, which are selected from an appropriate policy. By construction, the expected free energy strikes the Bayes-optimal balance between goal-directed and information-seeking behavior under some prior preferences. It is this particular aspect of active inference that subsumes Bayesian decision theory and optimal Bayesian design principles as limiting cases (Da Costa, Parr, et al., 2020; Friston et al., 2020). To make the connections between these clearer, we highlight the different ways of unpacking expected free energy (eq. 3):

$$G(\pi, \tau) = E_{\tilde{Q}}\left[\log Q(s_\tau|\pi) - \log P(o_\tau, s_\tau)\right]$$

$$= \underbrace{D_{KL}[Q(s_\tau|\pi)||P(s_\tau)]}_{Risk} + \underbrace{E_{Q(s_\tau|\pi)}[H[P(o_\tau|s_\tau)]]}_{Ambiguity}$$

$$\geq -\underbrace{E_{Q(o_\tau|\pi)}[D_{KL}[Q(s_\tau|o_\tau,\pi)||Q(s_\tau|\pi)]]}_{Intrinsic\ value} - \underbrace{E_{Q(o_\tau|\pi)}[\log P(o_\tau)]}_{Extrinsic\ value} \qquad (5)$$

The second equality presents expected free energy as a balance between risk and ambiguity (Da Costa, Parr, et al., 2020). Here, risk is the difference between predicted and prior beliefs about future latent states. Thus, policies will be more probable if they lead to states that align with prior preferences – that is, risk-minimizing policies. This part of expected free energy underwrites KL control (Todorov, 2008; van den Broek et al., 2010). Conversely, ambiguity – the expectation of the conditional entropy – is the uncertainty about future outcome given beliefs about future latent states. This can also be interpreted as the expected inaccuracy of future predictions. Low ambiguity means that observed outcomes are uniquely informative about the latent states. Therefore, ambiguity minimization corresponds to selecting policies that lead to unambiguous and salient outcomes.

Equivalently, the expected free energy bounds the difference between intrinsic value (about states) and extrinsic value (eq. 5; third equality). These terms capture the imperative to maximize intrinsic value (i.e., information gain), from interactions with the environment, about the latent states, whilst maximizing extrinsic value (i.e., expected value), in relation to prior beliefs. Extrinsic value is encoded by log prior preferences over outcomes and is analogous to a cost or reward function in reinforcement learning (Barto, Mirolli, & Baldassarre, 2013; Cullen, Davey, Friston, & Moran, 2018; Sajid et al., 2021; Sutton & Barto, 1998). This encourages exploitative behavior such that policies are more likely if they help the agent solicit preferred outcomes. Maximizing intrinsic value promotes curious, information-seeking behavior as the agent seeks out salient latent states to minimize its uncertainty about the environment. This term underwrites artificial curiosity (Schmidhuber, 1991a; Schmidhuber, 2006), and for particular generative model parameterizations it can be further decomposed to include expected information gain about model parameters (i.e., novelty; Schwartenbeck et al., 2019). This particular decomposition of expected free energy speaks to the two aspects of goal-directed, information-seeking behavior.

6.3.1 *Optimal Bayesian Design and Expected Free Energy*

Optimal Bayesian design is concerned with maximizing information gain – that is, resolving uncertainty about the latent states that generated particular outcomes (Chaloner & Verdinelli, 1995;

Lindley, 1956; Pukelsheim, 2006; Stone, 1959). Therefore, maximizing intrinsic value or expected information gain – pertaining latent states or model parameters – has a direct correspondence to optimal Bayesian design principles. Thus, if we were to remove prior preferences about outcomes – the extrinsic value component of expected free energy (eq. 5; third equality) – active inference reduces to optimal Bayesian design:

$$
\begin{aligned}
E_{Q(o_\tau|\pi)}[\log P(o_\tau)] &= 0 \Rightarrow \\
G(\pi, \tau) &\geq - E_{Q(o_\tau|\pi)}[D_{KL}[Q(s_\tau|o_\tau,\pi)\|Q(s_\tau|\pi)]] \\
&= -D_{KL}[Q(s_\tau,o_\tau|\pi)\|Q(s_\tau|\pi)Q(o_\tau|\pi)] \\
&= -I(\pi)
\end{aligned}
\tag{6}
$$

This is mathematically equivalent to expected Bayesian surprise, and mutual information that underwrites salience in visual search (Itti & Baldi, 2009; Sun, Gomez, & Schmidhuber, 2011) and the deployment of our visual epithelia with saccadic eye movements (Barlow, 1961; Barlow, 1974; Linsker, 1990; Optican & Richmond, 1987).

Within optimal Bayesian design principles, policies are regarded as a consequence of observed outcomes. This enables policy selection to maximize the evidence for a generative model, under which policies maximize information gain. To further elucidate this connection to active inference, we first establish a free energy functional of the predictive distribution that furnishes an upper bound on the expected log evidence of future outcomes. From this, posterior over policies can be evaluated:

$$
\begin{aligned}
Q(\pi) &= \arg \min_Q F_\tau[Q(s_\tau,\pi)] \\
F_\tau &= E_Q[\log Q(s_\tau,\pi) - \log P(o_\tau,s_\tau)] \\
&= E_{Q(\pi)}[G(\pi, \tau) + \log Q(\pi)] \\
&= E_{Q(\pi)}[G(\pi, \tau)] - H[Q(\pi)] \\
&\Rightarrow -\log Q(\pi) = G(\pi, \tau)
\end{aligned}
\tag{7}
$$

This renders the posterior surprisal of a policy its expected free energy $G(\pi, \tau)$ (Da Costa, Parr, et al., 2020). Consequently, under prior beliefs that the log probability of a policy corresponds to information gain, the expected free energy of a policy provides an upper bound on the expected log evidence (i.e., marginal likelihood) over outcomes and policies. This can be shown by rearranging the expected free energy summands and introducing an expected evidence bound:

$$G(\pi, \tau) = E_{Q(o_\tau, s_\tau | \pi)}[\log Q(s_\tau | \pi) - \log P(o_\tau, s_\tau)]$$

$$= \underbrace{-E_{Q(o_\tau | \pi)}[D_{KL}[Q(s_\tau | o_\tau, \pi) || Q(s_\tau | \pi)]]}_{\text{Expected information gain}} - \underbrace{E_{Q(o_\tau)}[\log P(o_\tau)]}_{\text{Expected log evidence}}$$

$$+ \underbrace{E_{Q(o_\tau | \pi)}[D_{KL}[Q(s_\tau | o_\tau, \pi) || P(s_\tau | o_\tau)]]}_{\text{Expected evidence bound}}$$

$$\geq \underbrace{-E_{Q(o_\tau | \pi)}[\log P(\pi | o_\tau)]}_{\text{Expected information gain}} - \underbrace{E_{Q(o_\tau)}[\log P(o_\tau)]}_{\text{Expected log evidence}}$$

$$= \underbrace{-E_Q[\log P(o_\tau, \pi)]}_{\text{Expected marginal likelihood}}$$

$$(8)$$

where:

$$\log P(\pi | o_\tau) = \underbrace{D_{KL}[Q(s_\tau | o_\tau, \pi) || Q(s_\tau | \pi)]}_{\text{Information gain}}$$

In short, policies depend on the final outcomes, and are more likely when outcomes reduce uncertainty about latent states. That is, the expected free energy of a policy is an upper bound on the expected log evidence for a model that generates outcomes, and Bayes-optimal policies from those outcomes. Consequently, when the expected evidence bound is minimized, the predictive posterior becomes the posterior under the generative model.

6.3.2 *Bayesian Decision Theory and Expected Free Energy*

Bayesian decision theory – that is, Bayesian formulations of maximizing expected utility under uncertainty – is predicated on the optimization of some expected cost or utility function (Berger, 2011; Harsanyi, 1978; Savage, 1972). Therefore, maximizing the extrinsic value (or expected value) in relation to some prior beliefs under active inference has a direct correspondence to Bayesian decision theory. This can be derived in two ways. First, by removing the expected information gain from the expected free energy objective (eq. 5; third equality), active inference reduces to Bayesian decision theory:

$$E_{Q(o_\tau | \pi)}[D_{KL}[Q(s_\tau | o_\tau, \pi) || Q(s_\tau | \pi)]] = 0 \Rightarrow$$
$$G(\pi, \tau) \geq - E_{Q(o_\tau | \pi)}[\log P(o_\tau)]$$

$$(9)$$

Now, we are left with extrinsic value or expected utility in economics (Von Neumann & Morgenstern, 1944). This is mathematically equivalent to the (reward) objectives employed in reinforcement learning and behavioral psychology (Da Costa, Sajid, Parr, Friston, & Smith, 2020; Sajid et al., 2021; Sutton & Barto, 1998). Note that here the expected utility is formulated in terms of outcomes. Conversely, expected utility can also be derived in terms of latent states by removing ambiguity and the posterior entropy from the expected free energy objective (eq. 5):

$$E_{Q(s_\tau, o_\tau | \pi)}[\log Q(s_\tau | \pi) \underbrace{- \log P(o_\tau | s_\tau)}_{\text{Ambiguity}}] = 0 \Rightarrow$$
$$G(\pi, \tau) = -E_{Q(s_\tau | \pi)}[\log P(s_\tau)] \tag{10}$$

This reduced formulation entails the maximization of some utility function, expected under predictive posterior beliefs about the consequences of action, and:

$$E_Q[\log P(s_\tau)] \leq E_Q[\log P(o_\tau)] \tag{11}$$

This equivalence shows that maximizing expected utility under uncertainty can be defined as the optimization of some expected cost, either in terms of latent states or observed outcomes. By definition, both formulations should yield comparable behavior. However, by only maximizing the expected value, Bayesian decision theory is only optimal when specific conditions (those before the implications in Equations 9 or 10) are met. Specifically, from an active inference perspective, Bayes optimality is a direct consequence of making decisions that maximize the expected free energy, not expected utility.

6.4   Simulations

In the previous section, we saw that both Bayesian decision theory and optimal Bayesian design are special cases of minimizing expected free energy. Specifically, Bayesian decision theory is predicated on optimizing some expected cost, and optimal Bayesian design on maximizing information gain. In active inference, we directly optimize both these distinct objectives:

Active inference = Bayes decision theory + optimal Bayesian design   (12)

To illustrate how behavioral differences arise under these separable imperatives, we consider inference using simulations of foraging in a maze, where the agent selects the next action by optimizing the following: 1) expected utility, 2) expected information gain, or 3) expected free energy. For ease of exposition, we have purposely chosen a simple paradigm. More complex active inference simulations can be seen in narrative construction and reading (Friston et al., 2020; Friston, Rosch, Parr, Price, & Bowman, 2018), saccadic searches and scene construction (Mirza, Adams, Mathys, & Friston, 2016; Parr, 2019), 3D mazes (Fountas et al., 2020), etc.

First, we describe the maze foraging environment and the accompanying generative model from (Friston et al., 2017; Friston et al., 2015). We then present the simulation results of how behavior differs when removing different constituents of expected free energy.

6.4.1   Maze Foraging Environment

In this setup, a mouse starts at the center of the T-maze: it can either move directly to the right or left arms – which contain some cheese – or to the lower arm that contains cues about whether the cheese is in the upper right or left arm. The agent can only move twice and upon entering the upper right or left arms cannot leave – that is, these are absorbing states. Thus, the optimal behavior is to first go to the lower arm to find the reward location and then retrieve the reward. If the agent follows this path, it is given a performance score of +5 from the environment; if it goes directly to the correct cheese location it receives a score of +10 but failure to find the correct cheese location results in −10. These scores allow us to record the agent's performance and play no part in the agent's decision-making process: see Figure 6.1. Consequently, what the agent considers to be optimal (defined by its prior preferences over outcomes) may or may not coincide with a high "performance" score.

6.4.2   Generative Model of Maze Foraging

We define the generative model as follows: four control states that correspond to visiting the four locations (the center and three arms – we assume each control state takes the agent to the associated location), eight latent states (four locations factorized by two contexts), and seven possible outcomes. The outcomes correspond to being in the center, plus the (two) outcomes at each of the (three) arms that are determined by the context, namely whether the right or the left arm has the cheese. We define

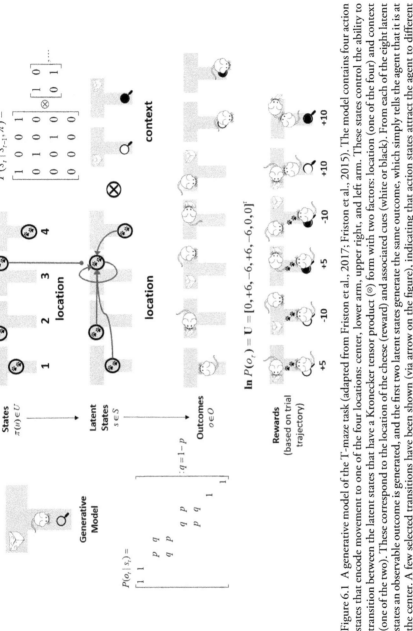

Figure 6.1 A generative model of the T-maze task (adapted from Friston et al., 2017; Friston et al., 2015). The model contains four action states that encode movement to one of the four locations: center, lower arm, upper right, and left arm. These states control the ability to transition between the latent states that have a Kronecker tensor product (⊗) form with two factors: location (one of the four) and context (one of the two). These correspond to the location of the cheese (reward) and associated cues (white or black). From each of the eight latent states an observable outcome is generated, and the first two latent states generate the same outcome, which simply tells the agent that it is at the center. A few selected transitions have been shown (via arrow on the figure), indicating that action states attract the agent to different locations, where outcomes are sampled. Categorical parameters that define the generative model – A (latent states to outcomes) and B (state transitions) – have been explicitly included. Additionally, $ln\ P(o)$ corresponds to prior preferences. A preference of 6 or –6 is allocated to the correct or incorrect cheese location, respectively (with preferences of 0 otherwise). These values relate to the unnormalized log

the likelihood, $P(o_\tau | s_\tau)$, such that the ambiguous cue is at the center (first) location and a definitive cue at the lower (fourth) location (see Figure 6.1). The remaining locations provide a reward with probability $p = 98\%$ determined by the context. The transition probabilities, $P(s_\tau | s_{\tau-1}, \pi)$, encode how the mouse might move, except for the second and third locations, which are absorbing latent states that it cannot leave. We define the mouse as having precise beliefs about all contingencies, except the current context. Each context is equally probable. Additionally, we remove the agent's capacity to learn these contingencies based on interactions with the environment. In other words, historic trials have no bearing on the current trial. The utility of the outcomes is 6 and −6 for identifying the correct and incorrect cheese location, respectively (and 0 otherwise). Having specified the state-space and contingencies, we can perform gradient descent on the free energy functionals to simulate behavior. Relative prior beliefs about the initial state were initialized to 128 for the central location for each context and 0 otherwise.

6.4.3   Simulations of Maze Foraging

To illustrate the relationship between planning and behavior under active inference, optimal Bayesian design, and Bayesian decision theory, we simulated three agents performing the maze foraging task. The active inference agent optimized expected free energy, the optimal Bayesian design optimized expected information gain, and the Bayesian decision theory optimized expected utility. Each simulation comprised fifty trials, with shifting context, namely occasionally moving the cheese from the right to the left arm. The context, indicated by the (black or white) cue in the lower arm, was white until trial 9, black from trial 10 to 12, white again from trial 13 to 29, and black again at trial 30. After trial 30, it remained white until the end of the simulation. These switches allowed us to evaluate behavioral shifts from information-seeking to goal-directed policies. Everything else was kept constant, including the initial conditions. Belief updating and behavior were simulated using the variational message passing scheme implemented in SPM::spm_MDP_VB_X.m.[2]

During the first trial, we observe marked differences in behavior (Figure 6.2; action selection). Unsurprisingly, the active inference agent can trade-off between information-seeking (i.e., go to the cue at epoch 2) and extrinsic value (i.e., go to the left arm to collect the cheese at epoch 3).

[2] www.fil.ion.ucl.ac.uk/spm/.

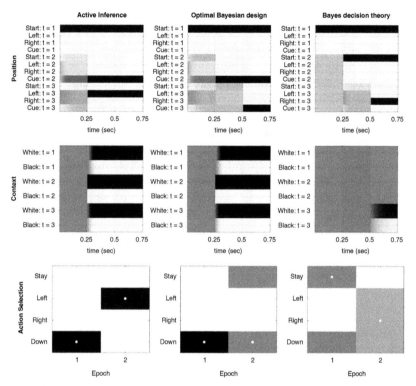

Figure 6.2   Belief updating and action selection. The graphics present the belief updates and action selection for the first simulated trial. The first two rows report belief updating over three epochs of a single trial, for the latent states position and context. The bottom row presents the actions selected during the same trial. Each column represents a simulated agent: active inference, optimal Bayesian design, and Bayesian decision theory. Here, white is an expected probability of zero, black of one, and gray indicates gradations between these. For the belief updating figures, the x-axis represents time in seconds (divided into 3 epochs), and the y-axis represents posterior expectations about each of the associated states at different epochs (in the past or future). For example, for the position latent state (first row), there are 4 states (start, left, right, and cue), and a total of 4 x 3 (states times epochs) posterior expectations; similarly, for the context latent state (second row), there are 2 levels, and a total of 2 x 3 expectations. For example, the first four rows for the position belief updates correspond to expectations about the agent's position, in terms of the four alternatives for the first epoch. The second four rows are the equivalent expectations for the second epoch, and so on. This means that at the beginning of the trial the second four rows report beliefs about the future: namely, the next epoch. However, later in time, these beliefs refer to the past, i.e., beliefs currently held about the first epoch. Note that most beliefs persist through time (along the x-axis), endowing the agents with a form of working memory that is both predictive and postdictive. In the action selection panels, the x-axis represents the 2 epochs, and the y-axis represents the four allowable actions with their posterior expectations at each epoch: stay center, go down, turn left, or right. In each graphic, the action with the circle marker indicates the selected action.

Conversely, the optimal Bayesian design agent exhibits purely information maximizing behavior, going to the cue at epoch 2, and then remaining there till the end of the trial. This follows directly from resolving its uncertainty about the trial context, as there is no further information to be gained: anecdotally, the agent gets bored and does nothing after exploring its environment. This behavior can be regarded as Bayes-optimal: when given uniform prior preferences, purely epistemic, information-seeking behavior is the only appropriate way to forage the maze. The Bayesian decision theory agent follows a different strategy: it remains in the central location till epoch 2, after which it goes to the right arm (i.e., the arm without the cheese). This is expected since the agent does not care about the information inferred and is indifferent about going to the cue location or remaining at the central location.

Predictably, these behavioral differences influence both the position and context latent state estimations (Figure 6.2; position and context). As the agents select different actions to navigate the maze, their location estimates differ along with their beliefs about the current context. The active inference agent estimates its location to be in the left arm at epoch 3 and can accurately infer that the current context is white. On the other hand, the Bayesian decision theory agent infers itself to be at the right arm at epoch 3. This inference is underwritten by the fact that it collects a reward, which also has epistemic value. Whilst the optimal Bayesian design agent believes itself, correctly, to be in the lower arm at epoch 3, having resolved its uncertainty about the current states of affairs.

Subsequent trials reveal comparable behavior (Figure 6.3; policy selection). The active inference agent pursues an epistemic policy throughout the fifty trials: first, go to the cue and then the cheese location. This is entirely appropriate since at the start of each trial the agent does not know where the cheese is located and the only way to resolve its uncertainty is to go to the cue location. This is the only agent that consistently selects information-seeking, goal-directed policies, as reflected by the high accumulated score (Figure 6.3; score).

In contrast, the Bayesian decision theory agent (i.e., maximizing expected utility), entertains all sorts of policies. However, the pattern is consistent. First, it chooses between remaining at the central location or going to the cue location with equal probability. If the agent goes to the cue location, then the only plausible action chosen is to go to the left arm. Instead, if it decides to remain at the central location, it can decide to go to the left, right, or lower arm. This is because it is unable to resolve uncertainty about the current context.

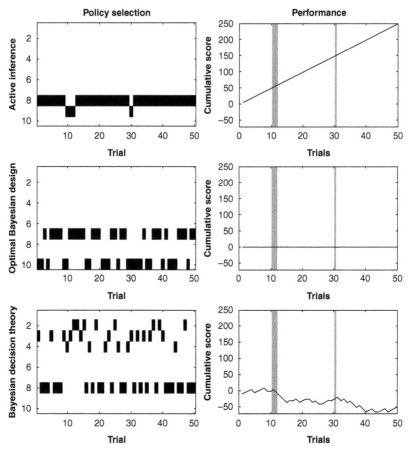

Figure 6.3 Policy selection and performance. The graphics report the selected policies, accumulated score, and optimization trajectory during the fifty simulated trials. The first column reports the conditional expectations over policies for each agent (the corresponding rows); the second column reports the accumulated score evaluated using the scoring presented in Figure 6.1. For the policy selection panels on the left, the x-axis represents trials, and the y-axis represents the final posterior expectations about the ten policies across the fifty trials. The ten policies are: 1 – continue to stay at the starting location, 2 – stay at the center and then to go the left arm, 3 – stay at the center and then to go the right arm, 4 – stay at the center and then to go the lower arm, 5 – go to the left arm and stay, 6 – go the right arm and stay; 7 – go to the cue and then back to the center, 8 – go to the cue and then left arm, 9 – go to the cue and then right arm and 10 – go to the cue and stay. Here, white is an expected probability of zero, black of one, and gray indicates gradations between these. For the score panels on the right, the x-axis represents trials, and the y-axis represents the cumulative score. The gray rectangles denote a black context, while their absence reflects a white context.

The optimal Bayesian design agent selects information-seeking policies, but, unsurprisingly, does not prefer to end the trial by going to either the left or right arm. Instead, it chooses to remain at the cue location or go to the central location again. This intrinsically motivated behavior is reflected in the low accumulated score (Figure 6.3; score). None of the agents selected the exploitative policies – that is, go to either the left or right arm at epoch 2 and stay there. This is due to the uncertainty about which latent states generated the particular observations, namely an inability to *learn* the context, which would be appropriate if the cheese were located randomly for every trial.

6.5   Concluding Remarks

Active inference scores the consequences of action in terms of the expected free energy that can be decomposed into two parts. The first part corresponds to the information gain that underwrites optimal Bayesian design. Thus, by removing any prior preferences over observations from the expected free energy, we are left with optimal Bayesian design imperatives – namely, minimizing uncertainty about states of affairs. This can be operationalized as maximum entropy sampling (Mitchell, Sacks, & Ylvisaker, 1994; Sacks, Welch, Mitchell, & Wynn, 1989; Shewry & Wynn, 1987), augmented with ambiguity aversion. The second part encodes expected model evidence – or marginal likelihood – that can be associated with an expected utility in Bayesian decision theory. Consequently, active inference subsumes Bayesian decision theory and optimal Bayesian design. Notably, expected free energy can be further decomposed to derive other special cases, including maximum entropy principle (Jaynes, 1957), Occam's principle, etc. (Friston et al., 2020). This speaks to the potentially ubiquitous nature of active inference as realizing a large class of sentient systems that self-organize themselves to some nonequilibrium steady-state (Friston, 2019; Parr et al., 2020). This means that a certain class of systems at steady-state will appear to operate Bayes-optimally – both in terms of optimal Bayesian design (i.e., information-seeking or explorative behavior) and Bayesian decision theory (goal-directed or exploitative behavior) (Da Costa, Parr, et al., 2020).

This way of characterizing active inference, and the expected free energy, speaks to a natural emergence of epistemic behavior. Information-seeking means that the agent seeks out states that afford observations, which minimize uncertainty about latent states. The maze foraging simulations highlight this property of active inference. Due to uncertainty about the context, and causes of observed outcomes, the agent engages in exploratory behavior. This curiosity is manifest by choosing policies that first lead to the lower arm to disclose the cue, which allowed the agent to determine the cheese location. In other words, the agent first engages in exploratory, epistemic foraging and then exploits its beliefs about states of affairs. Note that even though the cheese is left in the same place for several trials, the agent sticks to its preferred policy, since we do not equip it with the ability to learn that the context can persist over several trials. In the absence of uncertainty, the agent would choose exploitative policies (forego its epistemic foraging; Friston et al., 2017; Schwartenbeck et al., 2019).

Accordingly, implementations of active inference depend entirely on the generative model – for example, the inclusion of particular priors, different hierarchical levels, etc. (Friston, Parr, & de Vries, 2017). Specifically, if one were to remove particular priors over the generative model, different types of behavior would emerge. For example, when no preferred state has been specified, active inference reduces to optimal Bayesian design principles. In contrast, when the distribution over preferred states is a point mass, active inference reduces to expected utility theory (Da Costa, Sajid, et al., 2020). This leads to suboptimal behavioral convergence by constraining agent interaction to specific parts of the environment (Tschantz et al., 2020). In the same spirit, one could also complexify the generative model with additional parameters that could be inferred. This could introduce a shift in the balance between intrinsic and extrinsic value. For example, depending on the context, or the environment, prior preferences could be emphasized by increasing their precision (Da Costa, Parr, et al., 2020).

Conversely, in the reinforcement learning literature, different types of information-seeking behaviors have been engineered by supplementing objective functions or aspects of the implicit model. In contrast to active inference, these augmented reinforcement learning schemes try to maximize the agent's surprise (i.e., inability to predict the future). In temporal difference learning, this is often achieved by encouraging exploration through $P(s_\tau | s_{\tau-1}, \pi)$-greedy policies, where actions are random with probability $1 - \varepsilon$ (i.e., random exploration). This reduces the probability of policy learning falling into local minima (Sutton & Barto, 1998). Other approaches focus on intrinsic motivation or curiosity rewards, and augment the objective function with entropy terms, thereby encouraging more entropic policies (A. G. Barto, 2013; Bellemare et al., 2016; Burda, Edwards, Storkey, & Klimov, 2018; Pathak, Agrawal, Efros, & Darrell, 2017; Schmidhuber, 1991a, 1991b). This encourages policies that increase information gain by exploring unpredictable states. Popular Bayesian reinforcement learning schemes – for inducing information-seeking behavior – include upper confidence bounds (UCB), optimistic Bayesian sampling and Thompson sampling, and variational inference approaches such as **v**ariational **i**nformation **m**aximization **e**xploration (VIME) and **vari**ational **B**ayes-**A**daptive **D**eep RL (variBAD) (Auer, 2002; Houthooft et al., 2016; Russo, Van Roy, Kazerouni, Osband, & Wen, 2017; Schulz & Gershman, 2019; Zintgraf et al., 2019). These variational approaches are perhaps closest to active inference in the way they are set up. However, differences arise in how actions are selected: for example, VIME selects future actions by minimizing the entropy of beliefs about transition probabilities (Houthooft et al., 2016). The VIME scheme assumes an observable MDP and therefore ignores an important source of uncertainty in relation to minimizing the expected free energy in active inference. Finally, note that reward maximizing schemes are a special case of active inference (Da Costa, Sajid, et al., 2020), when certain sources of uncertainty are ignored. In other words, in the absence of risk and ambiguity, the principle of least action – which underwrites active inference – reduces to the Bellman optimality principle (Friston et al., 2016).

In this chapter, we have discussed the natural emergence of information-seeking behavior under active inference. How this may be realized in sentient creatures remains an open, and interesting, research area (Gottlieb, Oudeyer, Lopes, & Baranes, 2013). For example, humans employ a combination of epistemic and extrinsic value policies when engaging with their environment, but their information-seeking behavior can be modified by changes in temporal resolution (Vasconcelos, Monteiro, & Kacelnik, 2015), and/or temporal horizon (Wilson, Geana, White, Ludvig, & Cohen, 2014). This suggests that future work should consider which structural or parametric aspects of generative models (Vértes & Sahani, 2018) best account for individual differences in information-seeking behavior.

Acknowledgments

NS is funded by Medical Research Council (MR/S502522/1). LD is supported by the Fonds National de la Recherche, Luxembourg (Project code: 13568875). KJF is funded by the Wellcome Trust (Ref: 088130/Z/09/Z).

References

Attias, H. (2003). *Planning by Probabilistic Inference*. Paper presented at the Proc. of the 9th Int. Workshop on Artificial Intelligence and Statistics. https://pro ceedings.mlr.press/r4/attias03a.html.

Auer, P. (2002). Using confidence bounds for exploitation-exploration trade-offs. *Journal of Machine Learning Research*, 3(Nov.), 397–422.

Barlow, H. (1961). Possible principles underlying the transformations of sensory messages. In W. Rosenblith (Ed.), *Sensory Communication* (pp. 217–234). MIT Press.

Barlow, H. B. (1974). Inductive inference, coding, perception, and language. *Perception*, 3, 123–134.

Barto, A. G. (2013). Intrinsic motivation and reinforcement learning. In G. Baldassarre & M. Mirolli, *Intrinsically motivated learning in natural and artificial systems* (pp. 17–47). Springer.

Barto, A., Mirolli, M., & Baldassarre, G. (2013). Novelty or Surprise? *Frontiers in Psychology*, 4. doi:10.3389/fpsyg.2013.00907. Retrieved from www .frontiersin.org/Journal/Abstract.aspx?s=196&name=cognitive_science&AR T_DOI=10.3389/fpsyg.2013.00907.

Beal, M. J. (2003). *Variational Algorithms for Approximate Bayesian Inference*. PhD. Thesis, University College London. www.proquest.com/docview/17752 15626?pq-origsite=gscholar&fromopenview=true.

Bellemare, M. G., Srinivasan, S., Ostrovski, G., Schaul, T., Saxton, D., & Munos, R. (2016). Unifying count-based exploration and intrinsic motivation. *arXiv preprint arXiv:1606.01868*.

Berger, J. O. (2011). *Statistical decision theory and Bayesian analysis*. Springer.

Blei, D. M., Kucukelbir, A., & McAuliffe, J. D. (2017). Variational inference: A review for statisticians. *Journal of the American Statistical Association*, 112 (518), 859–877.

Botvinick, M., & Toussaint, M. (2012). Planning as inference. *Trends in Cognitive Science.*, 16(10), 485–488.

Burda, Y., Edwards, H., Storkey, A., & Klimov, O. (2018). Exploration by random network distillation. *arXiv preprint arXiv:1810.12894*.

Çatal, O., Wauthier, S., Verbelen, T., De Boom, C., & Dhoedt, B. (2020). Deep active inference for autonomous robot navigation. *arXiv preprint arXiv:2003.03220*.

Chaloner, K., & Verdinelli, I. (1995). Bayesian experimental design: A review. *Statistical Science*, 273–304.

Cullen, M., Davey, B., Friston, K. J., & Moran, R. J. (2018). Active inference in OpenAI gym: A paradigm for computational investigations into psychiatric illness. *Biological Psychiatry: Cognitive Neuroscience and Neuroimaging*, 3(9), 809–818.

Da Costa, L., Parr, T., Sajid, N., Veselic, S., Neacsu, V., & Friston, K. (2020). Active inference on discrete state-spaces: A synthesis. *Journal of Mathematical*

Psychology, 99, 102447. Retrieved from www.sciencedirect.com/science/article/pii/S0022249620300857.

Da Costa, L., Sajid, N., Parr, T., Friston, K., & Smith, R. (2020). The relationship between dynamic programming and active inference: The discrete, finite-horizon case. *arXiv preprint arXiv:2009.08111.*

Fleming, W. H., & Sheu, S. J. (2002). Risk-sensitive control and an optimal investment model II. *Annals of Applied Probability*, 12(2), 730–767. Retrieved from https://projecteuclid.org:443/euclid.aoap/1026915623.

Fountas, Z., Sajid, N., Mediano, P. A., & Friston, K. (2020). Deep active inference agents using Monte-Carlo methods. *arXiv preprint arXiv:2006.04176.*

Friston, K. J. (2010). The free-energy principle: A unified brain theory? *Nature Reviews Neuroscience*, 11(2), 127–138. http://dx.doi.org/10.1038/nrn2787.

Friston, K. (2019). A free energy principle for a particular physics. *arXiv preprint arXiv:1906.10184.*

Friston, K., Da Costa, L., Hafner, D., Hesp, C., & Parr, T. (2020). Sophisticated inference. *arXiv preprint arXiv:2006.04120.*

Friston, K. J., Daunizeau, J., Kilner, J., & Kiebel, S. J. (2010). Action and behavior: A free-energy formulation. *Biological Cybernetics*, 102(3), 227–260.

Friston, K., FitzGerald, T., Rigoli, F., Schwartenbeck, P., O'Doherty, J., & Pezzulo, G. (2016). Active inference and learning. *Neuroscience and Biobehavioral Reviews*, 68, 862–879. Retrieved from http://www.ncbi.nlm.nih.gov/pubmed/27375276.

Friston, K., FitzGerald, T., Rigoli, F., Schwartenbeck, P., & Pezzulo, G. (2017). Active inference: A process theory. *Neural Computation*, 29(1), 1–49. Retrieved from https://www.ncbi.nlm.nih.gov/pubmed/27870614.

Friston, K. J., Lin, M., Frith, C. D., Pezzulo, G., Hobson, J. A., & Ondobaka, S. (2017). Active inference, curiosity and insight. *Neural Computation*, 29(10), 2633–2683. Friston, K. J., Parr, T., & de Vries, B. (2017). The graphical brain: Belief propagation and active inference. *Network Neuroscience*, 1(4), 381–414. Retrieved from http://www.ncbi.nlm.nih.gov/pubmed/29417960.

Friston, K. J., Parr, T., Yufik, Y., Sajid, N., Price, C. J., & Holmes, E. (2020). Generative models, linguistic communication and active inference. *Neuroscience & Biobehavioral Reviews*, 118, 42–64. https://doi.org/10.1016/j.neubiorev.2020.07.005.

Friston, K. J., Rigoli, F., Ognibene, D., Mathys, C., Fitzgerald, T., & Pezzulo, G. (2015). Active inference and epistemic value. *Cognitive Neuroscience*, 6(4), 187–224. Retrieved from http://dx.doi.org/10.1080/17588928.2015.1020053.

Friston, K. J., Rosch, R., Parr, T., Price, C., & Bowman, H. (2018). Deep temporal models and active inference. *Neuroscience and Biobehavioral Reviews*, 90, 486–501.

Friston, K., Schwartenbeck, P., FitzGerald, T., Moutoussis, M., Behrens, T., & Dolan, R. J. (2014). The anatomy of choice: dopamine and decision-making.

Philosophical Transactions of the Royal Society B: Biological Sciences, 369 (1655). Retrieved from http://www.ncbi.nlm.nih.gov/pubmed/25267823.

Gottlieb, J., Oudeyer, P.-Y., Lopes, M., & Baranes, A. (2013). Information-seeking, curiosity, and attention: computational and neural mechanisms. *Trends in Cognitive Science*, 17(11), 585–593. Retrieved from https://www.sciencedirect.com/science/article/pii/S1364661313002052.

Harsanyi, J. C. (1978). Bayesian decision theory and utilitarian ethics. *The American Economic Review*, 68(2), 223–228. Retrieved from www.jstor.org/stable/1816692.

Houthooft, R., Chen, X., Duan, Y., Schulman, J., De Turck, F., & Abbeel, P. (2016). Vime: Variational information maximizing exploration. *Advances in Neural Information Processing Systems*, 29, 1109–1117.

Itti, L., & Baldi, P. (2009). Bayesian surprise attracts human attention. *Vision Research*, 49(10), 1295–1306.

Jaynes, E. T. (1957). Information theory and statistical mechanics. *Physical Review*, 106(4), 620.

Kahneman, D., & Tversky, A. (1979). Prospect theory: An analysis of decision under risk. *Econometrica*, 47(2), 263–291.

Kaplan, R., & Friston, K. J. (2018). Planning and navigation as active inference. *Biological Cybernetics*, 112(4), 323–343.

Laureiro-Martínez, D., Brusoni, S., & Zollo, M. (2010). The neuroscientific foundations of the exploration–exploitation dilemma. *Journal of Neuroscience, Psychology, and Economics*, 3(2), 95.

Lindley, D. V. (1956). On a measure of the information provided by an experiment. *The Annals of Mathematical Statistics*, 986–1005.

Linsker, R. (1990). Perceptual neural organization: some approaches based on network models and information theory. *Annual Review of Neuroscience*, 13, 257–281.

Millidge, B., Tschantz, A., & Buckley, C. L. (2020). Whence the expected free energy? *arXiv preprint arXiv:2004.08128*.

Mirza, M. B., Adams, R. A., Mathys, C. D., & Friston, K. J. (2016). Scene construction, visual foraging, and active inference. *Frontiers in Computational Neuroscience*, 10 (56). Retrieved from http://journal.frontiersin.org/Article/10.3389/fncom.2016.00056/abstract. Mitchell, T., Sacks, J., & Ylvisaker, D. (1994). Asymptotic Bayes criteria for nonparametric response surface design. *The Annals of Statistics*, 22(2), 634–651.

Optican, L., & Richmond, B. J. (1987). Temporal encoding of two-dimensional patterns by single units in primate inferior cortex. II Information theoretic analysis. *Journal of Neurophysiology*, 57, 132–146.

Parr, T. (2019). The computational neurology of active vision. UCL (Unpublished doctoral thesis, University College London). https://discovery.ucl.ac.uk/id/eprint/10084391/

Parr, T., Da Costa, L., & Friston, K. (2020). Markov blankets, information geometry and stochastic thermodynamics. *Philosophical Transactions of the Royal Society A*, 378(2164), 20190159.

Parr, T., & Friston, K. J. (2019a). Attention or salience? *Current Opinion in Psychology*, 29, 1–5.

Parr, T., & Friston, K. J. (2019b). Generalised free energy and active inference. *Biological Cybernetics*, 113(5–6), 495–513.

Parr, T., Markovic, D., Kiebel, S. J., & Friston, K. J. (2019). Neuronal message passing using Mean-field, Bethe, and Marginal approximations. *Scientific Reports*, 9(1), 1889. Retrieved from https://doi.org/10.1038/s415 98-018-38246-3.

Pathak, D., Agrawal, P., Efros, A. A., & Darrell, T. (2017). *Curiosity-driven exploration by self-supervised prediction.* Paper presented at the International Conference on Machine Learning.

Pukelsheim, F. (2006). *Optimal design of experiments*: SIAM.

Russo, D., Van Roy, B., Kazerouni, A., Osband, I., & Wen, Z. (2017). A tutorial on Thompson sampling. *arXiv preprint arXiv:1707.02038*.

Sacks, J., Welch, W. J., Mitchell, T. J., & Wynn, H. P. (1989). Design and analysis of computer experiments. *Statistical Science*, 4(4), 409–423.

Sajid, N., Ball, P. J., Parr, T., & Friston, K. J. (2021). Active inference: Demystified and compared. *Neural Computation*, 33(3), 674–712.

Savage, L. J. (1972). *The foundations of statistics*: Courier Corporation.

Schmidhuber, J. (1991a). Curious model-building control systems. In *Proc. International Joint Conference on Neural Networks, Singapore. IEEE*, 2, 1458–1463. https://mediatum.ub.tum.de/doc/814953/file.pdf.

Schmidhuber, J. (1991b). *A possibility for implementing curiosity and boredom in model-building neural controllers.* Paper presented at the Proc. of the international conference on simulation of adaptive behavior: From animals to animats. https://mediatum.ub.tum.de/doc/814958/file.pdf

Schmidhuber, J. (2006). Developmental robotics, optimal artificial curiosity, creativity, music, and the fine arts. *Connection Science*, 18(2), 173–187. https://doi.org/10.1080/09540090600768658.

Schulz, E., & Gershman, S. J. (2019). The algorithmic architecture of exploration in the human brain. *Current Opinion in Neurobiology*, 55, 7–14.

Schwartenbeck, P., Passecker, J., Hauser, T. U., FitzGerald, T. H., Kronbichler, M., & Friston, K. J. (2019). Computational mechanisms of curiosity and goal-directed exploration. *eLife*, 8, e.41707. https://doi.org/10 .7554/eLife.41703.

Shewry, M. C., & Wynn, H. P. (1987). Maximum entropy sampling. *Journal of Applied Statistics*, 14(2), 165–170.

Stone, M. (1959). Application of a measure of information to the design and comparison of regression experiments. *The Annals of Mathematical Statistics*, 30 (1), 55–70.

Sun, Y., Gomez, F., & Schmidhuber, J. (2011). Planning to be surprised: Optimal Bayesian exploration in dynamic environments. In J. Schmidhuber, K. R. Thórisson, & M. Looks (Eds.), *Artificial General Intelligence: 4th International Conference, AGI 2011, Mountain View, CA, USA, August 3–6,2011. Proceedings* (pp. 41–51). Springer.

Sutton, R. S., & Barto, A. G. (1998). *Introduction to Reinforcement Learning*. MIT Press.

Todorov, E. (2008). *General duality between optimal control and estimation*. In *2008 47th IEEE Conference on Decision and Control* (pp. 4286–4292). IEEE.

Tschantz, A., Seth, A. K., & Buckley, C. L. (2020). Learning action-oriented models through active inference. *PLoS Computational Biology*, 16(4), e1007805. Retrieved from https://doi.org/10.1371/journal.pcbi.1007805.

van den Broek, J. L., Wiegerinck, W. A. J. J., & Kappen, H. J. (2010). Risk-sensitive path integral control. *UAI*, 6, 1–8.

van der Himst, O., & Lanillos, P. (2020). *Deep Active Inference for Partially Observable MDPs*. In *International Workshop on Active Inference* (pp. 61–71). Springer.

Vasconcelos, M., Monteiro, T., & Kacelnik, A. (2015). Irrational choice and the value of information. *Scientific Reports*, 5(1), 13874. Retrieved from https://doi.org/10.1038/srep13874.

Vértes, E., & Sahani, M. (2018). Flexible and accurate inference and learning for deep generative models. *arXiv preprint arXiv:1805.11051*.

Von Neumann, J., & Morgenstern, O. (1944). *Theory of games and economic behavior*. Princeton University Press.

Wilson, R. C., Geana, A., White, J. M., Ludvig, E. A., & Cohen, J. D. (2014). Humans use directed and random exploration to solve the explore–exploit dilemma. *Journal of Experimental Psychology: General*, 143(6), 2074.

Zintgraf, L., Shiarlis, K., Igl, M., Schulze, S., Gal, Y., Hofmann, K., & Whiteson, S. (2019). VariBAD: A very good method for Bayes-adaptive deep RL via meta-learning. *arXiv preprint arXiv:1910.08348*.

CHAPTER 7

Exploration Beyond Bandits

Franziska Brändle, Marcel Binz, and Eric Schulz

7.1 Introduction

Reinforcement learning is the study of how an agent – be it human, animal, or a machine – can learn to choose actions that maximize rewards (Sutton & Barto, 2018). To maximize long-term rewards, the agent must seek out information about the environment, even if it comes at the cost of temporarily missing out on more rewarding actions. How to strike the balance between maximizing immediate and long-term rewards is referred to as the *exploration–exploitation dilemma* (Cohen et al., 2007). On the one hand, the agent should focus on gaining as many rewards as currently possible. The maximization of rewards given the agent's current knowledge is called exploitation. On the other hand, the agent should search for further information to increase their knowledge, which could help to generate more rewards later on. The search for information in the context of reinforcement learning is called exploration.

How intelligent organisms explore has been predominantly studied in multiarmed bandit tasks (Krebs et al., 1978; Mehlhorn et al., 2015), although other paradigms have also been investigated (Hills et al., 2015). The term "multiarmed bandit" stems from a colorful casino metaphor, in which the agent interacts with a row of slot machines, each associated with an unknown reward distribution. It is the agent's goal to maximize rewards by repeatedly sampling arms and collecting the resulting rewards. Ideal agents should explore by combining the immediate reward and the value of information for each action by thinking through future actions and calculating how much rewards would increase if more knowledge about the reward distributions is collected. However, such optimal exploration strategies are wildly intractable beyond a few special cases (Whittle, 1980). This is because the value of information depends on how information affects choices later on, which may also lead to new information, creating a scenario in which the complexity of planning increases as an exponential function of the agent's planning horizon.

Because optimal solutions to the exploration–exploitation dilemma are computationally intractable, humans, as well as other intelligent agents, must employ heuristics. Research on human exploration strategies has centered around two such heuristics (Gershman, 2018; Schulz & Gershman, 2019; Wilson et al., 2021). The first heuristic is to engage in *directed exploration*: seeking out options that are highly informative about the underlying reward distribution. Directed exploration can, for example, be implemented by adding an information bonus to the estimates of expected reward (Auer, 2002). This bonus will then encourage the agent to explore arms with high uncertainty. The second heuristic is *random exploration*: injecting stochasticity into one's sampling behavior. One widely adopted instantiation of random exploration applies a fixed source of stochasticity without caring about arms' uncertainty (Daw et al., 2006). More sophisticated random exploration strategies, however, are uncertainty-guided and sample options relative to their probability of being optimal (Thompson, 1933). This approach may be viewed as a form of hypothesis testing, where the agent keeps track of multiple hypotheses and acts at each point in time as if a particular hypothesis was true.

We argue that the repertoire of human exploration strategies has itself not been well explored. We believe that there are two reasons for this, opening up two paths toward extending current theories. The first one is that studies on human exploration have almost exclusively focused on multiarmed bandit tasks. However, multiarmed bandits only constitute a small part of the problems that people typically encounter. In particular, bandits do not include a mechanism to control the state of one's environment, yet this very mechanism is omnipresent in everyday exploration scenarios. For example, imagine that you want to navigate from location *A* to location *B*. To be successful at this task, you certainly need to know where – that is, in which state of the world – you are right now. Likewise, if you want to cook a particular meal, let us say a stew, it might be a good idea to know what is already in the pot – that is, you need to be aware of its state. We believe, therefore, that extending studies on human exploration to more complex paradigms can bring scientific experiments closer to the real world. To this end, we suggest that future work should move toward exploration problems that can be modeled as Markov Decision Processes (MDPs), in which an agent can control the state of the environment. The second reason is that past studies have focused almost exclusively on the two exploration strategies of random and directed exploration.

However, people can engage in exploratory behaviors that cannot easily be captured by these two simple mechanisms: for example, when children are freely exploring how to build block towers, or when scientists explore theories to create better explanations of the observed data. Thus, we propose studying more sophisticated algorithms of exploration, such as empowerment and goal-conditioned exploration, in terms of their ability to describe human behavior. Importantly, many of these strategies cannot be expressed within multiarmed bandit problems, but require the more expressive setting offered by MDPs.

This chapter is divided into three sections. In the first section, we review a subset of past studies on human exploration in multiarmed bandit tasks, with a particular focus on random and directed exploration. In the second section, we describe the shortcomings of multiarmed bandits and argue that we need to move toward more expressive tasks (i.e. MDPs) to understand the full breadth of human exploration. In this part, we outline the challenges that arise when extending random and directed exploration strategies to MDPs and discuss several new exploration strategies that can be studied in MDPs. In the final section, we speculate about novel paradigms to chart a path toward studying exploration beyond bandits.

7.2   Prior Work on Multiarmed Bandits

Given its notorious difficulty, how do people actually cope with the exploration–exploitation dilemma? As previously mentioned, past studies on human exploration have mostly focused on the multiarmed bandit case, in which participants can sample between different options to maximize monetary rewards. We review a subset of these studies and summarize the main results in Table 7.1.

In a simple variant of multiarmed bandit tasks, the reward distributions are stationary and independent of each other. In this setting, Steyvers et al. (2009) analyzed the data of 451 participants. Their results showed that, rather than following an optimal exploration strategy, people largely applied simple heuristics. Zhang and Yu (2013) also used a stationary bandit task to compare human behavior with models of different degrees of sophistication, including the optimal exploration strategy. Their results showed that a nonoptimal but "forgetful" Bayesian iterative learning model described human behavior best. Thus, people seem to follow heuristic strategies of exploration, even in simple bandit tasks.

As mentioned earlier, two of the most frequently studied exploration strategies are random and directed exploration, which use the uncertainty

Table 7.1 *Overview of past studies on human exploration the multiarmed bandit setting*

Paper	Bandit Type	Optimal	Uncertainty	Directed	Random
Steyvers et al. (2009)	Simple	✗	?	?	?
Zhang and Yu (2013)	Simple	✗	✓	✓	?
Gershman (2018)	Simple	?	✓	✓	✓
Binz and Endres (2019)	Simple	✗	✓	✓	✓
Wilson et al. (2014)	Simple	?	?	✓	✓
Daw et al. (2006)	Restless	?	✗	✗	✓
Speekenbrink and Konstantinidis (2015)	Restless	?	✓	✗	✓
Wimmer et al. (2012)	Correlated	?	?	?	✓
Borji and Itti (2013)	Correlated	?	✓	✓	?
Wu et al. (2017, 2018, 2020)	Correlated	?	✓	✓	✓
Stojić et al. (2015, 2020)	Contextual	?	✓	✓	✓
Frank et al. (2009)	Contextual	?	✓	✓	?

Crosses (✗) mark the absence of empirical evidence for a particular exploration strategy. Check marks (✓) indicate that evidence for a particular exploration strategy was obtained by a study. Gray question marks (?) indicate that a particular exploration strategy was not investigated.

of the arms' rewards to guide exploration. Whereas directed exploration applies an information bonus to seek out options with higher uncertainty, random exploration predicts that choice stochasticity increases with higher uncertainty across all arms. Gershman (2018) tested these predictions in a stationary two-armed bandit task. In his task, rewards were generated from a Gaussian distribution with a fixed mean and standard deviation. This allowed for the manipulation of the total and relative uncertainty of the two arms by increasing the variance of either both or only one of the arms. The results of these experiments showed that participants applied a mix of both random and directed exploration. Binz and Endres (2019) demonstrated that participants exhibit individual differences in how they explore in the same two-armed bandit task, and that traces of both random and directed exploration can emerge from optimal reasoning under limited computational resources. In the canonical "Horizon task," Wilson et al. (2014) manipulated the number of samples participants could draw from a two-armed stationary bandit on each round. The results of these experiments showed that participants increased their exploration in the long-horizon condition and applied both directed as well as random exploration strategies. Together, these studies indicate that participants seem to rely on a mix of both random and directed exploration in simple, stationary multiarmed bandit tasks.

All bandit tasks described so far involved a stationary distribution of rewards. However, in plenty of real-life scenarios the reward distribution can change over time: for example, if your favorite restaurant is continuously decreasing in terms of quality. Researchers have therefore looked at human behavior in another class of paradigms called "restless bandits." In these paradigms, the mean of an arm's reward distribution changes during the experiment. Daw et al. (2006) investigated the underlying strategies and cortical substrates of exploration in a restless bandit task. In their task, participants had to choose one of four arms whose expected values changed over time, following a decaying Gaussian random walk. They found no evidence for directed or uncertainty-guided, random exploration. In contrast to this finding, a study by Speekenbrink and Konstantinidis (2015) found evidence for uncertainty-guided, random exploration in a restless bandit task. In their experiment, participants also had to choose between four arms in a restless bandit task. Their results showed that subjects followed a random exploration strategy by choosing arms according to their probabilities of producing the maximum reward. Findling et al. (2019) argued that many exploratory choices in a restless bandit task can be explained by randomness in the learning process, showing that random exploration cannot only be induced by noise in the decision-making step, but also by noise during learning. While these studies found strong evidence for random exploration in restless bandit tasks, they found no evidence for directed exploration strategies. It could, however, still be possible that richer paradigms could reveal signatures of directed exploration.

The previously described paradigms assumed independent distributions of rewards between all available arms. However, naturally occurring scenarios often involve options whose rewards co-vary, for example when ordering food online from restaurants in the same district. A natural extension of past paradigms is therefore to consider scenarios with correlated arms. Wimmer et al. (2012) let participants perform a four-armed bandit task with binary rewards. Unknown to participants, the reward probabilities for pairs of arms were correlated across trials. Results showed that participants learned to take into account this correlational structure and built up an "acquired equivalence" between arms. Borji and Itti (2013) studied how people searched for the maximum of a one-dimensional function. Functions provide an interesting set-up in which nearby options (inputs) co-vary naturally since they will produce similar outputs. Borji and Itti found that human behavior was in line with a Bayesian optimization algorithm that used a mechanism of generalization combined with an uncertainty-guided search strategy to find high functional outputs. Wu et al. (2017, 2018) extended this paradigm further, studying one and two-dimensional functions in a spatially correlated multiarmed bandit. In these tasks, nearby arms produced similar rewards, which provided traction for generalization to speed up participants' search for highly rewarding options. They found that the same Bayesian model of generalization together with upper confidence bound sampling (i.e. a directed exploration strategy) predicted participants' search behavior best. In a follow-up study, Wu et al. (2020) used two correlated bandit paradigms to research commonalities and differences in spatial and conceptual information search. In the spatial task, participants had to samples arms on a grid in which rewards were correlated according to their position. In the conceptual task, participants were shown Gabor patches with different numbers of stripes and tilts, and patches with similar features produced similar rewards. As before, they found that exploration was guided by participants' ability to generalize over similar arms. Additionally, whereas participants employed directed exploration in the spatial task, they explored more randomly in the conceptual task. Taking these results together, there is substantial evidence that participants engage in both random and directed exploration in correlated bandit tasks. This is intuitive because the presence of correlational structure enhances the benefits of these exploration strategies (Brändle et al., 2020).

The concept of contextual bandits extends these paradigms further. In contextual bandits, different arms can come with features that relate to an arm's expected rewards. This paradigm was used in several experiments and implemented in a diverse set of tasks. Stojić et al. (2015) created a task that displayed options as red boxes and used vertical and horizontal lines as the features of each arm: the shorter the lines, the higher the rewards. They found that participants indeed took these contextual features into account to direct their exploration to more promising options. Moreover, they found evidence for directed exploration, since participants preferred options with the same expected average reward but higher relative uncertainty (Stojić et al., 2020). A different version of a contextual bandit task was put forward by Frank et al. (2009). In a so-called "clock task" participants could stop a clock running down to gain rewards. The rewards varied as a function of the position of the clock's arm and, depending on the condition, either increased, decreased, or stayed constant with time. This study produced strong evidence for directed exploration strategies. Another version of a contextual bandit was studied by Rich and Gureckis (2018). In their foraging task, participants had to decide whether or not to sample different species of mushrooms. Each species had different probabilities of containing edible mushrooms (i.e. positive rewards) or poisonous mushrooms (i.e. negative rewards). Participants explored more given a longer horizon and took the frequency of encountered mushrooms into account. Taking the results of past studies using contextual bandits together, there is strong evidence that participants apply directed and random exploration strategies in such tasks. Moreover, they seem to combine these strategies with more elaborate mechanisms of learning and generalization.

Summarizing past work on human exploratory behavior in multiarmed bandits, we can see that the following two main results emerge:

1. Even in the simplest bandit problems (i.e. two-armed bandits with stationary reward distributions) people deviate from the optimal exploration strategy.
2. People often use uncertainty estimates to guide their exploratory behavior using a combination of directed and random strategies.

7.3 Extending Multiarmed Bandit Tasks

Multiarmed bandits have served as a fertile ground for past studies on human exploration. Even though they can be extended to incorporate nonstationary rewards, correlated arms, and contextual features, the resulting paradigms might still fall short in describing the rich repertoire of human exploration strategies. We argue that one reason for the dearth of evidence for more sophisticated exploration strategies could be that multiarmed bandits do not contain a mechanism to control the state of one's environment. Many real-world problems, however, require a deliberate manipulation of the environment to achieve success. Imagine, for example, a child playing with differently sized and shaped building blocks. By constructing new objects, they are clearly able to influence their environment, changing not only the current state but perhaps even what options are available. It is not possible to capture this example in a bandit paradigm.

MDPs offer a natural extension to multiarmed bandits that *can* capture problems which involve the manipulation of an environment (Bellman, 1957). Formally, an MDP is defined as a tuple (S, A, T, p). S is a set of states, which, in our building block example, describe the current assembly of the blocks. A is a set of actions that express how the child can act on the environment. T is the planning horizon of the agent and p defines a probability distribution $p(s_{t+1}, r_t | s_t, a_t)$ over the next state and an associated reward given that the agent has executed action a_t in state s_t. In the building blocks example, this probability distribution describes what happens when the child adds a new part to an existing assembly. From the joint distribution over transition and reward probabilities, we can extract several other useful quantities:

$$p(s_{t+1}, r_t | s_t, a_t) = \int p(s_{t+1}, r_t | s_t, a_t) dr_t \qquad (1)$$

$$r(s_t, a_t) = \int r_t \sum_{s_{t+1}} p(s_{t+1}, r_t | s_t, a_t) dr_t \qquad (2)$$

Here, $p(s_{t+1} | s_t, a_t)$ defines a distribution over the state at time t + 1 given that the agent selects action a_t in state s_t, while $r(s_t, a_t)$ is the reward obtained when selecting action a_t in state s_t. The goal of an agent is then to find the policy $\pi^*(a_t | s_t)$, that is, a probabilistic mapping from states to actions, that maximizes the expected sum of rewards obtained over its planning horizon:

$$\pi^* = argmax_\pi E_{\pi,p} \left[\sum_{t=1}^{T} r(s_t, a_t) \right] \qquad (3)$$

If p is known, Equation 3 can be solved using dynamic programming (Sutton & Barto, 2018). However, it is typically assumed that the agent does not have access to the true distribution over transition and reward probabilities. It is this uncertainty in the agent's knowledge that causes the need for exploration.

MDPs can be viewed as a generalization of the multiarmed bandit paradigm, which means that each bandit problem may be formulated as an MDP. For example, a stationary bandit with independent reward functions can be expressed as an MDP with a single state, and therefore adheres to trivial transition probabilities (from the single state to itself with probability one). A contextual bandit can be expressed as an MDP in which the agent has no control over transition. In this case, $p(s_{t+1}|s_t, a_t)$ simplifies $p(s_{t+1}|s_t)$.

7.3.1   New Challenges

Exploration algorithms for MDPs have been extensively studied in computer science. We review several of these algorithms. First, we describe how algorithms of random and directed exploration can be extended to MDPs. We then discuss how MDPs allow us to capture even richer forms of exploration. The discussed algorithms are illustrated in Figure 7.1.

7.3.1.1   Random Exploration
Let us first look at random exploration. Osband et al. (2013) discussed how Thompson sampling (i.e., exploration based on randomly drawn beliefs)

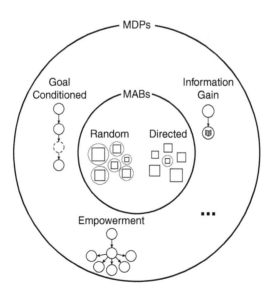

Figure 7.1 Overview of exploration strategies. While multiarmed bandits (MABs) can only capture directed and random exploration strategies, Markov Decision Processes (MDPs) are able to describe a wider range of strategies.

can be implemented in MDPs. To this end, they suggested an algorithm called *posterior sampling for reinforcement learning* (PSRL). PSRL keeps track of a posterior distribution over environment parameters θ, which is constantly updated via Bayes' rule as the agent interacts with the environment:

$$\underbrace{p(\theta|s_{1:t+1}, a_{1:t}, r_{1:t})}_{\text{posterior}} \propto \underbrace{p(s_{t+1}, r_t|s_t, a_t, \theta)}_{\text{likelihood}} \underbrace{p(\theta|s_{1:t}, a_{1:t-1}, r_{1:t-1})}_{\text{prior}} \quad (4)$$

At the beginning of each episode, the agent draws a random sample from this posterior distribution and computes the optimal policy for the sampled parameters by solving Equation 3. An agent applying PSRL assumes a randomly sampled hypothesis for an entire episode, and tests whether that particular hypothesis is true by using an exploration strategy that is consistent over a period of time (Strens, 2000). Coming back to our building block example, if a child applied PSRL as an exploration strategy, then they would maintain different hypotheses about what happens when you stack one block onto another. They might believe that one can stack only two blocks on top of each other, or that one can put pieces on top of each other indefinitely. The child would then sample one of these hypotheses and act as if the sampled hypothesis was true for an extended period. If, for example, the second hypothesis is sampled, the child might end up stacking blocks on top of each other until the resulting building crashes, and then a different hypothesis will be considered.

Resampling the parameters only at the beginning of an episode comes with advantages and disadvantages. It avoids erratic behavior that could arise if parameters were instead constantly resampled. However, it also implies that even if the agent obtains new information during an interaction with an environment, it has to wait until the end of the episode to actually use this information. If people applied a PSRL-like strategy, they would presumably also need a good set of heuristics to decide when to sample a new hypothesis. This could happen when they have a moment of insight (Köhler, 1925) or more gradually as parts of a hypothesis are proven incorrect (Bramley et al., 2017).

7.3.1.2 Directed Exploration

What about directed exploration? There exist several implementations of the principle of uncertainty-directed exploration in the context of MDPs (e.g., Jaksch et al., 2010; Strehl & Littman, 2008). Here, we focus on a particular example called *model based interval estimation with exploration bonus* (MBIE-EB) (Strehl & Littman, 2008). MBIE-EB keeps track of point estimates of environment parameters that are constantly updated. Based on these estimates it constructs, and solves, a new MDP with an optimistic reward function:

$$r_{\text{MBIE-EB}}(s_t, a_t) = r(s_t, a_t) + \frac{\beta}{\sqrt{N(s_t, a_t)}}, \tag{5}$$

where $N(s_t, a_t)$ denotes the number of times the agent has taken action a_t in state $N(s_t, a_t)$ and β is a hyperparameter that controls the degree of exploration. An agent that applies MBIE-EB assigns higher rewards to rarely encountered state–action pairs, essentially directing it to explore situations in which uncertainty is high. When playing with building blocks, this would encourage the child to modify a building in a way they have never done before. If, for example, a child has already built many towers with four blocks, but has never considered putting a fifth block on top of it, they would be encouraged to do so under an MBIE-EB-based exploration strategy.

MBIE-EB comes with its own challenges when considering it as a model of human exploration. Most importantly, it assumes that the optimistic reward function $r_{\text{MBIE-EB}}$ changes after each interaction with the environment. In turn, this means that an agent would have to run an expensive reinforcement learning algorithm to solve Equation 3 on each time-step, which seems like an unrealistically strong requirement when considering that human processing power is limited. One way to potentially implement a cognitively more plausible version of MBIE-EB could be to assume that people approximate the reward function by a finite number of mental samples (Sanborn & Chater, 2016).

7.3.2 New Opportunities

So far, we have described possible implementations of random and directed exploration in MDPs. PSRL keeps track of a posterior distribution over transition and reward probabilities and acts greedily with respect to sampled beliefs, thereby implementing a form of random exploration. MBIE-EB, on the other hand, keeps track of point estimates over transition and reward probabilities and uses these to construct and solve an optimistic MDP, thereby implementing a form of directed exploration. However, MDPs can also be approached using other exploration strategies, some of which we will discuss next.

7.3.2.1 *Information Gain*

Imagine a child who just got their first set of building blocks as a birthday present. When they start playing with the blocks, they first need to figure out how they work: How do blocks stack on top of each other? What determines the stability of a tower? How much does stepping on a block hurt your parents? Children are able to learn about all of these questions by exploring their new toy. How do they accomplish this?

Intuitively, children are great explorers because they reward themselves for learning new things about the environment; frequently, learning itself is the reward for curious agents. Being rewarded for learning per se is also at the core of several theories of curiosity, including computational accounts of "learning progress" (Kaplan & Oudeyer, 2004) and "learning as fun" (Schmidhuber, 2010). The core idea behind the "Learning Progress Hypothesis" put forward by Oudeyer and colleagues is that agents should be most curious about, and therefore most likely to sample, options that lead to maximal learning progress. This is well-aligned with Schmidhuber's "Theory of Fun," which argues that options produce the most fun if they create maximal learning progress. Maximizing learning progress naturally leads to a preference for problems of medium complexity (Oudeyer et al., 2007): if a problem is too easy, then there is nothing to be learned from it; if a problem is too difficult, people cannot solve it and also will not learn from it. A preference for options of medium complexity is known to be present in children (Kidd et al. 2012) and adults (Geana et al., 2016). In simple binary classification tasks, it is even possible to show that selecting stimuli of intermediate difficulty is provably optimal (Wilson et al., 2019).

Multiple algorithmic approaches have been proposed to further formalize this idea in MDPs (Houthooft et al., 2016; Lopes et al., 2012; Oudeyer & Kaplan, 2009; Schmidhuber, 1991; Sun et al., 2011). The main idea behind all of these approaches is to reward the agent for taking actions that maximize the reduction of uncertainty about the dynamics of the environment. To illustrate how an agent could find the reduction of uncertainty rewarding in an MDP set-up, we will focus on one such approach here, which has been put forward by Houthooft et al. (2016). Their algorithm assumes that the agent expresses beliefs about environment parameters through a probability distribution, which is constantly updated via Bayes' rule as the agent interacts with the environment (as described in Equation 4). How uncertain the agent currently is about the true environment parameters can be expressed in terms of the prior entropy $H[\theta|s_{1:t}, a_{1:t-1}, r_{1:t-1}]$. We may then express the expected reduction in uncertainty as the difference between entropies across two successive time-steps:

$$H[\theta|s_{1:t}, a_{1:t-1}, r_{1:t-1}] - E_{s_{t+1}, r_t \sim p(s_{t+1}, r_t|s_t, a_t)}[H[\theta|s_{1:t+1}, a_{1:t}, r_{1:t}]] \quad (6)$$

Equation 6 can be interpreted as a measure of the agent's information gain about the environment's dynamics. It is common practice to use this term as an intrinsic bonus reward, which then encourages the agent to take actions that maximize its learning progress (Houthooft et al., 2016). In the context of the earlier example, such a mechanism could offer an explanation for how a child explores after getting their first set of building blocks as a birthday present. Naturally, the child wants to figure out how the new toy works and does so by seeking to construct things that reduce their uncertainty about the toy's mechanics. This process then enables the child to find out, after playing with the toy for a while, how blocks stack on top of each other and what determines the stability of a tower.

7.3.2.2 Empowerment

After a child has learned the simple rules of how to combine building blocks, how could they continue learning about how to build more complex things? They could, for example, decide that knowing how to build robust walls will help them to construct many different buildings, such as homes, castles, or bridges. By figuring out how to construct elements that can be used in many different assemblies, children can empower themselves to further improve their abilities.

Inspired by examples from the animal kingdom, social sciences, and games, researchers have suggested the concept of *empowerment* to capture this kind of behavior (Klyubin et al., 2005). Honey bees, for example, try to be mobile because it allows them to forage at multiple sides, people strive for money because it enables them to do a variety of activities, and board game players often play in a way that keeps their options open. In all of these cases, empowerment "[motivates] an agent to move to states of maximum influence" (Mohamed & Rezende, 2015: 2127). Empowerment is also a useful signal for exploration because it enables the agent to explore large parts of the state space in a short time. In simple multiarmed bandit problems, an agent cannot apply an empowerment-based strategy, because states do not exist or there is no control over them. Thus, studying empowerment necessitates the use of MDP scenarios.

Mathematically, one can construct an agent that implements empowerment-based exploration by encouraging the maximization of the information contained in actions about future states (Mohamed & Rezende, 2015; Salge et al., 2014). Leibfried et al. (2019) suggested using one-step empowerment as an intrinsic bonus added to external rewards.[1] One-step empowerment is defined as the mutual information between actions and future states conditioned on the current state: $I[a_t; s_{t+1}|s_t]$. To gain an intuition of why this leads to the desired behavior, it is useful to consider the decomposition of the mutual information in terms of the marginal and the conditional entropy:

$$I[a_t; s_{t+1}|s_t] = H[s_{t+1}|s_t] - E_{a_t \sim \pi(a_t|s_t)}[H[s_{t+1}|a_t, s_t]] \quad (7)$$

The marginal entropy $H[s_{t+1}|s_t]$ will be high when the agent visits states that lead to a diverse set of future states, whereas the conditional entropy $E_{a_t \sim \pi(a_t|s_t)}[H[s_{t+1}|a_t, s_t]]$ will be low when the agent takes actions for which it can predict the outcome perfectly. Therefore, incorporating Equation 7 as an intrinsic bonus reward causes the agent to visit states of maximum influence. However, it also leads to a challenging optimization problem:

$$\pi^* = argmax_\pi E_{\pi,p}\left[\sum_{t=1}^{T} r(s_t, a_t) + \beta\, I[a_t; s_{t+1}|s_t]\right] \quad (8)$$

Maximizing Equation 8 is difficult because the augmented reward function depends on the optimal policy, and, vice versa, the optimal policy depends on the augmented reward function. How people would solve such a problem is an interesting avenue for future research.

7.3.2.3 Goal-Conditioned Exploration

Now that the child has acquired a basic set of construction skills, they might have a bigger goal – building the biggest castle the world has ever seen. While this goal is clearly not attainable, the child might still learn useful things along the way. For example, they could discover how to build towers, rooftops, or drawbridges.

Goal-conditioned reinforcement learning equips an agent with the ability to reach arbitrary goals (Colas et al., 2020; Pong et al., 2018; Schaul et al., 2015; Sutton et al., 2011). In this framework, the agent learns a policy $\pi(a|s, g)$ that is not only conditioned on the current state s but also on a goal g. The additional conditioning on a goal enables the

---

[1] Empowerment is typically defined in terms of multistep policies (Salge et al., 2014; Mohamed & Rezende, 2015). Leibfried et al. (2019) demonstrated that maximizing the cumulative one-step empowerment leads to similar behavior without the necessity to maintain multistep policies.

agent to exhibit different behaviors, depending on what goal is currently attempted. Typically, goals are defined in terms of the state space. In the simplest case, goals are just elements of the state space itself: that is, $g \in S$. More sophisticated implementations learn a goal embedding as a function of the state space – that is, $g \in \phi(S)$ – and perform goal-directed reasoning in latent space defined by the embedding (Nair et al., 2018; Zhu et al., 2017). In both cases, the agent is rewarded for reaching a given goal instead of following the original reward function. As this definition of goals relies heavily on the notion of states, such a strategy is not available in the multiarmed bandit paradigm.

While goal-conditioned reinforcement learning is not a method for exploration on its own, reasoning about goals can facilitate exploration. It has, for example, been demonstrated that the combination of goal-conditioned reinforcement learning with random exploration can speed up the time it takes to visit all states in the environment (Jinnai et al., 2019). If, for example, the child's goal is to build a big castle but they do not know how to get there, it will be useful to explore how potential subcomponents work. This type of exploration does not happen purely at random, because the child has a particular goal in mind. It is also not purely directed toward situations with high uncertainty, but instead attempts to explore things that are useful for the goal you are trying to accomplish. Future studies on human exploration could therefore assess if giving participants unobtainable but useful goals can improve their overall task performance later on.

7.4 Paradigms Beyond Bandits

We have argued that the standard multiarmed bandit setting is not rich enough to study the large repertoire of human exploration strategies. But how can we test whether people actually use the described types of exploration strategies? Advancing the study of human exploration will require the use of novel experimental paradigms. Here, we present some examples of such paradigms.

A straightforward extension to multiarmed bandits are grid-world problems. In a grid-world environment, an agent needs to navigate on a two-dimensional grid in an attempt to solve a specific task: for example, to find a goal or to escape from an intricate maze. Grid-world environments have been frequently used as paradigms to compare artificial reinforcement learning agents (Chevalier-Boisvert et al., 2018; Sutton & Barto, 2018), and could therefore help to disentangle more complex human exploration strategies. For example, Zheng et al. (2020) showed that different exploration strategies lead to intrinsic reward functions with varying properties. In particular, they found that directed exploration strategies can lead to over-exploration even after a goal has been found. This and other predictions could be easily tested in human participants.

Video-games can provide another interesting direction for future studies on human exploration. Video-games can easily incorporate different levels of complexity, ranging from simple Atari games, to modern physical game engines, all the way to realistic virtual reality environments. Frequently, data sets of people's behavior in video-games can be accessed via the internet, and available data sets are much bigger than data sets collected in standard in-lab experiments (Griffiths, 2014; Stafford & Dewar, 2014). Furthermore, video-games are rich enough to capture all exploration strategies discussed in the last section. To illustrate this point, let us take a look at a classic role-playing game example: You are a hero, traveling through a fantasy world, completing missions by fighting against monsters. To choose which mission to complete next, you may apply different strategies. You could try to improve your sword fighting skills by combating a monster with a difficulty level that provides just the right challenge – not too easy and not too hard. This corresponds to an exploration strategy based on information gain. Alternatively, you could buy a horse to explore new areas faster. This corresponds to an empowerment-based exploration strategy. Lastly, you could decide to set yourself the goal of fighting against a dangerous vampire king. While you are not able to beat him at the moment, you could try to find out a lot about vampires and start by training against weaker ones to prepare yourself for the big fight. This is an example of a goal-conditioned exploration strategy. Of course, it might still be a while until psychologists could reliably study human exploration in such scenarios. Moreover, the sheer complexity of the available action spaces makes it hard to trace model player's behavior back to individual factors in such games, leading to a loss of internal validity. However, it is possible to study human exploration in simpler games. For example, Matusch et al. (2020) used a precollected data-set of different Atari games and looked at how strongly intrinsic reward functions of different exploration algorithms correlated with human behavior. Their results showed that intrinsic objectives such as information gain and empowerment correlated more strongly with human behavior than just the simple reward in each task, thereby providing initial evidence that more complex exploration strategies govern human game play. If it turns out that existing video-games are too complex to be investigated with our currently available tools, then it could be worthwhile to specifically design simplified games for research purposes.

In an ideal world, we would also like to directly study human exploration in realistic scenarios, including our running example of a child playing with building blocks. However, measuring human behavior in such settings constitutes a highly nontrivial challenge, especially since it is not always clear when a new state or action has occurred. Nevertheless, it might still be possible to gain insights into how people explore in everyday situations by studying largescale data sets. For example, Schulz et al. (2019) looked at 1.5 million orders from an online food delivery service and analyzed the customers' exploration behavior. They found that customers used uncertainty-guided exploration to decide where to order next. One drawback with large online data sets is that they lack clear control over the factors that can influence people's behavior. This limits the conclusions that can be drawn from these settings. However, we believe that one way to partially address this concern is to study quasi-experiments in which changes to different users happened randomly, for example because new options were introduced to different users at different times.

While all these paradigms have their unique benefits and drawbacks, they can jointly allow us to look for more sophisticated strategies than just uncertainty-guided exploration. Eventually, we believe that these paradigms could be added into the experimentalist's toolkit and – together with more traditional paradigms – enrich our understanding of human information search in the context of reinforcement learning.

7.5 Conclusion

The attempt to find actions that maximize long-term rewards is a powerful tool to describe intelligent behavior. Yet any sufficiently complex reinforcement learning problem is also an information-seeking problem in disguise. This is because the drive to reap immediate rewards is always juxtaposed with the drive to seek out knowledge about one's environment that can lead to higher rewards later on. Finding the right balance between information-seeking and maximizing rewards according to one's current knowledge frames the exploration–exploitation dilemma, a canonical problem studied in humans and machines.

In this chapter, we have reviewed past studies on human exploration, which have primarily focused on multiarmed bandit tasks. In the multiarmed bandit paradigm, people seem to use a mix of two heuristic strategies. The first strategy is random exploration which induces some form of stochasticity in the decision-making process. The latter is directed exploration, which optimistically seeks out options with higher relative uncertainty. We then argued that using multiarmed bandits to study human exploration behavior can be unnecessarily restrictive. This could explain why past studies have only ever found evidence for random and directed exploration, and why – even for these two rather simple strategies – the evidence has occasionally been mixed. We have therefore proposed extending current paradigms to study human exploration by including scenarios in which people can also affect the state of their environment. This leads to the set-up of MDPs, which have been widely studied in the machine learning community.

The two classic exploration strategies can easily be extended to MDPs. Moreover, MDPs lend themselves well to the study of other, more sophisticated exploration strategies as well. These strategies include, but are not limited to, strategies driven by information gain, algorithms that try to empower themselves to explore even more, and goal-conditioned exploration. We believe that all of these strategies could be considered in richer environments that more closely resemble the real world, such as videogames, real world behavior such as tasks of physical construction, as well as online consumer behavior.

Taken together, this chapter may inspire future work focused on more advanced exploration strategies, and eventually lead to new insights on the human drive to seek out knowledge in reinforcement learning problems. In the end, further extending our descriptions of human exploration will also require us to extend our own exploration of experimental paradigms.

References

Auer, P. (2002). Using confidence bounds for exploitation-exploration trade-offs. *Journal of Machine Learning Research*, 3(Nov.), 397–422.

Bellman, R. (1957). A Markovian decision process. *Journal of Mathematics and Mechanics*, 6(5), 679–684.

Binz, M., & Endres, D. (2019). Where do heuristics come from? In *Proceedings of the 41st Annual Conference of the Cognitive Science Society*, (pp. 1402–1408). Montreal, QB: Cognitive Science Society.

Borji, A., & Itti, L. (2013). Bayesian optimization explains human active search. *Advances in Neural Information Processing Systems*, 26, 55–63.

Bramley, N. R., Dayan, P., Griffiths, T. L., & Lagnado, D. A. (2017). Formalizing Neurath's ship: Approximate algorithms for online causal learning. *Psychological Review*, 124(3), 301.

Brändle, F., Wu, C. M., & Schulz, E. (2020). What are we curious about? *Trends in Cognitive Sciences*, 24(9), 685–687.

Chevalier-Boisvert, M., Willems, L., & Pal, S. (2018). *Minimalistic gridworld environment for openai gym.* https://github.com/maximecb/gym-minigrid. GitHub.

Cohen, J. D., McClure, S. M., & Yu, A. J. (2007). Should I stay or should I go? How the human brain manages the trade-off between exploitation and exploration. *Philosophical Transactions of the Royal Society B: Biological Sciences*, 362(1481), 933–942.

Colas, C., Karch, T., Sigaud, O., & Oudeyer, P.-Y. (2020). Intrinsically motivated goal-conditioned reinforcement learning: a short survey. *arXiv preprint arXiv:2012.09830.*

Daw, N. D., O'Doherty, J. P., Dayan, P., Seymour, B., & Dolan, R. J. (2006). Cortical substrates for exploratory decisions in humans. *Nature*, 441(7095), 876–879.

Findling, C., Skvortsova, V., Dromnelle, R., Palminteri, S., & Wyart, V. (2019). Computational noise in reward-guided learning drives behavioral variability in volatile environments. *Nature Neuroscience*, 22(12), 2066–2077.

Frank, M. J., Doll, B. B., Oas-Terpstra, J., & Moreno, F. (2009). Prefrontal and striatal dopaminergic genes predict individual differences in exploration and exploitation. *Nature Neuroscience*, 12(8), 1062.

Geana, A., Wilson, R. C., Daw, N., & Cohen, J. D. (2016). Boredom, information-seeking and exploration. In A. Papafragou, D. Grodner, D. Mirman, & J. C. Trueswell (Eds.), *Proceedings of the 38th Annual Conference of the Cognitive Science Society* (pp. 1751–1756). Austin, TX: Cognitive Science Society.

Gershman, S. J. (2018). Deconstructing the human algorithms for exploration. *Cognition*, 173, 34–42.

Griffiths, T. (2014, 12). Manifesto for a new (computational) cognitive revolution. *Cognition*, 135. https://doi.org/10.1016/j.cognition.2014.11.026.

Hills, T. T., Todd, P. M., Lazer, D., Redish, A. D., Couzin, I. D., Group, C. S. R., et al. (2015). Exploration versus exploitation in space, mind, and society. *Trends in Cognitive Sciences*, 19(1), 46–54.

Houthooft, R., Chen, X., Duan, Y., Schulman, J., De Turck, F., & Abbeel, P. (2016). Vime: Variational information maximizing exploration. *Advances in Neural Information Processing Systems*, 29, 1109–1117.

Jaksch, T., Ortner, R., & Auer, P. (2010). Near-optimal regret bounds for reinforcement learning. *Journal of Machine Learning Research*, 11(4), 1563–1600.

Jinnai, Y., Park, J. W., Abel, D., & Konidaris, G. (2019). Discovering options for exploration by minimizing cover time. *arXiv preprint arXiv:1903.00606.*

Kaplan, F., & Oudeyer, P.-Y. (2004). Maximizing learning progress: an internal reward system for development. In Iida, F., Pfeifer, R., Steels, L., & Kuniyoshi. Y. (Eds.), *Embodied artificial intelligence* (pp. 259–270). Springer. https://doi.org/10.1007/978-3-540-27833-7_19.

Kidd, C., Piantadosi, S. T., & Aslin, R. N. (2012). The Goldilocks effect: Human infants allocate attention to visual sequences that are neither too simple nor too complex. *PLoS One*, 7(5), e36399.

Klyubin, A. S., Polani, D., & Nehaniv, C. L. (2005). All else being equal be empowered. In Capcarrère, M. S., Freitas, A. A., Bentley, P. J., Johnson, C. G., & Timmis, J. (Eds.), *Advances in Artificial Life. ECAL 2005. Lecture Notes in Computer Science*, vol. 3630. Springer, Berlin, Heidelberg. https://doi.org/10.1007/11553090_75.

Köhler, W. (1925). *The mentality of apes* (Vol. 74). K. Paul, Trench, Trubner & Company, Limited.

Krebs, J. R., Kacelnik, A., & Taylor, P. (1978). Test of optimal sampling by foraging great tits. *Nature*, 275(5675), 27–31.

Leibfried, F., Pascual-D´ıaz, S., & Grau-Moya, J. (2019). A unified Bellman optimality principle combining reward maximization and empowerment. *Advances in Neural Information Processing Systems*, 32, 7869–7880.

Lopes, M., Lang, T., Toussaint, M., & Oudeyer, P.-Y. (2012). Exploration in model-based reinforcement learning by empirically estimating learning progress. *Advances in Neural Information Processing Systems*, 25, 206–214.

Matusch, B., Ba, J., & Hafner, D. (2020). Evaluating agents without rewards. *arXiv preprint arXiv:2012.11538.*

Mehlhorn, K., Newell, B. R., Todd, P. M., Lee, M. D., Morgan, K., Braithwaite, V. A., ... Gonzalez, C. (2015). Unpacking the exploration–exploitation tradeoff: A synthesis of human and animal literatures. *Decision*, 2(3), 191.

Mohamed, S., & Rezende, D. J. (2015). Variational information maximisation for intrinsically motivated reinforcement learning. In *Advances in neural information processing systems* (pp. 2125–2133).

Nair, A., Pong, V., Dalal, M., Bahl, S., Lin, S., & Levine, S. (2018). Visual reinforcement learning with imagined goals. *arXiv preprint arXiv:1807.04742.*

Osband, I., Russo, D., & Van Roy, B. (2013). (More) efficient reinforcement learning via posterior sampling. In *Advances in neural information processing systems* (pp. 3003–3011).

Oudeyer, P.-Y., & Kaplan, F. (2009). What is intrinsic motivation? A typology of computational approaches. *Frontiers in Neurorobotics*, 1, 6.

Oudeyer, P.-Y., Kaplan, F., & Hafner, V. V. (2007). Intrinsic motivation systems for autonomous mental development. *IEEE Transactions on Evolutionary Computation*, 11(2), 265–286.

Pong, V., Gu, S., Dalal, M., & Levine, S. (2018). Temporal difference models: Model-free deep RL for model-based control. *arXiv preprint arXiv:1802.09081.*

Rich, A. S., & Gureckis, T. M. (2018). Exploratory choice reflects the future value of information. *Decision*, 5(3), 177.

Salge, C., Glackin, C., & Polani, D. (2014). Empowerment–an introduction. In Prokopenko, M. (ed.), *Guided self-organization: Inception* (pp. 67–114). Springer. https://doi.org/10.1007/978-3-642-53734-9_4.

Sanborn, A. N., & Chater, N. (2016). Bayesian brains without probabilities. *Trends in Cognitive Sciences*, 20(12), 883–893.

Schaul, T., Horgan, D., Gregor, K., & Silver, D. (2015). Universal value function approximators. In *International conference on machine learning* (pp. 1312–1320). https://proceedings.mlr.press/v37/schaul15.html.

Schmidhuber, J. (1991). Curious model-building control systems. In *Proc. international joint conference on neural networks* (pp. 1458–1463). https://doi.org/10.1109/IJCNN.1991.170605.

Schmidhuber, J. (2010). Formal theory of creativity, fun, and intrinsic motivation (1990–2010). *IEEE Transactions on Autonomous Mental Development*, 2(3), 230–247.

Schulz, E., Bhui, R., Love, B. C., Brier, B., Todd, M. T., & Gershman, S. J. (2019). Structured, uncertainty-driven exploration in real-world consumer choice. *Proceedings of the National Academy of Sciences*, 116(28), 13903–13908. https://doi.org/10.1073/pnas.1821028116.

Schulz, E., & Gershman, S. J. (2019). The algorithmic architecture of exploration in the human brain. *Current Opinion in Neurobiology*, 55, 7–14.

Speekenbrink, M., & Konstantinidis, E. (2015). Uncertainty and exploration in a restless bandit problem. *Topics in Cognitive Science*, 7(2), 351–367.

Stafford, T., & Dewar, M. (2014). Tracing the trajectory of skill learning with a very large sample of online game players. *Psychological Science*, 25(2), 511–518. https://doi.org/10.1177/0956797613511466.

Steyvers, M., Lee, M. D., & Wagenmakers, E.-J. (2009). A Bayesian analysis of human decision-making on bandit problems. *Journal of Mathematical Psychology*, 53(3), 168–179.

Stojić, H., Analytis, P. P., & Speekenbrink, M. (2015). Human behavior in contextual multi-armed bandit problems. In Noelle, D. C., et al. (Eds.), *Proceedings of the 37th Annual Meeting of the Cognitive Science Society* (pp. 2290–2295). Cognitive Science Society.

Stojić, H., Schulz, E., P Analytis, P., & Speekenbrink, M. (2020). It's new, but is it good? How generalization and uncertainty guide the exploration of novel options. *Journal of Experimental Psychology: General*, 149(10), 1878.

Strehl, A. L., & Littman, M. L. (2008). An analysis of model-based interval estimation for Markov decision processes. *Journal of Computer and System Sciences*, 74(8), 1309–1331.

Strens, M. (2000). A Bayesian framework for reinforcement learning. In *Proceedings of the Seventeenth International Conference on Machine Learning* (ICML-2000), Stanford University, California, June 29–July 2, 2000. (Vol. 2000, pp. 943–950).

Sun, Y., Gomez, F., & Schmidhuber, J. (2011). Planning to be surprised: Optimal Bayesian exploration in dynamic environments. In *International conference on artificial general intelligence* (pp. 41–51).

Sutton, R. S., & Barto, A. G. (2018). *Reinforcement learning: An introduction*. MIT Press.

Sutton, R. S., Modayil, J., Delp, M., Degris, T., Pilarski, P. M., White, A., & Precup, D. (2011). Horde: A scalable real-time architecture for learning knowledge from unsupervised sensorimotor interaction. In *Proc. of 10th Int. Conf. on*

Autonomous Agents and Multiagent Systems (AAMAS 2011), May, 2–6, 2011,
Taipei, Taiwan (pp. 761–768).

Thompson, W. R. (1933). On the likelihood that one unknown probability exceeds another in view of the evidence of two samples. *Biometrika*, 25(3/4), 285–294.

Whittle, P. (1980). Multi-armed bandits and the Gittins Index. *Journal of the Royal Statistical Society: Series B (Methodological)*, 42(2), 143–149.

Wilson, R. C., Bonawitz, E., Costa, V. D., & Ebitz, R. B. (2021). Balancing exploration and exploitation with information and randomization. *Current Opinion in Behavioral Sciences*, 38, 49–56.

Wilson, R. C., Geana, A., White, J. M., Ludwig, E. A., & Cohen, J. D. (2014). Humans use directed and random exploration to solve the explore–exploit dilemma. *Journal of Experimental Psychology: General*, 143(6), 2074.

Wilson, R. C., Shenhav, A., Straccia, M., & Cohen, J. D. (2019). The eighty five percent rule for optimal learning. *Nature Communications*, 10(1), 1–9.

Wimmer, G. E., Daw, N. D., & Shohamy, D. (2012). Generalization of value in reinforcement learning by humans. *European Journal of Neuroscience*, 35(7), 1092–1104.

Wu, C. M., Schulz, E., Garvert, M. M., Meder, B., & Schuck, N. W. (2020). Similarities and differences in spatial and non-spatial cognitive maps. *PLoS Computational Biology*, 16(9), e1008149.

Wu, C. M., Schulz, E., Speekenbrink, M., Nelson, J. D., & Meder, B. (2017). Mapping the unknown: The spatially correlated multi-armed bandit. *bioRxiv*, 106286.

Wu, C. M., Schulz, E., Speekenbrink, M., Nelson, J. D., & Meder, B. (2018). Generalization guides human exploration in vast decision spaces. *Nature Human Behaviour*, 2(12), 915–924.

Zhang, S., & Yu, A. J. (2013). Forgetful Bayes and myopic planning: Human learning and decision-making in a bandit setting. In *NIPS* (pp. 2607–2615). https://proceedings.neurips.cc/paper/2013/file/6c14da109e294d1e8155be8 aa4b1ce8e-Paper.pdf.

Zheng, Z., Oh, J., Hessel, M., Xu, Z., Kroiss, M., Van Hasselt, H., . . . Singh, S. (2020, 13–18 Jul). What can learned intrinsic rewards capture? In H. Duamé . III & A. Singh (Eds.), *Proceedings of the 37th international conference on machine learning* (Vol. 119, pp. 11436–11446). PMLR.

Zhu, Y., Mottaghi, R., Kolve, E., Lim, J. J., Gupta, A., Fei-Fei, L., & Farhadi, A. (2017). Target-driven visual navigation in indoor scenes using deep reinforcement learning. In *2017 IEEE international conference on robotics and automation (ICRA)* (pp. 3357–3364), Singapore.

CHAPTER 8

Representational Exchange in Human Social Learning
Balancing Efficiency and Flexibility

Charley M. Wu, Natalia Vélez, and Fiery A. Cushman

8.1 Introduction

Many animals can learn from each other, but not like us. If chimpanzee social learning were a simple tune carried by a single voice, ours would be the exuberant chorus of a twelve-piece ragtime marching band. Naturally, anybody who wants to understand human learning and behavior must confront a central question: Why do they *sing*, while we *swing*?

Our social learning abilities span a wide spectrum of different capacities, and so researchers have prioritized figuring out which ones matter the most, identifying the "small difference that . . . made a big difference" (Tomasello et al., 2005, p. 690). To some, human social learning is powerful primarily because we are uniquely disposed toward high-fidelity imitation of socially observed behaviors, granting us the capability to transmit and innovate upon cultural knowledge (Boyd & Richerson, 1988; Henrich, 2017; Tennie et al., 2009). When learning to bake a loaf of bread, for instance, we might imitate each individual action of an artisanal baker, faithfully replicating the same motor responses. We might do this even if we cannot understand the rationale behind her movements and choices (Lyons et al., 2007); Indeed, the artisan herself might be unaware of the rationale, having inherited some techniques through cultural transmission (Derex et al., 2019; Henrich, 2017). In sum, perhaps the key difference is that humans can transmit cultural knowledge of specific behaviors and action representations with precision.

To others, human social learning is powerful because we can copy not just actions, but also more abstract goals, beliefs, and values, which can be reassembled productively into new behaviors. Unlike actions, these mental states are not directly observable. Thus, copying them depends on our ability to draw rich social inferences about the unobservable mental states of other people (Apperly, 2010; Gweon, 2021; Jara-Ettinger, 2019; Scott-Phillips, 2017; Strachan et al., 2020). On this view, the uniqueness of human social learning owes less to high-fidelity copying and transmission of concrete behaviors, but, rather, shifts the focus to our ability to reconstruct abstract knowledge and values (Morin, 2016; Sperber, 2006). When observing someone bake a loaf of bread, we can acquire knowledge about the leavening power of yeast and the extensibility of well-developed gluten, and can emulate goals such as achieving airy expansion of the loaf in the oven. In sum, perhaps the key difference is that humans can both infer and emulate the hidden rationale of others' actions.

These are both plausible candidates. Compared to other primates, humans are more disposed to high-fidelity imitation (Horner & Whiten, 2005; McGuigan et al., 2007) and have more sophisticated capacities for mental-state inference (Herrmann et al., 2007; Tomasello et al., 2005). Nobody seriously believes that human social learning is limited exclusively to one form, whether copying actions or learning abstract, generative structure. The debate is over which form predominates: Both instruments are in the band, but which carries the melody?

At its heart, our proposal rejects the premise of this question. We propose that the power of human social learning comes not from any single instrument, but from their harmonization. We don't mean this in the banal sense that you can blow harder on two horns than one. Rather, like a musical arrangement, the things we learn must be effectively and efficiently combined. Humans, then, are uniquely masterful composers – social learners with an unrivaled ability to integrate across different levels of representation, from specific behaviors to the hidden generative structure behind them.

Our argument is structured around an analogy to *non*-social learning. It is an apt analogy because, here too, humans have a variety of instruments at our disposal. (In fact, we argue, the representations involved in social and nonsocial learning are the same.) Sometimes we rely on habit, recycling past actions or repeating what has been rewarded in the past. Other times, we plan new actions based on a representation of their likely future consequences. Decades of psychological theorizing were spent arguing over which of these things humans do, or which is more important (e.g., Skinner, 1950; Tolman, 1948). However, there is a growing recognition that the essence of human intelligence is not contained within one of these methods individually, but rather in the way that we arbitrate and integrate between them (Cushman & Morris, 2015; Huys et al., 2015; Keramati et al., 2016; Kool, Cushman, et al., 2018; Russek et al., 2017). A baker, for instance, relies at times on skills "in the hands" – a certain way of shaping a loaf, which is a learned behavior that has solidified into habit through countless hours of practice. At other times, she relies on domain knowledge and goals that allow her to adapt to variations in the ingredients, humidity, temperature, and so forth – or to plan out an entirely new recipe. A debate over whether "habit" or "planning" is more important misses the point: What is most remarkable is her ability to compose these elements into a whole that is both practiced and productive; both efficient and flexible (Botvinick & Weinstein, 2014; Rozenblit & Keil, 2002).

We argue that the same is true for social learning. High-fidelity imitation is a close homolog to certain forms of cheap-but-inflexible learning and decision-making, such as habit. Meanwhile, mentalizing and emulation are a close homolog to goal-directed planning. The first part of this chapter describes these homologies in detail. Just as a baker prepares her loaf in a way that integrates across diverse processes of decision-making, the baker's apprentice faces the task of learning representations at multiple levels, from concrete actions to abstract knowledge and goals. To be successful, she must arbitrate between imitation and emulation for each part of the bread-making process, and integrate these learned representations with her own preexisting knowledge, skills, and goals, across multiple levels of representation. The heart of our chapter addresses the processes of arbitration and integration, which is essential to the power of human social learning.

For simplicity, we focus on observational learning, where we perceive a person's action and the setting in which they are performing it, but without direct access to the underlying causes of their action (e.g., via explicit communication). We will also assume a relatively naïve observer is observing a relatively experienced expert, and attempts to learn how to act in more expert ways themselves (like a baker and her apprentice). Clearly, human social learning involves much more than this specific form of observational learning. It also involves teaching, talking, rewarding, punishing, and much more. Nevertheless, our case study of observational learning aims to inform theories of human social learning more broadly.

8.2 Mechanisms of Social Learning and Decision-Making

There is a close relationship between different forms of individual and social learning (Morris & Cushman, 2018; Najar et al., 2020). Theories of observational social learning have been broadly divided into two approaches: imitation and emulation. With imitation, the learner copies the observed *action* (Bandura, 1962; Heyes, 2001; N. E. Miller & Dollard, 1941). With emulation, the learner decomposes the observed behavior into a set of reconstructed primitives. This could be the *value* of the action, or it could be the *beliefs* and ultimate *rewards* that dictate the expected value of an action with respect to some goal (Tomasello et al., 1987; Whiten & Ham, 1992). This defines a hierarchy of inferences an observer can draw from a demonstrator's actions, and a corresponding set of mental representations that the observer can potentially adopt via social learning.

Analogously, when deciding how to act, a person can rely on any of several strategies. They can draw directly from a representation of which *action* to perform (i.e., a cached policy or stimulus-response repertoire); they can draw from a representation of the instrumental *value* of the actions available to them (from cached values); or, they can select potential actions by considering the likely future consequences of those actions given their *beliefs* about the environment and intrinsic *rewards* (i.e., model-based planning). This defines a hierarchy of individual decision-making mechanisms.[1]

In this section, we will introduce a taxonomy of social learning that draws an analogy between well-understood mechanisms of individual learning (Figure 8.1, left), and the hierarchy of inferences that an observer can draw in social learning (Figure 8.1, right). When an individual performs an action, observes a change in the world, and receives some reinforcement, she faces at least three ways to learn from this. She can update her *cached policy*, her representation of the *value* of the action performed, or her *world model*. Similarly, when an individual observes someone else's actions, there are several ways that she could use that observation to guide her own behavior. At the simplest level, she could take on that person's action as her own, directly imitating the person's behavioral policy (*policy imitation*). Moving up the hierarchy, she could infer the unobservable mental states that produced the action – namely, she could use her inferences about that person's value to update her own representations of the instrumental value of certain actions (*value inference*), her inferences about that person's beliefs to update her own beliefs about the world (*belief inference*), or even her inferences about what the

---

[1] Following convention in reinforcement learning (Sutton & Barto, 2018), we use "reward" for intrinsic objectives, such as eating food, and "value" for things of learned instrumental utility, such as planting seeds.

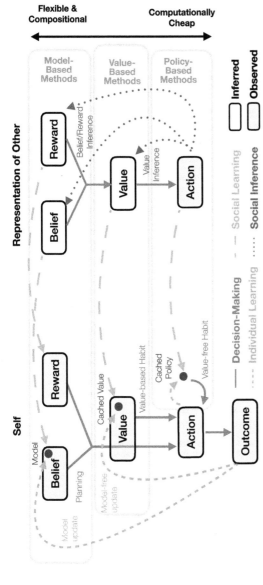

Figure 8.1 Different forms of social and individual learning share a similar tradeoff involving computational complexity and flexibility, which both increase as we ascend the decision-making hierarchy (solid arrows). *Left*: In individual learning (short dashed arrows), we can update a cached policy, a cached value representation, or our model of the environment. *Right*: Similarly, different forms of social learning (long dashed arrows) draw upon different representational formats: directly adopting the actions or policy of another agent, adopting their inferred value representations, or adopting their inferred beliefs or intrinsic reward function. Value-based and model-based methods of social learning require inferring hidden mental states from observed actions (dotted arrows), which incur added computational costs. However, they also afford increased flexibility, since learning from these primitives of the decision-making process allows us to deploy them in an adaptive and compositional fashion.

person finds intrinsically rewarding to update her own experience of reward (Cushman & Morris, 2015; Zaki et al., 2011).

This connection is useful because it allows us to export well-studied features of individual learning to better characterize social learning. We focus on three key ideas. First, these mechanisms of individual learning exhibit different tradeoffs between computational efficiency, on the one hand, and both flexibility and compositionality, on the other. Relying on cached representations of policy or value is computationally cheap, but it is less flexible and less compositional than full model-based planning, which can adapt to new goals and contexts, and can reassemble representational elements into novel behavior. Second, due to this tradeoff, people arbitrate between different forms of learning and decision-making, selecting computationally cheap methods when possible and more complex approaches when necessary. Third, complex real-world behaviors depend on the adaptive integration of different representations (e.g., policies, values, and beliefs). This in turn depends on processes such as planning and inference, which can transfer information across levels of representation. In the remainder of the chapter we address the implications of each of these points for theories of social learning.

8.2.1   Imitation and Policy Caching

In the simplest case, observing a behavior by another individual will often make us more likely to also adopt it (Figure 8.2). In other words, social learning often involves action imitation (Hoppitt & Laland, 2013; Legare & Nielsen, 2015; Whiten & Ham, 1992). You might simply choose a restaurant based on its popularity (Boyd & Richerson, 1988), or you might follow one of many widely studied imitation biases to selectively imitate the actions of prestigious (Henrich & Gil-White, 2001; Jiménez & Mesoudi, 2019) or previously successful individuals (Atkisson et al., 2012;

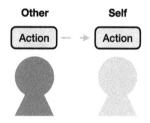

Figure 8.2 Schematic of policy imitation.

Rendell et al., 2010). Paired with an appropriate rate of even random variability (akin to "mutations") in the copying process, imitation has been proposed to be a key driver of human cultural evolution (Henrich, 2017; Heyes, 2018; Tennie et al., 2009).

Imitation is often considered computationally cheaper and simpler compared to other forms of social learning, since no inference is needed about the other person's goals or intentions (Catmur et al., 2009; Heyes, 2002). Rather, their behavioral policy can simply be copied verbatim. Thus, a useful analogy can be made to individual learning, where we often deploy a "cached policy" in the form of habitual behaviors (Dezfouli & Balleine, 2013; Gershman, 2020; K. J. Miller et al., 2019). Habits are patterns of behaviors that are learned through exercise and repetition, rather than reinforced through rewarding outcomes (Thorndike, 1932). For instance, we can take our usual route to work in the morning or order our usual meal at our favorite restaurant, without having to iterate over possible plans or weigh the benefits of different options on the basis of expected value. Sometimes referred to as "amortization" (Dasgupta et al., 2018), we can avoid costly computations simply by caching and redeploying solutions that have worked in the past.

In exchange for its simplicity, pure imitation lacks flexibility. Suppose you meet a friend for lunch at a restaurant with a confusing and sprawling menu. Since your friend is a regular, you could always copy their lunch order, saving you the trouble of blundering your way through trial and error. However, you are likely to reach the limits of this strategy on subsequent visits, where you may miss out on new, higher-reward options (e.g., a changing daily special), or you may have no idea what to get when your friend's usual order is out of stock. Thus, compared to more sophisticated forms of social learning, imitation generalizes poorly and lacks compositionality, since one cannot pluck an action out of its original context and expect it to be equally useful when placed in a new situation.

8.2.2 *Value Inference and Cached Value*

Another form of observational learning is to infer the instrumental value another person assigns to different actions by observing their behavior, and then to adopt this value representation oneself (Figure 8.3; Collette et al., 2017; Ho et al., 2017; Jern et al., 2017). Inferring values from social observation is closely related to the well-established use of cached value representations or value-based habits in individual learning (Daw et al., 2005; Keramati et al., 2016; Kool, Cushman, et al., 2018; Solway &

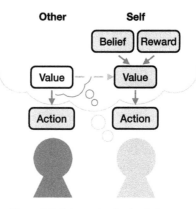

Figure 8.3 Schematic of value inference.

Botvinick, 2012). Like the use of a cached policy, caching value representations allows an agent to reuse costly computations, although this process takes place one step higher up the decision-making hierarchy (Figure 8.1), since observed actions first need to be "unpacked" into inferred value representations. Developing a representation of instrumental value – such as the instrumental value of trading a knight for a bishop in chess – is generally costly since it requires some amount of thinking, learning, and/or practice. Having earned this insight, it makes sense to "cache" it for reuse in future games. While not as cheap as caching policies, caching value representations offers superior generalizability and flexibility.

We can formally characterize social value inference as inverse reinforcement learning (IRL; Jara-Ettinger, 2019). Standard reinforcement learning (RL) models (Sutton & Barto, 2018) are used to understand how agents (biological or artificial) learn through interactions with the environment in nonsocial settings. As the agent interacts with the environment, they receive rewards, which update the value representations for different states and actions, which in turn guides future behavior. IRL inverts this model using Bayes' rule to infer hidden value representations given observed actions.

While IRL illuminates how humans reason about others' preferences, goals, and beliefs (Baker et al., 2017; Collette et al., 2017; Jern et al., 2017), it is computationally costly. For most interesting problems IRL is computationally intractable (Jara-Ettinger et al., 2016; Vélez & Gweon, 2021). Nevertheless, as a rational framework it can be used to uncover inductive biases that simplify the required computations. For instance, the *principle of efficient action* (Gergely & Csibra, 2003; Jara-Ettinger et al., 2015; Liu et al., 2019) assumes that other agents are acting in the most efficient manner toward achieving their aims, greatly constraining the hypothesis space for IRL inference.

A key advantage of cached value, rather than cached policy, is its superior generalization. Consider, for instance, an experiment in which participants are given repeated choices between two options that pay off with (A) 20% and (B) 30% probability, and also between options that pay off with (C) 70% and (D) 80% probability. Naturally, the proper policy is to choose B and D, respectively. But now suppose that a person is given the novel choice between B and C. Having cached a *policy* representation, they might choose B over C – after all, they have frequently chosen B, and rarely C (Hayden & Niv, 2021; K. J. Miller et al., 2019). In contrast, having cached a *value* representation, they should choose C over B, because C has been associated with greater historical rewards. This captures the key respect in which value representation affords greater compositionality than policy representation.

The same point applies to social learning. When imitating behavior at the level of policy representations, one does not distinguish between a person who chooses to eat a *dax* (some unknown fruit) when they could have eaten a ripe peach, versus someone who chooses to eat a *dax* given the alternative of a dirty hotdog. When learning from inferred value representations, however, one will likely assign greater value to the *dax* in the first case than the second. This, in turn, will help the learner to make adaptive choices about when to eat a *dax* herself – a key form of flexibility.

Importantly, cached value can be assigned not only to actions, but also to more abstract representations such as goal–subgoal relations (Botvinick & Weinstein, 2014; Cushman & Morris, 2015; Keramati et al., 2016; Maisto et al., 2019). For instance, the superordinate goal "make coffee in the morning" can be assigned value, but can also induce a set of value representations over subordinate goals: When valuing morning coffee, one should assign value to grinding beans, heating water, and so forth. This kind of cognitive architecture is naturally suited to "goal emulation" (Tomasello, 1996), in which the observer imputes goals to the actor and then adopts those goals, but uses novel planning to derive her own policy for attaining the goal.

8.2.3 *Belief Inference and Model-Based Planning*

Another method of social learning is to update one's own model of the world (i.e., beliefs) when observing another person's actions (Figure 8.4).

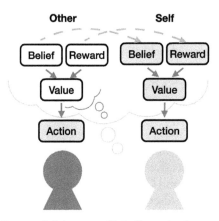

Figure 8.4 Schematic of belief/reward inference.

For instance, you might infer that it is likely to rain later by observing someone on the street carrying an umbrella. This observation could then inform you that you can skip watering the garden in the evening or that you should reschedule a planned picnic in the park.

Belief inference affords great flexibility and compositionality. Copying another person's actions, or adopting their representations of instrumental value, may not always be useful to you: those actions and values depend on the actor's unique circumstances, goals, or desires. In contrast, facts about the world are equally true for all of us. This affords maximal flexibility. Socially learned beliefs can be seamlessly composed with existing beliefs and, via planning, used to generate novel actions that reflect the specific circumstances, abilities, and desires of the actor.

Just as with values, an actor's unobserved beliefs can be inferred by Bayes' rule, given observation of their actions (Baker et al., 2017; Jara-Ettinger et al., 2016; Shafto et al., 2012). However, this may be computationally costlier than inferring the more direct linkage between actions and instrumental values. It is often possible to infer a person's values from their actions without considering their beliefs: for instance, concluding that someone like apples when you see them bite into one. But it is much harder to infer a person's beliefs from their action without performing a joint inference over their values (or rewards) as well. If a person opens a cabinet, you cannot know what they *believe* is in the cabinet without a hypothesis about what they *want* to retrieve from it. This may help to explain why very young infants are relatively adept at inferring the goals or values of other people, whereas robust inference about the beliefs of others comes much later (Gergely & Csibra, 2003).

There is a natural relationship between model-based social inference and model-based planning in individual learning, in terms of both the underlying representations and the computational demands of using them (K. J. Miller et al., 2017; Vikbladh et al., 2019). People often make decisions by computing the expected values of candidate actions given a model of their likely outcomes – in other words, their world model or beliefs. This is more computationally demanding than working from cached value or cached policy, but it affords the greatest degree of behavioral flexibility. Whereas cached policies and cached values are insensitive (without update) to changes in one's knowledge about the world or one's preferences, the process of planning over a world model maintains full sensitivity.

8.2.4   Reward Inference

When inferring the mental causes of observed actions, we can impute not only people's instrumental values ("she thinks it is useful to buy broccoli at the grocery store"), but also their intrinsic reward specification ("she loves the taste of broccoli"). Intrinsic rewards have been argued to be an important and useful target for social learning (Ho et al., 2017), since they may reveal elements of social partners' reward specifications that confer valuable fitness benefits (e.g., adopting a colleague's healthier food preferences). And, consistent with this possibility, a large social psychological literature documents examples of adopting others' preferences as "normative conformity" or "internalization" (Morris & Cushman, 2018). For instance, learning which faces other people find most attractive will influence one's own preferences (Zaki et al., 2011). Like the inference of beliefs and instrumental values, the inference of intrinsic rewards can be accomplished by IRL.

What are the costs and benefits of socially learning intrinsic rewards (e.g., "broccoli is delicious")? There are two sources of computational cost: inference and decision-making. Like inferring instrumental values or beliefs, inferring rewards can be accomplished by IRL, which requires costly computation. Then, after adopting a new reward, this can influence behavior in a variety of ways. The agent can use computationally expensive model-based methods to immediately update their policy via planning, or they can use computationally cheap model-free methods to gradually update their policy. Current research indicates that people can also use methods that blend model-free and model-based elements (Momennejad et al., 2017). Meanwhile, there are key benefits of socially learning new rewards. Like learning new beliefs, this form of learning is maximally compositional in the sense that a new optimal policy can be computed or learned following any arbitrary change to the reward function or the environment.

8.2.5   Interim Summary

Compared to information gained through firsthand interaction with the environment, social information has a rich structure built on hidden mental states. When observing your friend order a sandwich, you can infer information about both the world (e.g., the available menu options) and your friend (her values and beliefs). This information is implicitly "packed" into every socially observed action. We have defined a hierarchy of social-learning mechanisms that differ in how the learner "unpacks" observed actions to guide her own behavior. Each of these social learning mechanisms trades off the cost of performing the computation against the flexibility and compositionality of its outputs. It is computationally cheap to copy the "packed" information in the same format we observed it – that is, to use our observations of others' actions to guide our own actions directly. But, by "unpacking" the latent structure that gave rise to the action, this information can be productively composed with unique features of our own circumstances (e.g., our goals, abilities, and situational context). For example, you might infer that your friend's choice of sandwich is tastier than other options currently on the menu, but pass it up when the restaurant announces an exciting daily special. Drawing on this framework, our central proposal is that human social learning is powerful not because of any of these mechanisms, but rather because of how information is shared and composed across different mechanisms and levels of representation. Next, we consider how this is accomplished.

8.3   Representational Exchange in Social Learning

Our representational exchange framework of social learning (Figure 8.1) organizes different forms of social and nonsocial learning based on the representations involved. This focus on representational levels allows us to address two important problems within the same framework: how humans arbitrate among social learning mechanisms, and how information is exchanged and integrated across representations. Together, arbitration and integration enable humans to produce complex behaviors that efficiently blend cached representations with those that are computed online.

8.3.1   Arbitration

To some, the idea that humans arbitrate among social learning mechanisms may seem puzzling. Humans can make incredible inductive leaps from sparse social information by reasoning about the beliefs and values of other people (Vélez & Gweon, 2021). Why not always use the most sophisticated instrument in our repertoire?

One promising answer to this question comes from resource-rational theories of cognition (Bhui et al., 2021; Gershman et al., 2015; Lieder & Griffiths, 2020). Human minds are fundamentally limited – we have access to limited data, both from the world and from other people, and we have limited time and resources for performing computations. Resource-rational theories formalize how agents should make optimal use of limited minds. A common thread that runs through these theories is that people select strategies by balancing the effort required to perform a computation against the payoffs or precision of its outputs. This general principle shapes the arbitration between model-free habits (cached policy or value) versus model-based planning in individual decision-making (Kool et al., 2017; Kool, Gershman, et al., 2018). In tasks where model-based control generates little advantage in expected reward, people favor computationally cheaper model-free methods instead. When model-based control reliably produces a reward advantage, the degree to which they rely on it scales with the magnitude of the extra rewards.

We speculate that a similar principle might govern arbitration among social learning mechanisms: One should trade off the cost of performing a computation against the flexibility and compositionality of its outputs. A prediction that follows from this framework is that learners may deploy different social learning mechanisms based on the incentives of the task. Indeed, work on nonsocial learning and decision-making suggests that people engage in more effortful, controlled forms of reasoning when they are offered higher payoffs (Kool et al., 2017). Conversely, when people make decisions under stress (Otto, Raio, et al., 2013), strict time limits (Wu et al., 2021), or increased cognitive load (Cogliati Dezza et al., 2019), they fall back on cheaper, habitual behaviors instead (Kool, Cushman, et al., 2018; Otto, Gershman, et al., 2013; see Shenhav et al., 2013 for a review). Similarly, we might expect people to engage in more costly forms of social learning (e.g., belief inference) when they are incentivized to get it right, and to fall back on less costly forms (e.g., policy imitation) under increased task demands. If your friend orders a sandwich, you *could* compare the sandwich to other menu options to infer their preferences and beliefs in order to flexibly plan the best possible order – but if you are tired and need a quick bite to eat, you might get whatever she's having instead.

Further, more sophisticated inferences may miss the mark when they are based on insufficient evidence or when our model of the world is incomplete (Gigerenzer & Gaissmaier, 2011). Policy imitation does not only save computational costs, it also provides a way for learners to hedge their bets. For instance, if your friend demonstrates how to operate a very complex, delicate, and expensive Magnetic Resonance Imaging (MRI) scanner, it may be safer to faithfully reproduce her button presses than to use your limited knowledge to infer which steps can be skipped. Recent behavioral and neuroimaging evidence suggests that when comparing choice imitation against value inference (called goal emulation in the paper), people preferred the strategy that produced the most reliable predictions about outcomes (Charpentier et al., 2020). Activity in the bilateral temporoparietal junction and right ventrolateral prefrontal cortex tracked the trial-by-trial reliability of predictions generated through value inference; this activity is hypothesized to provide a control signal, regulating which of these predictions guides behavior.

In sum, humans face two fundamental challenges when arbitrating between social learning mechanisms: whether to engage in costlier forms of inference at all, and which outputs to use to guide behavior. How humans navigate these challenges has been largely unexplored (but see Charpentier et al., 2020). We hypothesize that humans decide whether to deploy costlier forms of inference by balancing the cost of the computation against the precision or payoff of its outputs, and they adjudicate the outputs of different computations based on their reliability.

8.3.2   Integration

So far we have emphasized three "horizontal pathways" for social learning (Figure 8.1): the direct copying of policy, the adoption of imputed values, and the adoption of imputed beliefs and rewards. Having discussed how information is transferred between minds, we now turn to the "vertical pathways" for exchanging information across representational formats within one's mind (Cushman, 2020). This includes ascending from observed actions to imputed mental states via inference, and also descending from mental states into actions via value-guided decision-making. The success of human social

learning is not only in our ability to acquire the right form of social information, but also to productively exchange information between levels of representation and to integrate it with our own experiences.

8.3.2.1   Descending: Amortization and Offline Planning

The simplest representational exchange is ordinary decision-making.
For instance, planning involves the compression of one's model of the
environment into a value representation, and then implementing
a policy to select actions on the basis of value (Sutton & Barto,
2018). Each of these steps creates new representations that can be
stored or "cached" for reuse in similar future episodes (Cushman &
Morris, 2015; Keramati et al., 2016; Maisto et al., 2019), such that
the computational burden can be distributed over time (i.e., amortization; Dasgupta et al., 2018).

This process can occur without actually taking any actions at all, but
merely through the act of planning and simulating action (Gershman et al.,
2014). For instance, a downhill skier can form a mental model of the
course and visualize the process of navigating it in the safety of her hotel
room, acquiring cached representations through mental simulations.
There is evidence that this kind of "offline planning" can occur without
conscious effort, and even during sleep (Foster, 2017; Momennejad et al.,
2018), helping to generate compressed representations that facilitate rapid
performance on the course.

These ideas naturally extend to social learning, since a skier can also
learn by observing an expert performance. If we adopted the view that
"imitation" and "emulation" are exclusively competing strategies, then our
skier would face a difficult choice. Should she copy the precise actions of an
expert, hoping that the differences between their bodies, skills, and moun-
tains are not too great? Or should she fully decompose the observed
behavior into its causal primitives: the beliefs, rewards, and values that
shaped the expert's performance? This offers more flexibility, but it's
difficult to imagine she could make it down the mountain at any reasonable speed while computing the best moves from first principles. Offline
planning, then, may play a key role in making emulation feasible. Rather
than having to recompute her plan while on the slope, she can integrate
whatever she has learned from the expert with her own knowledge in
advance, through offline planning.

Of course, we don't always "unpack" observed behavior into its most
elemental components and then fully replan new policies. Rather, we likely
employ a mixture of different social strategies, guided by the principles of

arbitration: using cheap methods whenever possible and more costly methods when more reliable. Offline planning – like ordinary experience – can be used to reassemble these components into a new and better trajectory down the hill.

8.3.2.2 Ascending: Inference and Rationalization

When we observe another person's actions, we can infer the hidden mental states that gave rise to those actions, including their beliefs, reward function, and computations of instrumental value. This is a basic form of "ascent" in our model (Figure 8.1). And, in the social cognition literature, this kind of thing is said so frequently that it can be easy to overlook its hidden premise: that, when we observe another person's actions, those actions really were caused by their beliefs, reward function, and computations of instrument value – namely, by rational planning.

But, often, they aren't. People's actions are also the product of habit (cached values or cached policies), instinct (innate behavioral responses), or conformity to cultural norms (when they imitate what other people do without reasoning why they do it). In these cases, what would it mean if an observer imputed beliefs, a reward function, and computations of instrumental value to the actor? It would mean that the observer is constructing a fiction – a "rationalization" of behavior – which can nevertheless be quite useful (Cushman, 2020). This fiction furnishes a key method of representational exchange, extracting implicit information from the cached policies or values of other people.

Suppose, for instance, that an aspiring baker wishes to improve the flavor of her loaves. She notices that in her culture people let their dough rise overnight, and she imputes the belief that this is a superior method – perhaps because the cool temperatures allow flavor to build during a longer fermentation. So, she tries putting her loaves in especially cool spots, even during the daytime. Now, it might be the case that in her culture, nobody knows why they let the bread rise overnight, they just do it because "that's how it's done." Nevertheless, by imputing beliefs, values, and rational choice, the aspiring baker might learn useful information from cultural practices that she can generalize productively.

The rationalization of cultural practices is ubiquitous. Its basic structure is depicted in Figure 8.5: A cultural norm is transmitted at the level of cached policy, but then later it is rationalized, yielding putative representations of values and beliefs. Parents and schoolteachers constantly find themselves attempting to "make sense" out of cultural practices for inquisitive children. Sometimes we are honest with ourselves, acknowledging that nobody really knows why we do things a certain way, although there may be implicit wisdom we can extract nevertheless. But just as often, we are less honest with ourselves

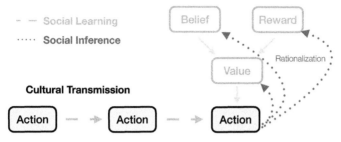

Figure 8.5 "Rationalization" of cultural knowledge. Behaviors may be transmitted through cultural norms, but because observed actions are rich in implicit information, they can be "unpacked" into imputed mental states. These mental states may not belong to the other individual (who directly acquired the behavior through imitation), yet they provide a useful fiction, exchanging an inflexible cultural norm for flexible and compositional representations to solve new problems.

(and with children), acting as if we had either chosen this behavior – or some forgotten designer had created it – for precisely the reasons we articulate to the child. In this case we are constructing a fiction, but a potentially useful one. The resulting representations may enable flexible and compositional thinking where, formerly, an inflexible cultural norm prevailed.

Of course, we rationalize not only other's behaviors, and "culture" more generally, but also our own behavior. Insofar as our own behavior is caused by nonrational processes (e.g., habits, instincts or norms), we can falsely impute reasoning processes to ourselves, assigning beliefs, values, and rewards as if the behaviors we perform were rational. Insofar as our behaviors are often guided by social learning, this is another pathway by which socially acquired information can propagate across levels of representation within our own mind (Cushman, 2020). For instance, having learned the motor routines involved in bread-making (a form of policy imitation), we can rationalize our own actions and thus extract useful values or beliefs about the bread-making process for further innovation.

8.3.3   Summary: Balancing Productivity and Reuse

Complex human behavior strikes a remarkable balance between flexible productivity and efficient reuse. This is true of the way we learn theories (Rozenblit & Keil, 2002), make plans (Cushman & Morris, 2015; Keramati et al., 2016; Solway et al., 2014), and speak (O'Donnell, 2015). This balance of productivity and reuse can be viewed as a variety of resource-rational cognition (Lieder & Griffiths, 2020). If we brought all of our knowledge and thinking to bear on every single problem, we'd never be able to make any decisions in time. Thus, wherever possible, we reuse the outputs of computations from relevant past episodes, while devoting our most powerful but precious cognitive resources to the specific elements of a behavior that require revision or improvement (Dasgupta & Gershman, 2021). To develop a complete theory of human social learning, we must understand how humans decompose observed behavior into disparate elements, each of which is represented at the appropriate level for efficient composition.

8.4   Conclusion

Social learning is central to the human experience. But rather than trying to pick out a single distinguishing feature of what makes humans special, we have argued that the distinction is in how the different mechanisms of social learning interact. In this we have drawn inspiration from the literature on nonsocial decision-making, where there is emerging consensus that human intelligence arises from the productive cooperation of diverse strategies for learning and decision-making (Huys et al., 2015; Kool, Cushman, et al., 2018; Solway & Botvinick, 2015). This is a natural source of inspiration because the hierarchy of inferences that we can draw from during observational social learning mirrors the hierarchy of learning and decision-making systems available to an individual. Both of these hierarchies can be characterized as points on a tradeoff between computational efficiency on the one hand and representational flexibility and compositionality on the other. The connection between social learning and individual decision-making is also natural because we integrate what we have learned with our preexisting policies, values, and beliefs. To do this, we exchange information between different formats of representation. This involves "descending" pathways (moving from more flexible and compositional representations toward compressed policy-relevant representations), as well as "ascending" pathways (extracting information implicit in policy-relevant representations into more flexible and compositional elements).

We study social learning because we want to understand real human behaviors – the kinds we perform every day, such as baking a loaf of bread or choosing what to eat. These behaviors are paradigmatic of human intelligence, partly because we are able to blend strategies we've learned from others with strategies we've developed ourselves. Yet, they are also paradigmatic because they involve skills and representations spanning from very specific, concrete behaviors to very abstract, general principles. Our ability to build harmony across these levels is essential to the virtuosic performances of the human mind.

Acknowledgments

CMW is supported by the German Federal Ministry of Education and Research (BMBF): Tübingen AI Center, FKZ: 01IS18039A and funded by the Deutsche Forschungsgemeinschaft (DFG, German Research Foundation) under Germany's Excellence Strategy–EXC2064/1–390727645. NV is supported by grant 8K00MH125856-02 from the National Institute of Mental Health. FAC is supported by grant N00014-19-1-2025 from the Office of Naval Research and grant 61061 from the John Templeton Foundation.

References

Apperly, I. (2010). *Mindreaders: The cognitive basis of "theory of mind."* Psychology Press.

Atkisson, C., O'Brien, M. J., & Mesoudi, A. (2012). Adult learners in a novel environment use prestige-biased social learning. *Evolutionary Psychology: An International Journal of Evolutionary Approaches to Psychology and Behavior,* 10(3), 519–537.

Baker, C. L., Jara-Ettinger, J., Saxe, R., & Tenenbaum, J. B. (2017). Rational quantitative attribution of beliefs, desires and percepts in human mentalizing. *Nature Human Behaviour,* 1(4), 1–10.

Bandura, A. (1962). Social learning through imitation. *Nebraska Symposium on Motivation,* 330, 211–274.

Bhui, R., Lai, L., & Gershman, S. J. (2021). Resource-rational decision making. *Current Opinion in Behavioral Sciences,* 41, 15–21.

Botvinick, M., & Weinstein, A. (2014). Model-based hierarchical reinforcement learning and human action control. *Philosophical Transactions of the Royal Society of London. Series B, Biological Sciences,* 369(1655). https://doi.org/10.1098/rstb.2013.0480.

Boyd, R., & Richerson, P. J. (1988). *Culture and the Evolutionary Process.* University of Chicago Press.

Catmur, C., Walsh, V., & Heyes, C. (2009). Associative sequence learning: The role of experience in the development of imitation and the mirror system. *Philosophical Transactions of the Royal Society of London. Series B, Biological Sciences,* 364(1528), 2369–2380.

Charpentier, C. J., Iigaya, K., & O'Doherty, J. P. (2020). A neuro-computational account of arbitration between choice imitation and goal emulation during human observational learning. *Neuron,* 106(4), 687–699.e7.

Cogliati Dezza, I., Cleeremans, A., & Alexander, W. (2019). Should we control? The interplay between cognitive control and information integration in the resolution of the exploration-exploitation dilemma. *Journal of Experimental Psychology. General*, 148(6), 977–993.

Collette, S., Pauli, W. M., Bossaerts, P., & O'Doherty, J. (2017). Neural computations underlying inverse reinforcement learning in the human brain. *eLife*, 6. https://doi.org/10.7554/eLife.29718.

Cushman, F. (2020). Rationalization is rational. *The Behavioral and Brain Sciences*, 43, e28.

Cushman, F., & Morris, A. (2015). Habitual control of goal selection in humans. *Proceedings of the National Academy of Sciences of the United States of America*, 112(45), 13817–13822.

Dasgupta, I., & Gershman, S. J. (2021). Memory as a computational resource. *Trends in Cognitive Sciences*, 25(3), 240–251.

Dasgupta, I., Schulz, E., Goodman, N. D., & Gershman, S. J. (2018). Remembrance of inferences past: Amortization in human hypothesis generation. *Cognition*, 178, 67–81.

Daw, N. D., Niv, Y., & Dayan, P. (2005). Uncertainty-based competition between prefrontal and dorsolateral striatal systems for behavioral control. *Nature Neuroscience*, 8(12), 1704–1711.

Derex, M., Bonnefon, J.-F., Boyd, R., & Mesoudi, A. (2019). Causal understanding is not necessary for the improvement of culturally evolving technology. *Nature Human Behaviour*, 3(5), 446–452.

Dezfouli, A., & Balleine, B. W. (2013). Actions, action sequences and habits: Evidence that goal-directed and habitual action control are hierarchically organized. *PLoS Computational Biology*, 9(12), e1003364.

Foster, D. J. (2017). Replay comes of age. *Annual Review of Neuroscience*, 40, 581–602.

Gergely, G., & Csibra, G. (2003). Teleological reasoning in infancy: The naive theory of rational action. In *Trends in Cognitive Sciences* (Vol. 7, Issue 7, pp. 287–292). https://doi.org/10.1016/s1364-6613(03)00128-1.

Gershman, S. J. (2020). Origin of perseveration in the trade-off between reward and complexity. *Cognition*, 204, 104394.

Gershman, S. J., Horvitz, E. J., & Tenenbaum, J. B. (2015). Computational rationality: A converging paradigm for intelligence in brains, minds, and machines. *Science*, 349(6245), 273–278.

Gershman, S. J., Markman, A. B., & Otto, A. R. (2014). Retrospective revaluation in sequential decision making: A tale of two systems. *Journal of Experimental Psychology. General*, 143(1), 182–194.

Gigerenzer, G., & Gaissmaier, W. (2011). Heuristic decision making. *Annual Review of Psychology*, 62, 451–482.

Gweon, H. (2021). Inferential Social Learning: How humans learn from others and help others learn. https://doi.org/10.31234/osf.io/8n34t.

Hayden, B. Y., & Niv, Y. (2021). The case against economic values in the orbitofrontal cortex (or anywhere else in the brain). *Behavioral Neuroscience*, 135(2), 192–201.

Henrich, J. (2017). *The Secret of Our Success: How Culture Is Driving Human Evolution, Domesticating Our Species, and Making Us Smarter*. Princeton University Press.

Henrich, J., & Gil-White, F. J. (2001). The evolution of prestige: Freely conferred deference as a mechanism for enhancing the benefits of cultural transmission. *Evolution and Human Behavior: Official Journal of the Human Behavior and Evolution Society*, 22(3), 165–196.

Herrmann, E., Call, J., Hernàndez-Lloreda, M. V., Hare, B., & Tomasello, M. (2007). Humans have evolved specialized skills of social cognition: the cultural intelligence hypothesis. *Science*, 317(5843), 1360–1366.

Heyes, C. (2001). Causes and consequences of imitation. *Trends in Cognitive Sciences*, 5(6), 253–261.

Heyes, C. (2002). Transformational and associative theories of imitation. *Imitation in Animals and Artifacts*, 607, 501–523.

Heyes, C. (2018). *Cognitive Gadgets: The Cultural Evolution of Thinking*. Harvard University Press.

Ho, M. K., MacGlashan, J., Littman, M. L., & Cushman, F. (2017). Social is special: A normative framework for teaching with and learning from evaluative feedback. *Cognition*, 167, 91–106.

Hoppitt, W., & Laland, K. N. (2013). *Social Learning: An Introduction to Mechanisms, Methods, and Models*. Princeton University Press.

Horner, V., & Whiten, A. (2005). Causal knowledge and imitation/emulation switching in chimpanzees (Pan troglodytes) and children (Homo sapiens). *Animal Cognition*, 8(3), 164–181.

Huys, Q. J. M., Lally, N., Faulkner, P., Eshel, N., Seifritz, E., Gershman, S. J., Dayan, P., & Roiser, J. P. (2015). Interplay of approximate planning strategies. *Proceedings of the National Academy of Sciences of the United States of America*, 112(10), 3098–3103.

Jara-Ettinger, J. (2019). Theory of mind as inverse reinforcement learning. *Current Opinion in Behavioral Sciences*, 29, 105–110.

Jara-Ettinger, J., Gweon, H., Schulz, L. E., & Tenenbaum, J. B. (2016). The Naïve Utility Calculus: Computational Principles Underlying Commonsense Psychology. *Trends in Cognitive Sciences*, 20(8), 589–604.

Jara-Ettinger, J., Gweon, H., Tenenbaum, J. B., & Schulz, L. E. (2015). Children's understanding of the costs and rewards underlying rational action. *Cognition*, 140, 14–23.

Jern, A., Lucas, C. G., & Kemp, C. (2017). People learn other people's preferences through inverse decision-making. *Cognition*, 168, 46–64.

Jiménez, Á. V., & Mesoudi, A. (2019). Prestige-biased social learning: Current evidence and outstanding questions. *Palgrave Communications*, 5(1), 20.

Keramati, M., Smittenaar, P., Dolan, R. J., & Dayan, P. (2016). Adaptive integration of habits into depth-limited planning defines a habitual-goal-directed spectrum. *Proceedings of the National Academy of Sciences of the United States of America*, 113(45), 12868–12873.

Kool, W., Cushman, F. A., & Gershman, S. J. (2018). Competition and cooperation between multiple reinforcement learning systems. In R. Morris, A. Bornstein, & A. Shenhav (Eds.), *Goal-directed decision making* (pp. 153–178). Academic Press.

Kool, W., Gershman, S. J., & Cushman, F. A. (2017). Cost-benefit arbitration between multiple reinforcement-learning systems. *Psychological Science*, 28(9), 1321–1333.

Kool, W., Gershman, S. J., & Cushman, F. A. (2018). Planning complexity registers as a cost in metacontrol. *Journal of Cognitive Neuroscience*, 30(10), 1391–1404.

Legare, C. H., & Nielsen, M. (2015). Imitation and innovation: The dual engines of cultural learning. *Trends in Cognitive Sciences*, 19(11), 688–699.

Lieder, F., & Griffiths, T. L. (2020). Resource-rational analysis: Understanding human cognition as the optimal use of limited computational resources. In *Behavioral and Brain Sciences* (Vol. 43). https://doi.org/10.1017/s0140525x1900061x.

Liu, S., Brooks, N. B., & Spelke, E. S. (2019). Origins of the concepts cause, cost, and goal in prereaching infants. *Proceedings of the National Academy of Sciences of the United States of America*, 116(36), 17747–17752.

Lyons, D. E., Young, A. G., & Keil, F. C. (2007). The hidden structure of overimitation. *Proceedings of the National Academy of Sciences of the United States of America*, 104(50), 19751–19756.

Maisto, D., Friston, K., & Pezzulo, G. (2019). Caching mechanisms for habit formation in active inference. *Neurocomputing*, 359, 298–314.

McGuigan, N., Whiten, A., Flynn, E., & Horner, V. (2007). Imitation of causally opaque versus causally transparent tool use by 3- and 5-year-old children. *Cognitive Development*, 22(3), 353–364.

Miller, K. J., Botvinick, M. M., & Brody, C. D. (2017). Dorsal hippocampus contributes to model-based planning. Nature Neuroscience. https://doi.org/10.1101/096594.

Miller, K. J., Shenhav, A., & Ludwig, E. A. (2019). Habits without values. *Psychological Review*, 126(2), 292–311.

Miller, N. E., & Dollard, J. (1941). *Social Learning and Imitation* (Vol. 55). Yale University Press.

Momennejad, I., Otto, A. R., Daw, N. D., & Norman, K. A. (2018). Offline replay supports planning in human reinforcement learning. *eLife*, 7. https://doi.org/10.7554/eLife.32548.

Momennejad, I., Russek, E. M., Cheong, J. H., Botvinick, M. M., Daw, N. D., & Gershman, S. J. (2017). The successor representation in human reinforcement learning. *Nature Human Behaviour*, 1(9), 680–692.

Morin, O. (2016). *How Traditions Live and Die*. Oxford University Press.

Morris, A., & Cushman, F. (2018). A common framework for theories of norm compliance. *Social Philosophy & Policy*, 35(1), 101–127.

Najar, A., Bonnet, E., Bahrami, B., & Palminteri, S. (2020). The actions of others act as a pseudo-reward to drive imitation in the context of social reinforcement learning. *PLoS Biology*, 18(12), e3001028.

O'Donnell, T. J. (2015). *Productivity and Reuse in Language: A Theory of Linguistic Computation and Storage.* MIT Press.

Otto, A. R., Gershman, S. J., Markman, A. B., & Daw, N. D. (2013). The curse of planning: Dissecting multiple reinforcement-learning systems by taxing the central executive. *Psychological Science*, 24(5), 751–761.

Otto, A. R., Raio, C. M., Chiang, A., Phelps, E. A., & Daw, N. D. (2013). Working-memory capacity protects model-based learning from stress. *Proceedings of the National Academy of Sciences of the United States of America*, 110(52), 20941–20946.

Rendell, L., Boyd, R., Cownden, D., Enquist, M., Eriksson, K., Feldman, M. W., . . . & Laland, K. N. (2010). Why copy others? Insights from the social learning strategies tournament. *Science*, 328(5975), 208–213.

Rozenblit, L., & Keil, F. (2002). The misunderstood limits of folk science: An illusion of explanatory depth. *Cognitive Science*, 26(5), 521–562.

Russek, E. M., Momennejad, I., Botvinick, M. M., Gershman, S. J., & Daw, N. D. (2017). Predictive representations can link model-based reinforcement learning to model-free mechanisms. *PLoS Computational Biology*, 13(9), e1005768.

Scott-Phillips, T. C. (2017). A (simple) experimental demonstration that cultural evolution is not replicative, but reconstructive – and an explanation of why this difference matters. *Journal of Cognition and Culture*, 17(1–2), 1–11.

Shafto, P., Goodman, N. D., & Frank, M. C. (2012). Learning from others: The consequences of psychological reasoning for human learning. *Perspectives on Psychological Science: A Journal of the Association for Psychological Science*, 7(4), 341–351.

Shenhav, A., Botvinick, M. M., & Cohen, J. D. (2013). The expected value of control: An integrative theory of anterior cingulate cortex function. *Neuron*, 79(2), 217–240.

Skinner, B. F. (1950). Are theories of learning necessary? *Psychological Review*, 57(4), 193–216.

Solway, A., & Botvinick, M. M. (2012). Goal-directed decision making as probabilistic inference: A computational framework and potential neural correlates. *Psychological Review*, 119(1), 120–154.

Solway, A., & Botvinick, M. M. (2015). Evidence integration in model-based tree search. *Proceedings of the National Academy of Sciences of the United States of America*, 112(37), 11708–11713.

Solway, A., Diuk, C., Córdova, N., Yee, D., Barto, A. G., Niv, Y., & Botvinick, M. M. (2014). Optimal behavioral hierarchy. *PLoS Computational Biology*, 10(8), e1003779.

Sperber, D. (2006). Why a deep understanding of cultural evolution is incompatible with shallow psychology. In N. J. Enfield & Stephen C. Levinson (Ed.), *Roots of human sociality* (pp. 431–449). Routledge.

Strachan, J., Curioni, A., Constable, M., Knoblich, G., & Charbonneau, M. (2020). A methodology for distinguishing copying and reconstruction in cultural transmission episodes. In S. Denison, M. Mack, Y. Xu, A. Yang and C. B. Armstrong (Eds.), *Proceedings of the 42nd Annual Conference of the Cognitive Science Society*. https://researchportal.northumbria.ac.uk/ws/files/32 896647/0831.pdf.

Sutton, R. S., & Barto, A. G. (2018). *Reinforcement Learning, second edition: An Introduction*. MIT Press.

Tennie, C., Call, J., & Tomasello, M. (2009). Ratcheting up the ratchet: On the evolution of cumulative culture. *Philosophical Transactions of the Royal Society of London. Series B, Biological Sciences*, 364(1528), 2405–2415.

Thorndike, E. L. (1932). *The fundamentals of learning*. https://psycnet.apa.org/r ecord/2006-04535-000.

Tolman, E. C. (1948). Cognitive maps in rats and men. *Psychological Review* (Vol. 55, Issue 4, pp. 189–208). https://doi.org/10.1037/h0061626.

Tomasello, M. (1996). Do apes ape. In C. M. Heyes & B. G. Galef, Jr. (Eds.), *Social Learning in Animals: The Roots of Culture*, (pp. 319–346). Academic Press. https://doi.org/10.1016/B978-012273965-1/50016-9.

Tomasello, M., Carpenter, M., Call, J., Behne, T., & Moll, H. (2005). Understanding and sharing intentions: The origins of cultural cognition. *The Behavioral and Brain Sciences*, 28(5), 675–691; discussion 691–735.

Tomasello, M., Davis-Dasilva, M., Camak, L., & Bard, K. (1987). Observational learning of tool-use by young chimpanzees. *Human Evolution*, 2(2), 175–183.

Vélez, N., & Gweon, H. (2021). Learning from other minds: An optimistic critique of reinforcement learning models of social learning. *Current Opinion in Behavioral Sciences*, 38, 110–115.

Vikbladh, O. M., Meager, M. R., King, J., Blackmon, K., Devinsky, O., Shohamy, D., Burgess, N., & Daw, N. D. (2019). Hippocampal contributions to model-based planning and spatial memory. *Neuron*, 102(3), 683–693.e4.

Whiten, A., & Ham, R. (1992). Kingdom: Reappraisal of a century of research. *Advances in the Study of Behavior*, 21, 239.

Wu, C. M., Schulz, E., Gerbaulet, K., Pleskac, T. J., & Speekenbrink, M. (2021). Time to explore: Adaptation of exploration under time pressure. *PsyArXiv*. https://doi.org/10.31234/osf.io/dsw7q.

Zaki, J., Schirmer, J., & Mitchell, J. P. (2011). Social influence modulates the neural computation of value. *Psychological Science*, 22(7), 894–900.

PART III

Which Machinery Supports the Drive for Knowledge?

CHAPTER 9

Information-Seeking in the Brain

Caroline J. Charpentier and Irene Cogliati Dezza

9.1 Introduction

Humans exhibit a strong preference for information (Gottlieb, Oudeyer, Lopes, & Baranes, 2013) and spend a substantial amount of time seeking information (e.g., asking questions, reading, internet browsing). In our modern, connected societies, we are very often bombarded with information, coming from different sources and with different levels of veracity. As a result, we have to actively weigh the pros and cons of seeking information (versus refraining from doing so), depending on what we expect that information will provide us with (e.g., good or bad news, better understanding of reality, etc.).

Information is needed to guide people's decisions and actions, but it is also necessary to better comprehend and predict the physical and social world. Information may also satisfy an internal need, such as a desire for novelty (Gottlieb et al., 2013), curiosity (Kidd & Hayden, 2015), or uncertainty reduction (Gershman, 2019). Additionally, information can impact the current mood and affective states of the information-seeker (Sharot & Sunstein, 2020). For example, receiving information about a positive HIV test result may induce sadness, while receiving a job offer may induce joy. As such, information-seeking is a complex behavior which drives intellectual development, is integral to social interactions (Evans & Chi, 2010; Evans, Kairam, & Pirolli, 2009), and is crucial for learning, decision-making, and goal-directed processing (Gottlieb et al., 2013).

Given the complexity associated with the human pursuit of knowledge, understanding its underlying mechanisms is inherently challenging. Many motives (see Table 9.1 for definitions) can play a role in driving information-seeking (e.g., satisfy internal or external needs, as described above and in other chapters in this book, such as Chapters 1, 2, 10). These motives also influence individual expectations during the anticipation of information, as well as the goals that can be achieved if the information is

Table 9.1 *Information-seeking: a multifaceted process*

Information-seeking motives	Definition
Instrumentality	The potential of information to improve future decisions, actions, and outcomes. Preference for/value of information increases the more 'useful' the resulting knowledge is.
Curiosity	The potential of information to satisfy an internal drive for knowledge. Preference for/value of information increases when subjective desire to know something is high.
Valence	The potential of information to influence mood and affective states. Preference for/value of information increases with the desirability of the information provided.
Uncertainty reduction	The potential of information to reduce uncertainty in the environment and to increase understanding of the world. Preference for/value of information increases when uncertainty or entropy is high.

Many motives can drive information-seeking behavior, making it a complex process to study. As shown, information can improve people's actions and decisions (instrumentality), and it can satisfy an internal drive for knowledge (curiosity), affective states (valence) and the understanding of reality (uncertainty reduction). The table provides definitions for each of these motives.

consumed (e.g., impact on internal or external states). Only recently in the information-seeking field, researchers have started to better characterize these behaviors (Zurn & Bassett, 2018; Kobayashi, Ravaioli, Baranes, Woodford, & Gottlieb, 2019; Murayama, 2019a; Sharot & Sunstein, 2020), as well as their underlying computational and algorithmic principles (Cogliati Dezza, Yu, Cleeremans, & Alexander, 2017; Friston et al., 2017; Oudeyer, 2018; Wu, Schulz, Speekenbrink, Nelson, & Meder, 2018; Schulz & Gershman, 2019; Dubey & Griffiths, 2020).

As a consequence, understanding how the brain implements information-seeking is still in its early stages. Moreover, the experimental paradigms and computational frameworks that have been used thus far to understand the neurocognitive processes associated with information-seeking have varied widely across studies. Some studies have used "observing" paradigms, whereby information is clearly noninstrumental (Bromberg-Martin & Hikosaka, 2009; Bromberg-Martin & Hikosaka, 2011; Blanchard, Hayden, & Bromberg-Martin, 2015; Charpentier, Bromberg-Martin, & Sharot, 2018), allowing researchers to isolate how information is valued in and of itself, as well as the role of specific noninstrumental motives. Other studies have focused on both instrumental and noninstrumental motives (Kobayashi & Hsu, 2019; Cogliati Dezza, Cleeremans, & Alexander, 2020) or have quantified information-seeking behavior through measuring and modeling exploratory behavior during learning (e.g. the explore–exploit dilemma, foraging problems; Wilson, Geana, White, Ludvig, & Cohen, 2014; Cogliati Dezza et al., 2017; Gershman, 2019). In exploratory paradigms, for example, the information gathered is instrumental, since it helps improve future actions and outcomes, but it also helps to better understand the environment. In this context, it is much harder to dissociate the specific drivers and mechanisms of information-seeking, since motives may be more confounded (unless computational modeling techniques are adopted; Cogliati Dezza et al., 2020). Overall, it is important to highlight that the level of variability in experimental approaches, for what is a relatively nascent field, makes it quite difficult to interpret current findings within a fully coherent picture.

Nevertheless, recent advances in the neuroscience of information-seeking all seem to converge on a key principle: information is valuable, similar to primary or monetary rewards (Murayama, 2019a). Humans and other animals are often willing to incur a cost for obtaining information (Pierson & Goodman, 2014; Blanchard et al., 2015; Charpentier et al., 2018), even if the information provides no or few instrumental benefits. This is reflected in the brain via a common neural code for reward and information (Kobayashi & Hsu, 2019), which seems to be a universal mechanism across many information-seeking behaviors, encompassing a general preference for information as well as information driven by instrumentality or valence. However, when people seek information to better understand the surrounding environment and reduce their uncertainty about the world, information-seeking appears to be implemented in the brain through distinct neural circuits. This idea of dissociable networks is consistent with a recent review suggesting distinct roles for anterior and posterior regions of the prefrontal cortex in information-seeking processes (Kaanders, Juechems, O'Reilly, & Hunt, 2021).

This chapter will review the main findings from the field, which show both *shared* and *independent* networks underlying how information-seeking is implemented in the brain. We will then conclude the chapter by presenting a possible mechanism based on recent theories (Bromberg-Martin & Monosov, 2020; Murayama, 2019a; Sharot & Sunstein, 2020), which suggests that the neural mechanisms of information-seeking are controlled by a unique network, with some mechanisms shared with reward processing and others independent of it.

9.2 Shared Neural Correlates for Information and Reward Processing: A Domain-General Preference for Information?

A large body of literature examining how the brain processes information has converged on the finding that the opportunity to gain information relies on the same neural circuitry as the opportunity to gain rewards (Figure 9.1A).

Considerable empirical evidence in neuroeconomics and decision neuroscience suggest that when learning and assigning value to outcomes, the brain relies on a prefrontal-mesolimbic network (Bartra, McGuire, & Kable, 2013; Lopez-Persem et al., 2020). Key regions of this network include the ventromedial prefrontal cortex (vmPFC), the orbitofrontal cortex (OFC), the ventral striatum, and the dopaminergic midbrain (substantia nigra and ventral tegmental area – SN/VTA). Activity in prefrontal regions tends to reflect the economic value of decision options as well as the difference in value prior to a choice (Bartra et al., 2013; Pessiglione & Lebreton, 2014; Padoa-Schioppa & Conen, 2017). In parallel, activity in SN/VTA and ventral striatum updates the expected value of an outcome by computing a prediction error. This signal is reflected in dopaminergic neurons, which fire up when an outcome is better than expected and decrease their firing rate when outcomes are worse than expected (Schultz, Dayan, & Montague, 1997; Diederen & Fletcher, 2021). We note, however, that these regions are extensively connected with each other, both anatomically and functionally (Goldman-Rakic et al. 1992; Chib, Yun, Takahashi, & Shimojo, 2013; Morris et al., 2016), and thus reward-related signals are encoded across the entire network more so than within each single region independently.

Interestingly, recent findings in the literature suggest that each of these regions also plays a role in encoding the opportunity to gain information, independent of its reward value (**Figure 9.1A**).

First, the OFC has been implicated in representing information gain, both at the single-neuron level in nonhuman primates, and in the BOLD signal in humans. In a seminal study (Blanchard et al., 2015), monkeys made sequential choices between two gambles displayed on the left and right sides of the screen. One gamble was informative as it always led to a cue which predicted the gamble's outcome. The other gamble led to a noninformative cue. OFC neural populations were found to use different

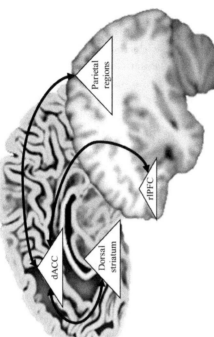

A   Shared Network   **B**   Independent network

Figure 9.1 Two main brain networks are recruited during information-seeking. Here we hypothesize some connections based on anatomical and functional connectivity usually found in the literature among the regions involved in information-seeking. However, the function and directionality of these connections is mostly unknown. A) A prefrontal-mesolimbic *"shared"* network appears to encode both the value of information and the value of primary and monetary rewards, as well the effect of valence on information-seeking. B) Uncertainty reduction, another motive for information-seeking, is represented in an *"independent"* fronto-parietal network.

neural codes to signal the opportunity to gain information about rewards versus the value of the rewards themselves. In other words, information and rewards were signaled with independent neural codes in OFC neurons. Interestingly, this distinct encoding of reward and information allowed for expectations about reward and information values to be adjusted separately depending on internal drives, which in turn influenced decisions and actions. For example, this would allow an agent to seek food when hungry, but to seek information when uncertain. In human fMRI, the lateral OFC was also found to represent informational signals (Jessup & O'Doherty, 2014), which encode whether an outcome is rewarding or punishing (compared to a neutral outcome), regardless of its valence, utility, or magnitude. More recently, a cluster in the medial portion of OFC was found to exhibit increased activity during the presentation of cues that predict the upcoming delivery of information, relative to the presentation of ignorance cues signaling that no information would be delivered (Charpentier et al., 2018). Importantly, this signal was again independent from the valence of the information (i.e., whether the information was about a reward, a loss, no reward, or no loss). This suggests that the OFC plays a possible role in signaling a general preference for knowledge over ignorance, in both human and nonhuman primates.

Another line of work has also provided evidence for a role of the dopaminergic system, specifically the lateral habenula (LHb), SN/VTA, and nucleus accumbens (a portion of the ventral striatum), in general information preference. Bromberg-Martin and Hikosaka (2009) recorded data from macaques' midbrain dopamine neurons while the animals performed a task in which they viewed either informative cues (cues that deterministically predict whether a small or a large reward is coming) or noninformative cues (random cues that each lead to the small or the big reward with 50 percent chance). Prior to these cues, the animals either chose from or were passively presented with one of two other cues, which this time predicted whether or not information (i.e., the cues that deterministically predict the reward) would be shown next. Behaviorally, the animals exhibited a strong preference for receiving advance information about the size of their reward. This preference was reflected in the response of midbrain dopamine neurons, which were found to signal the expectation of receiving information. Importantly, contrary to the OFC neurons identified in Blanchard et al. (2015)'s study, which signaled reward independently from information, here those same midbrain dopamine neurons that signaled expected information were found to signal expected reward, suggesting a common neural code in dopamine neurons. In humans, consistent with the idea of a shared neural code, fMRI BOLD responses in the nucleus accumbens encoded two properties of the outcome (Smith, Rigney, & Delgado, 2016): the affective component (number of points earned), and the informative component (amount of knowledge gained from feedback). Additionally, the strength of the informative – but not affective – signal predicted subsequent performance in using the information to obtain rewards, suggesting a role for the nucleus accumbens in processing instrumental information. Similarly, in a recent study (Filimon, Nelson, Sejnowski, Sereno, & Cottrell, 2020), the nucleus accumbens was found to respond not only to the valence of feedback (positive versus negative), but also to the expectation of a more informative stimulus (high versus low information to help stimulus categorization).

Thus, evidence from both human and nonhuman primate studies point toward a clear role of the brain's reward system in processing the value of information. Yet, the specific computations that underlie this shared neural code remain unclear. Several studies provide some initial key insights into these possible computations. Similar to reward prediction errors, which rely on the dopaminergic system and allow learning about rewards in the environment, an early theory posited that the dopaminergic system may also encode an information prediction error (IPE) – that is, the difference between the delivery or denial of information and the initial expectation of information. Following up on their earlier work, Bromberg-Martin and Hikosaka (2011) modified their task design in order to be able to quantify and detect the presence of information prediction errors. They added the presence of an initial cue, which led to the delivery of informative cues vs. noninformative cues 50 percent of the time. This allowed for the comparison of neural responses for expected information vs. unexpected information. Recording from the lateral habenula (LHb), which contains dopamine neurons and encodes reward prediction errors (Matsumoto & Hikosaka, 2007), they found that the neurons encoded an information prediction error (IPE). Specifically, LHb neurons responded more strongly when the delivery of informative or noninformative cues was unexpected compared to when it was expected. In humans, fMRI evidence for a domain-general IPE is still lacking; however, a study using EEG (Brydevall, Bennett, Murawski, & Bode, 2018) found that feedback-related negativity signals when informative cues are revealed can represent both an information prediction error and a reward prediction error. While it is difficult to assess whether these two signals come from the same source, this is nonetheless an additional piece of evidence for a similarity in the type of neural signal the brain uses to represent reward and information. In other words, given EEG evidence only, the source could be different, but the computational code (prediction error) appears to be the same for reward and information. With additional evidence coming from monkey recording studies and human fMRI studies, current findings seem to converge around the theory that both the source and the code of neural signals are shared between reward and information processing.

The most convincing evidence for shared neuro-computational signals for information and reward in the human brain comes from a recent study (Kobayashi et al., 2019), which examined the role of both vmPFC and ventral striatum in human decisions to buy information about the true probability associated with a lottery. Activity in both regions correlated with the subjective value of information (SVOI), a trial-by-trial variable from a computational model that integrates the influence of both instrumental and noninstrumental motives on information-seeking decisions. That is, the more valuable information is to an individual, the stronger the vmPFC and ventral striatum responses will be. Using multivariate analysis, the authors additionally showed that a decoder trained on reward-related responses (specifically, the expected utility signal; EU) could predict information-related responses (SVOI signal) and vice-versa. This suggests a common code for the subjective value of information and for the expected utility of the lotteries. While the aforementioned SVOI signal did not separate the contribution of instrumental and noninstrumental information (rather reflecting the integration of the two), the finding of a recent study (Cogliati Dezza et al., 2020) suggests (albeit in a different task) that it is the *instrumental* value of information that is expressed in reward regions. This study additionally shows the convergence of reward and information signals in the striatum region, consistent with Smith et al. (2016).

In summary, this body of literature has led to the now widely accepted assumption that information is intrinsically rewarding. The shared neural correlates described earlier provide a possible explanation for why individuals (both humans and other animals) exhibit a strong preference for information, and why they are often willing to incur a cost for obtaining such information, even when it provides no or few instrumental benefits. In the following sections, we will focus on the neural mechanisms for two main motives of these information-seeking decisions: valence and uncertainty reduction.

9.3 Valence-Dependent Information-Seeking: Neural Mechanisms of the Preference for Good News

While the opportunity to gain information carries value in and of itself, independent of the valence of the information, studies have demonstrated a clear bias whereby information likely to induce positive affect (desirable information) is preferred over information likely to induce negative affect (undesirable information; Sharot & Sunstein, 2020). Note that this valence-dependent information preference is present even when information has no instrumental use, namely when it cannot be used to influence one's outcomes (Charpentier et al., 2018; Kobayashi et al., 2019). In other words, an individual is more likely to open an envelope containing the results of a medical test if they expect the result to be good than if they expect it to be bad. This preference can be explained by belief utility theory (Bénabou, 2016; Loewenstein & Molnar, 2018), which is a theory from behavioral economics positing that our beliefs (e.g., the belief that my medical test result will carry good news), as well as the ability to anticipate the experience of outcomes, have utility, similar to goods or monetary rewards. Therefore, seeking desirable over undesirable information allows one to maintain positive belief utility by anticipating positive future outcomes (Loewenstein, 1987; Caplin & Leahy, 2001). This is thought to contribute to higher mood and well-being. Dread, on the other hand, would lead to negative belief utility (Berns et al., 2006 Story et al., 2013) and to the tendency to avoid undesirable information (Karlsson, Loewenstein, & Seppi, 2009; Golman, Hagmann, & Loewenstein, 2017) – for example, leaving the envelope unopened if I expect the medical test result to carry bad news.

One possible mechanism for such valence-dependent information-seeking behavior is through the computation of valence-dependent information prediction errors (VD-IPE). This represents an IPE signal (i.e., error in predicting the opportunity to receive information) that scales with the desirability of the outcome. In Charpentier et al. (2018), participants had to decide between a high and a low probability of receiving information about the outcome of a probabilistic lottery. Behaviorally, participants' propensity to choose the high-information probability increased with the probability of winning the lottery and decreased with the probability of losing the lottery. This valence-dependent information-seeking behavior was mirrored in the brain by VD-IPEs, which were detected in the SN/VTA, such that IPEs were represented more strongly in the gain domain than in the loss domain. In the nucleus accumbens – one of the regions SN/VTA dopaminergic neurons project to – the strength of the VD-IPE signal predicted the effect of valence on participants' information-seeking decisions. In other words, the more IPE signals differed for desirable versus undesirable information, the more participants' decisions to seek information were biased by the valence of the lottery.

Another mechanism contributing to the influence of hedonic motives on the valuation of information involves the notion of savoring – that is, the propensity for advanced knowledge of an upcoming reward to increase our anticipation of it. Computationally, a mechanism was proposed for this process (Iigaya, Story, Kurth-Nelson, Dolan, & Dayan, 2016), such that the anticipatory utility associated with knowledge of a future outcome is boosted by the reward prediction error (RPE). In a recent neuroimaging study, Iigaya et al. (2020) proposed that a network including the vmPFC, hippocampus and midbrain regions underlies this boosting of anticipatory utility by RPEs. Specifically, the vmPFC tracks the value of anticipatory utility, the SN/VTA and medial posterior cingulate cortex (mPCC) represent information that enhances anticipation (the anticipatory RPE), and the hippocampus encodes the absolute anticipatory RPE or surprise (independent of valence). These three regions were found to be functionally connected, such that the hippocampus–SN/VTA connectivity was modulated by the anticipatory utility predicted by the model, and the hippocampus-vmPFC connectivity was modulated by the anticipatory RPE. In addition to the typical reward processing areas, the hippocampus appears to play an integral role in integrating the effect of valence (here RPE) on information (here anticipatory utility). This study is also noteworthy for examining temporal aspects of the fMRI signals, with vmPFC activity found to be ramping up in anticipation of a reward in a way that is boosted by the surprise (RPE) associated with the information, rather than simply ramping up proportionally to the reward expected value. This finding raises the intriguing possibility of a bidirectional interaction between reward and information. Not only can expected reward increase information preference, but unexpected information can increase reward anticipation in the brain.

An obvious question following from this line of work is whether dopamine plays a role in underlying hedonic motivations during information-seeking. In a recent pharmacology study administering L-DOPA (a precursor to dopamine) or a placebo to human participants (Vellani, de Vries, Gaule, & Sharot, 2021), L-DOPA was actually found to eliminate the valence bias that is typically observed during information-seeking. Specifically, participants under L-DOPA preferred information equally for gains and losses. The difference was specifically driven by an increased preference for information about losses in the L-DOPA group relative to the placebo group. A possible mechanistic explanation for this finding is that L-DOPA administration may help reduce the anticipated negative affect or dread associated with the anticipation of a loss. Therefore, dopamine may influence how expected negative outcomes are processed in the midbrain or ventral striatum, in turn making information about these outcomes less aversive. Using ^{18}F-FDOPA PET scanning to quantify individual dopamine synthesis capacity, Van Lieshout et al. (2020) replicated the behavioral finding that curiosity increases as a function of outcome valence (i.e., higher for expected gains than for expected losses). However, they found no evidence that individual differences in curiosity or the sensitivity to outcome valence was related to dopamine synthesis in the ventral striatum, caudate, or putamen. This suggests that more work is needed to examine the role of dopamine in valence-dependent information-seeking.

In summary, the influence of valence on information-seeking appears to also rely on neural mechanisms shared with reward processing, such as those identified in the first part of the chapter. This shared network between reward and information, as we have discussed, is assumed to play a role in assigning value to the opportunity to gain information, independently of the valence of the information. However, it is perhaps unsurprising that outcome valence, which is known to be represented within this same network, would recruit these same mesolimbic and prefrontal regions to influence the value of information (Figure 9.1A). While the existing (yet limited) literature on this topic suggests converging evidence for a role of the reward, and possibly dopaminergic, systems in valence-dependent information-seeking, several mechanistic accounts have been proposed, and further investigations are needed to paint a more coherent picture of the exact computations performed by these brain regions.

9.4 Uncertainty Reduction: An Independent Information-Seeking Network

While humans seek information that makes them feel good or improves future actions, they also seek information that helps them to better understand the world by reducing subjective uncertainty. Uncertainty reduction is therefore a key motivational factor in seeking information (Berlyne, 1957; Gershman, 2019; Sharot & Sunstein, 2020). Different parameterizations of uncertainty reduction are often added in computational models for human cognition and behavior or in artificial agents to motivate information-seeking (Wilson et al., 2014; Oudeyer, Lopes, Kidd, & Gottlieb, 2016; Cogliati Dezza et al., 2017; Gershman, 2018; Schwartenbeck et al., 2019). This drive continues to prevail even in situations where information is noninstrumental (Kobayashi et al., 2019; White et al., 2019) and is linked to an intrinsic motivation to reduce entropy in a system (Oudeyer & Kaplan, 2007; Friston et al., 2015).

While both instrumental and valence-dependent motives for seeking information mostly recruit brain networks typically involved in reward processing (Figure 9.1A), the motivation to reduce uncertainty when seeking information seems to rely on a separate and independent neural network (Figure 9.1B). This independent network includes regions of the prefrontal cortex, such as the dorsal anterior cingulate cortex (dACC) and the rostrolateral prefrontal cortex (rlPFC), as well as portions of the parietal cortex and the dorsal striatum. In what follows, we present studies which have individuated key nodes of this network. It is worth mentioning that information-seeking driven by uncertainty and exploration often overlaps in the literature. For the sake of this chapter, however, we only focus on exploration findings in which uncertainty reduction is explicitly identified as the drive for exploration, in contrast with exploratory behaviors that are driven by randomness in the learning or decision process.

Evidence for the involvement of dACC in processing information-seeking motivated by uncertainty reduction comes from recent studies on humans (Cogliati Dezza et al., 2020; Kaanders, Nili, O'Reilly, & Hunt, 2020) and monkeys (Hunt et al., 2018; White et al., 2019). A first study conducted on human subjects highlighted the existence of independent systems for information and reward in the prefrontal cortex (Cogliati Dezza et al., 2020). In particular, human subjects were asked to make sequential choices among three decks of cards. Cards varied in terms of the level of information (i.e., how much the subject was ignorant about an option due to prior experience) and reward. In this task, subjects sought information about options they were more uncertain about (noninstrumental information) even in the absence of an instrumental benefit to seek information. Subsequent fMRI analysis showed that the dACC and anterior insula encoded the *noninstrumental* value of information after controlling for the variance explained by the reward value of an option and the instrumental value of information. On the contrary, the vmPFC and PCC encoded the reward value of the chosen option after controlling for the variance explained by noninstrumental information. This study identifies regions in the brain, including the dACC, which encode the noninstrumental value of information independently of the reward value associated to the options. The involvement of the dACC in information processing has also been shown in a second fMRI study, in which a portion of the medial frontal cortex (encompassing the dACC and presupplementary motor cortex) was found to encode the willingness to sample information to reduce reward uncertainty (Kaanders et al., 2020). Evidence for the involvement of the dACC in information processing also comes from nonhuman primate studies. For example, White et al. (2019) identified an intricate network, including the anterior cingulate cortex (ACC) and the dorsal striatum, which specifically signaled information-seeking but not reward-seeking. In particular, researchers presented monkeys with visual conditioned stimuli predicting reward information (i.e., 100%, 50% and 0%). ACC neurons (alongside neurons in the dorsal striatum) were strongly activated when the cue predicting reward was uncertain, with increased activation until information to resolve uncertainty was delivered. The strength of this ramping caused the gaze to shift toward information-related cues before receiving information to resolve uncertainty, and was specifically related to anticipating information and not to reward value or uncertainty per se. ACC neurons were the earliest predictor of gaze shifts. This suggests that ACC may have a supervisory role in sustaining information-seeking. A similar role for ACC in sustaining information-seeking was observed in an additional study (Hunt et al., 2018), in which monkeys' ACC neurons, primarily recorded in the dorsal bank of the cingulate sulcus, tracked how each piece of information reduced the uncertainty associated with the chosen action.

Another region involved in information-seeking driven by uncertainty reduction is the rlPFC. This region seems to track the amount of surprise humans recently experienced in a given context (Ligneul, Mermillod, & Morisseau, 2018). Additionally, the rlPFC encodes trial-by-trial changes in relative uncertainty, which increases exploration for uncertain options (Badre, Doll, Long, & Frank, 2012; Tomov, Truong, Hundia, & Gershman, 2020). In particular, Badre et al. (2012) asked participants to stop a rotating clock to win points. To maximize rewards, participants needed to learn the optimal speed (either "fast" or "slow" responses). Computational models were then adopted to compute the relative uncertainty associated with response time, with the assumption that subjects explore uncertain response times to reduce their uncertainty. Interestingly, the rlPFC not only tracked trial-by-trial changes in relative uncertainty associated with exploratory decisions, but this pattern also distinguished individuals who were using uncertainty as a drive for exploration from those who did not. A later study (Tomov et al., 2020) showed that activity in the rlPFC correlates with exploration to seek information (i.e., directed exploration), while activity in the dorsolateral prefrontal cortex was associated with a different type of exploration (i.e., random exploration; Wilson et al., 2014). It is worth noting that other regions may play a role in processing directed exploration, including the frontopolar cortex (Zajkowski, Kossut, & Wilson, 2017).

Another important region involved in information-seeking driven by uncertainty reduction is the parietal cortex. Van Lieshout et al. (2018) showed that humans were particularly curious when information had a greater impact in reducing subjective uncertainty, and this increase in uncertainty-driven curiosity was associated with BOLD responses in the parietal cortex. Parietal neurons in monkeys appear to also encode information gain based on changes in uncertainty (Horan, Daddaoua, & Gottlieb, 2019), as well as how much information reduces uncertainty (Foley, Kelly, Mhatre, Lopes, & Gottlieb, 2017). Interestingly, parietal neurons specifically encoded information-related signals but not reward-related signals. Similar results were found in human subjects, where by bilateral activation of the intraparietal sulcus encoded the willingness to sample additional information in order to reduce uncertainty about rewards (Kaanders et al., 2020). This suggests a role of the parietal cortex in encoding uncertainty-driven information-seeking.

In summary, when humans decide to seek information to reduce uncertainty, a network comprised of the dACC, the dorsal striatum, the rlPFC and the parietal cortex intervenes at different stages of the process. Key nodes of this network are also consistent with the animal literature. While uncertainty reduction seems to rely on an independent network compared to other information-seeking drives, more research is needed to identify the reciprocal connections between key nodes of this network.

9.5   Conclusion

Information-seeking is a complex behavior. To be implemented, it requires a wide range of neural circuitry. Both general preference for information and valence depended information-seeking appear to rely on similar neural mechanisms to those involved in processing primary or monetary rewards. A recent review (Bromberg-Martin & Monosov, 2020) proposed a hypothetical network for information-seeking, suggesting that the value of information and the value of rewards are encoded in the same brain areas

(OFC & ACC, projecting to striatum and pallidum) but in different neurons, thus allowing for the separate pursuit of information and rewards depending on individual motivations and the environment. These two value signals would then be integrated in the striatal and mesolimbic areas, possibly relying on dopaminergic neurons, to compute a total value signal integrating both information prediction and reward prediction (Cogliati Dezza et al., 2020). In parallel, an independent network, recruiting the dACC, rlPFC and parietal regions, seems to drive information-seeking to reduce uncertainty. To date, however, how uncertainty reduction signals could also be integrated into the computations of value signals discussed earlier remains to be established.

A novel theory (Sharot & Sunstein, 2020) and recent empirical evidence (Kelly & Sharot, 2021; Cogliati Dezza & Sharot, 2021) point toward a joint influence of instrumental utility, valence, and uncertainty reduction in motivating information-seeking. In other words, when humans decide to seek information, the value of information (or information prediction) is computed as the weighted sum of different motives. It is therefore possible that some level of interactions among these networks occurs when humans decide to seek information. This would suggest that the neural mechanisms of information-seeking are controlled by a unique network, with some mechanisms shared with reward processing and others independent of it.

In Figure 9.2, we describe a possible mechanism for how the "overall information-seeking network" may operate. Expectations for uncertainty reduction, valence, and instrumental utility are computed in distinct brain regions. These expectations may then be integrated in the OFC to compute the information prediction, which then guides behavior. While the OFC seems to be involved in processing information predictions, it is still unknown whether it also computes the weighted sum of the three motives (Sharot & Sunstein, 2020), or, instead, if other regions are involved in this process. If the resulting behavior is to seek information, information feedback is provided and used to update the information expectations computed in the brain. It is worth noting that the neural mechanisms by which the three motives are updated are still unclear. A recent framework suggests that knowledge can be learned and updated following similar reinforcement learning mechanisms as those used to learn about rewards (Murayama, 2019b; Chapter 2, this volume). And, neural evidence suggests that the brain computes information prediction error (IPE; Bromberg-Martin & Hikosaka, 2011) and valence-dependent IPE (VD-IPE; Charpentier et al., 2018). However, how these information

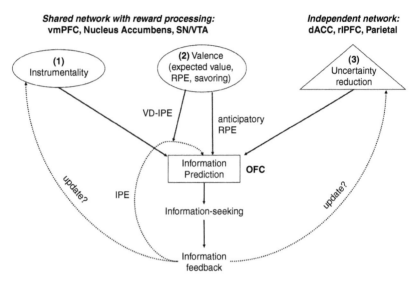

Figure 9.2 Overall information-seeking network. According to this hypothesized
integrated network, information-seeking motives (instrumentality, valence,
uncertainty reduction) are computed in distinct regions across the brain, and
influence information predictions. While these regions probably interact in ways
that are yet to be established, current evidence suggests that (1) the vmPFC may
compute the instrumentality of the information signal, (2) other reward-related
regions (such as the nucleus accumbens and dopaminergic midbrain) underlie
valence-driven information-seeking, and (3) a network independent from reward
processing regions, including the dACC, rlPFC, and parietal cortex, may encode
the drive to reduce uncertainty. These motives can all influence information
predictions (rectangle shown in the picture), with a possible integration in the
OFC to compute information value. Depending on the value of the information
prediction, a decision to seek or avoid information is made. If information is
received, information feedback is delivered and the value associated with each
motive is updated (dashed lines in the figure). The exact nature of these update
signals remains mostly unknown, although limited evidence suggests that updates
could be achieved through the computation of a prediction error, such as a general
information prediction error (IPE) influencing information prediction, and being
modulated by valence (VD-IPE).

prediction errors interact with the value associated with each motive is still
unknown.

Several other substantial questions remain unanswered in this nascent
field of information-seeking neuroscience.

First, there are few causal studies so far examining how necessary these
networks, and the regions within them, are for driving information-seeking

decisions. Preliminary evidence suggests a possible causal role for dopamine in motivating information-seeking about negative outcomes (Vellani et al., 2021), for the rlPFC in information-driven exploration (Zajkowski et al., 2017), and for the basal ganglia (dorsal striatum and pallidum) on the speed at which information is acquired (White et al., 2019). Yet, the causal involvement of some of the key regions of our proposed network, such as the vmPFC, ventral striatum, dopaminergic midbrain, dACC or parietal regions, has not been investigated at this point. Future pharmacology or lesion studies are needed to address this gap.

Second, whether and how the dynamics of information-seeking are represented in the brain is an open question. In other words, how does the brain track and update the value of information over time in order to adapt its decisions to seek or avoid information? One study provides preliminary evidence that the dlPFC, a region not implicated so far in the processes described in this chapter, may be involved in this dynamic process of tracking the value of information over time (Kobayashi et al., 2021). How this region is integrated in the information-seeking network will hopefully be examined in more details in future studies.

Lastly, the neurochemical mechanisms underlying the information-seeking network(s) remain to be established. Recent converging evidence appears to suggest an involvement of dopamine not only in valence-dependent information-seeking (Vellani et al., 2021), but also in uncertainty-driven exploration (Frank, Doll, Oas-Terpstra, & Moreno, 2009). An intriguing possibility is that dopamine signals could play a role in tying the "overall information-seeking network" together, and strengthening the interaction between motive-specific processes, such as valence and uncertainty reduction. Further evidence is needed to test this possibility, as well as to identify the role of other neurotransmitters such as serotonin and norepinephrine in information-seeking behaviors.

To sum up, recent advances in neuroscience all converge on the notion that information is intrinsically valuable. Some information-seeking behaviors indeed do share a common neural code with reward processing and general valuation mechanisms. However, when people seek information to reduce uncertainty a different route of implementation seems to be taken. These different routes could actually provide very useful bottom-up constraints to help refine our understanding of the algorithmic and computational implementation of information-seeking, which in turn will help to better characterize the neural mechanisms underlying information-seeking.

References

Badre, D., Doll, B. B., Long, N. M., & Frank, M. J. (2012). Rostrolateral prefrontal cortex and individual differences in uncertainty-driven exploration. *Neuron*, 73(3), 595–607. https://doi.org/10.1016/j.neuron.2011.12.025.

Bartra, O., McGuire, J. T., & Kable, J. W. (2013). The valuation system: A coordinate-based meta-analysis of BOLD fMRI experiments examining neural correlates of subjective value. *Neuroimage*, 76, 412–427. https://doi.org/10.1016/j.neuroimage.2013.02.063.

Bénabou, R. (2016). Mindful economics: The production, consumption, and value of beliefs. *Journal of Economic Perspectives*, 30, 141–164.

Berlyne, D. E. (1957). Uncertainty and conflict: A point of contact between information-theory and behavior-theory concepts. *Psychological Review*, 64(6), 329–339.

Berns, G. S., Chappelow, J., Cekic, M., Zink, C. F., Pagnoni, G., & Martin-Skurski, M. E. (2006). Neurobiological substrates of dread. *Science*, 312(5774), 754–758. https://doi.org/10.1126/science.1123721.

Blanchard, T. C., Hayden, B. Y., & Bromberg-Martin, E. S. (2015). Orbitofrontal cortex uses distinct codes for different choice attributes in decisions motivated by curiosity. *Neuron*, 85(3), 602–614. https://doi.org/10.1016/j.neuron.2014.12.050.

Bromberg-Martin, E. S., & Hikosaka, O. (2009). Midbrain dopamine neurons signal preference for advance information about upcoming rewards. *Neuron*, 63 (1), 119–126. https://doi.org/10.1016/j.neuron.2009.06.009.

Bromberg-Martin, E. S., & Hikosaka, O. (2011). Lateral habenula neurons signal errors in the prediction of reward information. *Nature Neuroscience*, 14(9), 1209–1216. https://doi.org/10.1038/nn.2902.

Bromberg-Martin, E. S., & Monosov, I. E. (2020). Neural circuitry of information seeking. *Current Opinion in Behavioral Sciences*, 35, 62–70, https://doi.org/10.1016/j.cobeha.2020.07.006.

Brydevall, M., Bennett, D., Murawski, C., & Bode, S. (2018). The neural encoding of information prediction errors during non-instrumental information seeking. *Scientific Reports*, 8(1), 6134. https://doi.org/10.1038/s41598-018-24566-x.

Caplin, A., & Leahy, J. (2001). Psychological expected utility theory and anticipatory feelings. *The Quarterly Journal of Economics*, 116(1), 55–79.

Charpentier, C. J., Bromberg-Martin, E. S., & Sharot, T. (2018). Valuation of knowledge and ignorance in mesolimbic reward circuitry. *Proceedings of the National Academy of Sciences of the United States of America*, 115(31), E7255-E7264. https://doi.org/10.1073/pnas.1800547115.

Chib, V. S., Yun, K., Takahashi, H., & Shimojo, S. (2013). Noninvasive remote activation of the ventral midbrain by transcranial direct current stimulation of prefrontal cortex. *Translational Psychiatry*, 3, e268. https://doi.org/10.1038/tp.2013.44.

Cogliati Dezza, I., Cleeremans, A., & Alexander, W. (2020). Independent and interacting value systems for reward and information in the human brain. *bioRxiv*.

Cogliati Dezza, I., & Sharot, T. (2021). People adaptively use information to improve their internal and external states. *PsyArXiv*. https://psyarxiv.com/f5vyq.

Cogliati Dezza, I., Yu, A. J., Cleeremans, A., & Alexander, W. (2017). Learning the value of information and reward over time when solving exploration-exploitation problems. *Sci Rep*, 7(1), 16919. https://doi.org/10.1038/s41598-017-17237-w.

Diederen, K. M. J., & Fletcher, P. C. (2021). Dopamine, prediction error and beyond. *Neuroscientist*, 27(1), 30–46. https://doi.org/10.1177/1073858420907591.

Dubey, R., & Griffiths, T. L. (2020). Reconciling novelty and complexity through a rational analysis of curiosity. *Psychological Review*, 127(3), 455–476. https://doi.org/10.1037/rev0000175.

Evans, B. M., & Chi, E. H. (2010). An elaborated model of social search. *Information Processing & Management*, 46, 656–678.

Evans, B. M., Kairam, S., & Pirolli, P. (2009). Do your friends make you smarter? An analysis of social strategies in online information seeking. *Information Processing & Management*, 46(6), 679–692.

Filimon, F., Nelson, J. D., Sejnowski, T. J., Sereno, M. I., & Cottrell, G. W. (2020). The ventral striatum dissociates information expectation, reward anticipation, and reward receipt. *Proceedings of the National Academy of Sciences of the United States of America*, 117(26), 15200–15208. https://doi.org/10.1073/pnas.1911778117.

Foley, N. C., Kelly, S. P., Mhatre, H., Lopes, M., & Gottlieb, J. (2017). Parietal neurons encode expected gains in instrumental information. *Proceedings of the National Academy of Sciences of the United States of America*, 114(16), E3315–E3323. https://doi.org/10.1073/pnas.1613844114.

Frank, M. J., Doll, B. B., Oas-Terpstra, J., & Moreno, F. (2009). Prefrontal and striatal dopaminergic genes predict individual differences in exploration and exploitation. *Nature Neuroscience*, 12(8), 1062–1068. https://doi.org/10.1038/nn.2342.

Friston, K., Rigoli, F., Ognibene, D., Mathys, C., Fitzgerald, T., & Pezzulo, G. (2015). Active inference and epistemic value. *Cognitive Neuroscience*, 6(4), 187–214. https://doi.org/10.1080/17588928.2015.1020053.

Friston, K. J., Lin, M., Frith, C. D., Pezzulo, G., Hobson, J. A., & Ondobaka, S. (2017). Active inference, curiosity and insight. *Neural Computation*, 29(10), 2633–2683. https://doi.org/10.1162/neco_a_00999.

Gershman, S. J. (2018). Deconstructing the human algorithms for exploration. *Cognition*, 173, 34–42. https://doi.org/10.1016/j.cognition.2017.12.014.

Gershman, S. J. (2019). Uncertainty and exploration. *Decision*, 6(3), 277–286.

Goldman-Rakic, P. S., Lidow, M. S., Smiley J. F., & Williams M. S. (1992). The anatomy of dopamine in monkey and human prefrontal cortex. In Stricker, E. M., Tuma A. H., & Gershon S. (Eds.), *Advances in neuroscience and schizophrenia*. Vienna: Springer.

Golman, R., Hagmann, D., & Loewenstein, G. (2017). Information avoidance. *Journal of Economic Literature*, 55(1), 96–135.

Gottlieb, J., Oudeyer, P. Y., Lopes, M., & Baranes, A. (2013). Information-seeking, curiosity, and attention: computational and neural mechanisms. *Trends in Cognitive Science*, 17(11), 585–593. https://doi.org/10.1016/j.tics.2013.09.001.

Horan, M., Daddaoua, N., & Gottlieb, J. (2019). Parietal neurons encode information sampling based on decision uncertainty. *Nature Neuroscience*, 22 (8), 1327–1335. https://doi.org/10.1038/s41593-019-0440-1.

Hunt, L. T., Malalasekera, W. M. N., de Berker, A. O., Miranda, B., Farmer, S. F., Behrens, T. E. J., & Kennerley, S. W. (2018). Triple dissociation of attention and decision computations across prefrontal cortex. *Nature Neuroscience*, 21(10), 1471–1481. https://doi.org/10.1038/s41593-018-0239-5.

Iigaya, K., Hauser, T. U., Kurth-Nelson, Z., O'Doherty, J. P., Dayan, P., & Dolan, R. J. (2020). The value of what's to come: Neural mechanisms coupling prediction error and the utility of anticipation. *Sci Adv*, 6 (25), eaba3828. https://doi.org/10.1126/sciadv.aba3828.

Iigaya, K., Story, G. W., Kurth-Nelson, Z., Dolan, R. J., & Dayan, P. (2016). The modulation of savouring by prediction error and its effects on choice. *Elife*, 5. https://doi.org/10.7554/eLife.13747.

Jessup, R. K., & O'Doherty, J. P. (2014). Distinguishing informational from value-related encoding of rewarding and punishing outcomes in the human brain. *European Journal of Neuroscience*, 39(11), 2014–2026. https://doi.org/10.1111/ejn.12625.

Kaanders, P., Juechems, K., O'Reilly, J. X., & Hunt, L. T. (2021). Dissociable mechanisms of information sampling in prefrontal cortex and the dopaminergic system. *Current Opinion in Behavioral Sciences*, 41, 63–70.

Kaanders, P., Nili, H., O'Reilly, J. X., & Hunt, L. T. (2020). Medial frontal cortex activity predicts information sampling in economic choice. bioRxiv preprint. https://doi.org/10.1101/2020.11.24.395814.

Karlsson, N., Loewenstein, G., & Seppi, D. (2009). The ostrich effect: Selective attention to information. *Journal of Risk and Uncertainty*, 38(2), 95–115.

Kelly, C. A., & Sharot, T. (2021). Individual differences in information-seeking. *Nature Communications* 12(7062). https://doi.org/10.1038/s41467-021-27046-5.

Kidd, C., & Hayden, B. Y. (2015). The psychology and neuroscience of curiosity. *Neuron*, 88(3), 449–460. https://doi.org/10.1016/j.neuron.2015.09.010.

Kobayashi, K., & Hsu, M. (2019). Common neural code for reward and information value. *Proceedings of the National Academy of Sciences of the United States of America*, 116(26), 13061–13066. https://doi.org/10.1073/pnas.1820145116.

Kobayashi, K., Lee, S., Filipowicz, A., McGaughey, K., Kable, J. W., & Nassar, M. R. (2021). Dynamic Representation of the Subjective Value of Information. *bioRxiv*.

Kobayashi, K., Ravaioli, S., Baranes, A., Woodford, M., & Gottlieb, J. (2019). Diverse motives for human curiosity. *Nature Human Behavior*, 3(6), 587–595. https://doi.org/10.1038/s41562-019-0589-3.

Ligneul, R., Mermillod, M., & Morisseau, T. (2018). From relief to surprise: Dual control of epistemic curiosity in the human brain. *Neuroimage*, 181, 490–500. https://doi.org/10.1016/j.neuroimage.2018.07.038.

Loewenstein, G. (1987). Anticipation and the valuation of delayed consumption. *The Economic Journal*, 97(387), 666–684.

Loewenstein, G., & Molnar, A. (2018). The renaissance of belief-based utility in economics. *Nature Human Behavior*, 2, 166–167.

Lopez-Persem, A., Bastin, J., Petton, M., Abitbol, R., Lehongre, K., Adam, C., . . . Pessiglione, M. (2020). Four core properties of the human brain valuation system demonstrated in intracranial signals. *Nature Neuroscience*, 23(5), 664–675. https://doi.org/10.1038/s41593-020-0615-9.

Matsumoto, M., & Hikosaka, O. (2007). Lateral habenula as a source of negative reward signals in dopamine neurons. *Nature*, 447(7148), 1111–1115. https://doi.org/10.1038/nature05860.

Morris, L. S., Kundu, P., Dowell, N., Mechelmans, D. J., Favre, P., Irvine, M. A., . . . Voon, V. (2016). Fronto-striatal organization: Defining functional and microstructural substrates of behavioural flexibility. *Cortex*, 74, 118–133. https://doi.org/10.1016/j.cortex.2015.11.004.

Murayama, K. (2019a). A reward-learning framework of autonomous knowledge acquisition: An integrated account of curiosity, interest, and intrinsic-extrinsic rewards. preprint. https://doi.org/10.31219/osf.io/zey4k.

Murayama, K. (2019b). A reward-learning framework of autonomous knowledge acquisition: An integrated account of curiosity, interest, and intrinsic-extrinsic rewards. OSFPREPRINTS. https://doi.org/10.31219/osf.io/zey4k.

Oudeyer, P.-Y. (2018). Computational theories of curiosity-driven learning. In G. Gordon (Ed.), *The new science of curiosity* (pp. 43–72). Nova Science Publishers.

Oudeyer, P.-Y., Lopes, M., Kidd, C., & Gottlieb, J. (2016). Curiosity and intrinsic motivation for autonomous machine learning. *ERCIM News*, 107, 34–35.

Oudeyer, P. Y., & Kaplan, F. (2007). What is intrinsic motivation? A typology of computational approaches. *Frontiers in Neurorobotics*, 1, 6. https://doi.org/10.3389/neuro.12.006.2007.

Padoa-Schioppa, C., & Conen, K. E. (2017). Orbitofrontal cortex: A neural circuit for economic decisions. *Neuron*, 96(4), 736–754. https://doi.org/10.1016/j.neuron.2017.09.031.

Pessiglione, M., & Lebreton, M. (2014). From the reward circuit to the valuation system: How the brain motivates behavior. In G. H. E Gendolla, S. L. Koole. & M. Tops (Eds.), *Handbook of biobehavioral approaches to self-regulation*. New York: Springer.

Pierson, E., & Goodman, N. (2014). Uncertainty and denial: A resource-rational model of the value of information. *PLoS One*, 9(11), e113342. https://doi.org/10.1371/journal.pone.0113342.

Schultz, W., Dayan, P., & Montague, P. R. (1997). A neural substrate of prediction and reward. *Science*, 275(5306), 1593–1599. Retrieved from https://www.ncbi.nlm.nih.gov/pubmed/9054347.

Schulz, E., & Gershman, S. J. (2019). The algorithmic architecture of exploration in the human brain. *Current Opinion in Neurobiology*, 55, 7–14. https://doi.org /10.1016/j.conb.2018.11.003.

Schwartenbeck, P., Passecker, J., Hauser, T. U., FitzGerald, T. H., Kronbichler, M., & Friston, K. J. (2019). Computational mechanisms of curiosity and goal-directed exploration. *Elife*, 8. https://doi.org/10.7554/eLife.41703.

Sharot, T., & Sunstein, C. R. (2020). How people decide what they want to know. *Nature Human Behavior*, 4(1), 14–19. https://doi.org/10.1038/s41562-019-0793 -1.

Smith, V. D., Rigney, A. E., & Delgado, M. R. (2016). Distinct reward properties are encoded via corticostriatal interactions. Scientific Reports. https://doi.org /10.1038/srep20093.

Story, G. W., Vlaev, I., Seymour, B., Winston, J. S., Darzi, A., & Dolan, R. J. (2013). Dread and the disvalue of future pain. *PLoS Computational Biology*, 9 (11), e1003335. https://doi.org/10.1371/journal.pcbi.1003335.

Tomov, M. S., Truong, V. Q., Hundia, R. A., & Gershman, S. J. (2020). Dissociable neural correlates of uncertainty underlie different exploration strategies. *Nature Communications*, 11(1), 2371. https://doi.org/10.1038/s41 467-020-15766-z.

van Lieshout, L. L. F., van den Bosch, R., Hofmans, L., de Lange, F. P., & Cools, R. (2020). Does dopamine synthesis capacity predict individual variation in curiosity? bioRxiv.

van Lieshout, L. L. F., Vandenbroucke, A. R. E., Muller, N. C. J., Cools, R., & de Lange, F. P. (2018). Induction and relief of curiosity elicit parietal and frontal activity. *Journal of Neuroscience*, 38(10), 2579–2588. https://doi.org/10.1523/JN EUROSCI.2816-17.2018..Vellani, V., de Vries, L. P., Gaule, A., & Sharot, T. (2021). A selective effect of dopamine on information-seeking. Elife, 9, e59152.

White, J. K., Bromberg-Martin, E. S., Heilbronner, S. R., Zhang, K., Pai, J., Haber, S. N., & Monosov, I. E. (2019). A neural network for information seeking. *Nature Communications*, 10(1), 5168. https://doi.org/10.1038/s41467-0 19-13135-z

Wilson, R. C., Geana, A., White, J. M., Ludvig, E. A., & Cohen, J. D. (2014). Humans use directed and random exploration to solve the explore-exploit dilemma. *Journal of Experimental Psychology: General*, 143(6), 2074–2081. https://doi.org/10.1037/a0038199.

Wu, C. M., Schulz, E., Speekenbrink, M., Nelson, J. D., & Meder, B. (2018). Generalization guides human exploration in vast decision spaces. *Nature Human Behavior*, 2(12), 915–924. https://doi.org/10.1038/s41562-018-0467-4.

Zajkowski, W. K., Kossut, M., & Wilson, R. C. (2017). A causal role for right frontopolar cortex in directed, but not random, exploration. *Elife*, 6. https://doi .org/10.7554/eLife.27430.

Zurn, P., & Bassett, D. S. (2018). On curiosity: A fundamental aspect of personality, a practice of network growth. *Personality Neuroscience*, 1, e13. https://doi.org/10.1017/pen.2018.3.

CHAPTER 10

Attention as Rational Choice

Jacqueline Gottlieb

10.1 Introduction

Selective attention has long been a fundamental yet controversial concept in cognitive science. On one hand, the meaning of attention is easily grasped. Every 4-year-old knows what her teacher means when she says "pay attention to me!" and every adult understands William James' definition of attention as "the focusing of the mind." On the other hand, this apparently obvious concept seems stubbornly resistant to rigorous research. In different experiments and contexts, attention seems to take so many forms and be so ubiquitous – involved in every behavior – as to be "everywhere," nearly synonymous with the functioning of the brain.

In this chapter, I argue that this longstanding conundrum is due in large part to a shortcoming in our operationalization of attention control. While psychologists and neuroscientists offer abundant evidence *that* animals focus on sources of information, they give no satisfactory answer to the computational question of *why* – to what end – they do so. What is the computational role of allocating attention? What benefit do we obtain from focusing our mind?

In some ways, attention seems to be so incontrovertible, so obvious, so *needed*, that even posing the question seems strange. After all, our intuition tells us, we must attend to be conscious, just as we must breathe in order to live. And yet, in a decision-theoretic perspective, a more principled answer reveals itself. Because attention focuses on sources of information and because it is capacity limited, its allocation amounts to a rational choice. We invest resources in some information based on the costs of doing so and the benefits this investment is expected to bring.

As I review in this chapter, despite the availability of well-defined decision-theoretic frameworks, the cost–benefit tradeoffs involved in allocating attention have been largely eschewed in our field. Instead, traditional frameworks describe attention control as being *exogenous* – specified by a process that is not subject to the decision-maker's cost–benefit trade-offs. Fortunately, this gap is alleviated by recent studies of information demand, similar to those that are used to investigate curiosity, which allow participants to choose their sources of information.

Here, I focus on the significance of studies of information demand for understanding selective attention. I briefly review the current view of visual selective attention and how the traditional concepts of "top-down" and "bottom-up" allocation refer to exogenous forms of attention control. I then present a decision-theoretic analysis of endogenous attention control based on the costs and benefits of gathering information, followed by neuroscientific evidence regarding the neural implementation of these tradeoffs. I end by considering the significance of these findings for realistic decisions in which animals must contend with vast amounts of information and actively construct their reality – that is, control their perception and the information they act on.

10.2   The Need for Understanding Endogenous Attention Control

"My experience is what I agree to attend to," William James famously wrote in the *Principles of Psychology* (James, 1890). Contrary to our intuition, James boldly claims, the information we act on is not simply out there and *given* to us, but is *constructed* and *created* by us.

The core factor driving the need for construction is the limited capacity of physical organisms. It is a fundamental reality for every physical agent – be it biological or man-made – that the set of signals that the agent can sense far exceeds the set of signals that the agent can process. Put differently, information processing is a *resource-limited* rather than a *data-limited* process. The crucial decision facing a biological system is not necessarily how to find information but how to allocate scarce resources to it. Which subset of the information should one discard and which (much smaller) subset should one process for behavioral benefits?

Attention is one solution to this critical question of information selection, but before we proceed, let us note that it is only one of many types of selection that the brain implements. Other forms of selection are implemented in early sensory representations by individual cells that are tuned to sensory features such as visual motion or auditory frequency. While selective attention is dynamic and responds to immediate context, sensory representations do not change much across behavioral contexts. Nevertheless, the features that are represented in sensory areas are species-specific, and efficient coding theories propose that they reflect evolutionary adaptations to the long-term global statistics of the sensory inputs that optimize the ability of a species to use the information in its ecological niche (Wei & Stocker, 2015). How information selection is optimized to serve behavioral needs is thus a deep question for all types of neural processing.

Attention is a specific form of information selection that rapidly adapts to behavioral context. A voluminous literature, focusing largely on the visual system of humans and monkeys, has shown that attention modulates visual processing in several ways. *Spatial attention* modulates visual responses at selected locations in the visual field, while *feature attention* modulates responses to specific features (e.g., color or motion) distributed across the visual field. In addition, attention may be deployed *covertly*, without motor output, or *overtly*, by physically orienting to specific locations. In humans and monkeys, visual orienting relies on saccades – rapid eye movements that place the highest-acuity portion of the retina (the fovea) on selected portions of a visual scene. Importantly, for all types of attention, improving the perception of one item entails reduced perception of others. Even when the eye remains still and visual acuity is controlled, unattended stimuli show lower perceptual discriminability and slower processing speed relative to attended stimuli (Carrasco, Eckstein, Verghese, Boynton, & Treue, 2009). Studies of *inattentional blindness* show that people can remain unaware of large, salient items or changes in visual scenes even when they directly look at these items, dramatically illustrating the profound limitations of processing capacity (Simons, 2000).

In parallel with this literature on the effects of attention, other studies examined attention control: that is, how attention is deployed in the first place. Traditionally, these studies relied on the dichotomy between "bottom-up" and "top-down" modes of control – which allocate attention to, respectively, salient or behaviorally relevant stimuli. However, there is increasing realization that this is an insufficient dichotomy (Awh, Belopolsky, & Theeuwes, 2012; Gottlieb & Oudeyer, 2018). The limitation is due, I propose, to the fact that both modes of control are described as being *exogenous* to the demands of a task (Figure 10.1A, left).

"Bottom-up" attention control is by definition exogenous, defined as the ability of external stimuli to gain access to neural processing regardless of the observer's intentions or goals. The most straightforward form of bottom-up capture is triggered by high-contrast stimuli, such as a red apple in a pile of green apples (Figure 10.1A, left). "Top-down" attention, on the other hand, refers to focusing on stimuli that are relevant to one's goals. But, strikingly, even this paradigmatically endogenous mode of control is

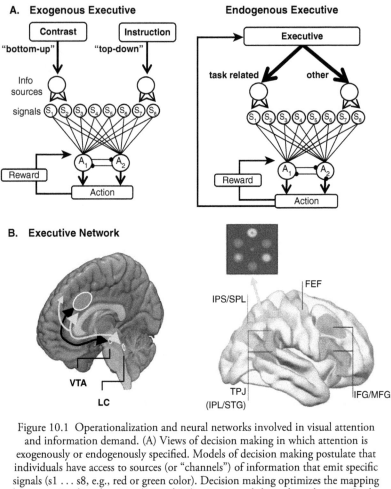

Figure 10.1 Operationalization and neural networks involved in visual attention and information demand. (A) Views of decision making in which attention is exogenously or endogenously specified. Models of decision making postulate that individuals have access to sources (or "channels") of information that emit specific signals (s1 . . . s8, e.g., red or green color). Decision making optimizes the mapping between stimuli and actions (A1 and A2) using reward-dependent plasticity. In the traditional view (left, "Exogenous Executive"), agents cope with overabundance of information by selecting sources identified by factors related to the experimental instruction ("top-down") or physical contrast ("bottom-up"). These factors are exogenous – that is, they are not optimized by the agent according to cost–benefit tradeoffs of a situation. In an alternative concept, rewards inform an executive that endogenously decides how to attend (right, "Endogenous Executive). The executive generates both task-related and task-unrelated ("other") attention commands based on the organisms preferences and cost–benefit tradeoffs, blurring the distinction between "top-down" and "bottom-up" modes of control. (B) Executive network in humans. (left) The dACC (blue oval) receives reward information from dopamine cells in the ventral tegmental area (VTA) and controls release of NE from the locus ceruleus (LC), which modulates responses throughout the brain to enhance information processing throughout the brain. (right) The dorsal attention network, consisting of the temporo parietal junction (TPJ), the inferior parietal lobule (IPL), the superior temporal junction (STJ), the intraparietal sulcus (IPS), the superior parietal lobule (SPL), the frontal eye field (FEF), and the inferior and medial frontal gyri (IFG and MFG). Parts of this network (in particular the IPS and FEF) encode "priority maps" – topographic visual representations that emphasize attention-worthy locations. This is shown schematically in the cartoon, as a map in which only 1 of the 8 locations containing visual stimuli are strongly represented.

operationalized as being exogenous to the decisions made in a task. In laboratory studies of task-related attention, the experimenter explicitly instructs participants about when and to what to attend. The participants are not asked to attend to what they consider relevant to the situation, and "top-down" control is de facto defined as obeying the experimenter's instructions.

The key to advancing our understanding of attention control, therefore, is to consider how participants endogenously deploy their attention based on feedback about the behavioral context. In canonical models, feedback about punishments or rewards modifies the mapping between stimuli and actions, but "information" is supplied exogenously, or *given* to the system (Figure 10.1A, left). The task before us, therefore, is to extend our models to specify how feedback also shapes the *information* we select when performing a task (Figure 10.1A, right).

As I discuss in the following sections, this approach will allow us to develop computational accounts of top-down attention control based on the observer's goals and constraints. In addition, it can explain the abundant evidence that bottom-up salience is not purely stimulus-driven but also strongly dependent on learning and behavioral context (Awh et al., 2012). In an exogenous operationalization, we are limited to hand-coding an ever-growing list of features that make an input "salient" – for example, related to reward associations, frequency of occurrence, habits, etc. Under an endogenous operationalization, we can attempt to explain these phenomena based on the observer's constraints – that is, her goals, her understanding of the situation, or her preferences that may differ from the experimenter's instructions.

A second great benefit from exploring the endogenous control of attention is for understanding its neural mechanisms. Converging evidence suggests that the control of attention depends on a distributed executive network that monitors the rewards of a task and a related network that implements the attentional policy that is appropriate for the task. Converging evidence shows that monitoring depends on a circuit centered on the dorsal anterior cingulate cortex (dACC) that receives input from valuation areas such as midbrain dopamine cells (Shenhav et al., 2017; Shenhav, Botvinick, & Cohen, 2013) (Figure 10.1B, left). A mechanistic model (Silvetti, Vassena, Abrahamse, & Verguts, 2018) proposes that, upon detecting a "need for control," the dACC sends descending commands to a brainstem nucleus called the locus ceruleus (LC), calling for the release of norepinephrine (NE), which enhances processing efficiency at different sites in the brain. However, a boost of NE is costly, representing the *cognitive effort* involved in a task, and is thus only called for in proportion to its potential to produce gains in utility.

The dACC circuit, therefore, may implement a cost–benefit tradeoff for allocating cognitive resources, including selective attention. Yet, strikingly, this circuit has been studied separately from a lateral fronto-parietal network that implements attentional policies (Figure 10.1B, right). This network includes visual and oculomotor areas, including the frontal eye field and the lateral intraparietal area, which encode spatial "priority maps" that selectively represent the locations of attention-worthy visual stimuli and guide spatial attention and gaze toward those stimuli (Bisley & Goldberg, 2010; Gottlieb, Kusunoki, & Goldberg, 1998; Krauzlis, Lovejoy, & Zenon, 2013; Thompson & Bichot, 2005). While the allocation of cognitive effort in response to incentives has been studied in tasks that require the optimization of learning rates, memory, or physical effort (Silvetti et al., 2018) and not in relation to attentional priority. Priority maps are described as being driven exogenously by stimulus contrast and experimental instructions (Bisley & Goldberg, 2010), reflecting the gap at the computational level, which eschews description of the endogenous mechanisms controlling attention (Figure 10.1A). Thus, closing this computational gap will provide a theoretical framework for understanding the interactions among distinct parts of the executive network.

Having pinpointed the question we need to address, we can delve into some of the answers to it that emerge from studies of information demand. Before we do so, let us consider a simpler theoretical question. How would one *optimally* allocate attention in a situation?

10.3   A Decision-Theoretic Analysis of Information Demand

If we think of information as exogenously given, we implicitly understand it to mean *any* sensory stimulus. A moment's reflection, however, shows that this definition is not very meaningful because the set of all stimuli is practically infinite. If everything is information, then information becomes a psychologically useless concept. Consider the likely fate of a fictitious organism that processes all the information while looking at pebbles strewn on a beach. Consumed by the desire to process *all* the information given to it, the organism will strive to represent and remember the infinite gradations of shapes, locations, sizes, and colors that it sees in the pebbles with endless precision, only to perish with no resources left to fulfill basic needs.

A decision-theoretic perspective, by contrast, provides a much more restrictive and meaningful definition of "information" as a reduction of uncertainty – with uncertainty defined by the probability distribution over options that are relevant to the organism's utility. This definition avoids overload by defining information through a small set of *internal* goal states. Under this definition, a sailor at the beach is no longer a slave to the external inputs available to her senses. Instead, she need only be concerned with her immediate goals. If the sailor wants to go boating, she will pay attention to the height of the waves, seeking to arbitrate between two relevant hypotheses: are the waves safe for boating or not? Other sensory inputs become momentarily meaningless and can be readily discarded (ignored). Information processing is thus no longer about engaging with stimuli. It is about resolving uncertainties – answering questions – that agents consider relevant to their goals.

The Bayesian framework formalizes this view by providing a mathematical prescription for updating beliefs – that is, optimally estimating the *posterior probabilities* given a set of *prior beliefs* and *new information*. Let us consider a common situation in which an observer weighs two hypotheses, H1 and H2. In the example above, a sailor may try to decide if the state of the waves is such that it is safe to boat (H1) or is safer to wait (H2). For simplicity we assume that the alternatives are exhaustive and mutually exclusive – that is, their probabilities add up to 1, and we can arbitrarily choose to discuss only one: for example, P(H1), with P(H2) = 1 - P(H1).

In a Bayesian framework, the sailor is depicted as having a prior guess – an estimate of P(H1) – based on her knowledge of the situation. For instance, the sailor may not have listened to the forecast and may believe that boating and waiting are equally likely (P(H1) ~ P(H2) ~ 0.5). Alternatively, the sailor may have clear clues from a forecast or from watching the clouds that waiting is the much safer alternative (P(H1) ~ 0.0). To refine her beliefs, the sailor can obtain new information by driving to the beach and observing the waves. There, she may see whether the waves are low – a signal (s1) that favors boating (H1), or, alternatively, that they are high – a signal (s2) that favors H2.

The Bayesian formula states that the sailor should optimally update her beliefs by combining her prior estimate with the new information, weighting each term in proportion to its reliability (the inverse of uncertainty). If the probabilities are expressed as log-odds ratios (logits; the log of the ratio of the two probabilities) this operation is a simple sum:

$$\log \left(\frac{P'(H1 \mid s1)}{P'(H2 \mid s1)}\right) = \log\left(\frac{P(H1)}{P(H2)}\right) + \log \left(\frac{P(s1 \mid H1)}{P(s2 \mid H1)}\right) \qquad \text{(eq.1)}$$

The term on the left-hand side of the equation is the *posterior probability* given that the observer saw signal s1 (P'(H1 | s1)). The first term on the right-hand side is the prior probability (P(H1)). The second term on the right-hand side is the reliability (likelihood) of the signal: the conditional probability that the observer sees s1 when the true state is H1 and s2 when the true state is H2.

The logit operator weights each term according to its certainty. If the probabilities defining a term are similar to each other (e.g., both close to 0.5) their ratio tends toward 1 and its log tends toward 0, indicating that the term contributes little to the posterior estimates. In contrast, if the probabilities strongly favor an alternative, the absolute value of the logit becomes very large and the term contributes strongly to the posterior beliefs. For example, a highly reliable signal s1 produces a large value of P(s1 | H1) and small value of P(s2 | H1) resulting in a large positive logit that strongly favors H1. A reliable signal s2 produces a strongly negative logit that strongly favors H2.

Note that this canonical form of the Bayesian equation describes what should happen after the agent gained access to signals s1 and s2. In our example, eq. 1 describes how the sailor should update her beliefs *after* becoming cognizant of the height of the waves. Our question, however, is how should the sailor *decide to look at the waves*? Since observing the waves may be costly (e.g., the sailor may need to drive to the beach), how should she estimate the benefits that the information may bring? This is precisely the computational question of attention control: how one decides to attend to a source of information (e.g., the waves) in order to discriminate the signals that are emitted by the source (e.g., high or low)?

With a few reasonable assumptions, eq. 1 can be extended to answer this question. Critical for this calculation is that, although the observer cannot know the precise signal (s1 or s2) before inspecting a source, she can know which signals a source is likely to emit and the likelihoods (reliabilities) of these signals. For instance, the sailor knows that the waves may be high or low (s1 or s2) and that height is a reliable predictor for the boating decision (i.e., the likelihoods in eq. 1 approach 1: P(s1 | H1) ~ P(s2 | H2) ~ 1.0). Based on this knowledge, she can estimate the posterior beliefs she would have *if* she were to encounter each possible signal (i.e., solving eq. 1 for s1 and s2) and the posterior certainty/uncertainty she can expect across all the possible signals. The expected information gain (EIG) is then defined as the difference between the expected posterior uncertainty and the prior uncertainty.

Information and uncertainty can be measured with several metrics, the best known of which is Shannon entropy, but empirical evidence shows that in simple two-alternative situations humans use a less complex metric based on accuracy (Coenen, Nelson, & Gureckis, 2018; Nelson, McKenzie, Cottrell, & Sejnowski, 2010). Figure 10.2A thus shows accuracy-based measures of information, defined as the probability of being correct if choosing the hypothesis favored by a distribution. Prior uncertainty ranges from 0.5 (indicating maximal prior uncertainty with a 50% chance of being correct) to 1.0 (certainty of being correct). Stimulus reliability is captured by %validity, a simple transformation of the likelihood that ranges from 0.5 for a source that makes random predictions to 1.0 for one that is perfectly accurate. Finally, EIG is defined as the difference in accuracy if the agent were to act based on her posterior versus her prior beliefs.

As shown in Figure 10.2A, EIG depends on an interaction between prior uncertainty and %validity. For each level of prior accuracy, EIG increases as a function of %validity. However, EIG is positive only if %validity exceeds the prior accuracy – namely, is larger if one starts with higher prior uncertainty. Thus, a perfectly Bayesian sampler will have maximal information demand if two conditions are met: she has high prior uncertainty *and* has access to information with sufficiently high %validity.

10.4   Likelihood and Uncertainty Modulate the Fronto-Parietal Network

A handful of studies suggest that, when visually gathering information, humans direct their saccades to locations that are expected to maximize EIG (Najemnik & Geisler, 2008; Yang, Lengyel, & Wolpert, 2016), providing behavioral evidence that EIG influences the control of gaze and attention. However, little is known about the neural mechanisms of EIG-based attention control. To examine this question we conducted a series of studies in the monkey lateral intraparietal area (LIP), a node of the fronto-parietal network that encodes visual priority (Figure 1B), to determine if the neurons are sensitive to prior uncertainty and %validity, the two quantities that determine Bayesian EIG.

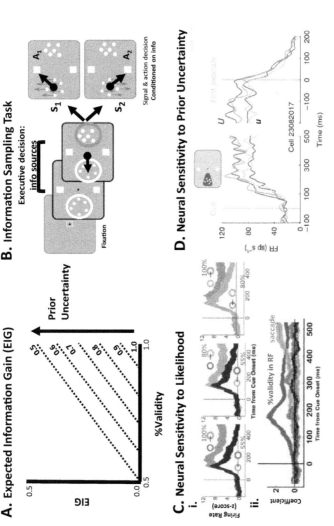

Figure 10.2 Neurophysiological evidence of sensitivity to likelihood and uncertainty in the parietal cortex. (A) Expected Information Gains (the increase in accuracy of the posterior relative to the prior expectations) in a two-alternative forced choice task, as a function of %validity (x-axis) and prior uncertainty (dashed lines). The numbers above each trace indicate the accuracy of a guess based on the prior and are inversely related to the prior uncertainty. EIG for prior certainty (1.0) is always 0. (B) Task of instrumental information demand in which the participant selects an information source (dots in a circular aperture), triggers information in the chosen source (100% coherent motion indicating a decision alternative, A1 or A2) and makes a second decision between an upper and lower target based on the information. Black arrows in each panel indicate eye movements. (C) (i) %validity is encoded by parietal neurons. Each trace shows the firing rates in a population of cells when an information source with different %validity (numbers) appears in the RF. In each panel, firing rates are higher when the higher relative to the lower %validity source is in the RF. In the cartoons, the faint dotted line shows the RF and the arrows show the monkey's saccade. (ii) Regression analysis across all the conditions identifies a clear response to the %validity of the RF source that precedes an encoding of saccade direction ("saccade"). Coefficients for saccade latency, velocity and accuracy (remaining traces) are not significant. (D) Uncertainty enhances parietal responses before a saccade. Firing rates of a representative LIP cell before a saccade to an information source in conditions of high prior uncertainty (U) and low prior

We used a behavioral task in which monkeys made two saccades to obtain a reward (Figure 10.2B). The first saccade was directed to a stimulus to obtain information. The second saccade reported a two-alternative choice based on the information and, if correct, received a reward. Our interest was in the mechanisms generating the initial, information sampling saccade (Figure 10.2B, "Executive Decision"). At this stage, the monkeys could choose to direct their gaze to one of two peripheral masks (round patches with stationary dots) to reveal the information concealed by the mask (motion toward one of the targets). This gaze-contingent procedure allowed us to isolate the presaccadic selection of an information source (during the "Sampling" step) from the postsaccadic discrimination and use of the information (Figure 10.2B, during the "signal and action decision" step).

In a first experiment using this task, we asked if LIP cells encode the % validity of competing visual cues by familiarizing monkeys with masks of three colors signaling high, medium, or low %validity (of, respectively, 100%, 80%, or 55% validity) (Foley, Kelley, Mhatre, Lopes, & Gottlieb, 2017). When the monkeys were allowed to choose among masks of different %validity, they had a strong preference for viewing the more reliable mask, showing that they were highly sensitive to %validity. Importantly, LIP cells encoded validity-based prioritization (Figure 10.2C). For all 3 possible pairs of masks, the neurons responded more strongly when the monkey inspected the mask that fell inside relative to opposite their receptive field (RF), and this selective response depended on the relative %validity of the available masks. When the masks were clearly distinct (100% vs. 55% validity), the neurons had a large response difference between the two mask locations (Figure 10.2Ci. left). In contrast, when the masks had more similar %validity (100% vs. 80%), the same locations elicited much lower activity difference, implying a weaker target selection response (Figure 10.2Ci, right). Regression analyses across all the conditions showed that the neurons clearly encoded the relative % validity of the available stimuli independently of the direction of the eventual saccade (which was only signaled at a later time point; Figure 10.2Cii).

These results are consistent with the view that priority maps rank possible target locations and are read out in downstream areas to determine the final saccade. Importantly, they provide a partial answer to how the ranking arises, suggesting that stimuli are prioritized in proportion to their expected reliability, consistent with a Bayesian active sampling strategy.

In a second experiment we showed that the neurons are sensitive to prior uncertainty (Horan, Daddaoua, & Gottlieb, 2019), the second factor that would optimally specify EIG. We used a slightly different version of the task in which the monkeys sampled stimuli of 100% validity in conditions of high or low prior uncertainty. In high uncertainty trial blocks ("U") the two targets for the final decision had equal ex ante probability of being rewarded and the monkeys could expect that the motion would resolve this uncertainty (i.e., specify the correct final). In contrast, in low uncertainty blocks ("u"), a single alternative was correct in all trials. Thus, the monkeys could predict the correct decision in advance and expected that the motion would merely confirm (be redundant with) their prediction.

As described in Figure 10.2A, Bayesian logic dictates that information should have higher priority in U relative to u blocks. Consistent with this prediction, nearly 40% of LIP neurons had enhanced presaccadic responses on U relative to u blocks (Figure 10.2D). In a separate experiment we found that uncertainty enhances information transmission from the parietal to the frontal lobe, while suppressing transmission in the opposite direction (Taghizadeh et al., 2020), revealing an additional mechanism for enhancing the impact of new information under prior uncertainty.

These results provide proof of concept that the brain computes attentional priority based on %validity and uncertainty, consistent with theoretical principles of rational attention control.

10.5   Integrating Rewards

A salient aspect of the Bayesian formula (eq. 1) is that it refers only to probability and uncertainty with no mention of rewards or utility. However, the probabilities we consider are over *utility-relevant* hypotheses. Indeed, in the tasks that the monkeys performed the information was instrumental – it helped the monkeys obtain a reward by making a correct choice. This raises a critical question. Since rewards modulate visual and attentional networks (Leong, Radulescu, Daniel, DeWoskin, & Niv, 2017; Padmala & Pessoa, 2011), could the apparent responses to % validity and uncertainty be explained by reward gains? Our results show that while the monkeys were sensitive to information utility, this utility was not encoded in LIP cells, supporting the two-process (monitoring/ regulation) view of executive function (Figure 10.1B).

Using the task in Figure 10.2D, we randomly interleaved trials in which the monkeys could expect a small or large reward for a correct final choice in both U and u blocks. This orthogonally manipulated rewards and uncertainty and allowed us to test how LIP neurons encoded each factor.

In principle, the reward functions relevant in this task were the expected value (EV) and the expected value of information (EVOI). EV is defined as the product of reward magnitude and probability and, as shown in Figure 10.3Ai, increased with reward size by design. In addition, EV was negatively related to uncertainty – that is, was slightly higher in u relative to U blocks due to the fact that the monkeys' performance (and hence, the reward probability) was better when target location was fixed across trials. EVOI is defined as the *added* EV for taking informed versus uninformed actions and is the product of reward size and EIG (the increased probability of being correct after gathering information). As shown in Figure 10.3Aii, EVOI was minimal in u blocks, when the monkeys made accurate final decisions even when they received random motion, but was much higher in U blocks, particularly at a large reward size (Figure 10.3Aii).

Analysis of the neural responses showed that LIP neurons did not encode EV or EVOI (Figure 10.3Aiii). Although some neurons were sensitive to reward magnitude, this sensitivity was independent of the enhancement by uncertainty. Moreover, in the average population response, uncertainty and reward size combined additively rather than multiplicatively as would be expected for EV or EVOI. Third, and particularly strikingly, neural responses to reward and uncertainty had opposite polarity, as firing rates were enhanced by uncertainty but *reduced* by reward size, incompatible with EVOI. Finally, the neurons that were suppressed by rewards in this task switched their responses, becoming enhanced by reward in a standard saccade task in which the monkeys made simple saccades to gather rewards, showing that the cells had inconsistent reward sensitivity.

These results shed light on longstanding controversies about the significance of reward modulations in systems of selective attention (Maunsell, 2004). While initial findings that LIP neurons are enhanced by rewards were interpreted to indicate that the cells encode action values (Sugrue, Corrado, & Newsome, 2004), our results strongly question this hypothesis. The findings suggest that, rather than representing economic utility, these responses indicate intermediate cognitive states that the brain generates to obtain the desired utility by gathering information.

It is important to note that, despite the lack of value encoding by LIP cells, rewards clearly affected the monkeys' behavior. Consistent with a utility-based strategy, the monkeys made reward-dependent speed-accuracy tradeoffs, increasing or decreasing the time they spent viewing the motion to obtain

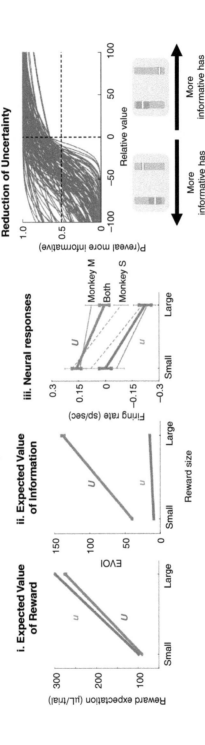

Figure 10.3 Complex interactions between uncertainty and reward (A) The expected value of rewards (i) or information (ii) cannot explain reward sensitivity in LIP (iii). (B) Rewards bias information demand in multi-attribute settings. The cartoons depict the task setting, in which participants receive random monetary prizes from two lotteries that differ in their relative value and have high or low variance. The high variance lottery is more informative regarding the total payoff. The traces are individual psychometric functions of representative participants who request information in proportion to the relative value of a lottery (the functions slope upward), with a bias toward the high uncertainty lottery (the functions are shifted upward).

higher or lower decision accuracy. LIP responses, however, did not correlate with the motion viewing time or its reward modulations, and instead correlated specifically with information processing *efficiency* – the accuracy of the monkeys' final decision at a fixed viewing time (Horan et al., 2019). Together, these findings strongly support the dual-process model of executive function (Figure 10.1B). LIP neurons, potentially alongside cells in other areas that encode visual priority, implement an attentional policy by facilitating the selection and processing of stimuli that reduce uncertainty. Tradeoffs between rewards and attentional effort, in contrast, may be governed by a distinct circuit potentially relying on the dACC.

10.6 Reward Misbehavior and Interference with Uncertainty Minimization

The discussion so far brings empirical evidence for reframing our understanding of executive function in terms of a resolution of uncertainty. But some readers may wonder if this is merely "passing the buck." After all, didn't we just swap two terms, substituting "information" with "reduction of uncertainty"? Surely, this substitution only has meaning if we have a concrete understanding of how animals estimate uncertainty.

The answer is that uncertainty depends on an agent's understanding of the situation – their "internal model" of the states that are possible in a situation and how these states are related to each other and to the agent's actions. For example, a sailor can only ascribe meaning to the height of the waves if she has an internal model of how she and her boat will react in a situation, and which wave is likely to be "too high" for her boat. Similarly, a physician can only order the appropriate test (request the best information) if she knows the possible causes of a patient's symptoms and the relative probabilities of these causes. It is only based on these models that an individual can identify uncertainty and request information. Should the individual start from the wrong premise, they will carry out a suboptimal investigation and fail to seek out the best information.

Although much remains unknown about the use of task models, laboratory investigations are consistent with their importance in guiding information demand. In the studies described in the previous sections, people and monkeys could acquire internal models guiding information demand through extensive training or instructions familiarizing them with the task. Consistent with a role for task-training, other studies have shown that people are remarkably inefficient when apparently natural information-seeking behaviors are tested in novel laboratory situations. People do not shift gaze to the most informative locations in a simple laboratory test despite routinely looking at task-relevant items when performing natural tasks (Morvan & Maloney, 2012; Tatler, Hayhoe, Land, & Ballard, 2011). Similarly, people generate mostly low-quality questions in a modified hide-and-seek ("Battleships") game, despite correctly ranking the informativeness of questions that are suggested to them and, of course, routinely asking questions in natural situations (Rothe, Lake, & Gureckis, 2016).

Emerging research suggests that model-based information demand may be challenging to compute even in apparently simple and clearly described situations. A recent study in our laboratory suggests that one source of difficulty is identifying the most informative feature in multi-dimensional situations (Kobayashi, Ravaioli, Baranès, Woodford, & Gottlieb, 2019). Imagine that you have a financial portfolio containing two items: a certificate of deposit and a stock. Both items contribute to your earnings, and they differ in their average value and uncertainty, with the certificate paying a fixed interest and the stock being volatile. Imagine also that you want to accurately estimate the total instantaneous value of your portfolio but, because of resource limitations, can only inquire about the current value of one of its items. Should you inquire about the certificate of deposit or about the stock? The theoretically optimal strategy is to inquire about the most uncertain component – the stock in this case – as this will minimize your uncertainty about the entire portfolio. Importantly, the relative value of a component does not impact your uncertainty and should thus irrelevant to your choice.

Kobayashi et al. emulated this scenario in a task in which people received two prizes, each of which was drawn from a probabilistic lottery, but had the opportunity to inquire about the precise value of one of the prizes. The information was noninstrumental, as people could not take actions to improve on their payoff. The two lotteries had, respectively, high and low uncertainty and independently differed in their average value (EV). Contrary to the prediction that people should request information strictly about the high uncertainty lottery, the vast majority of participants were sensitive to relative EV (Figure 10.3B). If the high uncertainty lottery also had higher EV, people typically inquired about the prize they obtained from this lottery. However, if the high uncertainty lottery had lower EV, people typically inquired about the higher EV (low-uncertainty) lottery, achieving worse estimates of the total payoff then if they had inquired about the high uncertainty lottery. Only ~30% of participants pursued the normative strategy, while the remainder were influenced by value and uncertainty to different degrees.

Understanding the mechanisms of deviations from optimal information demand is a crucial goal for future research. Two proposed explanations are that people prioritize information based on conditioned reward associations (perhaps related to the salience of reward-associated stimuli; Daddaoua, Lopes, & Gottlieb, 2016; Kobayashi et al., 2019) or are driven by anticipatory utility: the desire to anticipate positive outcomes(Iigaya, Story, Kurth-Nelson, Dolan, & Dayan, 2016; Loewenstein, 1987; Sharot & Sunstein, 2020). Future research can test the contributions of these mechanisms in different situations.

10.7   Information Demand and Realistic Decisions

Having discussed selective attention, let us briefly consider, in closing, the importance of information demand for decision research. As mentioned in the opening sections, experiments in neuroscience and psychology have traditionally studied decisions based on a small set of preselected information (Figure 10.1A). Interest is now growing in decisions made in realistic conditions, such as shopping at a supermarket, when correctly controlling attention is clearly central to the eventual choice. Models of eye movements during economic decisions show that directing attention to an item enhances the leverage that the item exerts on the choice but, in the absence of extensive knowledge of endogenous attention control, such models continue to rely on the simplistic assumption that attention is randomly allocated (Krajbich, Armel, & Rangel, 2010).

The evidence discussed in this chapter will be critical in specifying how attention supports decisions of realistic complexity (Callaway, Rangel, & Griffiths, 2021). As we saw, initial evidence shows that attention and information demand are sensitive to prior uncertainty and likelihood consistent with Bayesian predictions and, perhaps more important, also systematically violates these predictions. Suboptimal sampling is present in noninstrumental conditions (when individuals merely predict future outcomes; Charpentier, Bromberg-Martin, & Sharot, 2018; Kobayashi et al., 2019) but persists in instrumental conditions when it adversely impacts incentivized choices (Hunt, Rutledge, Malalasekera, Kennerley, & Dolan, 2016; Morvan & Maloney, 2012). This has the important implication that apparent decision anomalies – in which choices differ from what a normative theory would predict – may be due not only to individual preferences, as has been traditionally assumed, but have deeper roots in nonnormative attentional and information-gathering strategies.

Thus, a crucial question for decision research is to understand the constraints that limit the efficiency of attention and information processing, whether they stem from cognitive biases (an inaccurate specification or use of models of the situation), emotional biases (the desire to avoid thinking about negative outcomes), or fundamental processes in attention control (which enhance the weight of high-reward observations).

10.8　Conclusions

Curiosity, the phenomenon reviewed in this volume, is a complex construct with social, emotional, and cognitive aspects. Here, I have focused on the process of information demand that is central to curiosity but also for selective attention. I argued that a perspective based on information demand can spearhead a novel paradigm to understand how attention is endogenously optimized rather than exogenously dictated. This paradigm will fill longstanding gaps in our understanding of attention and executive function and support a significant expansion of decision research to explain how decisions in realistic conditions are explained by optimal or nonoptimal information-gathering policies.

Acknowledgments: The research described in this review was supported by a Human Frontiers Science Program (HFSP) Collaborative Research Grant, a National Eye Institute RO1, and National Institute of Mental Health RO1 to JG.

Disclosure statement:
The author declares that she has no conflict of interest.

References

Awh, E., Belopolsky, A. V., & Theeuwes, J. (2012). Top-down versus bottom-up attentional control: A failed theoretical dichotomy. *Trends in Cognitive Science*, 16(8), 437–443.

Bisley, J. W., & Goldberg, M. E. (2010). Attention, intention, and priority in the parietal lobe. *Annual Review of Neuroscience*, 33, 1–21.

Callaway, F., Rangel, A., & Griffiths, T. L. (2021). Fixation patterns in simple choice reflect optimal information sampling. *PLoS Comp Biol.* https://doi.org/10.1371/journal.pcbi.1008863.

Carrasco, M., Eckstein, M., Verghese, P., Boynton, G., & Treue, S. (2009). Visual attention: Neurophysiology, psychophysics and cognitive neuroscience. *Vision Research*, 49(10), 1033–1036. https://doi.org/10.1016/j.visres.2009.04.022.

Charpentier, C. J., Bromberg-Martin, E. S., & Sharot, T., S. (2018). Valuation of knowledge and ignorance in mesolimbic reward circuitry. *Proceedings of the*

National Academy of Sciences of the United States of America., 115(31), E7255–E7264.

Coenen, A., Nelson, J. D., & Gureckis, T. M. (2018). Asking the right questions about the psychology of human inquiry: Nine open challenges. *Psychonomic Bulletin & Review*, Jun. 4. https://doi.org/10.3758/s13423-018-1470-5. [Epub ahead of print]

Daddaoua, N., Lopes, M., & Gottlieb, J. (2016). Intrinsically motivated oculomotor exploration guided by uncertainty reduction and conditioned reinforcement in non-human primates. *Sci Rep*, 6(20202). https://doi.org/10.1038/srep20202.

Foley, N. C., Kelley, S. P., Mhatre, H., Lopes, M., & Gottlieb, J. (2017). Parietal neurons encode expected gains in instrumental information. *Proceedings of the National Academy of Science*, 114(16), E3315–E3323.

Gottlieb, J., Kusunoki, M., & Goldberg, M. E. (1998). The representation of visual salience in monkey parietal cortex. *Nature*, 391, 481–484.

Gottlieb, J., & Oudeyer, P. Y. (2018). Toward a neuroscience of active sampling and curiosity. *Nature Reviews Neuroscience*, 19(12), 758–770.

Horan, M., Daddaoua, N., & Gottlieb, J. (2019). Parietal neurons encode information sampling based on decision uncertainty. *Nature Neuroscience*, 22(8), 1327–1335. https://doi.org/10.1038/s41593-019-0440-1.

Hunt, L. T., Rutledge, R. B., Malalasekera, W. M., Kennerley, S. W., & Dolan, R. J. (2016). Approach-induced biases in human information sampling. *PLoS Biol.*, 14(11), e2000638. https://doi.org/10.1371/journal.pbio.2000638.

Iigaya, K., Story, G. W., Kurth-Nelson, Z., Dolan, R. J., & Dayan, P. (2016). The modulation of savouring by prediction error and its effects on choice. *eLife*, Apr. 21(5), e13747. https://doi.org/10.7554/eLife.13747.

James, W. (1890). *The principles of psychology.* Holt.

Kobayashi, K., Ravaioli, S., Baranès, A., Woodford, M., & Gottlieb, J. (2019). Diverse motives for human curiosity. *Nature Human Behavior.*, 3(6), 587–595. https://doi.org/10.1038/s41562-019-0589-3.

Krajbich, I., Armel, C., & Rangel, A. (2010). Visual fixations and the computation and comparison of value in simple choice. *Nature Neuroscience*, 13(10), 1292–1298. https://doi.org/nn.2635[pii]10.1038/nn.2635.

Krauzlis, R. J., Lovejoy, L. P., & Zenon, A. (2013). Superior colliculus and visual spatial attention. *Annual Review of Neuroscience*, 36, 165–182. https://doi.org/10.1146/annurev-neuro-062012-170249.

Leong, Y., Radulescu, A., Daniel, R., DeWoskin, V., & Niv, Y. (2017). Dynamic interaction between reinforcement learning and attention in multidimensional environments. *Neuron*, 93(2), 451–463.

Loewenstein, G. (1987). Anticipation and the valuation of delayed consumption. *The Economic Journal*, 97(387), 666–684.

Maunsell, J. H. (2004). Neuronal representations of cognitive state: reward or attention? *Trends in Cognitive Science*, 8(6), 261–265.

Morvan, C., & Maloney, L. (2012). Human visual search does not maximize the post-saccadic probability of identifying targets. *PLoS Computational Biology*, 8(2), e1002342. https://doi.org/10.1371/journal.pcbi.1002342.

Najemnik, J., & Geisler, W. S. (2008). Eye movement statistics in humans are consistent with an optimal search strategy. *Journal of Vision*, 8 (3), 1–14. https://doi.org/10.1167/8.3.4/8/3/4/ [pii].

Nelson, J., McKenzie, C., Cottrell, G., & Sejnowski, T. (2010). Experience matters: Information acquisition optimizes probability gain. *Psychological Science*, 21(7), 960–969.

Padmala, S., & Pessoa, L. (2011). Reward reduces conflict by enhancing attentional control and biasing visual cortical processing. *Journal of Cognitive Neuroscience*, 23(11), 3419–3432. https://doi.org/10.1162/jocn_a_00011.

Rothe, A., Lake, B., & Gureckis, T. M. (2016). Asking and evaluating natural language questions. In A. Papafragou, D. Grodner, D. Mirman, & J. C. Trueswell (Eds.), *Proceedings of the 38th Annual Conference of the Cognitive Science Society* (pp. 2051–2056). Austin, TX: Cognitive Science Society.

Sharot, T., & Sunstein, C. R. (2020). How people decide what they want to know. *Nature Human Behavior*, 4(1), 14–19. https://doi.org/10.1038/s41562-019-0 793-1.

Shenhav, A., Botvinick, M., & Cohen, J. (2013). The expected value of control: an integrative theory of anterior cingulate cortex function. *Neuron*, 79(2), 217–240.

Shenhav, A., Musslick, S., Lieder, F., Kool, W., Griffiths, T. L., Cohen, J. D., & Botvinick, M. M. (2017). Toward a rational and mechanistic account of mental effort. *Annual Review of Neuroscience*, 40, 99–124. https://doi.org/10.1146/a nnurev-neuro-072116-031526.

Silvetti, M., Vassena, E., Abrahamse, E., & Verguts, T. (2018). Dorsal anterior cingulate-brainstem ensemble as a reinforcement meta-learner. *PLoS Computational Biology*, 14(8), e1006370. https://doi.org/10.1371/journal .pcbi.1006370.

Simons, D. J. (2000). Attentional capture and inattentional blindness. *Trends in Cognitive Science*, 4(4), 147–155. https://doi.org/10.1016/s1364-6613(00)01455-8.

Sugrue, L. P., Corrado, G. S., & Newsome, W. T. (2004). Matching behavior and the representation of value in the parietal cortex. *Science*, 304(5678), 1782–1787.

Taghizadeh, B., Foley, N. C., Karimimehr, S., Cohanpour, M., Semework, M., Sheth, S. A., … Gottlieb, J. (2020). Reward uncertainty asymmetrically affects information transmission within the monkey fronto-parietal network. *Communications Biology*, 3(1), 594. https://doi.org/10.1038/s42003-020-01320-6.

Tatler, B. W., Hayhoe, M. N., Land, M. F., & Ballard, D. H. (2011). Eye guidance in natural vision: reinterpreting salience. *Journal of Vision*, 11(5), 5–25.

Thompson, K. G., & Bichot, N. P. (2005). A visual salience map in the primate frontal eye field. *Progress in Brain Research*, 147, 251–262.

Wei, X. X., & Stocker, A. A. (2015). A Bayesian observer model constrained by efficient coding can explain "anti-Bayesian" percepts. *Nature Neuroscience* 18 (10), 1509–1517.

Yang, S. C., Lengyel, M., & Wolpert, D. M. (2016). Active sensing in the categorization of visual patterns. *eLife*. https://doi.org/10.7554/eLife.12215.

CHAPTER 11

Seeking Inner Knowledge
Foraging in Semantic Space

Thomas T. Hills, Nancy B. Lundin, Mahi Luthra, and Peter M. Todd

11.1 Introduction

The first author of this chapter was once invited to give a talk at the Max Planck Institute for Human Development in Berlin, which had recently moved buildings without telling him. Dutifully following the latest online maps, he arrived in an empty building with vacant offices and unswept meeting rooms. A few faded flyers and office name tags confirmed that, in fact, this was a *version* of the correct destination. But it was as if the inhabitants had all left in a hurry. Or possibly Thomas had arrived several decades too late.

Search problems such as the one above typically have two stages: the part where you feel close to the resources you are looking for, and the part where you don't. More generally, this is an instance of the *exploration–exploitation trade-off* (Hills et al., 2015). The part where you think you feel close leads to a kind of exploitation of existing knowledge. In this phase, Thomas simply exploited an information trail, both online and in the physical world, because he believed that trail contained the answer to the where-will-I-give-my-talk question. It did not. This led to the second stage, which initially involved investigating different floors in the same building. This only compounded the Phillip K. Dickian nature of the experience (e.g., Dick, 1959). Indeed, here was the room identified as the location of the talk, with dusty desks and nary a soul in sight.[1]

The ability to look for things nearby when you expect to find them there, and to look further afield when you do not, is called *area-restricted search*. To a first approximation, roughly all organisms that move do area-restricted search, including bacteria, nematodes, ants, and lost speakers

---

[1] Having once slept on a train going the wrong way, only to awaken twice as far from his destination as when he started, Thomas didn't put it out of his mind that the problem was of his own creation. It just wasn't obvious to him how he had managed to slip into exactly *this* alternate reality.

(reviewed in Hills, 2006). Bacteria do area-restricted search via their run-and-tumble behavior, which allows them to exploit and "run" up resource gradients – to richer pastures – or to reverse their protein motors and "tumble" – randomly choosing a new direction – when their receptors signal they may be moving down a resource gradient. Nematodes perform a pirouette, touching their nose to their tail, to turn around abruptly when they suddenly find themselves away from food. Ants, even the path-integrating desert ant *Cataglyphis*, engage in area-restricted search, wandering slowly in increasingly wider spirals when they fail to find their home at its expected location.

Lost speakers can tumble and pirouette around buildings. But they can also search inside their heads to generate alternatives to moving through space – like recovering the identity of the person who sent the invitation and phoning them. The notion of embarking on an inner journey, as a surrogate for reality, is often associated with Tolman's (1948) concept of a *cognitive map*. Tolman, observing rats as they navigated through mazes, often observed in the rats' behavior what he thought was a kind of deliberation. Given prior experiences with shock in a dark environment, a rat provided with a choice between a dark and a light environment down two alternate arms of a maze would stop at the choice point and apparently consider the possibilities before choosing the light side. Tolman called this behavior *vicarious trial and error learning* and he imagined that the rat was also imagining running through alternative mazes in its head (Tolman & Gleitman, 1949).

More recent work has confirmed Tolman's suspicions by identifying the neural correlates of these cognitive maps and the internal searches they make possible. Using neuroimaging, we can now "watch" as animals search inside their heads, deliberating over possible alternative choices and investigating the outcomes of those choices in a simulated cognitive environment (Hills, 2019). Much evidence shows that the hippocampus contributes a great deal to the representation and navigation of internal maps, allowing for alternative pathways to be compared and for novel routes to be taken through internal space that have never been encountered before (O'Keefe & Nadel, 1978; Pezzulo, van der Meer, Lansink, & Pennartz, 2014). Curiosity-driven exploration of internal spaces is activated by choice points – as in Tolman's rat. But exploration is also driven in response to prediction errors, which appear to be encoded by both the hippocampus and the anterior cingulate cortex (ACC), which in turn engage the prefrontal cortex (PFC) in search guidance and assessment (Gruber & Ranganath, 2019;

Winstanley et al., 2012). Perhaps even more importantly, the hippocampus encodes information about not only space but also time and conceptual information, suggesting that search processes used to navigate internal space may also govern other forms of internal search, such as episodic and semantic memory search (Constantinescu, O'Reilly, & Behrens, 2016, Hills, 2003; Lundin, 2022; Mack, Love, & Preston, 2016; Morton, Sherrill, & Preston, 2017).

This naturally leads to the question of how internal and external foraging processes might be similar, both in terms of the problems they face – adaptively mediating the exploration–exploitation trade-off – but also in terms of their underlying neuroscience. This is what we explore next.

11.2 Semantic Memory Search as Internal Foraging

The need to search internally extends beyond searching internal representations of external space. In humans and some other species, rich stores of semantic and experiential (autobiographic) information are stored in memory and the structure of these representations has been shown to predict human judgments (e.g., Bhatia, Richie, & Zou, 2019). Though information from these memory representations can "pop" into one's mind, these representations may also require effortful search, as when coming up with a list of items to pack for a holiday trip. How these search processes work is an area of ongoing study.

One way to investigate these mechanisms is by taking a comparative evolutionary perspective and testing whether particular spatial search strategies seen in a range of species can account for human cognitive search patterns measured in experimental settings. As described, animals ranging from bacteria to lost speakers often employ foraging strategies in which they switch between local search within regions of clustered resources (patch exploitation) and global search between those regions (exploration for new patches). Charnov (1976) described this problem mathematically in what is called the Marginal Value Theorem (MVT). The MVT posits that organisms can maximize their foraging rewards by exploiting local patches until their rate of return drops below the average expectation across all patches, at which point they should transition to exploration for a new patch. Note that the MVT describes a relationship between the structure of resources and the strategic behaviors required to optimally exploit them. The MVT is indifferent to what those resources are or whether or not they lie inside or outside one's head.

How information is structured in long-term memory therefore makes predictions about the strategies people use to search memory. In particular, we expect transitions between exploration and exploitation that map onto the somewhat categorical structure of memory. Categorical structure in semantic memory corresponds to patchy resource structures in space – categories consisting of multiple items that are "nearby" (similar to) other items, and "more distant" (dissimilar to) items in other categories. And as the evolutionary associations predict, there is evidence suggesting that humans employ patch-like foraging strategies when searching semantic memory (Hills, Jones, & Todd, 2012): people "enter" regions (or patches) of memory that are resource-rich, near items with many close associations, and then transition to exploration when local resources in memory are depleted.

11.2.1 Naturalistic and Experimental Assays of Semantic Foraging

There are numerous naturalistic settings in which foraging-like patterns in semantic memory can be observed and potentially studied. A common example is generating items for a grocery shopping list (Boettcher, Drew, & Wolfe, 2018). A person may begin by adding foods from the produce section to their list, perhaps even by generating further subcategories within that category such as fruits (e.g., apples, bananas) and then vegetables (asparagus, zucchini, mushrooms), next onto grains (spaghetti, rice), and then dairy (milk, yogurt, butter). Others may generate items for their list based on meals of the day, such as breakfast foods, lunch foods, and ingredients for dinner. Still others may organize their list by the regions of the grocery store where they will be shopping. In all these cases, these cognitive processes aid the shopper in identifying and remembering desired food items to purchase. When all the food is prepared, one may need to invite guests to eat it, and the guest list requires searching for and selecting people based on how they are related to one another in an internally represented social network – first immediate family, next friends, then colleagues, etc. (see Hills & Pachur, 2012). Speech during a dinner conversation may also be viewed through a semantic foraging lens, in that people tend to search for a topic to discuss, exploit that area of conversation, and then may decide to switch to new topics when they run out of related things to say. These naturalistic examples showcase how people's tendencies to search their memories by transitioning between global and local searches may be beneficial for accomplishing tasks or creating positive social interactions. That being said, studying such search behavior in the wild brings with it the range of challenges of field research.

Research using laboratory-based tasks and internet search behavior has begun to quantify semantic foraging phenomena similar to those observed in these naturalistic settings. A recent study that bridges external and internal search examined curiosity-driven information seeking using Wikipedia (Lydon-Staley et al., 2021). In a relatively unconstrained task, participants were asked to spend 15 minutes a day for 21 days browsing Wikipedia and reading about topics of their choosing. Search behavior was analyzed using graph theoretic metrics, treating pages visited as nodes of a network and the semantic similarity between nodes as weighted edges. People with higher deprivation curiosity (or stronger motivation to fill gaps of knowledge) exhibited greater local search by exploiting relatively tighter networks of concepts and by more frequently returning to previously visited pages. This study and others (Wang & Pleimling, 2017; Fu & Pirolli, 2007) provide insight into individual differences in search behavior in a context highly relevant to today's technology-driven society.

Relatively simple and less time-consuming tasks frequently administered in research and clinical contexts can also provide a window into people's internal cognitive search. In semantic priming paradigms, participants respond to target words (e.g., "dog") after exposure to semantically related (e.g., "cat") and unrelated (e.g., "light") primes, typically exhibiting faster target responses after the semantically related prime (Meyer & Schvaneveldt, 1971). The verbal responses and timing during these tasks provide information about the structure of an individual's semantic associations. However, these tasks are essentially disconnected one-shot productions, with participants being required to quickly direct their attention to the next (usually unrelated) cue after providing a response; consequently, they tell us little about the extended ongoing process of search for multiple items in semantic memory (but see Abbot, Austerweil, & Griffiths, 2015; Jones, Hills, & Todd, 2015).

The category verbal fluency test (Bousfield & Sedgewick, 1944), on the other hand, provides a rich set of data useful for testing semantic foraging mechanisms, as it is an ongoing multiple-item search that involves decisions regarding local and global transitions. In this task, a participant is asked to verbally list as many different items as they can think of from a particular category (e.g., animals, foods, vehicles) within a designated amount of time (e.g., 1–3 minutes). Given the goal of producing as many words as possible, participants may employ a range of strategies to search their semantic memory. The data from this task enables researchers to operationalize participants' search processes by quantifying "where" they decide to search (semantic similarity between responses), for how long (inter-item response times), and their ultimate success (how many unique words were produced).

11.2.2   Modeling Foraging in Semantic Space

Early investigations into category verbal fluency performance reported that participants produced temporally clustered groups of semantically related words (Bousfield & Sedgewick, 1944). Participants were described as exhausting retrieval within a cluster, pausing, and then experiencing an "attainment of insight" in which a new cluster becomes available for retrieval. A later study noted that participants tended to take similar amounts of time to generate each of the items within a semantic cluster, but the gaps between clusters were longer and increased over time, suggesting rapid discovery of the words in one cluster (found in a corresponding "semantic field") interspersed with lengthening exploration for the next semantic field (Gruenewald & Lockhead, 1980). This seminal work informed conceptualizations of verbal fluency performance as a two-component process in which participants alternatingly "cluster" (produce a set of words within a subcategory) and "switch" (move to a new subcategory when associated words are less readily available in the first subcategory). Troyer and colleagues (1997) introduced a set of norms for particular category fluency tasks (e.g., animals), defining subcategories based on common participant responses (e.g., pets, farm animals, beasts of burden, water animals). While these Troyer norms were a useful first step in quantifying search behavior, their categorical coding scheme does not capture the continuous multidimensional measure of distance (or similarity) between fluency responses that is important for assessing how people may be "foraging" for nearby items in clusters or exploring to find more distant ones. More importantly from a cognitive perspective, it also does not provide a mechanistic explanation of why people decide to switch from one cluster to seek a new one.

Advances in natural language processing have increased researchers' ability to measure and model semantic memory search. Associative semantic models (such as latent semantic analysis [or LSA; Landauer & Dumais, 1997] and Bound Encoding of the Aggregate Language Environment [or BEAGLE; Jones & Mewhort, 2007]) learn associations between words in large text corpora (e.g., Wikipedia) based on direct and indirect word co-occurrence across contexts. They convert word tokens into vector representations, allowing for the calculation of semantic similarity between two words as the cosine of the angle between their vectors. This fine-grained assessment of similarity between words can be used quantitatively to assess "semantic distance" traveled during search processes, aiding in understanding people's search strategies in tasks such as verbal fluency.

This approach to measuring semantic distance has been used to test whether participants' behavior during semantic memory search can be modeled as a form of internal foraging in mind (Hills, Jones, & Todd, 2012; Todd & Hills, 2020). As briefly described earlier, Hills and colleagues found that people produced words in patches, with lower distance (higher similarity) between words within a Troyer-norm-defined subcategory and greater distance (lower similarity) when moving from one patch to the next. People also tended to leave a patch when there were few remaining words to produce nearby in semantic space and when their rate of producing words in the current patch fell below their average rate in the task, following the predictions of the MVT (Charnov, 1976). It remains to be determined whether their patch-leaving decisions are actually based on depletion or on other cues, such as the time since the previous item was found.

The foraging perspective thus provides a productive framework for studying and modeling the strategies people use during semantic search. It also suggests questions to be explored about the neural mechanisms involved and gives new directions for research into individual differences and suboptimal foraging strategies as a potential explanation for impaired verbal fluency performance in clinical populations, as described later.

11.2.3 *Alternative Models to Semantic Foraging*

Semantic foraging as an explanation for verbal fluency behavior is not without its critics, as other researchers have argued that a random walk through semantic networks can sufficiently explain participant word production patterns (Abbott et al., 2015). However, this critique has itself been questioned (Jones, Hills, & Todd, 2015) on the basis of the semantic structure underlying the random walks. Specifically, the random walks in Abbott et al., (2015) took place over semantic networks that were produced from free association data generated by human participants; thus, the representations embedded within the semantic structure were likely generated in a similar fashion to verbal fluency data – that is, via potential foraging search mechanisms. Therefore, there is not yet conclusive evidence as to whether an undirected random walk model explains patchy semantic search behavior in a way that differs from a strategic search process such as foraging. Nonetheless, what Abbott et al.'s (2015) work does suggest is that a large part of the semantic memory search may reflect an automatic search process similar to reporting the first word that comes to mind in a free association task, possibly leaving more effortful decisions for when and where to initiate the long-distance explorations.

Another related alternative for semantic search processes is the Lévy flight, derived from the ecological literatures. Lévy flights are a type of random walk where directions are chosen at random but path lengths are chosen from a power-law distribution – meaning they are heavy-tailed, such that most path lengths are short, but some are very long (Benhamou, 2007; Viswanathan et al., 1999). Rhodes & Turvey (2007) showed that the time intervals between retrievals in a semantic memory search task were power-law distributed, suggesting the possibility that they may be the outcome of a simple Lévy-like search process. Other research has reported similar relations between semantic memory search and heavy-tailed distributions (Montez et al., 2015; Thompson & Kello, 2014). An observation of heavy-tailed (or power-law) distributions is not sufficient to distinguish between Lévy-like search processes and more adaptive strategies such as area-restricted search. For example, Hills, Kalff, and Wiener (2013) showed that area-restricted search in space – which adaptively reduced path lengths when near clusters of resources – produced path-length distributions that were indistinguishable from Lévy flights. Nonetheless, the question of Lévy processes in memory search is still open, and new experiments are needed to formalize and disentangle Lévy processes from other forms of random walks and area-restricted search.

11.2.4   Neural Correlates of Internal Foraging

Investigating patterns of brain activity during search tasks is another way to understand the degree to which internal search aligns with foraging mechanisms. Theories of goal-directed cognition have posited overlap in the neural mechanisms of physical and cognitive foraging behavior, identifying, for example, similar neural circuitry across animals during internal and external search. Specifically, connectivity between the basal ganglia and prefrontal cortex may give rise to adaptive modulation of dopaminergic signaling, which promotes attribution of attentional salience to rewards found in the environment (Hills, 2006; Hills et al., 2015; Todd, Hills, & Robbins, 2012). As mentioned earlier, the hippocampus also serves roles in both external and internal search, with the posterior portion in humans (dorsal in rodents) critical to navigation in physical space, and the anterior portion (ventral in rodents) theorized to perform similar computations at a more conceptual level, enabling linking of semantic and episodic memory to form higher-level representations (Buzsáki & Moser, 2013; Eichenbaum, 2004; Strange et al., 2014).

Functional magnetic resonance imaging (fMRI) in humans and neuronal firing studies in nonhuman primates have demonstrated robust involvement of the anterior and posterior cingulate cortex in contexts of reward-based decision making (e.g., gambling tasks in humans: Kolling et al., 2012; reward-based motor tasks in monkeys: Shima & Tanji, 1998). Some researchers posit that the anterior cingulate encodes monitoring of foraging risk and reward value (Brown & Alexander, 2017; Kolling et al., 2012), while others suggest this region tracks choice difficulty (Shenhav et al., 2014; Shenhav et al., 2016) and post-decision evaluation of rewards not received (Blanchard & Hayden, 2014). The ventromedial prefrontal cortex has also been frequently implicated as encoding value in reward-based decision-making studies, with debate as to whether this is specific to economic choice between well-defined options (Kolling et al., 2012) or more broadly applicable to foraging contexts of unknown options (Mehta et al., 2019; Shenhav et al., 2016). These regions have also been conceptualized to work together in the context of curiosity-driven information seeking, through encoding and incorporating value information into a cognitive map by the orbitofrontal cortex and monitoring of environmental demands by the anterior cingulate (Wang & Hayden, 2021).

Less work has been done to understand whether neural activation during semantic search resembles foraging-like activity and whether this activity correlates with dopaminergic signaling. Several studies have conducted fMRI while participants perform verbal fluency tasks, revealing a widespread network of activation in frontal, temporal, parietal, insular, cingulate, cerebellar, and subcortical regions (Costafreda et al., 2006; Birn et al., 2010; Gauthier et al., 2009). However, most of these studies have measured brain responses associated with verbal fluency production in general, rather than mapping activation patterns to particular search strategies (e.g., clustering, switching). Preliminary evidence in small samples using brief covert (unspoken) verbal fluency tasks has revealed differential fMRI activation during switching and clustering, with increased switch-related activation in regions such as the inferior frontal gyrus, posterior cerebellum, and posterior parietal cortex, among others (Gurd et al., 2002; Hirshorn & Thompson-Schill, 2006). In a verbal fluency fMRI study with 3 minute periods of overt word generation, we more directly tested whether neural activation reflects patterns that align more strongly with foraging or random walk theories, in part by examining whether activation in particular regions differs in magnitude and localization during local and global semantic search and increases in a ramp-like fashion over a patch until reaching a switch (Lundin, 2022). In this study, both the anterior hippocampus and posterior cerebellum showed increasing activity leading up to the decision to switch, suggesting neural processes related to a strategic foraging process (e.g., switching based on monitoring search effort) as opposed to an undirected random walk.

11.2.5   *Individual Differences and Disruptions in Semantic Search*

Quantifying semantic search in terms of specific component processes such as exploration and exploitation opens up novel opportunities for investigations of individual differences in cognitive functioning. This can involve individual differences in strategy and differences associated with age (Hills, Mata, Wilke, & Samanez-Larkin, 2013), cognitive impairment, and/or psychopathology (Taler, Johns, Sheppard, & Jones, 2015). For example, while associative search accurately describes verbal fluency search behavior in some participants, other participants' response production may be better described by a categorical search process (Hills et al., 2012; Hills et al., 2015). In other words, some people may search their semantic memory by making decisions as to whether there are items readily available similar to the last item retrieved, whereas others may make decisions as to whether there are available items remaining within that subcategory (e.g., pets, farm animals). In conjunction with analyzing response production, directly asking participants about their search strategies could provide additional insight into individual differences in semantic search.

Studying semantic search within clinical populations could aid in diagnostic characterization. Impairments in verbal fluency production have been reported in individuals with neurological conditions such as dementia (Henry et al., 2004) and frontal and temporal lobe lesions (Troyer et al., 1998), as well as psychiatric illnesses such as schizophrenia (Bokat & Goldberg, 2003) and depression (Henry & Crawford, 2005). While individuals across these groups tend to generate fewer words in verbal fluency tests, different specific cognitive functions are likely impaired between groups. For example, particular types of dementia may be associated with a degradation of semantic representations in long-term memory (Laisney et al., 2009), whereas schizophrenia may be associated with disrupted executive and/or processing speed functions which impair fluid retrieval of semantically related words (Joyce et al., 1996; Lundin et al., 2020; van Beilen et al., 2004; Taler et al., 2015). More research is needed to disentangle the specific mechanisms of impaired semantic search in these heterogeneous clinical populations.

There is an additional challenge relevant to studying individual differences in search strategies. Because observable search responses result from an interaction between one's semantic representations and the strategies used to retrieve them (Jones et al., 2015), researchers need to evaluate both before assuming differences are caused exclusively by one or the other (for a more detailed discussion, see Hills & Kenett, 2021). Individuals may have different categorical (patch) knowledge and structures in semantic memory, as in the grocery shopping list example earlier, and the expert category knowledge of bird watchers or dog breeders, which could erroneously make their navigation of semantic space appear to operate differently from that of other people.

11.3   How Memory Search Changes the Internal Search Environment

The previous section showed how search strategies may be adapted to the distribution of resources (e.g., local-to-global search fitting patchy semantic memories). Much of the research on this topic investigates search behavior assuming a static distribution of resources. However, this assumption often does not hold for real-world systems – in most situations, distributions of resources are very much influenced by the search behavior of resource consumers – that is, search strategies and resource distributions mutually influence one another. In the current section, we consider this dynamical interaction between search and structure. We begin by describing the influence of memory search on memory networks – and hence, on subsequent searches. Based on this, we then consider possible explanations specifically for the patchy structure of semantic memory.

11.3.1   *Semantic Search Influences Semantic Network Structure*

We first illustrate the influence of search strategies on resource distributions using ecological examples – which, as the preceding sections argued, should then help us develop hypotheses that generalize from physical ecological environments to abstract mental environments. As stated earlier, ecological resources often come distributed in patches (Levin, 1992). Many ecologists indicate that such patchiness is a consequence of search processes themselves. For instance, phytoplankton are patchily distributed at multiple scales of measurement, and Levin (1992) suggests that this patchiness arises not only from physical processes such as drift diffusion or habitat events such as water currents, but also through the search behavior of plankton-consuming species such as krill. Using agent-based modeling simulations, Luthra, Izquierdo, and Todd (2020) studied mutual interactions of environmental patchiness and simple search strategies (exploration vs. exploitation with varying range of perception) that evolved among simulated plants and foragers. They found that patchiness emerged through the behavioral impact of searching consumers (foragers) on the spatial distribution of resources (plants) in the environment, and the patchiness in turn led to the evolution of more effective forager search strategies, creating an ongoing dynamical interaction between the two. Using similar methods, Luthra and Todd (2021) studied mutual interactions between social rather than individual search (i.e., consumers used information about the whereabouts of other consumers to locate resources) and resource patchiness, finding that each increased the level of the other up to a particular threshold.

Similar ideas of bidirectional interactions between search strategies and resource distributions can be applied to memory search. Unlike ecological spaces, memory spaces are not usually conceptualized as simple two- or three-dimensional Euclidean environments, but rather as higher-dimensional spaces or networks. Here, distance is the inverse of the strength of connections between concepts: the stronger a connection between two semantic concepts, the easier and quicker it is to traverse from one to the other (as with locations that lie physically close to one another). Hence, resource distributions in semantic memory can be quantified based on strength of memory connections (Rips, Shoben, & Smith, 1973).

Several studies indicate that semantic resources, like ecological resources, have a patchy distributional structure. Researchers have used tools from graph theory to analyze properties of human semantic networks derived from word association tasks, where participants generate words associated with presented cue words (Dubossarsky, De Deyne, & Hills, 2017; Morais, Olsson, & Schooler, 2013; Steyvers & Tenenbaum, 2005). Investigations find that these semantic networks have a high clustering coefficient – that is, groups of semantic concepts tend to be tightly knit, with a large density of within-group ties. Similar measures of aggregation are often used to estimate patchiness of ecological resources (Lloyd, 1967).

How are such structures in memory created and changed over time? That is, what processes influence the formation and ongoing strength of connections between concepts in memory? Some of the earliest research on long-term memory indicated that searching and retrieving semantic memories alters their structure (e.g., Jones, 1923). Most research has demonstrated the power of retrieval to improve recall – this effect has been found with nonsense words (Gates, 1917), pictures (Wheeler & Roediger, 1992), visual-auditory stimuli pairs (Nyberg et al., 2000), and word pairs (Pyc & Rawson, 2009). Other studies indicate that memory search can alter connections *between* concepts, strengthening those between arbitrary items that are activated simultaneously. For instance, in one study (Hupbach et al., 2007) participants learned two lists of words across two days. Researchers found that reminding participants of the first learning experience prior to studying the second list led to more confusion between the two lists than not recalling the first learning experience, indicating that memory retrieval strengthened the connections between the two arbitrary lists. Further, there is ample evidence to suggest that retrieval not only strengthens connections between activated concepts, but also weakens those between competing concepts. Across several studies on retrieval-induced failure, Anderson, Bjork, and Bjork (1994) found that connections between word pairs (e.g., *fruit–apple*) are weakened after retrieval practice with competing word pairs (e.g., making participants practice completion of *fruit–pe__* for *fruit–pear* weakens the *fruit–apple* connection). Thus, searching for and retrieving information can both strengthen and diminish semantic memory connections, actively influencing the structure of items distributed in memory, just as distributions of ecological resources are influenced by search and consumption.

To complement such behavioral studies, researchers have obtained neurological evidence of retrieval-based strengthening of memory connections. In experiments with rats, researchers found that proteins suspected to be involved in memory formation are synthesized in neurons not only during memory encoding, but also during retrieval, in a process of memory reconsolidation (Nader, Schafe, & Le Doux, 2000). Other studies have found that retrieval of memories involves brain structures similar to those used in encoding new ones (Gelbard-Sagiv et al., 2008; Chadwick et al., 2010). In support of Anderson, Bjork, and Bjork's (1994) classic studies of retrieval-induced forgetting, Wimber et al. (2015) reported that memory retrieval leads to active suppression of cortical patterns of competing memories, potentially produced by engaging regions of the prefrontal cortex. These studies imply that memory search and retrieval do not simply entail a passive read-out of information from the store of memory, but rather, similar to encoding, also involve reactivation of memory traces, suppression of competing ones, and thus overall alteration of connections.

As we interact with the external world, we are continually searching for, reactivating, and thereby altering stored concepts. For instance, when using a tool, we must search for and retrieve semantic information related to it. Further, not all stored information is needed at all times, hence memory structures need to be tuned to provide us with appropriate, context-relevant information when it is useful (Anderson & Schooler, 1991). As an important instance of this, concepts frequently encountered together in the real world and consequently frequently retrieved together will also have stronger connections between them in memory which facilitate their joint retrieval. This is demonstrated by extensive priming research: presentation of semantic concepts (e.g., *sleep*) typically leads to increased accessibility of contextually associated concepts (e.g., *pillow*) that are frequently encountered and recalled together in everyday life. Various models have been developed to account for such priming effects, including spreading activation (Anderson & Pirolli, 1984) and prime/target compound cue combination (Ratcliff & McKoon, 1988). Using language also requires repeated searching, retrieval, and recombination of concepts, again changing their internal structural configuration over time. Even more, our constant communication with others makes our semantic structures susceptible to the memory search performed by others which results in the concepts they communicate to us. Such effects are particularly important as children interact with adults to learn language. For instance, bilingual children's poorer performance on verbal fluency tasks and greater susceptibility to tip-of-the-tongue phenomena may reflect retrieval difficulties produced by unintended interference from the competing language (Sandoval et al., 2017).

Memory connections are therefore examples of stigmergic structures. Stigmergy is a mechanism of indirect coordination through which prior events perpetuate occurrence of future events. A popular example of stigmergy is that of ants producing pheromone trails to assist future ants in locating food. Researchers frequently distinguish between individualistic stigmergy (wherein the actions of a single agent perpetuate its own future actions) and collective stigmergy (wherein multiple agents indirectly coordinate to produce future events; Heylighen, 2016). Many stigmergic events can be imagined as a combination of both. For instance, pheromone trails not only enable a single ant to find food locations again, but also foster cooperation between ants for collectively finding food locations.

Memory traces are similar: connections left behind by previous activations enable the same person to retrieve the information again more efficiently, and when the connections of earlier activations are recorded externally as physical markers (e.g., in the form of verbal and written communication), they can influence and coordinate the behavior of others.

11.3.2   Explanations for Patchiness in Semantic Memory

So far, we have provided evidence to suggest that searching through semantic memory influences its network structure. But what is it about the way we search that specifically produces patchiness in semantic memories? We mentioned earlier that analyses of semantic networks indicate that they have high clustering coefficients – that is, they are patchy (Morais, Olsson, & Schooler, 2013; Steyvers & Tenenbaum, 2005). These same studies also find that semantic memories have a low average path length between two random nodes in the network. That is, it is possible to connect any two seemingly unrelated semantic concepts by traversing only a small number of connections. For instance, although *sleep* and *duck* might seem like distant concepts, it is possible to connect the two by following the path *sleep-pillow-feather-duck*. In graph theory, networks featuring these two features (patchiness and small path length) are known as small-world networks.

How do small-world structures in semantic memory develop? We have argued that connections in memory develop due to activations produced through encountering semantic concepts in the real world. This suggests that semantic structures come to resemble existing structures in the world, and so to the extent that the contents of the world have small-world structure, so too will some of the contents of mind. In fact, much recent research has focused on the discovery of small-world architectures across real-world network systems. Researchers find evidence for small-world features in human-constructed domains including language (Ferrer i Cancho & Solé, 2001), social groups (Davidsen et al., 2002), transport systems (Sen et al., 2003), and the world-wide web (Adamic, 1999), as well as in other naturally occurring systems such as pollination networks (Olesen et al., 2006) and food webs (Montoya & Solé, 2002). Hence, potentially, some internal semantic networks could reflect small-world structures of the external world. Furthermore, dynamical interactions between internal semantic structures and external social structures (e.g., language, social media) serve to reinforce small-world features in both – that is, small-world structures in semantic memory get reflected in social systems (e.g., distribution of words in language or connections on social media), which in turn reinforce the small-worldness of semantic memory.

Small-world patchy structures may thus arise internally in semantic memory through search processes that make memory reflect external structures. But these patchy semantic structures could also emerge through internal adaptive processes, independent of external structure, because of their high efficiency for information search and transmission. Since small-world networks have a high level of clustering, they foster efficient local interactions, and because of their low path distance, they also promote global search (Latora & Marchiori, 2001). These adaptive benefits perhaps encourage the emergence and selection of small-worldness in search networks, including semantic ones. Supporting this hypothesis, agent-based simulations by Williams (2019) showed that optimizing simple neural networks to perform lifelike search behaviors such as finding food and mates using genetic algorithms and Hebbian learning leads them to develop small-world architectures. Hence, features of small-worldness – high patchiness and low path length – are likely to also emerge in semantic memory, created by and optimized for the act of memory search.

11.4   Conclusions

External and internal searches share similar strategies. They also operate on spaces that share similar structure. More speculatively, the structure of inner space (like that of the external world) may be partly constructed by the mechanisms we use to search it. Together, this suggests that the similarities between inner and outer space are not only a function of the inner world reflecting the outer world. They are also a product of imposing search processes originally evolved for navigating the external spatial world onto our internal world. The inner world is clearly not a perfect reflection of the outer world; importantly, many things come out of our heads that do not (yet) exist outside, forming the basis of innovation (Hills, 2019). Consequently, the search processes we describe here for space and memory apply to problem solving and exploration more generally – domains where areas of the cognitive map are uncharted until we start looking. In that way, our internal and external search also governs what, just beyond the horizons of the known, we are likely to find.

References

Abbott, J. T., Austerweil, J. L., & Griffiths, T. L. (2015). Random walks on semantic networks can resemble optimal foraging. *Psychological Review*, 122(3), 558–569.

Adamic, L. A. (1999). The small world web. *International Conference on Theory and Practice of Digital Libraries*, 1696, 443–452.

Anderson, M. C., Bjork, R. A., & Bjork, E. (1994). Remembering can cause forgetting: Retrieval dynamics in long-term memory. *Journal of Experimental Psychology: Learning, Memory, and Cognition*, 20(5), 1063–1087.

Anderson, J. R., & Pirolli, P. L. (1984). Spread of activation. *Journal of Experimental Psychology: Learning, Memory, and Cognition*, 10(4), 791–798.

Anderson, J. R., & Schooler, L. J. (1991). Reflections of the environment in memory. *Psychological Science*, 2(6), 396–408.

Benhamou, S. (2007). How many animals really do the Lévy walk? *Ecology*, 88(8), 1962–1969.

Bhatia, S., Richie, R., & Zou, W. (2019). Distributed semantic representations for modeling human judgment. *Current Opinion in Behavioral Sciences*, 29, 31–36.

Birn, R. M., Kenworthy, L., Case, L., Caravella, R., Jones, T. B., Bandettini, P. A., & Martin, A. (2010). Neural systems supporting lexical search guided by letter and semantic category cues: A self-paced overt response fMRI study of verbal fluency. *Neuroimage*, 49(1), 1099–1107.

Blanchard, T. C., & Hayden, B. Y. (2014). Neurons in dorsal anterior cingulate cortex signal postdecisional variables in a foraging task. *Journal of Neuroscience*, 34(2), 646–655.

Boettcher, S. E., Drew, T., & Wolfe, J. M. (2018). Lost in the supermarket: Quantifying the cost of partitioning memory sets in hybrid search. *Memory & Cognition*, 46(1), 43–57.

Bokat, C. E., & Goldberg, T. E. (2003). Letter and category fluency in schizophrenic patients: A meta-analysis. *Schizophrenia Research*, 64(1), 73–78.

Bousfield, W. A., & Sedgewick, C. H. W. (1944). An analysis of sequences of restricted associative responses. *The Journal of General Psychology*, 30(2), 149–165.

Brown, J. W., & Alexander, W. H. (2017). Foraging value, risk avoidance, and multiple control signals: How the anterior cingulate cortex controls value-based decision-making. *Journal of Cognitive Neuroscience*, 29(10), 1656–1673.

Buzsáki, G., & Moser, E. I. (2013). Memory, navigation and theta rhythm in the hippocampal-entorhinal system. *Nature Neuroscience*, 16(2), 130–138.

Chadwick, M. J., Hassabis, D., Weiskopf, N., & Maguire, E. A. (2010). Decoding individual episodic memory traces in the human hippocampus. *Current Biology*, 20(6), 544–547.

Charnov, E. L. (1976). Optimal foraging, the marginal value theorem. *Theoretical Population Biology*, 9(2), 129–136.

Constantinescu, A. O., O'Reilly, J. X., & Behrens, T. E. (2016). Organizing conceptual knowledge in humans with a gridlike code. *Science*, 352(6292), 1464–1468.

Costafreda, S. G., Fu, C. H., Lee, L., Everitt, B., Brammer, M. J., & David, A. S. (2006). A systematic review and quantitative appraisal of fMRI studies of verbal fluency: Role of the left inferior frontal gyrus. *Human Brain Mapping*, 27(10), 799–810.

Davidsen, J., Ebel, H., & Bornholdt, S. (2002). Emergence of a small world from local interactions: Modeling acquaintance networks. *Physical Review Letters*, 88 (12), 128701.

Dick, P. K. (1959). *Time out of joint*. J. B. Lippencott & Co.

Dubossarsky, H., De Deyne, S., & Hills, T. (2017). Quantifying the structure of free association networks across the lifespan. *Developmental Psychology*, 53, 1560–1570.

Eichenbaum, H. (2004). Hippocampus: Cognitive processes and neural representations that underlie declarative memory. *Neuron*, 44(1), 109–120.

Ferrer i Cancho, R., & Solé, R. V. (2001). The small world of human language. *Proceedings of The Royal Society B*, 268, 2261–2265.

Fu, W. T., & Pirolli, P. (2007). SNIF-ACT: A cognitive model of user navigation on the World Wide Web. *Human–Computer Interaction*, 22(4), 355–412.

Gates, A. I. (1917). Recitation as a factor in memorizing. *Archives of Psychology*, 6, 40.

Gauthier, C. T., Duyme, M., Zanca, M., & Capron, C. (2009). Sex and performance level effects on brain activation during a verbal fluency task: A functional magnetic resonance imaging study. *Cortex*, 45(2), 164–176.

Gelbard-Sagiv, H., Mukamel, R., Harel, M., Malach, R., & Fried, I. (2008). Supporting online material internally generated reactivation of single neurons in human hippocampus during free recall. *Science Reports*, 322, 96–101.

Gruber, M. J., & Ranganath, C. (2019). How curiosity enhances hippocampus-dependent memory: The prediction, appraisal, curiosity, and exploration (PACE) framework. *Trends in Cognitive Sciences*, 23(12), 1014–1025.

Gruenewald, P. J., & Lockhead, G. R. (1980). The free recall of category examples. *Journal of Experimental Psychology: Human Learning and Memory*, 6(3), 225–240.

Gurd, J. M., Amunts, K., Weiss, P. H., Zafiris, O., Zilles, K., Marshall, J. C., & Fink, G. R. (2002). Posterior parietal cortex is implicated in continuous switching between verbal fluency tasks: An fMRI study with clinical implications. *Brain*, 125(5), 1024–1038.

Henry, J. D., & Crawford, J. R. (2005). A meta-analytic review of verbal fluency deficits in depression. *Journal of Clinical and Experimental Neuropsychology*, 27(1), 78–101.

Henry, J. D., Crawford, J. R., & Phillips, L. H. (2004). Verbal fluency performance in dementia of the Alzheimer's type: A meta-analysis. *Neuropsychologia*, 42(9), 1212–1222.

Heylighen, F. (2016). Stigmergy as a universal coordination mechanism II: Varieties and evolution. *Cognitive Systems Research*, 38, 50–59.

Hills, T. (2003). Towards a unified theory of animal event timing. In W. H. Meck (Ed.), *Functional and neural mechanisms of interval timing* (pp. 77–111). New York: CRC Press.

Hills, T. T. (2006). Animal foraging and the evolution of goal-directed cognition. *Cognitive Science*, 30(1), 3–41.

Hills, T. T. (2019). Neurocognitive free will. *Proceedings of the Royal Society B*, 286 (1908), 20190510.

Hills, T. T., Jones, M. N., & Todd, P. M. (2012). Optimal foraging in semantic memory. *Psychological Review*, 119(2), 431–440.

Hills, T. T., Kalff, C., & Wiener, J. M. (2013). Adaptive Lévy processes and area-restricted search in human foraging. *PLoS One*, 8(4), e60488.

Hills, T. T., & Kenett, Y. (2021). Is the mind a network? Maps, vehicles, and skyhooks in cognitive network science. *Topics in Cognitive Science*. https://onl inelibrary.wiley.com/doi/abs/10.1111/tops.12570

Hills, T. T., Mata, R., Wilke, A., & Samanez-Larkin, G. R. (2013). Mechanisms of age-related decline in memory search across the adult life span. *Developmental Psychology*, 49(12), 2396.

Hills, T. T., & Pachur, T. (2012). Dynamic search and working memory in social recall. *Journal of Experimental Psychology: Learning, Memory, and Cognition*, 38(1), 218.

Hills, T. T., Todd, P. M., Lazer, D., Redish, A. D., Couzin, I. D., & Cognitive Search Research Group (2015). Exploration versus exploitation in space, mind, and society. *Trends in Cognitive Science*, 19(1), 46–54. doi:10.1016/j. tics.2014.10.004

Hirshorn, E. A., & Thompson-Schill, S. L. (2006). Role of the left inferior frontal gyrus in covert word retrieval: Neural correlates of switching during verbal fluency. *Neuropsychologia*, 44(12), 2547–2557.

Hupbach, A., Gomez, R., Hardt, O., & Nadel, L. (2007). Reconsolidation of episodic memories: A subtle reminder triggers integration of new information. *Learning & Memory*, 14, 47–53.

Jones, H. E. (1923). The effects of examination on the performance of learning. *Archives of Psychology*, 10, 1–70.

Jones, M. N., Hills, T. T., & Todd, P. M. (2015). Hidden processes in structural representations: A reply to Abbott, Austerweil, and Griffiths (2015). *Psychological Review*, 122(3), 570–574.

Jones, M. N., & Mewhort, D. J. (2007). Representing word meaning and order information in a composite holographic lexicon. *Psychological Review*, 114(1), 1–37.

Joyce, E. M., Collinson, S. L., & Crichton, P. (1996). Verbal fluency in schizo-phrenia: Relationship with executive function, semantic memory and clinical alogia. *Psychological Medicine*, 26(1), 39–49.

Kolling, N., Behrens, T. E., Mars, R. B., & Rushworth, M. F. (2012). Neural mechanisms of foraging. *Science*, 336(6077), 95–98.

Laisney, M., Matuszewski, V., Mézenge, F., Belliard, S., de la Sayette, V., Eustache, F., & Desgranges, B. (2009). The underlying mechanisms of verbal fluency deficit in frontotemporal dementia and semantic dementia. *Journal of Neurology*, 256(7), 1083–1094.

Landauer, T. K., & Dumais, S. T. (1997). A solution to Plato's problem: The latent semantic analysis theory of acquisition, induction, and representation of knowledge. *Psychological Review*, 104(2), 211–240.

Latora, V., & Marchiori, M. (2001). Efficient behavior of small-world networks. *Physical Review Letters*, 87(19), 198701.

Levin, S. A. (1992). The problem of pattern and scale in ecology. *Ecology*, 73(6), 1943–1967.

Lloyd, M. (1967). Mean crowding. *Journal of Animal Ecology*, 36(1), 1–30.

Lundin, N. B. (2022). Disorganized speech in psychosis: Computational and neural markers of semantic foraging and discourse cohesion. Unpublished doctoral dissertation. Indiana University Bloomington.

Lundin, N. B., Todd, P. M., Jones, M. N., Avery, J. E., O'Donnell, B. F., & Hetrick, W. P. (2020). Semantic search in psychosis: Modeling local exploitation and global exploration. *Schizophrenia Bulletin Open*, 1(1), sgaa011.

Luthra, M., Izquierdo, E. J., & Todd, P. M. (2020). Cognition evolves with the emergence of environmental patchiness. In J. Bongard, J. Lovato, L. Herbert-Dufresne, R. Dasari, & L. Soros (Eds.), *Proceedings of the Artificial Life Conference 2020* (pp. 450–458). MIT Press. https://direct.mit.edu/isal/proceedings/isal2020/450/98395

Luthra, M. & Todd, P. M. (2021). Social search evolves with the emergence of clustered environments. In J. Čejková, S. Holler, L. Soros, & O. Witkowski (Eds.), *Proceedings of the Artificial Life Conference 2021* (pp. 182–190). MIT Press.

Lydon-Staley, D. M., Zhou, D., Blevins, A. S., Zurn, P., & Bassett, D. S. (2021). Hunters, busybodies and the knowledge network building associated with deprivation curiosity. *Nature Human Behaviour*, 5(3), 327–336.

O'Keefe, J., & Nadel, L. (1978). *The hippocampus as a cognitive map*. Oxford University Press.

Mack, M. L., Love, B. C., & Preston, A. R. (2016). Dynamic updating of hippocampal object representations reflects new conceptual knowledge. *Proceedings of the National Academy of Sciences*, 113(46), 13203–13208.

Mehta, P. S., Tu, J. C., LoConte, G. A., Pesce, M. C., & Hayden, B. Y. (2019). Ventromedial prefrontal cortex tracks multiple environmental variables during search. *Journal of Neuroscience*, 39(27), 5336–5350.

Meyer, D. E., & Schvaneveldt, R. W. (1971). Facilitation in recognizing pairs of words: Evidence of a dependence between retrieval operations. *Journal of Experimental Psychology*, 90(2), 227.

Montez, P., Thompson, G., & Kello, C. T. (2015). The role of semantic clustering in optimal memory foraging. *Cognitive Science*, 39(8), 1925–1939.

Montoya, J. M., & Solé, R. V. (2002). Small world patterns in food webs. *Journal of Theoretical Biology*, 214(3), 405–412.

Morais, A. S., Olsson, H., & Schooler, L. J. (2013). Mapping the structure of semantic memory. *Cognitive Science*, 37(1), 125–145.

Morton, N. W., Sherrill, K. R., & Preston, A. R. (2017). Memory integration constructs maps of space, time, and concepts. *Current Opinion in Behavioral Sciences*, 17, 161–168.

Nader, K., Schafe, G. E., & Le Doux, J. E. (2000). Fear memories require protein synthesis in the amygdala for reconsolidation after retrieval. *Nature*, 406(6797), 722–726.

Nyberg, L., Habib, R., Mcintosh, A. R., & Tulving, E. (2000). Reactivation of encoding-related brain activity during memory retrieval. *Proceedings of the National Academy of Sciences*, 97(20), 11120–11124.

Olesen, J. M., Bascompte, J., Dupont, Y. L., & Jordano, P. (2006). The smallest of all worlds: Pollination networks. *Journal of Theoretical Biology*, 240(2), 270–276.

Pezzulo, G., van der Meer, M.A., Lansink, C.S., & Pennartz, C.M. (2014). Internally generated sequences in learning and executing goal-directed behavior. *Trends in Cognitive Sciences*, 18, 647–657. doi:10.1016/j.tics.2014.06.011

Pyc, M. A., & Rawson, K. A. (2009). Testing the retrieval effort hypothesis: Does greater difficulty correctly recalling information lead to higher levels of memory? *Journal of Memory and Language*, 60(4), 437–447.

Ratcliff, R., & McKoon, G. (1988). A retrieval theory of priming in memory. *Psychological Review*, 95(3), 385–408.

Rhodes, T., & Turvey, M. T. (2007). Human memory retrieval as Lévy foraging. *Physica A: Statistical Mechanics and its Applications*, 385(1), 255–260.

Rips, L. J., Shoben, E. J., & Smith, E. E. (1973). Semantic distance and the verification of semantic relations. *Journal of Verbal Learning and Verbal Behavior*, 12(1), 1–20.

Sandoval, T. C., Gollan, T. H., Ferreira, V. S., & Salmon, D. P. (2017). What causes the bilingual disadvantage in verbal fluency? The dual-task analogy. *Bilingualism: Language and Cognition*, 13(2), 231–252.

Sen, P., Dasgupta, S., Chatterjee, A., Sreeram, P. A., Mukherjee, G., & Manna, S. S. (2003). Small-world properties of the Indian railway network. *Physical Review*, 67, 036106.

Shenhav, A., Straccia, M. A., Botvinick, M. M., & Cohen, J. D. (2016). Dorsal anterior cingulate and ventromedial prefrontal cortex have inverse roles in both foraging and economic choice. *Cognitive, Affective, & Behavioral Neuroscience*, 16(6), 1127–1139.

Shenhav, A., Straccia, M. A., Cohen, J. D., & Botvinick, M. M. (2014). Anterior cingulate engagement in a foraging context reflects choice difficulty, not foraging value. *Nature Neuroscience*, 17(9), 1249–1254.

Shima, K., & Tanji, J. (1998). Role for cingulate motor area cells in voluntary movement selection based on reward. *Science*, 282(5392), 1335–1338.

Steyvers, M., & Tenenbaum, J. B. (2005). The large-scale structure of semantic networks: Statistical analyses and a model of semantic growth. *Cognitive Science*, 29(1), 41–78.

Strange, B. A., Witter, M. P., Lein, E. S., & Moser, E. I. (2014). Functional organization of the hippocampal longitudinal axis. *Nature Reviews Neuroscience*, 15(10), 655–669.

Taler, V., Johns, B., Sheppard, C., & Jones, M. (2015, December). Determining the linguistic information sources underlying verbal fluency performance across aging and cognitive impairment. *Canadian Journal of Experimental Psychology-Revue Canadienne De Psychologie Experimentale*, 69(4), 369–369.

Thompson, G. W., & Kello, C. (2014). Walking across Wikipedia: A scale-free network model of semantic memory retrieval. *Frontiers in Psychology*, 5, 86.

Todd, P. M., & Hills, T.T. (2020). Foraging in mind. *Current Directions in Psychological Science*, 20(3), 309–315. https://doi.org/10.1177/0963721420915861

Todd, P. M., Hills, T. T., & Robbins, T. W. (Eds.). (2012). *Cognitive search: Evolution, algorithms, and the brain*. MIT Press.

Tolman, E. C. (1948). Cognitive maps in rats and men. *Psychological Review*, 55, 189–208.

Tolman, E. C., & Gleitman, H. (1949). Studies in learning and motivation: I. Equal reinforcements in both end-boxes, followed by shock in one end-box. *Journal of Experimental Psychology*, 39, 810–819.

Troyer, A. K., Moscovitch, M., & Winocur, G. (1997). Clustering and switching as two components of verbal fluency: Evidence from younger and older healthy adults. *Neuropsychology*, 11(1), 138–146.

Troyer, A. K., Moscovitch, M., Winocur, G., Alexander, M. P., & Stuss, D. O. N. (1998). Clustering and switching on verbal fluency: The effects of focal frontal- and temporal-lobe lesions. *Neuropsychologia*, 36(6), 499–504.

van Beilen, M., Pijnenborg, M., van Zomeren, E. H., van den Bosch, R. J., Withaar, F. K., & Bouma, A. (2004). What is measured by verbal fluency tests in schizophrenia? *Schizophrenia Research*, 69(2–3), 267–276.

Viswanathan, G. M., Buldyrev, S. V., Havlin, S., Da Luz, M. G. E., Raposo, E. P., & Stanley, H. E. (1999). Optimizing the success of random searches. *Nature*, 401(6756), 911–914.

Wang, M. Z., & Hayden, B. Y. (2021). Latent learning, cognitive maps, and curiosity. *Current Opinion in Behavioral Sciences*, 38, 1–7.

Wang, X., & Pleimling, M. (2017). Foraging patterns in online searches. *Physical Review E*, 95(3), 032145.

Wheeler, M. A., & Roediger, H. L. (1992). Disparate effects of repeated testing: Reconciling Ballard's (1913) and Bartlett's (1932) results. *Psychological Science*, 3(4), 240–245.

Williams, S. C. (2019). *Neural correlates of adaptive behavior: Structure, dynamics, and information processing* (Publication No. 27543239) [Doctoral dissertation, Indiana University Bloomington]. ProQuest Dissertations Publishing.

Wimber, M., Alink, A., Charest, I., Kriegeskorte, N., & Anderson, M. C. (2015). Retrieval induces adaptive forgetting of competing memories via cortical pattern suppression. *Nature Neuroscience*, 18(4), 582–589.

Winstanley, C. A., Robbins, T. W., Balleine, B. W., Brown, J. W., Büchel, C., Cools, R., ... & Seamans, J. K. (2012). Search, goals, and the brain. In P. M. Todd, T. T. Hills, & T. W. Robbins (Eds.), *Cognitive search: Evolution, algorithms, and the brain. Strüngmann Forum reports* (pp. 125–156). MIT Press.

CHAPTER 12

Edgework
Viewing Curiosity as Fundamentally Relational

Perry Zurn, Dale Zhou, David M. Lydon-Staley, and Dani S. Bassett

12.1 Introduction

The human mind is curious. It is strange, remarkable, and mystifying; it is eager, probing, and questioning. Despite the pervasiveness of curiosity and its relevance for our well-being, many of us still pause in attempting to answer the fundamental question: What is curiosity? The quandary of how to define curiosity, its places, and its actions is not a challenge that we newly face. Humanity has been attempting such definitions for centuries. In 1270, Aquinas suggested that curiosity is the desire to know (Aquinas, 1981). Descartes stated that curiosity is a desire to understand (Descartes, 1649). In 1889, William James wrote that curiosity is the impulse toward better cognition (James, 1925). John Dewey asserted that curiosity is an interest in problems provoked by the observation of things and the accumulation of material (Dewey, 1910/1933). Lowenstein suggested that curiosity is a feeling of deprivation produced by information gaps (Loewenstein, 1994). Even in modern science, Celeste Kidd writes that curiosity is a drive-state for information (Kidd & Hayden, 2015).

What is it precisely that we are desirous of, impulsive toward, interested in, deprived of, or driven toward? The answers—knowledge, information, solutions to problems, better cognition—are commonly thought of as items, which, when acquired, are satisfying. In fact, the analogy between hunger (thirst) and curiosity, as well as the analogy between food (drink) and information, underscores the acquisitional nature of our common conceptualizations (Cofer & Appley, 1964). Moreover, we think of curiosity as valuable to us because when we acquire the item of information, perhaps more often than not, our life gets better: our uncertainty about the world is reduced (Cohen et al., 2007) and we no longer feel deprived of information (Loewenstein, 1994). Upon reflection, the acquisitional account of curiosity seems intuitive. Yet, if we press the account, if we allow acquisitional actions of humans to play out upon the theater of experience, we quickly come to realize that we are missing a key piece of the puzzle. An acquisition (or collection) of informational bits does not constitute knowledge.

Knowledge requires something more. Knowledge requires an understanding of the relations between bits of information: relations of cause, of correlation, and of consequence, to name a few. How might we expand the current acquisitional account of curiosity to an explicitly connectional account of curiosity? And if we did so, what sorts of affordances might such an account offer? Here we frame curiosity as edgework. In doing so, we offer a justification, operationalization, investigation, and validation of a connectional account of curiosity. Our approach is explicitly interdisciplinary: we begin the discussion in philosophy, recast core notions in mathematics, and then exercise the ideas further in cognitive science, throughout drawing inspiration from physics and ethics as appropriate. The work we review ranges in inquisitorial processes from laboratory experiments to mathematical models, and capitalizes on the data of today and those of yesteryear. Against this backdrop, we will see that the edgework account of curiosity provides new explanations for human behavior, and inspires a unique set of future investigative directions in understanding how we build knowledge of our networked world.

12.2   From Acquisitional to Connectional Curiosity

For centuries, even millennia, curiosity has been defined in the Western intellectual tradition as the desire to know (Zurn, 2021). Following suit, the contemporary fields of psychology and neuroscience typically understand curiosity to be the intrinsic motivation to seek information (Kidd & Hayden, 2015; Begus & Southgate, 2018). Implicit in these definitions is an acquisitional model of curiosity. Curiosity is the desire to know something or a behavior to seek some piece of information. Curiosity is then quelled when knowledge is secured or information gaps are filled. But curiosity does not only acquire; it also, and perhaps more fundamentally, connects (León, 2020; Swanson, 2020). It puts two and two together. It builds relations between ideas in the mind and between things in the world, steadily crafting and recrafting the network architecture of individual and collective knowledge. This is the connectional model of curiosity. And while this model has uniquely promising applications in network science today (Zurn & Bassett, 2022), it also has underappreciated roots in the philosophies of yesteryear.

The acquisitional model of curiosity focuses, so to speak, on the nodes of knowledge to be obtained. This conceptualization has deep roots in the history of philosophy. Plutarch, for example, characterized the curious person as "passionate to find out" whatever is new or novel around town (Plutarch, 2005, 518c). Augustine similarly describes the curious person as "lusting to see" everything, from scientific marvels to religious wonders (Augustine, 1961, 10.35). In the early modern period, this inquisitive passion became precisely the appetite for knowledge that promised to loose human society from its chains of ignorance (Benedict, 2003). Today, philosophers still conceptualize curiosity as the motivation to find out information or acquire specific epistemic goods (Inan, 2011; Watson, 2018). Importantly, the acquisitional model is rooted in units of knowers and units of knowledge: "I want to know X" or "I desire to find out X" (Zurn & Bassett, 2022). In this model, the butterfly collector is paradigmatically curious because they aim to acquire elusive butterflies.

But where there are nodes, there are also edges. And, in fact, when the word curiosity (and its cognates in multiple languages) are tracked alongside words for "connection," "link," and "relation" within the Western intellectual tradition, another possibility appears: the connectional model. On this model, curiosity is edgework. As such, curiosity might collect information, track down answers, or imagine new possibilities, but it does so by building scaffolds or weaving webs. It builds connections, finds links, and follows threads. As Renaissance humanist Jean Luis Vives writes, curiosity tracks (and sometimes creates) the "threads" between things (Vives, 1531; 1913, p. 16). John Dewey similarly defines curiosity as the impulse to make the "connections" between things perceptible (Dewey, 1916/2011, pp. 115–116). That project will necessarily connect the curious person more deeply to their own interests and investments (Rousseau, 1762/1909), which shape the connections made and determine the disconnections chosen. But it will also, as William James astutely notes, necessarily "knit" new information together with the old (James, 1890/ 1918, p. 25). On this model, it is not the collector but the butterfly conservationist who best embodies curiosity, for the latter aims to know the butterfly precisely within the relations that best sustain it.

While the traditional model of curiosity characterizes it as a desire to acquire new information, amassing knowledge in an ever-growing pile of nodes, the connectional model of curiosity characterizes it as a practice of building connections, whether between things to know or between knowers themselves. From a network science perspective (Bassett, 2020), freeing curiosity from nodal gravity is priceless; it allows us to explore the curious energy of the edge.

12.3   Case Study of Curiosity as Edgework

How might the paradigm of curiosity as edgework manifest in the contemporary lives of humans today? Curious minds engage in a kinesthetic practice, by walking through knowledge space and picking up relations to structure their thought architectures (Zurn, 2019; Zurn & Bassett, 2018). We recently set out to watch humans walk on collective knowledge networks, thereby building their own individual knowledge networks (Lydon-Staley et al., 2019c). After providing informed consent for the study, participants browsed Wikipedia for 15 minutes a day for 21 days. While they browsed, a piece of software installed on their computer provided us with information about which pages they visited, in what order, and for how long. The data were then analyzed by treating each page as a node in a network, and by treating the transition from one page to another as a step along the edge connecting them (Scholtes, 2017; West & Leskovec, 2012). We defined long steps to be those taken between pages with dissimilar content, and short steps to be those taken between pages with similar content. The sequence of steps that each person took reflected their characteristic style of curiosity and thus of knowledge network building.

In the many hours of data collected, we saw clear evidence for a continuum of curiosity styles bookended by two archetypes: the busybody and the hunter (Zurn, 2019). The hunter "wishes [they] had a few hundred helpers and good, well-trained hounds that [they] could drive into the history of the human soul to round up [their] game" (Nietzsche, 1886/1989, §45, 59) in a targeted search for information; in contrast, the busybody will "frisk about, and rove about, at random, wherever they please" (Yonge & Philo, 1854, §34). These kinesthetic signatures of the hunter and the busybody naturally lead to the creation of different individual knowledge networks. Consistent with this expectation, we found that the hunters in the participant group took walks that traced out networks with high clustering, meaning that they navigated among sets of three or more pages with high similarity, taking short steps in a local neighborhood (Onnela et al., 2005). In contrast, the busybodies in the participant group took walks that traced out networks with low clustering and long path length, meaning that they navigated among pages that were dissimilar, taking long steps spanning many distinct neighborhoods.

Interestingly, one personality trait stood out in explaining the different network building practices of the busybodies and the hunters: their sensitivity to information deprivation (Litman, 2008; Litman & Jimerson, 2004; Loewenstein, 1994). In a separate testing session, participants had completed a scale measuring their deprivation sensitivity by determining the degree to which the following statements characterized them: "Thinking about solutions to difficult conceptual problems can keep me awake at night"; "I can spend hours on a single problem because I just can't rest without knowing the answer"; "I feel frustrated if I can't figure out the solution to a problem, so I work even harder to solve it"; "I work relentlessly at problems that I feel must be solved"; "It frustrates me not having all the information I need" (Kashdan et al., 2018, p. 147). Individuals high in deprivation sensitivity have a drive to eliminate the unknown as they encounter new information and recognize gaps in their knowledge. Consistent with this trait, we found that individuals high in deprivation sensitivity were hunters building densely clustered networks, while those low in deprivation sensitivity were busybodies building sparse and loopy networks. In other words, individual differences in deprivation sensitivity lead to the creation of knowledge networks with distinct architectures.

12.4 Curiosity as Edgework in a Changing Mental World

Does our mental state explain daily variation in the connectional knowledge structures that we build? Beyond trait deprivation sensitivity, might mental state affect the knowledge network structures we build? A rich literature considers the timescales over which the experience of curiosity unfolds (Pekrun, 2019; Hidi & Renninger, 2019). Beyond between-person differences in the tendency to consistently experience high levels of curiosity across months and years (Kashdan et al., 2018; Lydon-Staley et al., 2019d), curiosity can also be a transient experience, lasting only moments (Berlyne, 1960; Loewenstein, 1994) or days (Garrosa et al., 2017; Kashdan & Steger, 2007; Lydon-Staley et al., 2019d). These fluctuations in curiosity track dynamic mental states, including the waxing and waning of our emotional experiences (Diener & Diener, 1996; Reio & Callahan, 2004; Rodrigue et al., 1987). Positive affect facilitates an openness to experiences, even challenging ones, that is at the core of many definitions of curiosity (e.g., "I view challenging situations as opportunities to grow and learn", "I frequently seek out opportunities to challenge myself and grow as a person" [Kashdan et al., 2009]). By broadening individuals' behaviors and cognitive repertoires, positive affect states facilitate engagement in diverse and novel courses of action (Fredrickson, 2004). Negative emotions, in contrast, can promote a narrowing of behavior directed toward the immediate situation (Fredrickson & Branigan, 2005).

Probing edgework dynamics, we decomposed the 21 days of Wikipedia browsing into three one-week periods and found that curiosity styles exhibit both trait and state components. Focusing on the state component, we found, for example, that weeks of higher than usual sensation-seeking (Zuckerman, 1994), when participants had greater craving for excitement and new experiences than was typical for them (Lydon-Staley et al., 2019b), were also weeks during which participants browsed with longer steps than usual, traversing more dissimilar Wikipedia pages and building more spindly networks (Lydon-Staley et al., 2019c). Further, our unpublished data show that subclinical levels of depression are associated with the tendency to build close by, whereas less depressed participants built over wider spaces. This narrowing of search in depressed states parallels the narrowing of self-reported curiosity when experiencing negative affect (Fredrickson & Branigan, 2005). In the connectional curiosity view, this decrease in the tendency to seek diverse and novel information in the context of negative affect is a modulation of the type of edgework that is practiced rather than a reduction in curiosity.

Our observations that styles of edgework fluctuate across time alongside naturalistic fluctuations in mental state highlight the important role that our mental states play in the types of knowledge structures we build. Understanding the time-varying nature of edgework more deeply will require the acquisition of fine-grained measurements of each person's time-varying mental state concurrently with intensive assessment of edgework. Such investigations will benefit from increasingly feasible approaches for capturing dynamics in both mental state (Larson & Csikszentmihalyi, 2014; Lydon-Staley et al., 2019a) and media engagement (Reeves et al., 2019; George et al., 2018).

12.5 Curiosity as Edgework Reshapes Previous Theoretical Constructs

Does connectional curiosity validate the information gap or compression progress theories of curiosity? Framing curiosity as edgework not only raises new opportunities to study the internal landscape of mental experience, it also fundamentally reshapes the theoretical discourse. Prior theories often define curiosity as being composed of interactions among other constructs, such as those of learning, attention, reward, uncertainty, and exploration (Gottlieb & Oudeyer, 2018; Kidd & Hayden, 2015). According to these theories, curiosity is an emotion or drive defined by reward or uncertainty (Gruber et al., 2014; Kang et al., 2009; Kidd & Hayden, 2015; Loewenstein, 1994) and is explained by its ability to compel learning (Gruber et al., 2014; Oudeyer et al., 2016; Oudeyer, 2018), attention (Gottlieb, 2012; Gottlieb et al., 2014), play (Chu & Schulz, 2020), and exploration (Gershman & Niv, 2015; Gopnik, 2020). Yet, these explanations beg the question of whether (and how) curiosity is distinct from other constructs, being its own process rather than motivating other processes.

The notion of curiosity as edgework provides an answer to this question. Framing curiosity as a building process clarifies the compositional concepts: a system of knowledge composed of relations among informational units, which grows over time by relation-finding actions (Bassett, 2020; Zhou et al., 2020b). By operationalizing those compositional concepts within network science, the field has the opportunity to test two prior theories of curiosity: the information gap theory and the compression progress theory (Loewenstein, 1994; Schmidhuber, 2008). In the former, curiosity is the drive to fill an information gap, to find the missing piece of knowledge in a mental model (Kang et al., 2009; Loewenstein, 1994). In the latter, curiosity is the drive to seek information that improves the compression of a mental model, enhancing the compactness, efficiency, and flexible use of knowledge (Schmidhuber, 2008; Zhou et al., 2020b).

These two theories have proven difficult to validate, in part because the key concepts are difficult to describe and measure. The translation from concept to measure is a perennial challenge (Birhane, 2021), which can sometimes be addressed by choosing an appropriate mathematical model. What empirical and computational data could validate either or both frameworks? By framing curiosity as edgework operationalized as a network building process, we gain traction. First, an information gap can be explicitly defined as a cavity in the network, which is the absence of edges in a portion of the network; that absence forms a hole among concepts. Such a cavity can be detected using algebraic topology (Ju et al., 2020; Sizemore et al., 2018). Similarly, when curiosity is a network-building process, then compression progress can be quantified as a change in the network's compressibility (Lynn & Bassett, 2021).

Each theory makes distinct predictions. The growth of knowledge networks accompanied by a closing of cavities would support information gap theory. Evidence for such closing of cavities arises in the development of language in toddlers (Sizemore et al., 2018) and collective knowledge in

Wikipedia (Ju et al., 2020). The growth of knowledge networks accompanied by increasing compressibility would support compression progress theory. The framing of curiosity as edgework not only provides a way of validating a given theory, but also a way of testing whether the two theories are compatible. Tighter networks are created by filling in gaps, and some sorts of such gap-less networks are markedly compressible (Lynn & Bassett, 2021). Looser networks are created by leaving gaps open, and some sorts of such gap-full networks are less compressible. Do the relative rates of gap-filling align with (or diverge from) changes in the networks' compressibility? Such an investigation could elucidate whether the two theories are describing the same generative process, or distinct generative processes that can be engaged either synergistically or competitively.

12.6   Curiosity as Edgework Poses a Novel Theoretical Construct

Does connectional curiosity reframe curiosity's utility to the individual human? Beyond clarifying prior theories of curiosity, the framing of edgework suggests that networks may be built to enable conceptual flexibility. The relation between structure and flexibility is clear in mechanics. A triangle made from steel bars connected by hinges is rigid because pressure on any bar does not change the triangle's shape. Conversely, a square made from the same materials is flexible because pressure applied to any bar will collapse the square into a rhombus. By combining rigid and nonrigid motifs, networks can be built that allow both flexibility and stability. Moving from mechanics to cognitive science, we can ask: As we build our knowledge networks through curious practice, do we combine sections of rigid (triangular) conceptual relations with sections of flexible (squarish) conceptual relations, allowing our minds to bend as and when necessary? In isolation, the process of filling information gaps (closing triangles in the network) will create a rigid knowledge, whereas the process of disconnection (or the removal of edges) and the process of reaching out to the unknown (adding otherwise untethered concepts) will create a knowledge that can undergo shape-morphing. Is it perhaps by this flexibility that we gain insight, the "Aha!" moment as two seemingly distant concepts come close enough in our conceptual space to touch?

Such questions can be operationalized with measures of network conformability. Building on design principles for conformable materials (Kim et al., 2019b, 2019a), one can calculate the degrees of freedom of growing knowledge networks, reflecting the flexibility of a set of related concepts in d-dimensional concept space. Such calculable, theory-based measures can be applied to information-seeking experiments in single humans, and collective information seeking in groups of humans (Gray et al., 2016). Moreover, they can be used to assess how knowledge networks grow over development, as children mature into adulthood. The fact that looser and more fluid, as opposed to tighter and more crystalline, knowledge networks may be easier to reconfigure could explain why children are able to better learn and flexibly use information from abstract schema than adults (Gopnik, 2020). Evidence from neuroscience further suggests that the patterns of inter-regional connections in the human brain may increasingly prioritize less compressed transmission (less abstract) as development occurs (Zhou et al., 2020c), potentially altering the sorts of interconceptual connections made and carried within a mind into later life.

12.7 Curiosity as Edgework Embodies the Edgework of the Brain

How does the mind curious-ing build a network of knowledge using a network of neurons? Curiosity as edgework situates the seeker between their internal and external environments in building their model of the world (Zhou et al., 2020b). Behaviors that selectively deploy attention rely on the capacity of the brain to process information from the external environment and to transform that information within the internal environment of neural representations (Gottlieb, 2012). Seekers build network models of information (Bassett et al., 2018; Bassett, 2020; Karuza et al., 2016, 2017; Zurn & Bassett, 2020), which can be relational, social, and rewarding (Constantinescu et al., 2016; Garvert et al., 2017; Kahn et al., 2018; Karuza et al., 2019; Lynn et al., 2020; Ocko et al., 2018; Tompson et al., 2020). Ongoing efforts seek to understand where in the brain we represent each node and edge in the network, as well as where (and how) we encode the network's architecture. How are these representations and encodings dynamically created, modified, and (sometimes) forgotten (Ju & Bassett, 2020; Zhou et al., 2020c)? Answering this question requires us to understand not only the locations in the brain where the world leaves an impression (like a foot in wet sand), but also how those impressions relate to one another reflecting the trajectory of information (like the series of footprints in the sand reflecting the trajectory of the walker from beach to cove).

Understanding how brain regions and their respective encodings relate to one another, and share information with one another, is the purview of the nascent field of network neuroscience. Here, brain regions are represented as network nodes, and inter-regional relations or interactions are represented as network edges. Network neuroscience defines mathematical models and metrics that characterize the neural efficiency of information transfer and the spatial distribution of information gathered from within the brain and from the external environment (Bassett et al., 2018; Suárez et al., 2020). The approach reveals that the human brain network is characterized by a striking gradient of computations organized along a principal axis spanning the cortex (Huntenburg et al., 2018), from unimodal sensation to transmodal higher-order abstract processing. At the transmodal extreme of the gradient, localized regions in the frontoparietal, default-mode, and limbic systems have been associated with learning, abstraction, self-referential processing, semantic cognition, emotional regulation, uncertainty monitoring, and reward (Huntenburg et al., 2018; Margulies et al., 2016). In so far as curiosity has been traditionally defined as inextricable from some of these cognitive functions, it is therefore unsurprising that prior work has also found associations between curiosity-driven behavior and the neural activity of specific regions within these subnetworks (Gruber et al., 2014, 2019; Kang et al., 2009). However, it remains unclear how localized processes within separate brain regions or systems are fused together within the wider brain network, as prior theories necessitate.

Curiosity as edgework reframes this question by asking: How does the network of the human brain communicate the consequence of local computations (supporting processes ranging from sensation and emotion to cognition) in order to build a model situating oneself in relation to the world? One possible answer lies in a structural isomorphism between the brain and the world, which supports the development of internal mental models. It is now clear that the network organization that efficiently transmits and flexibly represents information is similar for the information processed by the human brain (Zhou et al., 2020c) and for the information processed during human behavior (Karuza et al., 2016; Lynn et al., 2020; Lynn & Bassett, 2021). Both the brain and behavior rely on the usage of hubs and hierarchical organization. Hubs are central landmarks that are highly connected to other units. Hierarchical organization is a hallmark of efficient spatial nesting of modules within modules and the formation of abstract categories of knowledge (Kemp & Tenenbaum, 2008; Zhou et al., 2020b). This interesting isomorphism between the edgework of brains and behavior could arise from shared evolutionary and developmental pressures for efficient yet flexible spatiotemporal information processing and representation (Lynn & Bassett, 2020; Zhou et al., 2020b). Shared constraints of efficiency and flexibility on the brain and behavior may shape the capacity to learn statistical relations, form a system of semantic categories, deploy attention, and explore new information (Gopnik, 2020; Gottlieb, 2012; Kemp & Tenenbaum, 2008; Schapiro et al., 2013; Stachenfeld et al., 2017). When we seek information, the ability of an external source to transmit information is intertwined with the ability to transmit and dynamically transform internal representations of information within the brain network (Ju et al., 2020; Lynn et al., 2020; Zhou et al., 2020c). In doing so, the brain network can shape and modify information to send only behaviorally relevant inputs to the hippocampal-entorhinal circuit for representation of statistical regularities, prediction, and planning (Constantinescu et al., 2016; Garvert et al., 2017; Ocko et al., 2018; Schapiro et al., 2017).

12.8   Curiosity as Edgework Is Valued

How does our culture value curiosity? Does it only value the acquisition of knowledge? Or is there evidence that our culture values the laying down of connections, and of some connections more than others? Two recent studies provide evidence for the latter, both in the recognition of scientific discoveries, and in the evaluation of classroom material. The first study reports that science progresses as much through identifying uncharted gaps as through advancing solutions within scientific communities; the latter, filling-the-gap (or tessellating-the-cavity) discoveries are more frequently awarded Nobel prizes than discoveries adding edges at the boundaries of collective knowledge (Ju et al., 2020). The second study reports that college-level mathematics textbooks are more likely to be rated highly on Good Reads when they progressively fill (rather than leave open) gaps in the knowledge network by connecting concepts introduced early with concepts introduced late (Christianson et al., 2020). Together, these studies suggest that there exist some domains of human inquiry wherein the act of placing a connection that fills a network cavity is more greatly valued than the act of placing a connection to the unknown at the frontiers of knowledge.

Is this same valuation strategy used in other aspects of our society? Consider, for example, the choice of whose ideas to discuss, as well as how (and whether) to attribute those ideas to the person who created them (Rossiter, 1993). Both the choice and the attribution are processes of valuation, and occur in verbal communication, social and mass media, and written documents (Ahmed, 2012, 2017, 2019; Crawford et al., 2014). In scientific articles and classroom textbooks, for example, new

270 ZURN, ZHOU, LYDON-STALEY AND BASSETT

material references older material, offering a record of the questions that have been and are being asked, and the answers of greatest import and value (Mott & Cockayne, 2017). Are articles or chapters that fill a network cavity in the space of scientific knowledge cited more frequently than those that add a new connection at the frontiers of that space? The field is poised to answer this question. And what makes this area of inquiry particularly exciting is the fact that it naturally interdigitates with the field of ethics: namely, the ethics of knowing, addressing epistemic justice and injustice (Fricker, 2009). Citation ethics seeks to understand and address existing biases in citation practices, including the bias against women and people of marginalized races and ethnicities (Bertolero et al., 2020; Caplar et al., 2017; Dion et al., 2018; Dworkin et al., 2020; Maliniak et al., 2013; Mitchell et al., 2013). Determining how we value the edges that knowers newly place will require both an understanding of the network placements we value (those tessellating or those expanding) and the placers we value (those privileged or those marginalized). Such an investigation could shed important new light on the factors that determine how our culture values curiosity (and curious minds embodied in gendered and racialized beings), simultaneously informing the development of an explicit and systematic ethics of citation practices germane to classroom learning and the scientific enterprise (Dworkin et al., 2020; Zurn et al., 2020). Importantly, connectional curiosity encompasses disconnection; biased information seeking may dismiss an edge just as easily as it lays one down (Enloe, 2004).

12.9 Conclusion

In being curious, we connect our minds to previously known knowns and to knowns just discovered. In acting curiously, we connect our bodies to previously existing knowers and to knowers alive today. We follow threads of ideas, weave lines of thought, and weld hinges among intersecting concepts. We create a scaffold of knowledge with the wrench of attention, the hammer of reward, the spirit level of exploration, the pliers of learning, and the screwdriver of uncertainty. Some of us shy away from the world, choosing instead to tinker in the bowels of the scaffold; others of us scale to the top and peer out at the world from above, or scramble to the edges and peek at the world from the side. We see a world of possibilities . . . a world of what could be when we exchange acquisition for connection, capture for construction, and conquest for relation. Curiosity as edgework offers a new lens into the constructs, affordances, and values of seeking communion with our world.

Acknowledgments

We thank Jason Kim, Shubhankar Patankar, and Pixel Xia, and acknowledge support from the MacArthur Foundation and the Center for Curiosity.

Citation Diversity Statement

Recent work has identified a bias in citation practices such that papers from women and other minorities are under-cited relative to the number of such papers in the field (Caplar et al., 2017; Dion et al., 2018; Dworkin et al., 2020; Maliniak et al., 2013; Mitchell et al., 2013). Here we sought to proactively consider choosing references that reflect the diversity of the field in thought, form of contribution, gender, and other factors. We obtained the predicted gender of the first and last author of each reference by using databases that store the probability of a name being carried by a woman (Dworkin et al., 2020; Zhou et al., 2020a). By this measure (and excluding self-citations to the first and last authors of our current paper), our references contain 25.68% woman/woman, 16.22% woman/man, 6.76% man/woman, and 51.35% man/man. This method is limited in that a) names, pronouns, and social media profiles used to construct the databases may not, in every case, be indicative of gender identity and b) it cannot account for intersex, nonbinary, or transgender people. We look forward to future work that could help us to better understand how to support equitable practices in science.

References

Ahmed, S. (2012). *On being included: Racism and diversity in institutional life.* Duke University Press.

Ahmed, S. (2017). *Living a feminist life.* Duke University Press.

Ahmed, S. (2019). *What's the use.* Duke University Press.

Aquinas, T. (1981). *Summa theologica* (p. Question 167). Christian Classics.

Augustine, S. (1961). *Confessions,* trans. W. Watts. London, 1631.

Bassett, D. S. (2020). A network science of the practice of curiosity. In P. Zurn & A. Shankar (Eds.), *Curiosity studies: A new ecology of knowledge* (pp. 57–74). Minnesota Press.

Bassett, D. S., Zurn, P., & Gold, J. I. (2018). On the nature and use of models in network neuroscience. *Nature Reviews Neuroscience,* 19(9), 566–578.

Begus, K., & Southgate, V. (2018). Curious learners: How infants' motivation to learn shapes and is shaped by infants' interactions with the social world. In *Active learning from infancy to childhood* (pp. 13–37). Springer.

Benedict, B. (2003). *Curiosity: A cultural history of early modern inquiry*. University of Chicago Press.

Berlyne, D. E. (1960). *Conflict, arousal, and curiosity*. McGraw-Hill.

Bertolero, M. A., Dworkin, J. D., David, S. U., Lloreda, C. L., Srivastava, P., Stiso, J., Zhou, D., ... Bassett, D. S. (2020). Racial and ethnic imbalance in neuroscience reference lists and intersections with gender. bioRxiv, 10.12.336230. https://doi.org/10.1101/2020.10.12.336230.

Birhane, A. (2021). The impossibility of automating ambiguity. *Artificial Life*, 27(1), 44–61.

Caplar, N., Tacchella, S., & Birrer, S. (2017). Quantitative evaluation of gender bias in astronomical publications from citation counts. *Nature Astronomy*, 1(6), 0141. https://doi.org/10.1038/s41550-017-0141.

Christianson, N. H., Blevins, A. S., & Bassett, D. S. (2020). Architecture and evolution of semantic networks in mathematics texts. *Philosophical Transactions of the Royal Society, A*, 476(2239), 20190741.

Chu, J., & Schulz, L. E. (2020). Play, curiosity, and cognition. *Annual Review of Developmental Psychology*, 2, 317–343.

Cofer, C. N., & Appley, M. H. (1964). *Motivation: Theory and research*. Wiley.

Cohen, J. D., McClure, S. M., & Yu, A. J. (2007). Should I stay or should I go? How the human brain manages the trade-off between exploitation and exploration. *Philosophical Transactions of the Royal Society B: Biological Sciences*, 362(1481), 933–942.

Constantinescu, A. O., OReilly, J. X., & Behrens, T. E. J. (2016). Organizing conceptual knowledge in humans with a gridlike code. *Science*, 352(6292), 1464–1468. https://doi.org/10.1126/science.aaf0941.

Crawford, K., Gray, M. L., & Miltner, K. M. (2014). Big data. Critiquing big data: Politics, ethics, epistemology. Special Section Introduction. *International Journal of Communication*, 8(10).

Descartes, R. (1649). Passions of the soul. In J. Cottingham (Ed.), *The philosophical writings of Rene Descartes* (p. sec. 88). Cambridge University Press, 1985.

Dewey, J. (1916/2011). *Democracy and education*. Simon and Brown.

Dewey, J. (1910/1933). *How we think*. D. C. Heath & Company.

Diener, E., & Diener, C. (1996). Most people are happy. *Psychological Science*, 7(3), 181–185.

Dion, M. L., Sumner, J. L., & Mitchell, S. M. (2018). Gendered citation patterns across political science and social science methodology fields. *Political Analysis*, 26(3), 312–327. https://doi.org/10.1017/pan.2018.12.

Dworkin, J. D., Linn, K. A., Teich, E. G., Zurn, P., Shinohara, R. T., & Bassett, D. S. (2020). The extent and drivers of gender imbalance in neuroscience reference lists. *Nature Neuroscience*, 23, 918–926.

Dworkin, J., Zurn, P., & Bassett, D. S. (2020). (In)citing action to realize an equitable future. *Neuron*, 106(6), 890–894.

Enloe, C. (2004). *The Curious Feminist*. University of California Press.

Fredrickson, B. L. (2004). The broaden–and–build theory of positive emotions. *Philosophical Transactions of the Royal Society of London. Series B: Biological Sciences*, 359(1449), 1367–1377.

Fredrickson, B. L., & Branigan, C. (2005). Positive emotions broaden the scope of attention and thought-action repertoires. *Cognition & Emotion*, 19(3), 313–332.

Fricker, M. (2009). *Epistemic injustice: Power and the ethics of knowing*. Oxford University Press.

Garrosa, E., Blanco-Donoso, L. M., Carmona-Cobo, I., & Moreno-Jiménez, B. (2017). How do curiosity, meaning in life, and search for meaning predict college students' daily emotional exhaustion and engagement? *Journal of Happiness Studies*, 18(1), 17–40.

Garvert, M. M., Dolan, R. J., & Behrens, T. E. (2017). A map of abstract relational knowledge in the human hippocampal–entorhinal cortex. *Elife*, 6, e17086.

George, M. J., Russell, M. A., Piontak, J. R., & Odgers, C. L. (2018). Concurrent and subsequent associations between daily digital technology use and high-risk adolescents' mental health symptoms. *Child Development*, 89(1), 78–88.

Gershman, S. J., & Niv, Y. (2015). Novelty and inductive generalization in human reinforcement learning. *Topics in Cognitive Science*, 7(3), 391–415. https://doi.org/10.1111/tops.12138.

Gopnik, A. (2020). Childhood as a solution to explore–exploit tensions. *Philosophical Transactions of the Royal Society B*, 375(1803), 20190502.

Gottlieb, J. (2012). Attention, learning, and the value of information. *Neuron*, 76(2), 281–295.

Gottlieb, J., & Oudeyer, P.-Y. (2018). Towards a neuroscience of active sampling and curiosity. *Nature Reviews Neuroscience*, 19(12), 758–770.

Gottlieb, J., Hayhoe, M., Hikosaka, O., & Rangel, A. (2014). Attention, reward, and information seeking. *Journal of Neuroscience*, 34(46), 15497–15504.

Gray, M. L., Suri, S., Ali, S. S., & Kulkarni, D. (2016, February). The crowd is a collaborative network. In *Proceedings of the 19th ACM conference on computer-supported cooperative work & social computing* (pp. 134–147).

Gruber, M. J., Gelman, B. D., & Ranganath, C. (2014). States of curiosity modulate hippocampus-dependent learning via the dopaminergic circuit. *Neuron*, 84(2), 486–496.

Gruber, M. J., Valji, A., & Ranganath, C. (2019). Curiosity and learning: A neuroscientific perspective. In Renninger, K. & Hidi, S. E. (Eds.), *The Cambridge handbook of motivation and learning* (pp. 397–417). Cambridge University Press.

Hidi, S. E., & Renninger, K. A. (2019). Interest development and its relation to curiosity: needed neuroscientific research. *Educational Psychology Review*, 31(4), 833–852.

Huntenburg, J. M., Bazin, P.-L., & Margulies, D. S. (2018). Large-scale gradients in human cortical organization. *Trends in Cognitive Sciences*, 22(1), 21–31.

Inan, I. (2011). *The philosophy of curiosity*. Routledge.

James, W. (1925). *Talks to teachers on psychology: And to students on some of life's ideals.* Henry Holt Company.

James, W. (1890; 1918). *The principles of psychology, vol.* 2. Dover Publications.

Ju, H., & Bassett, D. S. (2020). Dynamic representations in networked neural systems. *Nature Neuroscience,* 23(8), 908–917.

Ju, H., Zhou, D., Blevins, A. S., Lydon-Staley, D. M., Kaplan, J., Tuma, J. R., & Bassett, D. S. (2020). The network structure of scientific revolutions. *arXiv Preprint arXiv:2010.08381.*

Kahn, A. E., Karuza, E. A., Vettel, J. M., & Bassett, D. S. (2018). Network constraints on learnability of probabilistic motor sequences. *Nature Human Behaviour,* 2(12), 936–947.

Kang, M. J., Hsu, M., Krajbich, I. M., Loewenstein, G., McClure, S. M., Wang, J. T.-y., & Camerer, C. F. (2009). The wick in the candle of learning: Epistemic curiosity activates reward circuitry and enhances memory. *Psychological Science,* 20(8), 963–973.

Karuza, E. A., Kahn, A. E., & Bassett, D. S. (2019). Human sensitivity to community structure is robust to topological variation. *Complexity, 2019* (8379321).

Karuza, E. A., Kahn, A. E., Thompson-Schill, S. L., & Bassett, D. S. (2017). Process reveals structure: How a network is traversed mediates expectations about its architecture. *Scientific Reports,* 7(1), 1–9.

Karuza, E. A., Thompson-Schill, S. L., & Bassett, D. S. (2016). Local patterns to global architectures: Influences of network topology on human learning. *Trends in Cognitive Sciences,* 20(8), 629–640.

Kashdan, T. B., & Steger, M. F. (2007). Curiosity and pathways to well-being and meaning in life: Traits, states, and everyday behaviors. *Motivation and emotion,* 31(3), 159–173.

Kashdan, T. B., Gallagher, M. W., Silvia, P. J., Winterstein, B. P., Breen, W. E., Terhar, D., & Steger, M. F. (2009). The curiosity and exploration inventory-ii: Development, factor structure, and psychometrics. *Journal of Research in Personality,* 43(6), 987–998.

Kashdan, T. B., Stiksma, M. C., Disabato, D. J., McKnight, P. E., Bekier, J., Kaji, J., & Lazarus, R. (2018). The five-dimensional curiosity scale: Capturing the bandwidth of curiosity and identifying four unique subgroups of curious people. *Journal of Research in Personality,* 73, 130–149.

Kemp, C., & Tenenbaum, J. B. (2008). The discovery of structural form. *Proceedings of the National Academy of Sciences,* 105(31), 10687–10692.

Kidd, C., & Hayden, B. Y. (2015). The psychology and neuroscience of curiosity. *Neuron,* 88(3), 449–460.

Kim, J. Z., Lu, Z., & Bassett, D. S. (2019a). Design of large sequential conformational change in mechanical networks. *arXiv,* 1906, 08400.

Kim, J. Z., Lu, Z., Strogatz, S. H., & Bassett, D. S. (2019b). Conformational control of mechanical networks. *Nature Physics,* 15, 714–720.

Larson, R., & Csikszentmihalyi, M. (2014). The experience sampling method. In *Flow and the foundations of positive psychology* (pp. 21–34). Springer. https://link .springer.com/book/10.1007/978-94-017-9088-8.

León, C. (2020). Curious entanglements: Opacity and ethical relation in Latina/ or aesthetics. In Zurn, P. and Shankar, A. (Ed.), *Curiosity studies: A new ecology of knowledge* (pp. 167–187). University of Minnesota Press.

Litman, J. A. (2008). Interest and deprivation factors of epistemic curiosity. *Personality and Individual Differences*, 44(7), 1585–1595.

Litman, J. A., & Jimerson, T. L. (2004). The measurement of curiosity as a feeling of deprivation. *Journal of Personality Assessment*, 82(2), 147–157.

Loewenstein, G. (1994). The psychology of curiosity: A review and reinterpretation. *Psychological Bulletin*, 116(1), 75.

Lydon-Staley, D. M., Barnett, I., Satterthwaite, T. D., & Bassett, D. S. (2019a). Digital phenotyping for psychiatry: Accommodating data and theory with network science methodologies. *Current Opinion in Biomedical Engineering*, 9, 8–13.

Lydon-Staley, D. M., Falk, E. B., & Bassett, D. S. (2019b). Within-person variability in sensation-seeking during daily life: Positive associations with alcohol use and self-defined risky behaviors. *Psychology of Addictive Behaviors*, 34(2), 257–268.

Lydon-Staley, D. M., Zhou, D., Blevins, A. S., Zurn, P., & Bassett, D. S. (2019c). Hunters, busybodies, and the knowledge network building associated with curiosity. *Nature Human Behavior*, 6(3), 327–336.

Lydon-Staley, D. M., Zurn, P., & Bassett, D. S. (2019d). Within-person variability in curiosity during daily life and associations with well-being. *Journal of Personality*, 88(4), 625–641.

Lynn, C. W., & Bassett, D. S. (2020). How humans learn and represent networks. *Proceedings of the National Academy of Sciences of the United States of America*, 117(47), 29407–29415.

Lynn, C. W., & Bassett, D. S. (2021). Quantifying the compressibility of complex networks. *Proceedings of the National Academy of Sciences* 118(32): e2023473118. https://doi.org/10.1073/pnas.2023473118.

Lynn, C. W., Kahn, A. E., & Bassett, D. S. (2020). Abstract representations of events arise from mental errors in learning and memory. *Nature Communications*, 11(1), 2313.

Lynn, C. W., Papadopoulos, L., Kahn, A. E., & Bassett, D. S. (2020). Human information processing in complex networks. *Nature Physics*, 16, 965–973. https://doi.org/10.1038/s41567-020-0924-7.

Maliniak, D., Powers, R., & Walter, B. F. (2013). The gender citation gap in international relations. *International Organization*, 67(4), 889–922. https://doi .org/10.1017/S0020818313000209.

Margulies, D. S., Ghosh, S. S., Goulas, A., Falkiewicz, M., Huntenburg, J. M., Langs, G., Bezgin, G., . . . et al. (2016). Situating the default-mode network along a principal gradient of macroscale cortical organization. *Proceedings of the National Academy of Sciences*, 113(44), 12574–12579.

Mitchell, S. M., Lange, S., & Brus, H. (2013). Gendered citation patterns in international relations journals. *International Studies Perspectives*, 14(4), 485–492. https://doi.org/10.1111/insp.12026.

Mott, C., & Cockayne, D. (2017). Citation matters: Mobilizing the politics of citation toward a practice of "conscientious engagement." *Gender, Place and Culture*, 24(7), 954–973.

Nietzsche, F. W. (1886/1989). *Beyond good and evil*. Random House.

Ocko, S. A., Hardcastle, K., Giocomo, L. M., & Ganguli, S. (2018). Emergent elasticity in the neural code for space. *Proceedings of the National Academy of Sciences*, 115(50), E11798–E11806.

Onnela, J.-P., Saramäki, J., Kertész, J., & Kaski, K. (2005). Intensity and coherence of motifs in weighted complex networks. *Physical Review E*, 71(6), 065103.

Oudeyer, P.-Y. (2018). Computational theories of curiosity-driven learning. In Gordon, G. (Ed.), *The new science of curiosity* (pp. 43–72). Nova Science Publishers.

Oudeyer, P.-Y., Gottlieb, J., & Lopes, M. (2016). Intrinsic motivation, curiosity, and learning: Theory and applications in educational technologies. In *Progress in brain research* (Vol. 229, pp. 257–284). Elsevier.

Pekrun, R. (2019). The murky distinction between curiosity and interest: State of the art and future prospects. *Educational Psychology Review*, 31(4), 905–914.

Plutarch. (2005). On being a busybody. In *Moralia* VI (pp. 473–517). Harvard University Press.

Reeves, B., Ram, N., Robinson, T. N., Cummings, J. J., Giles, C. L., Pan, J., Chiatti, A., . . . & others. (2019). Screenomics: A framework to capture and analyze personal life experiences and the ways that technology shapes them. *Human–Computer Interaction*, 1–52.

Reio, T. G., & Callahan, J. L. (2004). Affect, curiosity, and socialization-related learning: A path analysis of antecedents to job performance. *Journal of Business and Psychology*, 19(1), 3–22.

Rodrigue, J. R., Olson, K. R., & Markley, R. P. (1987). Induced mood and curiosity. *Cognitive Therapy and Research*, 11(1), 101–106.

Rossiter, M. W. (1993). The Matthew/Matilda Effect in science. *Social Studies of Science*, 23(2), 325–341.

Rousseau, J.-J. (1762; 1909). *Emile*. Appleton & Company.

Schapiro, A. C., Rogers, T. T., Cordova, N. I., Turk-Browne, N. B., & Botvinick, M. M. (2013). Neural representations of events arise from temporal community structure. *Nature Neuroscience*, 16(4), 486–492.

Schapiro, A. C., Turk-Browne, N. B., Botvinick, M. M., & Norman, K. A. (2017). Complementary learning systems within the hippocampus: A neural network modelling approach to reconciling episodic memory with statistical learning. *Philosophical Transactions of the Royal Society B: Biological Sciences*, 372 (1711), 20160049.

Schmidhuber, J. (2008). Driven by compression progress: A simple principle explains essential aspects of subjective beauty, novelty, surprise, interestingness, attention, curiosity, creativity, art, science, music, jokes. *Workshop on Anticipatory Behavior in Adaptive Learning Systems*, 48–76. https://link.springer.com/chapter/10.1007/978-3-642-02565-5_4.

Scholtes, I. (2017). When is a network a network? Multi-order graphical model selection in pathways and temporal networks. *Proceedings of the 23rd ACM Sigkdd International Conference on Knowledge Discovery and Data Mining*, 1037–1046. https://dl.acm.org/doi/10.1145/3097983.3098145.

Sizemore, A. E., Karuza, E. A., Giusti, C., & Bassett, D. S. (2018). Knowledge gaps in the early growth of semantic networks. *Nature Human Behavior*, 2(9), 682–692.

Stachenfeld, K. L., Botvinick, M. M., & Gershman, S. J. (2017). The hippocampus as a predictive map. *Nature Neuroscience*, 20(11), 1643.

Suárez, L. E., Markello, R. D., Betzel, R. F., & Misic, B. (2020). Linking structure and function in macroscale brain networks. *Trends in Cognitive Sciences*, 24(4), 302–315.

Swanson, H. (2020). Curious ecologies of knowledge: More-than-human anthropology. In Zurn, P. and Shankar, A. (Eds.), *Curiosity studies: A new ecology of knowledge* (pp. 15–36). University of Minnesota Press.

Tompson, S. H., Falk, E. B., O'Donnell, M. B., Cascio, C. N., Bayer, J. B., Vettel, J. M., & Bassett, D. S. (2020). Response inhibition in adolescents is moderated by brain connectivity and social network structure. *Social Cognitive and Affective Neuroscience*, 15(8), 827–837.

Vives, J. L. (1531; 1913). *On education*. Cambridge University Press.

Watson, L. (2018). Curiosity and inquisitiveness. In Battaly, H. (Ed.), *The Routledge handbook of virtue epistemology* (pp. 155–166). Routledge.

West, R., & Leskovec, J. (2012). Human wayfinding in information networks. *Proceedings of the 21st International Conference on World Wide Web*, 619–628. https://dl.acm.org/doi/10.1145/2187836.2187920.

Yonge, C. D., & Philo. (1854). *The works of Philo Judaeus, the contemporary of Josephus* (Vol. 1). Bohn.

Zhou, D., Cornblath, E. J., Stiso, J., Teich, E. G., Dworkin, J. D., Blevins, A. S., & Bassett, D. S. (2020a). *Gender diversity statement and code notebook v1.0*. https://doi.org/10.5281/zenodo.3672110.

Zhou, D., Lydon-Staley, D. M., Zurn, P., & Bassett, D. S. (2020b). The growth and form of knowledge networks by kinesthetic curiosity. *Current Opinion in Behavirioral Sciences*, 35, 125–134. https://doi.org/10.1016/j.cobeha.2020.09.007.

Zhou, D., Lynn, C. W., Cui, Z., Ciric, R., Baum, G. L., Moore, T. M., Roalf, D. R., ... & others. (2020c). Efficient coding in the economics of human brain connectomics. *Network Neuroscience*.

Zuckerman, M. (1994). *Behavioral expressions and biosocial bases of sensation seeking*. Cambridge University Press.

Zurn, P. (2019). Busybody, hunter, and dancer: Three historical models of curiosity. In Papastephanou, M. (Ed.), *Toward new philosophical explorations of the epistemic desire to know: Just curious about curiosity* (pp. 26–49). Cambridge Scholars Press.

Zurn, P. (2021). *Curiosity and power: The politics of inquiry*. University of Minnesota Press.

Zurn, P., & Bassett, D. S. (2018). On curiosity: A fundamental aspect of personality, a practice of network growth. *Personality Neuroscience*, 1.

Zurn, P., & Bassett, D. S. (2020). Network architectures supporting learnability. *Philosophical Transactions of the Royal Society B*, 375(1796), 20190323.

Zurn, P. & Bassett, D. S., (2022). *Curious minds: The power of connection*. MIT Press.

Zurn, P., Bassett, D. S., & Rust, N. C. (2020). The citation diversity statement: A practice of transparency, a way of life. *Trends in Cognitive Science*, 24(9), 669–672.

Future Challenges

Irene Cogliati Dezza, Eric Schulz, and Charley M. Wu

This book has covered a wide range of new and exciting research in the science of information-seeking. Yet many open questions still remain. For example, how is information-seeking related to reward-seeking? What are the principles that enable us to acquire useful information with computational efficiency, despite possessing limited cognitive capacities and knowledge? Which aspects of our neural machinery are unique to information-seeking, and what is shared across other cognitive systems? How does the science of information-seeking inform important societal issues, such as fake news, conspiracy theories, and education?

In this closing chapter, we present a brief overview of future challenges and current puzzles in the field, organized around the same three questions used to structure the sections of this book: **What** drives humans to seek information? **How** do humans search for information? **Which** machinery supports the drive for knowledge? While our current theories and frameworks have answered many questions about information-seeking, many more still remain. At the end of this chapter, we address the social implications for the science of information-seeking. Like boats paddling against the current, the drive for knowledge will continue to propel us toward new and exciting questions to be curious about.

What Drives Humans to Seek Information?

Throughout this book, we have sought to answer the question of why humans seek information and how our desire for information stacks up against other primary rewards, such as food or water. One simple answer to this question is the old adage "knowledge is power," and that information allows us to acquire more rewards in the future. Yet, how far into the future do we need to reason when considering the instrumental value of information? This problem is often studied under the framework of the exploration–exploitation dilemma (Mehlhorn et al., 2015), where optimal solutions are typically intractable under finite time horizons. Indeed, even doing the math and computing expected information gain for short-run decisions is not necessarily informative for deciphering the optimal decision in the long run (Meder et al., Chapter 5). Thus, intrinsic motivations to seek information (e.g., curiosity; Ten et al., Chapter 3) might be an adaptive bias that ensures humans behave less myopically and introduce enough exploration into their decisions. Since we cannot tractably compute the value of information for long-run horizons, our innate curiosity may simply provide a blanket subsidy for knowledge-generating activities, similar to how governments and institutions support basic research without a guaranteed return of investment (Wojtowicz et al., Chapter 1). Nevertheless, as we move from simple bandit tasks to more sequential decision-making tasks (Brändle et al., Chapter 7), and connect short-term "curiosity" to long-term "interest" (Donnellan et al., Chapter 2), an important and still open question is what tractable computations people use to compute the value of information, as we discuss in the second section of this chapter.

Yet, acquiring future rewards alone does not entirely explain our drive for knowledge. An important component of information-seeking behaviors seems unrelated to rewards and can sometimes even run orthogonal or counter to it (Kobayashi, Ravaioli, Baranes, Woodford, & Gottlieb, 2019; Charpentier, Bromberg-Martin, & Sharot, 2018). One prominent idea featured in this book is that information may be desired for improving the coherency of internal models of the environment, where "sense-making" provides an alternative currency to rewards (Wojtowicz et al., Chapter 1). Sense-making is not some alien, nonfungible currency, but can be measured in terms of compressibility, where more coherent models require less computational bandwidth to use and maintain. Thus, information-seeking for acquiring rewards and information-seeking for reducing the computational costs of modeling the environment may ultimately be comparable through a cost–benefit trade-off within a resource-rationality framework (Lieder & Griffiths, 2019; Bhui, Lai, & Gershman, 2021; Wu et al., Chapter 8). We already have preliminary evidence that value representations for reward and information are computed by different populations of neurons in similar brain regions, allowing for different exchange rates depending on the environment and one's goals, but with both capable of being integrated downstream into a common currency (Charpentier & Cogliati Dezza, Chapter 9).

Even then, why do people still seek redundant information? Just as it can sometimes be difficult to avoid overeating unhealthy snacks or binging TV shows, controlling information-seeking behavior may itself incur cognitive costs (Gottlieb, Chapter 10). Thus, overactive information-seeking may simply be a result of more economical monitoring and control, which switches more lazily between different modes of exploration and exploitation or is perhaps biased toward a cognitively cheaper mode. Alternatively, the brain may regulate information-seeking, similar to other motivated behaviors (Pezzulo, Rigoli, & Friston, 2015; Keramati & Gutkin, 2014), by allowing the system to oscillate around a homeostatic attraction point. Alternations of behavior, characteristic of this style of regulation, may at times lead to redundant information-seeking. However, there are still many open questions regarding how information-seeking is regulated in the brain – for example, how humans balance their need for acquiring information for future rewards with their needs for acquiring information which makes them feel good or to help to increase understanding of reality. A better understanding of the adaptive role of information-seeking, and its regulation, will provide new tools for diagnosing and treating psychopathologies, such as reduced novelty-seeking in addiction (Cogliati Dezza, I., Noel, X., Cleeremans, A., Yu, A. (2021). Distinct motivations to seek out information in healthy individuals and problem gamblers. Transl Psychiatry 11, 408. doi.org/10.1038/s41398-021-0152 3-3) or increased information-seeking in obsessive-compulsive disorders (Hauser, Moutoussis, Consortium, Dayan, & Dolan, 2017).

A key resource in understanding the cognitive costs associated with information-seeking is studying how it changes over the lifespan. Childhood presents unique opportunities for learning, where children can expect pedagogical instruction in their environment (i.e., natural pedagogy; Csibra & Gergely, 2009). Yet children also have less developed cognitive representations and processes, making more complex inferences less accessible. One robust finding is that children have difficulty *producing* informative queries even though they are quite capable of *selecting* useful queries (De Simone & Ruggieri, Chapter 4). Despite their less developed cognitive capacities, children are nevertheless highly sensitive to which individuals are the most reliable sources of information (De Simone & Ruggieri, Chapter 4) and are capable of performing increasingly sophisticated inferences to learn not only from their actions, but also from imputed mental states (Wu et al., Chapter 8).

How Humans Search for Information

A recurring theme in this book is that optimal solutions to most interesting cognitive problems are intractable. This means that, practically, we humans must have developed various computational shortcuts or heuristics to guide our decisions, bound by the limits of our cognitive resources and the sparsity of our knowledge about a complex world. Perhaps nowhere is the need for heuristic solutions more important than in solving the exploration–exploitation dilemma, where acquiring information (benefiting future decisions) needs to be traded-off against acquiring immediate rewards. Here, the complexity of planning increases exponentially with the number of available choices (Brändle et al., Chapter 7), making it especially important to discover the computational principles of human learning and information search that balance efficiency and flexibility (Wu et al., Chapter 8).

One potential answer is that human behavior can be described as the attempt to optimize an information-enriched utility, integrating both information and reward-based value into a single currency (Charpentier & Cogliati Dezza, Chapter 9). For example, Meder et al. (Chapter 5) argue that this utility could be a de facto measure of information gain, normally computed either myopically or taking the agent's next few decisions into account. However, many measures exist for quantifying the value of information (Crupi, Nelson, Meder, Cevolani, & Tentori, 2018), and it is the topic of ongoing research to determine which measure best explains human behavior.

Another proposal for how bounded-rational agents could maximize information gain is to assume that they optimize free energy instead, which combines informational utility with a resource capacity component (Sajid et al., Chapter 6). Nevertheless, this Active Inference framework (Friston et al., 2016; Schwartenbeck et al., 2019), like other resource-rational optimization frameworks (e.g., Lieder & Griffiths, 2019), can still require a prohibitive amount of computation. Thus, humans may simply opt for heuristic computations instead, behaving "as-if" they maximize informational utility or minimize free energy. One such heuristic is to treat uncertainty as having utility of its own (Ten et al., Chapter 3) and to myopically sample options that both promise to produce high rewards and are highly uncertain (Brändle et al., Chapter 7). Even though these strategies are approximate, they nonetheless offer guarantees in some settings, such as sufficient regret bounds and convergence to the best possible option over time (Srinivas, Krause, Kakade, & Seeger, 2009).

Yet simply computing uncertainties over different options becomes expensive as the number of options or the planning horizon increases. Thus, across several chapters of this book, researchers have proposed that people might not act according to informational utilities at all, but rather have a general drive toward being curious (Wojtowicz et al., Chapter 1).

As explained in the previous section, such a drive for information might have emerged to allow better adaptation to the environment, since acquiring information is generally valuable in most human environments, even if computing the exact value is intractable. Evolution could have exerted pressure on agents to be generally curious, creating a general motivation to seek out information (Donnellan et al., Chapter 2). This can be formalized as a "bonus" (e.g., information bonus, novelty bonus, or curiosity bonus) added to the value function, which guarantees efficient information-seeking when tractable computations are unfeasible (Wilson, Geana, White, Ludwig, & Cohen, 2014; Cogliati Dezza et al., 2021)

Given the difficulties involved in computing informational utilities, another cost-saving solution is to use social information to augment one's own limited computational abilities (Wu et al., Chapter 8). By learning from other people, we can adopt effective solutions that would have been costly or impossible to discover on our own. Social learning is not merely limited to copying at the level of behaviors, but can also involve the inference of hidden mental states, such as imputing goals and beliefs to other agents. Here too exists a computational trade-off. Despite social learning at the level of copying behavior being cheap, learning from inferred goals and beliefs allows for more flexibility and better generalization when there is a mismatch between individual preferences, skills, or circumstances (Wu et al., Chapter 8).

Lastly, another crucial distinction is whether the process of information search is discriminative or generative, which maps onto the distinction between *selecting* and *producing* information, where the latter is observed as developing later in childhood (De Simone & Ruggieri, Chapter 4). This suggests that it is more cognitively demanding to use generative models of information-seeking rather than discriminative models. Whereas a discriminative approach assumes that people start out from different hypotheses and then seek out information to arbitrate between them, generative approaches assume that information search is driven by the attempt to build increasingly better models of the world. Plausible accounts of human information search will likely need both of these elements, where the generative component generates plausible hypotheses to be tested and the discriminative component arbitrates between which hypotheses are the most likely, with both systems complementing one another. Thus, a better understanding of the heuristics and approximate mechanisms people use to seek out information may help to bridge this gap (Hills et al. Chapter 11).

In summary, the study of information-seeking offers valuable insights into the computational principles and cognitive shortcuts that humans use to make intractable problems tractable. The proposals in this book are diverse, and include utility maximization under resource constraints, heuristics, a general drive toward being curious, as well as learning from other people. However, it is still an open question whether these diverse solutions proliferate like tools in a toolbox (Gigerenzer & Todd, 1999), or whether they point toward complementary and interacting systems.

Which Machinery Supports the Drive for Knowledge?

Information-seeking allows humans to select relevant information from a multitude of stimuli arriving from the environment (Gottlieb, Chapter 10) and compress them into a meaningful understanding of the world (Wojtowicz et al., Chapter 1). Despite these benefits, acquiring novel information is costly. Searching for information might take time away from other adaptive behaviors, such as consuming food or water or acquiring other primary rewards. Moreover, to implement information-seeking behaviors, the brain needs to assemble novel strategies and behavioral policies, or engage in expensive computations, thereby incurring metabolic and cognitive costs. Indeed, evidence suggests that people require more cognitive resources when seeking novel information compared to only exploiting known rewards or simply randomly exploring their environment (Cogliati Dezza, Cleeremans, & Alexander, 2019; Wu, Schulz, Pleskac & Speekenbrink, 2021). To facilitate information-seeking, therefore, the brain needs to rely on behavioral and cognitive control mechanisms. As shown in Chapter 9, brain regions typically involved in cognitive control, such as the dorsal anterior cingulate cortex (dACC) and anterior insula, are activated when humans seek novel information. Moreover, the fronto-parietal network controls information-seeking behaviors when information gathering relies on active sensing behaviors (Gottlieb, Chapter 10).

However, is information-seeking just a control mechanism which allows the brain to compress relevant stimuli into meaningful understanding (e.g., cognitive utility of information)? As shown throughout this book, information not only has a cognitive utility, it can also impact people's affective states (hedonic utility) and future decisions (instrumental utility; Sharot & Sunstein, 2020). These two latter utilities seem to activate a different network, which overlaps with reward processing (Charpentier & Cogliati Dezza, Chapter 9). For example, the vmPFC tracks the savoring of information (i.e., increased anticipation due to advance knowledge of an upcoming reward; Iigaya et al., 2020) and, together with the ventral striatum, it tracks a combination of instrumental and noninstrumental values of information (Kobayashi & Hsu, 2019).

These two different networks – one overlapping with reward processing and the other with control processing – may nevertheless work together to produce a single integrated value of information for implementing adaptive information-seeking. An intriguing hypothesis is that dopamine may facilitate this "integrative role" by strengthening the interaction between the two networks (Charpentier & Cogliati Dezza; Chapter 9). However, the exact mechanisms are still unknown, although one theory is that dopamine provides a signal of the weighted sum of cognitive, hedonic, and instrumental utility of information, integrating them into a common currency (Sharot & Sunstein, 2020). However, there are still many open questions, and it is not yet known what role other neurotransmitters such as norepinephrine and serotonin play within this process.

So far, we have seen that the neural machinery of information-seeking contains a mixture of reward and control mechanisms, which may oscillate between the two depending on one's motivational state, preferences, and needs. However, this also suggests that there might be nothing unique as to how this machinery is structured. Put differently, mechanisms developed to serve specific functions, such as processing primary needs (food, water, reproduction) or controlling behavior, could be "exapted" (extraneously adapted from one domain to another) to implement information-seeking behaviors (Hills et al., Chapter 11). Although it is difficult to assess which came first in evolutionary terms (i.e., information-seeking, cognitive control, or reward maximization), it is not a new phenomenon in biology for structures developed for certain adaptive functions to be then reused to serve other functions. This transfer of mechanisms from one domain to another is also observed in comparing searching for information in the environment to searching internally from memory (Hills et al., Chapter 11). The hippocampal-entorhinal system is one example, wherein similar neural activity facilitates navigation in spatial and conceptual environments (Constantinescu, O'Reilly, & Behrens, 2016), although with some notable differences in information-seeking (Ho et al., 2017). Similarly, mechanisms used in individual learning and decision-making may also be reused for learning in a social context (Wu et al., Chapter 8), facilitating the transfer of information between minds.

Information-Seeking and Society

We have discussed information-seeking as a behavior that allows humans to acquire novel information. However, as suggested by Zurn et al.

(Chapter 12), a more fundamental goal of information-seeking is to connect things we observe in the world to one another, weaving together our concepts and understanding. This background knowledge determines how individuals perceive reality, and also connects diverse perspectives into common narratives, shared across communities and societies. Narratives are at the core of societal structure, and can shape political discourse and policy (Jones, Shanahan, & McBeth, 2014; Esposito, Terlizzi, & Crutzen, 2020).

Narratives are also at the center of many societal problems, including radicalization, conspiracy theories, and pseudoscientific frameworks. As Wojtowicz et al. expressed in Chapter 1, these common narratives are "not always perfectly calibrated to the provision of long-term benefits in every situation." Individual information-seeking therefore plays a crucial role in the way societies or communities develop, and the way information connects individuals is at the core of many issues faced by modern societies. Synergy between researchers studying individual information-seeking (e.g., psychologists, neuroscientists, and computer scientists) and researchers studying human behavior at the macro-level of social inter-actions is required to advance our understanding of how groups jointly search for information.

In recent years, (mis)information played a pivotal role in developing narratives, which in some cases shaped the future of entire countries (e.g., the 2016 UK Brexit referendum and the 2016 US presidential election). Information (and therefore misinformation) is crucial for updating individ-ual beliefs (Bromberg-Martin & Sharot, 2020). Let us imagine a person who has no particular beliefs on matters related to climate change. However, suppose she encounters some theories about climate change denial online. Information denying the existence of climate change is good news, since it would lift the burden of existential dread about the extinction of the human species. Since people seek information that makes them feel good (Wojtowicz et al., Chapter 1; Charpentier et al., Chapter 9), she may seek out this positive information more often and be more likely to integrate it with her other beliefs (Sharot, Korn, & Dolan, 2011). This bias toward believing positive information is likely to occur in many scenarios unless the accuracy or reliability of the information source can be properly considered (Pennycook & Rand, 2021). Recent research suggests that shifting attention to the accuracy of the information shared between groups might reduce the spread of misinformation online (Pennycook et al., 2021). However, the ability to accurately judge the reliability of information is becoming increas-ingly more difficult, given the flood of information people are confronted with every day. While changing belief with novel information is possible when a person is less confident about a topic (Rollwage et al., 2020), it becomes much harder when the belief is stronger (Sunstein, Bobadilla-Suarez, Lazzaro, & Sharot, 2017). Thus, more research needs to be done on how the search for information can go astray and is susceptible to deception. How a better societal and collective search for information can be achieved, and which specific information-seeking processes should be involved when it comes to policy decisions, is a new challenge faced by researchers studying information-seeking.

Conclusion

This book discusses the most current theories and scientific research on human curiosity, and the nature of our propensity to seek out information. But how can the insights contained herein be translated to daily human experiences? Domains such as education, human–computer interaction, and clinical psychiatry seem to be ideal candidates for benefiting from advances in the science of information-seeking. For example, Donnellan et al. (Chapter 2) proposed a framework for knowledge acquisition that could be used to implement more efficient educational programs, allowing "unsuccessful" students to find their own interest and succeed in their academic career. The framework for social learning introduced by Wu et al., (Chapter 8), while targeted for understanding human interactions, could also be applied to enhance how artificial agents interact with humans, based on an understanding of how we perceive and use social information. Additionally, this book highlights several computational and neural mechanisms underlying information-seeking (Chapter 5–8). Can these processes be targeted to improve the living conditions of patients with information-seeking abnormalities? These opportunities and challenges, among many others, are what the nascent field of information-seeking will face in the coming years.

References

Bhui, R., Lai, L., & Gershman, S. J. (2021). Resource-rational decision making. *Current Opinion in Behavioral Sciences*, 41, 15–21.

Bromberg-Martin, E. S., & Sharot, T. (2020). The value of beliefs. *Neuron*, 106 (4), 561–565. https://doi.org/10.1016/j.neuron.2020.05.001.

Charpentier, C. J., Bromberg-Martin, E. S., & Sharot, T. (2018). Valuation of knowledge and ignorance in mesolimbic reward circuitry. *Proceedings of the*

National Academy of Sciences of the United States of America, 115(31), E7255–E7264. https://doi.org/10.1073/pnas.1800547115.

Cogliati Dezza, I., Cleeremans, A., & Alexander, W. (2019). Should we control? The interplay between cognitive control and information integration in the resolution of the exploration-exploitation dilemma. *Journal of Experimental Psychology: General*, 148(6), 977–993. https://doi.org/10.1037/xge0000546.

Cogliati Dezza, I., Noel, X., Cleeremans, A., & Yu, A. J. (2021). Distinct motivations to seek out information in healthy individuals and problem gamblers. *Translational Psychiatry*, 11(408). doi.org/10.1038/s41398-021-01523-3.

Constantinescu, A. O., O'Reilly, J. X., & Behrens, T. E. J. (2016). Organizing conceptual knowledge in humans with a gridlike code. *Science*, 352(6292), 1464–1468. https://doi.org/10.1126/science.aaf0941.

Crupi, V., Nelson, J. D., Meder, B., Cevolani, G., & Tentori, K. (2018). Generalized information theory meets human cognition: Introducing a unified framework to model uncertainty and information search. *Cognitive Science*, https://doi.org/10.1111/cogs.12613.

Csibra, G., & Gergely, G. (2009). Natural pedagogy. *Trends in Cognitive Science*, 13(4), 148–153. https://doi.org/10.1016/j.tics.2009.01.005.

Esposito, G., Terlizzi, A., & Crutzen, N. (2020). Policy narratives and mega-projects: the case of the Lyon-Turin high-speed railway. Public Management Review. https://doi.org/10.1080/14719037.2020.1795230.

Friston, K., FitzGerald, T., Rigoli, F., Schwartenbeck, P., O'Doherty, J., & Pezzulo, G. (2016). Active inference and learning. *Neuroscience and Biobehavioral Reviews*, 68, 862–879. https://doi.org/10.1016/j.neubiorev.2016.06.022.

Gigerenzer, G., & Todd, P. M. (1999). Fast and frugal heuristics: The adaptive toolbox. In G. Gigerenzer, P. M. Todd, & The ABC Research Group, *Simple heuristics that make us smart* (pp. 3–34). Oxford University Press.

Hauser, T. U., Moutoussis, M., Consortium, N., Dayan, P., & Dolan, R. J. (2017). Increased decision thresholds trigger extended information gathering across the compulsivity spectrum. *Translational Psychiatry*, 7(12), 1296. https://doi.org/10.1038/s41398-017-0040-3.

Ho, M. K., MacGlashan, J., Littman, M. L., & Cushman, F. (2017). Social is special: A normative framework for teaching with and learning from evaluative feedback. *Cognition*, 167, 91–106.

Iigaya, K., Hauser, T. U., Kurth-Nelson, Z., O'Doherty, J. P., Dayan, P., & Dolan, R. J. (2020). The value of what's to come: Neural mechanisms coupling prediction error and the utility of anticipation. *Sci Adv*, 6 (25), eaba3828. https://doi.org/10.1126/sciadv.aba3828.

Jones, M., Shanahan, E., & McBeth, M. (2014). *The science of stories*. Palgrave Macmillan.

Keramati, M., & Gutkin, B. (2014). Homeostatic reinforcement learning for integrating reward collection and physiological stability. *Elife*, 3. https://doi.org/10.7554/eLife.04811.

Kobayashi, K., & Hsu, M. (2019). Common neural code for reward and information value. *Proceedings of the National Academy of Sciences of the United States of America*, 116(26), 13061–13066. https://doi.org/10.1073/pnas.1820145116.

Kobayashi, K., Ravaioli, S., Baranes, A., Woodford, M., & Gottlieb, J. (2019). Diverse motives for human curiosity. *Nature Human Behavior*, 3(6), 587–595. https://doi.org/10.1038/s41562-019-0589-3.

Lieder, F., & Griffiths, T. L. (2019). Resource-rational analysis: Understanding human cognition as the optimal use of limited computational resources. *Behavioral and Brain Sciences*, 43, e1. https://doi.org/10.1017/S0140525X1900061X.

Mehlhorn, K., Newell, B. R., Todd, P. M., Lee, M. D., Morgan, K., Braithwaite, V. A., . . ., & Gonzalez, C. (2015). Unpacking the exploration–exploitation tradeoff: A synthesis of human and animal literatures. *Decision*, 2(3), 191–215.

Pennycook, G., Epstein, Z., Mosleh, M., Arechar, A. A., Eckles, D., & Rand, D. G. (2021). Shifting attention to accuracy can reduce misinformation online. *Nature*, 592(7855), 590–595. https://doi.org/10.1038/s41586-021-033442.

Pennycook, G., & Rand, D. G. (2021). The Psychology of Fake News. *Trends in Cognitive Science*, 25(5), 388–402. https://doi.org/10.1016/j.tics.2021.02.007.

Pezzulo, G., Rigoli, F., & Friston, K. (2015). Active Inference, homeostatic regulation and adaptive behavioural control. *Progress in Neurobiology*, 134, 17–35. https://doi.org/10.1016/j.pneurobio.2015.09.001.

Rollwage, M., Loosen, A., Hauser, T. U., Moran, R., Dolan, R. J., & Fleming, S. M. (2020). Confidence drives a neural confirmation bias. *Nature Communications*, 11(1), 2634. https://doi.org/10.1038/s41467-020-16278-6.

Schwartenbeck, P., Passecker, J., Hauser, T. U., FitzGerald, T. H., Kronbichler, M., & Friston, K. J. (2019). Computational mechanisms of curiosity and goal-directed exploration. *Elife*, 8. https://doi.org/10.7554/eLife.41703.

Sharot, T., Korn, C. W., & Dolan, R. J. (2011). How unrealistic optimism is maintained in the face of reality. *Nature Neuroscience*, 14(11), 1475–1479. https://doi.org/10.1038/nn.2949.

Sharot, T., & Sunstein, C. R. (2020). How people decide what they want to know. *Nature Human Behavior*, 4(1), 14–19. https://doi.org/10.1038/s41562-019-0793-1.

Srinivas, N., Krause, A., Kakade, S. M., & Seeger, M. (2009). Gaussian process optimization in the bandit setting: No regret and experimental design. *arXiv preprint*.

Sunstein, C. R., Bobadilla-Suarez, S., Lazzaro, S., & Sharot, T. (2017). How people update beliefs about climate change: Good news and bad news. Cornell Law Review. https://scholarship.law.cornell.edu/cgi/viewcontent.cgi?article=4736&context=clr.

Wilson, R. C., Geana, A., White, J. M., Ludvig, E. A., & Cohen, J. D. (2014). Humans use directed and random exploration to solve the explore-exploit dilemma. *Journal of Experimental Psychology: General*, 143(6), 2074–2081. https://doi.org/10.1037/a0038199.

Wu, C. M., Schulz, E., Pleskac, T. J., & Speekenbrink, M. (2021). Time pressure changes how people explore and respond to uncertainty *PsyArXiv*. https://doi.org/10.31234/osf.io/dsw7q.

Index

For EU product safety concerns, contact us at Calle de José Abascal, 56–1°,
28003 Madrid, Spain or eugpsr@cambridge.org.

www.ingramcontent.com/pod-product-compliance
Ingram Content Group UK Ltd.
Pitfield, Milton Keynes, MK11 3LW, UK
UKHW020358140625
459647UK00020B/2538